NEW AMERICANISTS

A Series Edited by Donald E. Pease

José David Saldívar

Trans-Americanity

Subaltern Modernities, Global

Coloniality, and the Cultures

of Greater Mexico

Duke University Press DURHAM & LONDON 2012

© 2012 Duke University Press
All rights reserved
Printed in the United States of America
on acid-free paper ∞
Designed by C. H. Westmoreland
Typeset in Arno Pro by Keystone Typesetting, Inc.
Library of Congress Cataloging-in-Publication Data
appear on the last printed page of this book.

To Laura Escoto Saldívar

Contents

Preface
Americanity Otherwise

The Américas were not incorporated into an already existing capitalist world-economy. There could not have been a capitalist world-economy without the Américas.—ANÍBAL QUIJANO and
IMMANUEL WALLERSTEIN, "Americanity as a Concept"

To embrace Americanity is to dwell in the erasures of coloniality.
—WALTER MIGNOLO, *The Idea of Latin America*

Aníbal Quijano's and Immanuel Wallerstein's prescient analysis "Americanity as a Concept" (1992) is in my mind as I begin to preview all of this book's chapters and theoretical idioms that have been produced under the framework of the various meetings, seminars, and conferences of the Modernity/Coloniality Research Program. Contemplating these many different and nuanced arguments about the book's keywords—the coloniality of power, transmodernity, and border thinking in Greater Mexico—I wonder if Quijano's and Wallerstein's collaborative essay "Americanity as a Concept" might also serve as a theoretical framing device for my book. How might Quijano's and Wallerstein's Global South–Global North trans-American collaboration help those of us working in mainline American studies, critical U.S. studies, Latin American studies, and U.S. Latino/a studies project a transnational, anti-national, and outernational model?[1] Why has Quijano's and Wallerstein's trans-American (even planetary) conceptualization of Americanity not been more central to the current vitality of these divergent fields? I suggest here that we may need to think more broadly of "Americanity as a Concept" and its connection to globalization.

What might it mean, then, to start off within the context of a relatively understudied essay the historical sociologists Aníbal Quijano and Immanuel Wallerstein co-published some seventeen years ago? "Americanity as a Concept, or the Américas in the Modern World-System" attempts to explain the impact, I believe, of how the invention of the Américas over the past five centuries developed what they call "the pattern," "the locus," and "the prime testing ground" of what today we mean by modernity and the "capitalist world-system" (Quijano and Wallerstein 1992, 549–50). In this, "Americanity as a Concept" might also serve as a crucial document for any comparative project that attempts to foreground the transnational and post-disciplinary impulses related to Chicano/a studies, Latin American studies, and American studies as interdisciplinary fields. While I believe that "Americanity as a Concept" has the potential to open up the emerging field-imaginary of trans-American studies to some dystopian and utopian futures (see Pease 1990),[2] I begin this book by underlining Quijano's and Wallerstein's prescience in constructing "Americanity" as a crucial geo-social space for our times and for the discipline's turn to hemispheric and trans-American studies. "Americanity" offers the area studies of Latin American studies and American studies an outernationalist approach to the cultures of the Américas in the modern world-system, the rediscovery of the Américas as the expansion of the world through what Quijano and Wallerstein (1992, 549) see as "variegated methods of labor control for different products and zones" of the planet's economy, and for the very construction of newness, progress, instrumentalized science, racism, and modernity themselves.

Overall, for Quijano and Wallerstein, "Americanity's invention" was a fourfold process, and each part was closely linked to the others. Hence, Quijano and Wallerstein intended their neologism "Americanity" to accomplish and perform a number of disparate and related functions. It would look at the cross-genealogy of the Américas as involved in an ongoing conflict with the provincialism of Europe (and Eurocentrism and the coloniality of power), for European hegemony (especially Iberian and British) created and crafted "a rank order" of social classification in the modern world-system, producing with this new dominant rank of order "a new set of rules" (Quijano and Wallerstein 1992, 550) for the interaction of the planet's cultures, societies, and states with each other. With the invention and so-called discovery of the Américas in 1492, Quijano and Wallerstein suggest, an essential boundary line was powerfully put in place for the first time: that of empire vis-à-vis other metropolitan empires.

If the Spanish viceroyalties, over the centuries, carved up in the process of the wars of independence to yield what Quijano and Wallerstein (1992, 550) describe as "the states [of Latin America] we know today," the very "stateness of the states" in the Américas also made it possible for the invention of ethnicity and for ethnicity's emergence in what they see as a crucial "building block" of the modern capitalist world-system.[3] Americanity as a historical self-fashioning matrix thus links up the idea of the coloniality–power couplet with that of ethnicity. For Quijano and Wallerstein (1992, 550), coloniality "as a set of states" articulated itself within a global interstate system in hierarchical layers. The formal colonies of the Américas were at the bottom of Europe's colonial modernity, and the few European metropolitan core states were at the top.

If the European hierarchy of coloniality manifested itself, as Quijano and Wallerstein (1992, 550) suggest, "in all domains—political, economic, and not least of all cultural" over the centuries, the coloniality of power "reproduced itself" over and over again. However, and this is crucial for trans-American historical sociologists and for those of us in U.S. Latino/a studies and American studies, when the formal colonial states ended through the wars of independence and what we today call decolonization, the coloniality of power did not end; instead, Americanity's coloniality of power continued "in the form of a socio-cultural hierarchy of European and non-European" (Quijano and Wallerstein 1992, 550). Moreover, as I have noted, the coloniality of power was itself essential glue in the articulation, interpellation, and integration of the interstate system within the modern and colonial world-system.

Throughout their essay, Quijano and Wallerstein closely identify coloniality, ethnicity, and racism with capitalism and with capital's consolidation in Europe and the Américas from the fifteenth century to the eighteenth century. Moreover, they propose, coloniality constitutes itself through the Iberian and British classification and reclassification of the planet's population—hence, the concepts of culture and ethnicity become foundational in this task of classifying and reclassifying. As they aptly put it, "All the major categories [of ethnicity and race] into which we ethnically divide today in the Américas and the world (Native Americans or 'Indians,' Blacks or 'Negroes,' Whites or 'Creoles'/Europeans, *Mestizos* or other names given to a so-called 'mixed' category)—all these categories did not exist prior to the modern world-system" (Quijano and Wallerstein 1992, 550) and, by extension, before the invention of Americanity. Additionally, the so-called ideological state apparatuses such as the church, the universities, and so on served to manage and control such classifications. Lastly, the Iberian and British coloniality the colonists brought with them from Europe's empires figured an epistemological standpoint and perspective from which they signified the ethnic and racialist absolutist meaning of this new matrix of power—or *patrón de poder* (coloniality of power). From my perspective, one could therefore conceptualize the coloniality of power as sharing axes of both domination and subjectification, articulated with labor, exploitation, and capital.[4] Ethnicity and coloniality from the perspective of Americanity delineated what the authors call "the social boundaries corresponding to the division of labor. And it justified the multiple forms of labor control, invented as part of Americanity: slavery for the Black Africans, various forms of coerced cash-crop (*repartimiento, mita,* peonage) for the Native Americans, indentured labor (*engagés*) for the European working class" (Quijano and Wallerstein 1992, 550–51).[5]

Thus envisaged, Quijano's and Wallerstein's "Americanity as a Concept," I believe, must be understood not simply as a cross-genealogy or critical manifesto of a new field of academic area studies but as a profound founding gesture provincializing Europe and its insidious worldview or philosophy of praxis, Eurocentrism, and as a founding gesture reorganizing the roots and routes of modernity, globalization, and the capitalist world-system.[6] Like most founding articulations, Quijano and Wallerstein gave foundational status to the Américas through their creation of the geo-social temporalities and outernational concept of Americanity. In so doing, they also sought to emphasize the ways the hierarchical relations of coloniality, power, ethnicity, racism, and scientific colonial modernity themselves shaped the Américas from their very invention. Hence, Americanity, for Quijano and Wallerstein (1992, 552; emphasis added) was the construction "of a gigantic ideological overlay to the modern world-system. It established a series of institutions and worldviews that sustained the system, and it invented all of this out of the *American crucible.*" For those of us teaching and writing from within traditional nationally oriented programs such as American studies, ethnic studies, and U.S. Latino/a studies, Quijano's and Wallerstein's conceptualization of Americanity might also help us broaden, open, and outernationalize our internally colonized horizons.

In the wake of this long colonial encounter within the context of the "American crucible"—that is, within the context of some five hundred years of the genocide of native peoples in the Américas, the hegemonic (infra-human) classification of humans into ethno-racial formations brought over from the metropole to the colonies of the Américas as a kind of set of rules for labor control, and an emerging capitalist world-system in which an enormous metallic colonial wealth in the Américas (gold and silver) was transferred to "central Euorpean bankers and to British, French, Dutch, and Flemish industrialists and merchants" (Quijano and Wallerstein 1992, 553)—Quijano and Wallerstein work hard to invent a different unit of analysis (not the traditional one of the nation-state) to comprehend and cognitively map the vast machinery of the Américas in the making of modernity, coloniality, and the world-system. The histories of coloniality, ethnicity, racism, and newness in the Américas were foundational for Quijano and Wallerstein for managing "the gigantic ideological overlay" of the Américas and for explaining the uneven histories of dystopia and utopia Americanity has had to grapple with over the past five centuries. In other words, Wallerstein's and Quijano's notion or theory (as a system of concepts aimed to give a global explanation to an area of knowledge) of Americanity emerged together with what they called the "modern world-system" and "coloniality of power." Further, Quijano's and Wallerstein's Americanity was a terrific emendation to the hegemonic history of the world, which had erased and silenced a large part of the planet—what became known as the geo-social construct of the Américas—because it was an unthinkable space to those writing universal history. The creation of the Américas was thus the "constitutive act" of the coloniality of power.[7]

From my perspective and standpoint as a scholar and critical social theorist in U.S. critical studies (particularly from the field-imaginary developed from the new social student movements of [proto]Chicano/a studies), Quijano's and Wallerstein's pan-Andean and U.S. prescience is slightly tempered by their stopping short of locating a coherent explanation of the Southwestern U.S.-Mexican borderlands within their gazes of Americanity and the coloniality–power couplet. If the Américas were initially hegemonized by Iberians and the

British, Wallerstein and Quijano suggest, they radically diverged in the nineteenth century. That is, North America developed and progressed through a largely Protestant-based (capitalist) culture and society, and Latin America was underdeveloped by Europe and North America. But the Southwestern U.S.-Mexican borderlands (from Texas to California) were never entirely the result of a British American colonial society, as they rightly suggest most North American culture and society were. After all, if the United States distinguished itself by following the path of Protestant development, it hegemonized the borderlands of Texas, New Mexico, Arizona, Utah, and California with its own imperial movements of Manifest Destiny. And, as the Chicano and Chicana historians David Montejano (1987), Ramón Gutiérrez (1991), and Emma Pérez (1991) have taught us over the past twenty-five years, did not Iberian conquistadors carry within them their Iberian seigniorial concepts of the coloniality of power into Nuevo Santander and Greater New Spain? But countering Quijano's and Wallerstein's project (by noting that Americanity's coloniality of power did not stop at the Rio Grande) at this late date is not the point of this preface. As a scholar and a critical social theorist in Chicano/a studies, I am more interested in foregrounding an outernationalist and post-exceptionalist critical impulse in the study of the Américas that my work begins to chart than in arguing with any of Quijano's and Wallerstein's substantive socio-temporal and socio-spatial claims. That is why I have included references in each of the book's chapters to the scholarship of both well-known Latinamericanists from the Global South and New Americanists from the Global North (and vice versa), and those whose theoretical frameworks, objects of study, and academic disciplinary inclinations challenge the border-patrolled area studies fields' historical understanding of themselves.

Although I certainly agree with Quijano and Wallerstein that the Américas were founded through the imperial differences and colonialities of power that the Iberians and the British brought with them in their creation of a gigantic geo-social concept of Americanity, I also finally agree with them that today, at the beginning of the twenty-first century, Latin America still occupies a "subordinate place" (Quijano and Wallerstein 1992, 556) in its relation to North America and that the United States continues to occupy the top place. The key historical and structural difference between Latin America and the United

States in the nineteenth century and today, in the twenty-first century, however, is that Latin America and the United States of America (through globalization) are now part of what Quijano and Wallerstein (1992, 556) presciently called a *single world order,* for the Americanization of the Américas is coming into "full bloom." Adding to this integration of the Américas (the North American Free-Trade Agreement and General Agreement on Tariffs and Trade notwithstanding) is, of course, a continuing massive migratory flux from Americanity's South to Americanity's North, whereby in the twenty-first century Euro-Americans in the United States will be a demographic minority and whereby U.S. Latinos/as will be the largest ethno-racial minority bloc, at 25 percent of the population. These demographic changes will bring about significant challenges at the very heart of the post-contemporary debates about political transformations in the United States and Latin America and around the planet. Against the neo-liberal bigotry and U.S. chauvinism exhibited throughout Samuel Huntington's *Who Are We?: The Challenges to America's National Identity* (2004), I side in my work with Quijano's and Wallerstein's utopian integration of the Américas.

It is in this sense of understanding the Américas through Quijano's and Wallerstein's "crucible of Americanity"—that is, through the crucible of coloniality, ethnicity, racism, and the reification of scientific progress—that I would like readers to understand *Trans-Americanity* as part of an unfinished encounter with Quijano's and Wallerstein's collaborative global North–South work. While all of the book's chapters share the vantage points of the Global South and of the invention of Americanity, and almost all of the chapters assume that the area studies field-imaginaries of Latin American studies, American studies, or U.S. Latino/a studies cannot be reduced to a single, mono-topical paradigm, all are arguing for a unit of analysis that is greater than that of the nation-state today. In situating *Trans-Americanity* in the context of the collaborative perspectives from the pan-Andes (Quijano) and the United States (Wallerstein), I hope that my book can be read as exploring and exploiting an emerging disposition of trans-Americanity studies. Can Americanity's dystopian five-hundred-year experiences in the crucible of coloniality, ethnicity, racism, and modernity build on what Quijano and Wallerstein (1992, 556–57) see as North America's "utopia of social equality and liberty" and Latin America's indigenous "utopia of reciprocity, solidarity, and direct democracy"?

The book's preface—"Amercanity Otherwise"—falls, too, outside the border-patrolled academic area studies of the Global North as a part of a dramatic shift in trans-American sociological, historical, and cultural acting and thinking from the nation-state level to a thinking and acting at the planetary and world-system levels. There is, then, something speculative and risky in reading through the critical and theoretical approaches of scholars, activists, and social theorists from America's (Global) South and North to this relatively understudied topic of Americanity, which, as I see it, is the intellectual property of no specific national field-imaginary yet which seems to concern the geosocial and temporal construction of the Américas and the coloniality of power in immediate ways. In "Americanity as a Concept," Wallerstein and Quijano sought to dismantle those imaginary figures of Europe and Eurocentrism that remain deeply embedded in shorthand forms in our everyday habits of thought. If the Iberian and British colonizers of the Américas preached a Renaissance humanism of scientific rationality, modernity, and popular sovereignty to the colonized of the Américas, they certainly, as Quijano and Wallerstein suggest, at the same time denied these ideals in their very practices and technologies of genocide, racism, social classification, and labor control. Through their concept of Americanity, Wallerstein and Quijano, almost by definition as post-contemporary scholars of the coloniality of power engage the universals—such as the abstract figure of the human in the Renaissance or that of Eurocentrism (with its denial of coevalness)[8]—that were forged in the Renaissance and, later, in Enlightenment Europe, and that underlie the human and social sciences in the modern world-system.

Like Quijano and Wallerstein, my work holds to emphasizing the hyphen in the phrase "the modern (capitalist) world-system," for by doing so I am attempting not to conceptualize systems of the whole world but, rather, to talk about systems, economies, and world empires that are a world (though possibly not encompassing the whole planet)" (Wallerstein 2004, 17). In organizing this book around the critical neologisms of "coloniality," "Americanity," and the cultures of "Greater Mexico" I have tried to show that, in interdisciplinary world-

system analysis and an emerging post-exceptionalist American studies, the neologism "Americanity" knows its own slippages, among
various zones of references, especially through the related code words
of "transmodernity" developed by the philosopher Enrique Dussel,
and that of *pensamiento fronterizo* (border thinking) formulated by
the semiotician of coloniality and critical social theorist Walter Mignolo and the Chicana feminist theorist Gloria Anzaldúa. As one can
see from the book's title, *Trans-Americanity*, I do not simply aim to
recover material that might be labeled "American" or "colonial" but
turn these adjectives into material nouns, identifying concepts,
thought processes, and definitions as the objects of my study. Yet this
level of abstraction does not replace the more direct and politically
driven aspect of my book. As I suggest later, I also try to listen to the
small voice of history and to challenge U.S. exceptionalist state fantasies and field-imaginaries. Nor do I abandon language, for I claim as
a particular subject of Americanity and the coloniality of power its
many idioms, syntax, grammar, rhetorical forms, and systems invented
by imaginative writers and theorists from the Global South.

Clearly enough, the concept of Americanity that I am using here
as a world-systemic unit of analysis reflects the sense of immense
enlargement of a planetary (trans)modernity, communication, and
zone of the economy that began with the first Iberian modernity and
hegemony of the Américas, as well as the beginning horizon of the
first modernity (as Dussel has been arguing for the past decade) of a
world-system market. The concept of Americanity at the beginning
of the twenty-first century, I suggest, can perhaps be reformulated
and repositioned from Quijano's and Wallerstein's construction as a
post-contemporary twofold process—to that of the localization of the
global and to that of the globalization of the local (see Robertson
1992, 177–78). We might also add a heavier dose of the negative (as
Theodor Adorno and Fredric Jameson might have proposed) to Quijano's and Wallerstein's already dystopian sense of Americanity and
hence define transnational Americanity as an "untotalizable totality,"
which intensifies the patrón de poder in its relation between its parts
—coloniality, power, ethnicity, racism, and newness, or instrumentalized scientific progress.

Briefly, in *Trans-Americanity* I propose that the geo-social and temporal space of Americanity and the coloniality of power involves us in

a number of different conceptual axes. At one level, is the dystopian evaluation by Quijano and Wallerstein of Americanity (as well as that of coloniality, ethnicity, racism, and labor control) a matter of planetary formations of the many idioms of dominance? Or is Quijano's and Wallerstein's conceptualization of Americanity a potentially utopian, dialectical, and revolutionary source and radical redefinition of "equality," "liberty," "reciprocity" and "direct democracy" of the United States and of Latin America, as Wallerstein and Quijano powerfully concluded at the end of their essay?

In what follows, I emphasize that the arguments in *Trans-Americanity* about subaltern studies and the coloniality of power are arguments *within* postcolonial studies. I say this to emphasize that neither the South Asian Subaltern Studies Group, founded in 1982, nor the largely Latinamericanist Modernity/Coloniality Research Program, established in 2001, can be defined by a single "program."[9] Rather, the South Asian and Latin American collectives are experimental spaces in which various agendas and cross-genealogical projects talk to each other around a common concern that is at the same time political, ethical, and pedagogic—that is, what Quijano calls decolonization as "epistemological reconstitution."[10] Throughout my study, I follow Ranajit Guha's succinct definition of the subaltern as the "name for the general attribution of subordination . . . whether this is expressed in terms of class, caste, age, gender, and office or in any other way" (Guha 1998, 35). In the same spirit, I hope that the subaltern might serve as a signifier for a variety of concerns in my book: the "unspeakable" in subalternized African American, U.S. Latino and Latina, Cuban, and South Asian literature; the rhetoric of form in postcolonial narratives; and the constructions of subalternized identities in our culture and society. Postcolonial studies, as I see it, involves listening to what Guha (1996, 1) calls "the small voice of history." Like many minoritized theorists in the United States who have taken an interest in subaltern studies and coloniality of power studies,[11] I am interested in mapping out the small voices of those positioned within a "subordinated particularity" and in the difficulty of representing—as the critical theorists Gayatri Chakravorty Spivak (1988) and John Beverley (1999) have both cogently argued—the subaltern in our discourses (academic, literary, and testimonial).

Specifically, my idea for *Trans-Americanity* arose from a passage I was teaching in Toni Morrison's postcolonial novel *Beloved* (1987), in which the protagonist Sethe, faced with the awesome circumstances surrounding her act of infanticide, admits to her mother-in-law, Baby Suggs, that the entire situation with the spectral "voices surrounding the house" was "unspeakable" (Morrison 1987, 235). These words led me to consider whether the story Morrison relates (based on a real story of social death, slavery, and infanticide) is finally caused less by Sethe's "rememories" than by her own attempts to represent an aspect of the ineffable of the subordinate in narrative.

What kind of "unspeakable" idiom of the subordinate was this, and what kind of comprehensible form does Morrison (through Sethe and the women of color of 124 Bluestone Road) provide? Late in the novel, Morrison (1987, 235) returns to this issue by writing, "The thoughts of the women of 124 [were] unspeakable thoughts, unspoken." At base, the questions seemed to involve not just the formal features of the narrative, but also the entire enterprise of the many idioms of dominance and subordination in postcolonial (subaltern) literature. Sethe could not understand the meaning of those "unspeakable" semiotics of U.S. dominance without first naming the "unspeakable thoughts, unspoken" and keeping as Morrison (1987, 51) says "the past at bay." This could be done only by constructing a "syntax" to organize the storytelling and to establish the most basic links between words and things. Morrison's task is to formulate the very possibility of a grammar of the subaltern by which the "unspeakable" individual and collective trauma of her vision might be meaningfully communicated.

It then struck me that it is this very possibility of expression and representation through narration that forms the fundamental assumption of much minoritized writing. All writers must be in fact first the authors of a system of expression before they can be the authors of a particular expression. In her own allegory of reading iconic American literature, *Playing in the Dark*, published after the appearance of *Beloved*, Morrison (1992, 15) expressed this idea in the following way: "The ability of writers to imagine what is not the self, to familiarize the strange and mystify the familiar, is the test of their power." Likewise, the late Gloria Anzaldúa (1987, 88) expressed this idea of systemic writing in similar terms in *Borderlands/La Frontera*: "In looking at this book that I'm almost finished writing, I see a mosaic pattern [Mexica-like] emerging, a weaving pattern, thin here, thick there. I see a preoccupation with deep structure, the underlying structure . . . that is red earth, black earth."

My book analyzes the assumptions and theories behind such statements by Morrison and Anzaldúa (among others) to examine the processes by which the following trans-American and South Asian diasporic and border writers and thinkers establish the grammar and syntax proper to the expression of their particular meanings. Following post-structuralists and postcolonialists such as Paul de Man, Judith Butler, and Ranajit Guha, I term these processes the creation of rhetorical form. This study investigates the enabling conditions of narrative (novels, memoirs, testimonies) by postcolonial, subaltern writers and the various ways in which their stories of global coloniality of power seek to create an epistemological ground on which coherent versions of the world may be produced.

The book involves careful readings of a series of nineteenth-, twentieth, and twenty-first-century trans-American and South Asian texts by José Martí, Miguel Barnet and Esteban Montejo, Gloria Anzaldúa, Victor Martínez, Toni Morrison, Gabriel García Márquez, Arundhati Roy, and Sandra Cisneros, among others. It includes eight chapters. The first chapters, originally published, respectively, in *American Literary History* and as the introduction to Julio Ramos's iconic *Divergent Modernities* (2001), are devoted to the re-contextualizing of Martí's essays and chronicles (*Escenas norteamericanas* [North American Scenes]), culturally and historically, and to a decolonial reading of two memoirs/testimonies about the Spanish–American War of 1898: Theodore Roosevelt's *The Rough Riders* and Barnet's and Montejo's *Biography of a Runaway Slave*. Other chapters consist of detailed readings of Gloria Anzaldúa's *Borderlands/La Frontera*, Victor Martínez's *Parrot in the Oven*, Toni Morrison's *Sula* and *Beloved*, Gabriel García Márquez's *The General in His Labyrinth*, Arundhati Roy's *The God of Small Things*, and Sandra Cisneros's *The House on Mango Street* and *Caramelo or Puro Cuento*. This book follows directly from my previous work on the transculturation of the inter-American novel (*The Dialectics of Our America* [1999]) and on Greater Mexico's border culture and literature (*Border Matters* [1997]).

Chapter 1, "Unsettling Race, Coloniality, and Caste in Anzaldúa's

Borderlands/La Frontera, Martínez's *Parrot in the Oven*, and Roy's *The God of Small Things*" is a study of the interplay between the performative border epistemologies of two award-winning Chicana/o writers and the changing subaltern discourses of American vernacular literatures and cultures. Gloria Anzaldúa's *Borderlands/La Frontera* and Victor Martínez's *Parrot in the Oven* explore the linguistic intermixture of ethnic and mainstream languages (English, Spanish, and Spanglish) to illustrate the changing languages of the United States. What vernacular varieties of English or Spanish will dominate in twenty-first-century América? Which *lingua rustica* will the some 30 million Latinos and Latinas in the United States (with more than 10 million in California) hegemonize in their testimonies, novels, poetry, and essays? What new literary genres will emerge in postcolonial American literature? If Anzaldúa sees the aesthetic (subalternized) structure of knowledge as a form of what she calls "nepantilism," a Mexica word signifying cultural in-betweenness, Martínez argues in his novel for a rhetorical reading based on mass-mediated youth culture. What Anzaldúa is proposing in *Borderlands/La Frontera* is that we must look for the place, *nepantla* (physical as well as theoretical), from which a given grammar is being pronounced. What are the desires, the interests, and the politics of intellectual inquiry in a work of art, as well as in a political discourse? I conclude chapter one by arguing that the complexities of South Asian identities and kinship are at the heart of Arundhati Roy's *The God of Small Things*. Central to the novel, I suggest, is a vision of the continuity between knowing the world through experience and struggle and changing the central relations of what I call (after Quijano and Guha) the global coloniality of power, which sustain and make the world what it is. Subaltern characters in Roy's novel, especially women, peasants, and children, defy bloodlines of kinship and caste to condemn the bloodshed of their everyday world in Kerala. In so doing, they defy the gods of both dominance and kinship to remember what they experienced and shared with their god of small things.

In chapter 2, "Migratory Locations: Subaltern Modernity and José Martí's Trans-American Cultural Criticism," I focus on the questions, How is the migratory subject, in an inter-American politics of location, to be conceptualized as revolutionary and antimilitaristic, Latin American and North American at the same time? What are the limits of our

modern notions of citizenship, identity, and residence for activist
intellectuals involved in intense processes of de-territorialization?
How does José Martí's residence in New York City and the United
States (1880–95) generate a "grammar" of (outer)nationalist and local modernist discursive practices? Martí's ruminations on subaltern
cultures throughout the Américas took many forms in his hybrid and
experimental chronicle *Escenas norteamericanas* (North American
Scenes). As an émigré in an alien Anglo-American environment, Martí
often took the role of a cultural anthropologist engaged in what James
Clifford and George Marcus (1986) call the production of "writing
culture." As I argue, Martí's scores of modern chronicles, prologues,
and essays thematize, among other things, the unfamiliar rituals, ceremonies, and daily practices of his host country. Briefly stated, my
emphasis is on what I call Martí's "subaltern modernity." His resistance
to the modern rationality of the enlightened *letrados* (lettered elites),
as well as to the commodification and racialization of U.S. mass culture, might also be labeled the Martí differential—calling for a cultural
critique—appropriate to an uneven aesthetic modernity.

In chapter 3, "Looking Awry at the War of 1898: Theodore Roosevelt
versus Miguel Barnet and Esteban Montejo," I juxtapose Theodore
Roosevelt's mainline memoir *The Rough Riders* (1999 [1899]) against
the grain of the Cuban *novela testimonial Biografía de un cimarrón*
(1966), by Miguel Barnet and Esteban Montejo, to expand the expression "subaltern studies." Here I argue that Roosevelt's, Barnet's, and
Montejo's texts are intensely involved in a struggle of dominance and
subordination over the history of the Spanish–American War of 1898.
My approach is to pick my way through two of the foundational
memoirs and *testimonios* of the war of 1898 and ask, Who writes or tells
the history of the subordinate? In the case of the Cubans Barnet and
Montejo, the question resonates with a response to Roosevelt's pen.
Did conquest of Cuba by Roosevelt and the United States empower
them to impose on the conquered a past written from a metropolitan
point of view? Can war function as an imperial semiosis? Did Roosevelt's gun confer a right on his pen, as well?

Chapter 4, "In Search of the 'Mexican Elvis': *Border Matters*, Americanity, and Post-State-centric Thinking," starts where I ended *Border
Matters* to point to the limits of state-centric thinking of much of post-
contemporary American cultural studies. Here I take two examples

of Chicano cultural production—the novel *The Miraculous Day of Amalia Gómez* (1992), by John Rechy, and the performances and songs of the Mexican Elvis, El Vez—to illustrate an important shift that has been occurring in Chicano and Chicana cultural production. What has been happening (and what we would do well to register), I argue, is the making of cultural artifacts that, because they reflect the embeddedness of the subaltern subject in a variety of cultural discourses and material practices as they have been produced by the flows of global capital, think beyond the state. By describing the works I analyze as participants in a kind of "borderlands epistemology," I suggest that minoritized authors and artists in the United States, such as Rechy and El Vez, are creating a subaltern knowledge that challenges, from below, the supposed homogeneity and presumed boundedness of the U.S. public sphere. But I am also making a second polemical point to an audience that in some ways is closer to home in Chicano/a literary and cultural studies. By noting and describing the diverse cultural discourses signified in Rechy's novel and El Vez's performances, I point to the limits of a Chicano/a cultural studies that adheres for its categories of analysis too narrowly to the imagined Chicano and Chicana nation. By refusing the geographic, cultural, and national categories that have been handed to us by scholars that preceded us, and by attending to those artistic, cultural, and political influences that do not respect national (or cultural nationalist) borders, I point readers to a trans-American and even global cultural studies that attends to the multiple and overlapping levels of cultural production and critique that circulate in the new global marketplace.

Some of my initial critical thoughts in chapter 5 on *The Miner's Canary: Enlisting Race, Resisting Power, Transforming Democracy* (2002), by the critical race theorists Lani Guinier and Gerald Torres, were first cobbled together in a University of California, Berkeley, graduate seminar on cultural studies and on social structure that I co-taught a few years ago with the sociologist Michael Omi. In our seminar's discussion of *The Miner's Canary*, I confessed that as an undergraduate literature major at Yale I had met and collaborated with Gerald Torres, who was then completing his law degree at the Yale Law School, on an experimental Spanglished literary journal. Preparing chapter 5, titled "Making U.S. Democracy Surreal: Political Race, Transmodern Realism, and the Miner's Canary," stirred up memories of my discussions with Torres about approaching the problems of Chicano/a multiculture and *mestizaje* from a different angle, about "bare life" and the structuring of law and violence, and about our divergent readings of our favorite imaginative writers at the time from the Global South, especially Gabriel García Márquez and Toni Morrison. My transdisciplinary graduate students at Berkeley, hearing again the elusive soundings Torres and I heard many years ago down the mean streets of New Haven about Chicano/a multiculture, tended to dislike my literary (figural) reading of this legal and activist book—for instance, my claims concerning Torres's dystopian melancholic take on mestizaje and his utopian faith in *lo real maravilloso* and magical realism.[12] In the difference between my reading and theirs, I now see that Guinier's and Torres's book on political race still interests me deeply.

In chapter 6, "The Outernational Origins of Chicano/a Literature: Paredes's Asian-Pacific Routes and Hinojosa's Cuban Casa de las Américas Roots," I argue that Américo Paredes's journalistic Asian-Pacific writings for the *Pacific Stars and Stripes* during the Second World War foreshadow the subject of global coloniality and modernity in his mature writings about ballads of intercultural conflict, or *corridos*. Moreover, I suggest that we need to re-examine this outernational literary and journalistic terrain that U.S.–Mexico borderland scholars are only now beginning to take into account in their understanding of Paredes's minor and iconic literary and cultural texts *"With His Pistol in His Hand": A Border Ballad and Its Hero* (1958) and *George Washington Gómez: A Mexicotexan Novel* (1990). With Rolando Hinojosa's iconic novel *Klail City y sus alrededores* (1976), I will go back over the literary and ideological terrain of this South Texas text's winning of the prestigious Cuban Casa de las Américas Prize that I described in my previous work (via the dialectics of Roberto Fernández Retamar's school of Calibán). But *Klial City y sus alrededores* deals more directly with Cuba's vernacular culture (via the roots of the Cuban vernacular aesthetic of the *choteo* or humor) than I first recognized. It was not until I visited Cuba in 1997 as a judge of the inaugural Casa de las Américas' *premio extraordinario* in U.S. Latino/a literature that I was able to improve my understanding of the history of the Cuban choteo and begin formulating its impact on Hinojosa's novels about Greater Mexico. Instead of viewing Paredes and Hinojosa as exclusively local South Texas writers, I propose to take an alternative route and attempt to read the planetary Asian-Pacific and Cuban roots and routes that helped form these great minoritized writers.

In chapter 7, "Transnationalism Contested: On Sandra Cisneros's *The House on Mango Street* and *Caramelo or Puro Cuento*," I argue that the "Disclaimer," or prologue, to Cisneros's *Caramelo or Puro Cuento* (2003) allegorizes how the metaphoric act involves the repression of itself. Concepts generated by the figurative odds and ends of string of the *caramelo rebozo* (by metaphor) conceal their origins and stage themselves as being literal language. The metaphoric and the literal, however, in *Caramelo or Puro Cuento* are part of the same process of the Reyes family's use of what the narrator calls "healthy lies." The process then generates a variety of *"puros cuentos,"* illusions, and pleasures and pains in the novel. But like Jorge Luis Borges before her, Cisneros alludes in her "Disclaimer" to the dominant principles that regulate not only the development of her own transnational fiction but also of the genre of the novel itself.[13] And apart from the text's "Disclaimer," *Caramelo or Puro Cuento,* I argue, offers readers a series of post-contemporary literary and mass-mediated cultural discussions, commentaries, and even scholarly footnotes on Greater Mexico's icons, such as Raquel Welch (born Raquel Tejada); Elia Kazan's film *Viva Zapata*; Gabriel Vargas's comic book *La familia Burrón*; and the young Chicana starlet Yolanda Móntez, straight out of Oakland, California, who transformed herself into the ethnic Mexican film icon Tongolele. Despite their random dispersal, the icons travel toward a single topic: that of defining what the narrator calls "inventing" a proper and exemplary figural language of Greater Mexico's novel.

This preoccupation with Greater Mexico's figural border language reveals a portrait of a Chicana feminist artist profoundly situated within the philosophic and aesthetic ideologies of her time. In fact, one might even argue that the intersubjective and spatio-temporal dimensions explored by the transnational novel are also indicated in *Caramelo or Puro Cuento*. As Celaya narrates the melancholy, racial melodrama of her Awful Grandmother's pleasure and pains to live the ideals of traditional Mexican romance, she also reveals the conditions under which the immanent potential of Greater Mexico's figural language to be meaningful might be actualized. To begin my rhetorical reading of *Caramelo or Puro Cuento*, I suggest that new perspectives concerning Cisneros's use of Greater Mexico's figural language might be gained by reading some instances of this transnational novel where the issues of the truth and "healthy lies" of literature—and, more broadly, where the dysfunctionality of language as such—are dramatized for us. By directing attention to the "Disclaimer" and to the novel's recurring metaphors of the numerous discourses on the nature of Greater Mexico's "proper literary language," we can begin to recognize the features and applications of the hermeneutic model the text *Caramelo or Puro Cuento* constructs for its own proper reading.

In the appendix, I include an experimental trans-American cultural conversation the Chilena scholar and journalist Mónica González García conducted with me titled, "On the Borderlands of U.S. Empire: The Limitations of Geography, Ideology, and Disciplinarity." The wide-ranging conversation covers all of the major coordinates of the continental map, a context that allows me to suggest that Chicano and Chicana imaginative writers belong equally to the dialectics of the Américas—that is, from both the Global North and the Global South. This cultural conversation also intends to encompass the intellectual and cognitive mapping of Amercanity, embracing a variety of topics, such as the boundaries of the imperial history of the United States; the role of Cuba's Casa de las Américas in modifying the geopolitics of knowledge; the recent manifestations of U.S. immigration law; Rodrigo Dorfman's film *Los Sueños de Angélica* (2007) about Mexican immigrants in North Carolina; and the drama *Fukú Americanus* (2009), which debuted in San Francisco and is based on Junot Díaz's Pulitzer Prize–winning novel *The Brief Wondrous Life of Oscar Wao* (2007).

I have elaborated this theoretical scenario of Americanity to explain how we might move away from a nationalist American studies to an outernational comparative critical U.S. studies. I have solicited the insights not only of Quijano's and Wallerstein's invention of Americanity but also of a range of intercultural and transdisciplinary scholars to articulate this explanation, because they arrived at an understanding of the workings of the outernational from within the precincts of comparative and intercultural studies of diasporas and borders. For those familiar with my work in Chicano/a studies, it should come as no surprise that I see the study of Americanity and its interscultures and literatures as more promising and more politically urgent than the study of traditional field-imaginaries such as comparative literature or comparative history organized around the existence of (Eurocentric) national boundaries. No disciplinary taxonomy, of course, is free of flaws, but I agree with the recent work of both oceanic circum–(Black) Atlantic scholars, such as Joseph Roach, Ian Baucom, Marcus Rediker, and Paul Gilroy, and planetary, land-based (trans-American) scholars working on the Global South, such as Kirsten Gruesz-Silva, Gayatri Chakravorty Spivak, Wai-Chi Dimock, and Anna Brickhouse, among others, that deeply hegemonic divisions within American studies between U.S. studies and British studies have shut down what Roach (1996, 183) calls the rich "historic relationships in a particularly invidious way." Some of these intercultural contact zones, as I emphasize and use them in different places in the book, are notably oceanic, spectral circum-Atlantic, such as the Afro-Asian-Pacific, and some are geo-topically land-based, such as the Global South, Other Asias, Hemispheric Islam, and Greater Mexico.[14] These recent analyses of the planet's geo-cultural formations, I suggest, do not simply open up an isolated core or peripheral intercultural zone; rather, they help us radically reorganize our ways of thinking about how performative intercultural productions interact dialectically. By foregrounding Wallerstein's and Quijano's comparative work on Americanity, my book seeks to combine what the insights of the oceanic circum-Atlantic and land-based trans-American work encourages: both a spatial and a temporal analysis in rethinking the outernational as disciplinary strategy and critical model. Like Wallerstein and Quijano, I am, therefore, interested in what follows in stretching the mainline and (traditional) comparative structures of "American studies"—its disciplines and methods, as well as its objects of study; its regional and national units and border and diaspora counter-units. How do Americanity's many idioms of spatio-temporality provide a way to think "otherwise" about the new comparative and post-exceptional American studies? What does it mean to consider Americanity as a spatial and temporal conjunction?

By assembling the various zigzags of these outernational contact zones in the book's case studies of Anzaldúa, Roy, Martí, Morrison, Paredes, García Márquez, Ramos, Dorfman, Cisnersos, and Díaz (among others), I hope to provide an alternative way to think beyond what Benedict Anderson (1998) has called "the specter of comparisons" and thus to re-engage the iconic works of Martí, Anderson, Spivak, Wallerstein, and Quijano. My focus on the "comparative" as a strategy for the study of the United States, Latin America, and the hemisphere and beyond means not the familiar model of comparative literature or comparative history but, rather, a structure of comparability based on what Wallerstein and Quijano call Americanity's "spatiotemporal" matrix. I am using the idea of "comparability" in *Trans-Americanity* to see how comparability also entails a theory of space and time that recognizes the quality of the conjunctural present—where multiple times exist simultaneously within and across the same planetary location or co-exist as uneven, subaltern temporalities.

Acknowledgments

Most of what follows was written for various occasions—invitations to participate in transcontinental conferences in Havana, Cuba, Mexico City, Guadalajara, and Madrid and at Dartmouth's Institute on the Futures of American Studies, or to contribute to the seminars and workshops of the Modernity/Coloniality Research Program held at the University of California, Berkeley, and Duke University. But several years ago—when I was chair of the Department of Ethnic Studies and taught in the Department of English at the University of California, Berkeley—I began to feel that there was enough common entanglement among the projects in Chicano/a studies, critical U.S. studies, global coloniality, and transmodernity to begin gathering them into a book. Later, when I moved to Duke University to become the director of the Program in Latino/a Studies in the Global South, I was delighted that Ken Wissoker, editor-in-chief, and J. Reynolds Smith, executive editor, at Duke University Press, found the book project doable. They only asked me to explicate the shared entanglements and tensions among the chapters in the introduction. I am deeply indebted to Steven Cohn, J. Reynolds Smith, Ken Wissoker, Jade Brooks, and the editorial staff at Duke University Press, who made publishing this book a long, wondrous trip. Donald E. Pease and an anonymous reviewer read the manuscript with great care and offered many important suggestions for revision.

The essays were written and revised between 2000 and 2010 at the University of California, Berkeley; Duke University; and Stanford University. Although some of them were published in earlier form, they have been substantially revised for this book. An earlier version of chapter 1 was published as "Unsettling Race, Coloniality, and Caste in Anzaldúa's *Borderlands/La Frontera*, Martínez's's *Parrot in the Oven*, and Roy's *The God of Small Things*," *Cultural Studies* 21, nos. 3–4 (March–May 2007), 339–67. Chapter 2 draws on my essay "Migratory Locations: Subaltern Modernity and Inter-American Cultural Criticism," the introduction to Julio Ramos's *Divergent Modernities: Culture and Politics in Nineteenth-Century Latin America*, trans. John D.

Blanco (Duke University Press, 2001), xi–xxxiv. Chapter 3 was published as "Looking Awry at 1898: Roosevelt, Montejo, Paredes, and Mariscal," *American Literary History* 12, no. 3 (2000), 386–406. A version of chapter 4 was published as "In Search of the 'Mexican Elvis': *Border Matters*, 'Americanity,' and Post–State-centric Thinking," *Modern Fiction Studies* 49, no. 1 (2003), 84–100. Part of chapter 5 draws from "Making Democracy Surreal: Political Race and the Miner's Canary," *American Literary History* 20, no. 3 (Summer 2008), 609–21. A version of the first half of chapter 6 was published as "Los orígenes transnacionales de la literatura chicana: El itinerario de Américo Paredes en Asia y el Pacífico," *Revista Casa de las Américas* 252 (July–September 2008), 76–83. The book's extended coda appeared in an earlier and truncated form as "On the Borderlands of América: The Limit(ations) of Geography, Ideology, and Discipline (an Interview with José David Saldívar by Mónica González García)," *Lucero* 17 (2006), 204–17. I thank the editors and publishers for permission to reprint this material. During the 2000s, I benefited enormously from the transcontinental debates among the members of the Modernity/Coloniality Research Program.

I am grateful for the discussions I have had with many interlocutors over the years that informed and changed my thinking: Munia Bahumik, John Beverley, Anna Brickhouse, Héctor Calderón, Maria Cantú, Guadalupe Carillo, Angie Chabram-Dernersesian, James Clifford, María DeGuzman, Junot Díaz, Enrique Dussel, Roberto Fernández Retamar, Winfried Fluck, Susan Gillman, Ramón Grosfoguel, Kirsten Gruesz-Silva, Carl Gutierrez-Jones, Monica Hanna, Nigel Hatton, Adam Lifshey, Eric Lott, Amy Kaplan, George Lipsitz, Nelson Maldonado-Torres, China Medel, Walter Mignolo, Rafael Pérez-Torres, Mary Louise Pratt, Aníbal Quijano, Ralph Rodriguez, John Carlos Rowe, Rosaura Sánchez, Lyn Di Irio Sandin, Gerald Torres, and Jennifer Harford Vargas. Ramón Saldívar, Laura Escoto Saldívar, and Sonia Saldívar-Hull's *pensamiento fronterizo* are also, in one way or another, a major part of this book.

I thank my graduate research assistants at the University of California, Berkeley, Frank Cruz, Mónica González-García, Teresa G. Jimenez, and Abraham Ramírez, who helped with specific items of information, books, articles, newspapers, CDs and DVDs, and for their meticulous proofreading of the manuscript. Alma Granado, Sara Ramirez, and María Villaseñor helped me set straight my views on

Junot Díaz's *Fuku Americanus,* the theatrical adaptation of *The Brief Wondrous Life of Oscar Wao.*

I also thank David X. Saldívar and Gabriel J. Saldívar, who, more than they realize, were able and constructive advisors, especially on Sky Computing and planetary (Googled) cultural matters.

All errors, however, are mine.

I also express my gratitude to the people who came to hear me talk at the various universities and research institutions where I first presented these ideas. The most valuable of these sessions were at the Centro Casa de las Américas, Havana; the Institute for the Futures of American Studies, Dartmouth University, Hanover, New Hampshire; the Kenan Institute for Ethics, Sanford School of Public Policy, Duke University; the National Association for Chicana and Chicano Studies Conference (NACCS), Guadalajara; the Universidad Cumpletense, Madrid; the Center for Comparative Studies in Race and Ethnicity, Stanford University; the Institute for Latino/a Public Policy, University of California, Berkeley; the Departments of English and Comparative Literature at the University of Virginia, University of Notre Dame, University of Pennsylvania, Duke University, Princeton University, and Stanford University; and the stimulating session Héctor Calderón organized at his home with some of Rock en Español's artists, filmmakers, and intellectuals in Coyoacán, Mexico City.

I thank my colleagues and students at Duke University; the University of California, Berkeley; and Stanford University. At Duke, I thank Srinavas Aravemudan, Ian Baucom, Cathy Davidson, Ariel Dorfman, Thomas Ferraro, Karla Holloway, Michael Hardt, Fredric Jameson, Frank Lentricchia, Wahneema Lubiano, Walter Mignolo, Michael Valdez Moses, Fred Moten, Maureen Quilligan, Maurice Wallace, Robyn Wiegman, and Priscilla Wald. A lot of expert colleagues helped me in my duties as the director of Latino/a studies in the Global South Program at Duke: Lee Baker, Eduardo Bonilla-Silva, Lori Carlson-Hijuelos, Sarah Deutsch, Oscar Hijuelos, Pedro Lasch, George McLendon, Claudia Milian, Emilio Parrado, Antonio Viego, and Jenny Snead Williams. My ideas were refined in seminars and conversations at the University of California, Berkeley, with Mitchell Breitwiesser, Wendy Brown, Anthony Cascardi, Pheng Cheah, Ian Duncan, Cathy Gallagher, Marcial González, Patricia Hilden, Abdul JanMohamed, Martin Jay, Niklaus Largier, Colleen Lye, Beatriz Manz, David Montejano, Evelyn Nakano Glenn, Michael Omi, Genaro Padilla, Laura Pérez, Gautam Premath,

José Rabasa, Julio Ramos, Alex Saragoza, Hans Sluga, and James Grantham Turner. I especially thank Judith Butler for inviting me to co-chair the Berkeley Critical Theory Initiative with her.

I also thank my colleagues at Stanford University who responded to parts of this book: Russell Berman, Albert Camarillo, Roland Greene, Paula Moya, Franco Moretti, and David Palumbo-Liu.

My heartfelt gratitude goes to my former graduate students for their various forms of support and *convivencia*: Gerardo Arellano, Ingrid Banks, Nerrisa S. Balce, Kirstie Dorr, Vernadette Gonzalez, Mónica González-García, Michelle Habell-Pallán, Sara Kaplan, Josh Kun, Edrik Lopez, Victor Mendoza, Rani Neutill, Karina Oliva-Alvarado, Birgit Rasmussen, Jennifer Reimer, Hilda (Mercy) Romero, Anna Marie Sandoval, María Villaseñor, and Matt Wray.

Although I have done some major editorial and structural retrofitting, chopping, and sanding the body of the manuscript—like a Chevy lowrider—the book's style, tone, and method tend to twist and turn quite a bit. I have aimed to keep the anti-systematic aspect of the book to dispel a false impression that could be created by the emphases I have placed on the critical world-system analysis and the coloniality of power theories conjured by the historical sociologists Immanuel Wallerstein and Aníbal Quijano at the expense of the post-contemporary imaginative literature from Greater Mexico and South Asia—or what I call in the book the Global South. Just as I occasionally feel remote from what social scientists call nomothetic discourses, I disclaim any idiographic attempt to write a literary history of the Global South's multiculture and literature. I have consciously chosen to focus *Trans-Americanity* on novelists, poets, critics, and experimental autobiographers (autoethnographers) who are also adept traveling theorists. For, as Toni Morrison (1992, 15) suggests, are imaginative writers not "the most intellectually anarchic, most representative, most probing, of artists. . . . The languages they use and the social and historical context in which these languages signify are indirect and direct revelations of that power and its limitations"? So it is to them, the Global South's imaginative writers and theorists, that I look for clarification about Americanity and the coloniality of power.

Carlos Santana, Los Lobos, Café Tacvba, Freddy Fender, Ely Guerra, and Ceci Bastida supplied the soundscape for the book.

Unsettling Race, Coloniality, and
Caste in Anzaldúa's *Borderlands/La Frontera*,
Martínez's *Parrot in the Oven*, and Roy's
The God of Small Things

What is termed globalization is the cultural process that began with the
constitution of America and colonial/modern Eurocentered capitalism as
a new global power.—ANÍBAL QUIJANO, "Coloniality of Power,
Eurocentrism, and Latin America" (2000)

This comparative chapter on Chicano/a and South Asian narratives
and global coloniality has a somewhat sweeping character. It is a
preliminary attempt to link *pensamiento fronterizo* (border thinking)
in Chicano/a Studies and realist interpellations of the subject and
the politics of unsettling the coloniality of power on a planetary scale.
Pensamiento fronterizo emerges from the critical reflections of (undocumented) immigrants, migrants, *bracero/a* workers, refugees,
campesinos, women, and children on the major structures of dominance and subordination of our times. Thus envisaged, pensamiento
fronterizo is the name for a new geopolitically located thinking from
Greater Mexico's borderlands and against the new imperialism of the
United States.[1] Pensamiento fronterizo is a necessary and affiliated
tool for thinking about what the Peruvian historical social scientist
Aníbal Quijano calls the "coloniality of power" and identity at the
intersections (*los intersticios*) of our local *historias* and the double
logics of capitalism and the cultures of U.S. imperialism.[2]

Quijano's coloniality of power, I argue, can help us begin to account
for the entangled relations of power between the global division of
labor, racial and ethnic hierarchy, identity formation, and Eurocentric
epistemologies. Moreover, the coloniality of power can help us trace

the continuous forms of hegemonic dominance produced by colonial cultures and structures. As I use it, the coloniality of power is fundamentally a structuring process of identity, ethnicity, political race, experience, and knowledge production that articulates geo-strategic locations and subaltern (minor) inscriptions.

My emphasis will be on late-twentieth-century postcolonial narratives (Chicano/a and South Asian) and early-twenty-first century realist theories about identity, interculturality, and minoritized studies. So I will begin by discussing three of the most important paradigms of minoritized study as forms of culture that have shared experiences by virtue of their antagonistic relationship to the hegemonic culture, which seeks to marginalize and interpellate them as minor.[3] Then I will examine the issue of border thinking and braided languaging practices in Gloria Anzaldúa's celebrated *Borderlands/La Frontera: The New Mestiza* (1987) and Victor Martínez's National Book Award–winning novel *Parrot in the Oven: Mi Vida* (1996). Last, I will speculate on the issue of ethnic kinship trouble in Arundhati Roy's Booker Prize–winning novel *The God of Small Things* (1996).

Why propose a cross-genealogical (U.S. Latino/a and South Asian) treatment of differently structured histories of border and diaspora identity and minoritized writing? I hope the answer to this will emerge as I go along and, indeed, in the rest of the book, designed as it is to encourage in-depth, cross-cultural comparisons within the matrix of globalization's coloniality of power. But I begin by asserting some of the potential meanings and nuances of the minor as they have appeared on the scene of U.S. subaltern studies in the past fifteen years.

The Politics of "Becoming Minor"

In a landmark conference at the University of California, Berkeley, in 1987 the literary theorists Abdul JanMohamed and David Lloyd (1990, 1) called for a radical examination of the "nature and context of minority discourse." JanMohamed and Lloyd were specifically interested in rethinking the relationship between a "minor literature" and the canonical literatures of the majority. Schematically, their theory and practice of minority discourse involves "drawing out solidarities in the forms of similarities between modes of repression and struggles that all minorities experience separately but precisely as minorities" (Jan-Mohamed and Lloyd 1990, 9). Their project of minority discourse fundamentally supplemented Gilles Deleuze's and Félix Guattari's theorizing of a minor literature—a literature so termed by its "opposition to those which define canonical writing" (quoted in JanMohamed and Llyod 1990, 381). A minor literature entails, for them, "the questioning or destruction of the concept of identity and identification . . . and a profound suspicion of narratives of reconciliation and unification" (JanMohamed and Lloyd 1990, 381). In other words, Jan-Mohamed and Lloyd maintained that a "minority discourse should neither fall back on ethnicity or gender as an a priori essence nor rush into calculating some 'nonhumanist' celebration of diversity for its own sake" (JanMohamed and Lloyd 1990, 9). While some realists might take issue with their dismissal of the cognitive work of our identities and their over-reliance on the work of Deleuze and Guattari (the erasure of the cognitive aspects of racialized minority experiences and identities), the political project of minority discourse remains on target. "Becoming 'minor,' " they write, "is not a question of essence . . . but a question of position: a subject-position that in the final analysis can be defined only in political terms" (JanMohamed and Lloyd 1990, 9).

My sense of the future of minoritized studies within the context of our globalized coloniality owes much to the theoretical work of my colleagues at Berkeley, but it does not quite reproduce the nuances of how JanMohamed and Lloyd use the term "minor" (following the famous study of Kafka by Deleuze and Guattari [2002]). In my recent cross-genealogical work in Chicano/a and Americanity studies otherwise; on José Martí as a subaltern modernist; on the Cuban *testimonio* of Miguel Barnet and Esteban Montejo; and on "Greater Mexico's" border modernism of Américo Paredes, for example, I have used the terms "subaltern" and "minor" to cast doubt not so much on our "narratives of identity" as on the mainline narratives of the major, mainstream, and hegemonic (see Saldivar 1996, 2000a, 2000b, 2001). My emergent minority studies follows the lead of the Modernity/Coloniality Research Program (especially Walter Mignolo, Enrique Dussel, and Quijano) and the South Asian Subaltern Studies Group, particularly the work of historian Dipesh Chakrabarty. As Chakrabarty (2000, 101) suggests, the minor "describes relationships to the past that the rationality of the [mainstream] historian's methods necessarily makes 'minor' or 'inferior' as something 'irrational' in the course of, and as a result of, its own operation." The cultural and political work of the subaltern or minoritized historian, in Chakrabarty's words, is to "try to show how the capacity (of the modern person) to historicize actually depends on his or her ability to participate in nonmodern relationships to the past that are made subordinate in the moment of historicization. History writing assumes plural ways of being in the world."

This brings me to the third and most recent sense of minoritized studies: U.S. minority studies as a comparative "epistemic project" formulated by Satya Mohanty, Paula Moya, Michael Hames-García, and Linda Martín Alcoff. Against purely skeptical (postmodern and poststructuralist) attitudes toward identity, ethnic studies, and experience, they argue for a strong defense of critical multiculturalism and minority studies based on what they call "realist" views.[4] (As shorthand for this realist-inspired group of minority studies, I focus on what follows on the collective project *Reclaiming Identity* [Moya and Hames-García 2000].)

What Moya and Hames-García have done is to tease out—using Satya Mohanty's iconic realist view of identity—a new way to do literary, cultural, and comparative ethnic studies in the United States. *Reclaiming Identity* is at the very center of what the authors, after Mohanty (1997, xii), call a "post-positivist realism," an engaging method of philosophical, cultural, and literary interpretation that situates "identity" in both a "radical universalist" and a "multiculturalist" worldview. Briefly, *Reclaiming Identity*, like Mohanty's *Literary Theory and the Claims of History* (1997) and Moya's *Learning from Experience* (2002), is a sustained, eloquent, and rich exemplification of this innovative method, practice, and pedagogy. Moya puts the collective project this way: the realist view of identity can provide "a reconstructed universalist justification for the kind of work being done by . . . ethnic studies scholars" by supporters of multicultural education, as well as for the salience of the identities around which such minoritized programs are organized (Moya, 2).

Although the *Reclaiming Identity* project gracefully eschews righteous polemic, the work in which its authors are engaged demonstrates beyond dispute what a critically focused research collective and interdisciplinary project—that is, philosophy, social-science theory, and the philosophy of science—can bring to literary studies proper. Indeed, Mohanty ends his erudite *Literary Theory and the Claims of History* by calling for a new kind of literary studies. "We should go beyond the bounds of a purely text-based literary theory to engage more directly the findings of the various scientific disciplines. . . . We [need] to make serious contact with the growing knowledge about the natural and social world and come to terms with the empirical implications of our claims" (Mohanty 1997, 251–52). Thus envisaged, for Mohanty, Moya, and Hames-García literary theory must be a site in which scholars and activists "examine, debate, and specify the social implications of advances in the natural and social sciences" (Mohanty 1997, 252).

Ranging across issues involving philosophy, literature, and social theory, the essayists explore realist accounts of identity and experience by making linkages among social location, experience, epistemic privilege, and cultural identity.[5] All contemplate a world where cultural identity is both socially constructed and substantively real. By attempting to transcend the limits of postmodernism/poststructuralism and essentialism, the authors in *Reclaiming Identity* take seriously that (1) identities are real; and (2) experiences are epistemically crucial. As Alcoff (2000, 312) emphasizes, *Reclaiming Identity* "is an act of taking back . . . the term realism in order to maintain the epistemic significance of identity."

Because I am working under some spatial constraints, I focus in the remainder of this section on the essays by Mohanty, Moya, Hames-García, and Alcoff. *Reclaiming Identity* blasts off with Mohanty's minoritized philosphical exegesis of Toni Morrison's celebrated novel *Beloved*. "The community sought" in the novel, he argues, "involves as its essence a moral and imaginative expansion of oneself." Moreover, Morrison's "political vision of the oppressed . . . provides the context" in which her characters challenge each other's views "on the limits of mother-love" in specifically historical, gendered, and ethno-racial terms. Thus envisaged, Morrison's character's perspectives, Mohanty suggests, are "not only affective but also epistemic" (Mohanty 2000, 236). By reading Morrison's *Beloved* (1987), many of us are therefore put in the position of characters in the novel, like Paul D, who have inadequate understandings of the social world they live in. Briefly, Morrison teaches us in *Beloved,* among other things, how to read infanticide and the social roles of slave mothers, thereby widening the scope of the moral debates about slavery and the gendered division of labor in the modern-world systems' analysis of capitalism. At the end of chapter 5, I return to this idea and discuss Morrison's postcolonial *Beloved* in terms of political race and *lo real maravilloso* (marvelous realism).

Do slave mothers, like Morrison's Sethe, have a "special knowledge" (Mohanty 2000, 236)? Can a realist account of identity spell out the claim that members of a diaspora often have a privileged, albeit sharable, knowledge about their social world? What are the valuable implications that the epistemic privilege of the politically oppressed and socially underprivileged people have? These are the major interpretive questions Mohanty grapples with in his provocative essay. If diaspora implicitly refers to an identity, and Morrison elaborates it in narratological and descriptive terms, Mohanty argues persuasively that readers of *Beloved* have been slow to see how Morrison elaborates diasporic identity in unavoidably moral and theoretical terms. Thus, instead of seeing Morrison's characters as "empty signifiers" and therefore dismissing her take on identities on the grounds that they are, after all, rhetorically constructed and hence "spurious," Mohanty argues that identities in *Beloved* are not only descriptive and affective but also evaluative and epistemic. Hence, realists need to distinguish between different kinds of constructedness and at the same time see the politics of identities as enmeshed in competing social and ethical-theoretical worldviews. Last, Mohanty sets the *Reclaiming Identity* project in motion by arguing for a notion of "epistemic privilege": that our experiences have real cognitive content and that deconstructive suspicions of experience are unwarranted.

Building on Mohanty's realist view of identity and his ideas about epistemic privilege, Moya and Hames-García complement and enlarge the realist view of the project by reading Cherríe Moraga's *Loving in the War Years* (1983) and Michael Nava's *The Hidden Law* (1992) as contributing to understandings of how the minoritized "other" can change us and how issues that challenge identity such as heterogeneity, multiplicity, and hybridity do not have to be seen as separate entities but can be seen as "mutually constitutive." If Moraga, as Moya (2000, 69) suggests, "understands identities as relational and grounded in the historically produced social categories that constitute social location" and not as trapped in a cyborgian "signifying function" à la Donna Haraway (1991), Nava's work, Hames-García argues, "demands that we . . . take seriously the moral implications" of Henry Ríos's experiences. For Hames-García (2000, 113), taking Henry's experiences seriously does not make him a "strategic essentialist," à la Gayatri Chakravorty Spivak (1988a); rather, Henry bases his claim on the "moral sense of his right to participate in a Chicano community on the basis of his cultural upbringing and experience of racialization" (Hames-García 2000, 113).

In the book's conclusion, "Who's Afraid of Identity Politics?," Alcoff carefully defends the new post-postivist accounts of identity by discussing how approaches to the self developed by Hegel, Freud, Foucault, and Althusser have influenced the most important postcontemporary conceptions of identity and subjectification. The answer to the problems of essentialism and anti-essentialism, Alcoff argues, is not Wendy Brown's theory of "wounded attachments" (Brown 1995), where the cycle of blame is never transcended, but new, better formulations of identity produced by the essayists in *Reclaiming Identity*. Near her essay's ending, Alcoff (2000, 335) writes, "To say that we have an identity is just to say that we have a location in social space, a hermeneutic horizon that is both grounded in a location and an opening or site from which we attempt to know the world. Understood in this way, it is incoherent to view identities as something we would be better off without."

Given this précis of what I take to be one of the central aims of the *Reclaiming Identity* project, I end this section by raising two issues for further interrogation. The first concerns the issue of identity in relationship to what Quijano and Wallerstein call "Americanity" and what Quijano, Mignolo, Agustín Laó-Montes, Ramón Grosfoguel, and others are theorizing as "the coloniality of power."[6]

As I noted in the preface, Quijano and Wallerstein (1992) argue that the Américas were fundamental to the formation of the modern (colonial) world-system and that Americanity is a fundamental element of modernity. For our purposes, Quijano and Wallerstein identify four new categories that originated in the so-called discovery of the Americas. They are coloniality, ethnicity, racism, and the concept of newness itself. My first hesitation with the *Reclaiming Identity* project thus has to do with the way most of the contributors are generally silent about our identities in relationship to what Quijano and Wallerstein grapple with in their work—namely, coloniality.

In other words, if Mohanty, Moya, Hames-García, and Alcoff are right that to have an identity means that we have to understand that "we have a location in social space" (Moya and Hames-García 2000, 335), would it not be useful for us to ground these identities and locations in the history of the modern (colonial) world-system? Quijano and Wallerstein remind us that, after all, coloniality created a structure of hierarchy and drew new boundaries around and within the Américas. Moreover, coloniality was essential to the formation of states, and in his more recent work, such as "Coloniality of Power, Eurocentrism, and Latin America" (2002), Quijano makes the additional claim that, even in decolonization, the "stateness" of decolonized states re-centered the colonial structure of power. In "What is termed globalization," Quijano (2000b, 533) writes,

> is the cultural process that began with the constitution of America and colonial/modern Eurocentered capitalism as a new global power. One of the fundamental axes of power is the social classification of the world's population around the idea of race, a mental construction that expresses the basic experience of colonial domination and pervades the more important dimensions of global power, including its rationality. The racial axis has a colonial origin and character, but it has proven to be more durable and stable than colonialism in whose matrix it was established. Therefore the model of power that is globally hegemonic today presupposes an element of coloniality.

For Quijano and Wallerstein (1992, 550; emphasis added), ethnic identity fundamentally is

> the set of communal boundaries into which in part we are put by others [through coloniality], in part which we impose upon ourselves, serving to locate our *identity* and our rank within the state. . . . [Ethnic identities] are always contemporary constructs, and thus always changing. All the major categories, however, into which we ethnically divide today in the Américas and the world (Native Americans or Indians, Blacks or Negroes, Whites or Creoles/Europeans, *Mestizos* or other names given to a so-called mixed-category)—all these categories did not exist prior to the modern world-system. They are part of what makes up Americanity. They have become the cultural staple of the entire world-system.

If our identities are real and affective, they do come from somewhere. Any post-contemporary account of subjectification (e.g., Butler, Laclau, and Žižek 2000) and any post-postivist realist account of identity (Mohanty, Moya, and Hames-García), I believe, would have to grapple with the "colonial difference" that Quijano and Wallerstein, among others, outline for us. Perhaps to get back to Alcoff's concluding riffs on the realist view of identity, that is why it might not be so dizzying for some to view identities as something we might be better off without. Michel Foucault (1982, 212), for instance, noted that the point is "not to discover what we are but to refuse what we are." But here, too, I would stress that Foucault, especially in *The History of Sexuality*, tends to erase the crafty details of the colonial difference in his analysis of biopower. On the whole, however, I am largely in strong agreement with Alcoff's point about the political power of our identities. In our informational culture and society, our identities, Manuel Castells (2003, 361) insists, are crucial and important because "they build interests, values, and projects, around experience, and refuse to dissolve by establishing a specific connection between nature, history, geography, and culture." Identities, Castells concludes (in Marxist realist fashion), "anchor power in some areas of the social structure, and build their resistance or their offensives in the informational struggle about the cultural codes constructing behavior and, thus, new institutions." It is this new subject or identity project of the informational mode of production, I believe, that many "straight" Marxists have refused to grapple with in their engagement with the power of identity politics.

This issue of global "coloniality," then, leads to another hesitation I have with the rich *Reclaiming Identity* project of Mohanty, Moya, and Hames-Garcia, and Alcoff. In his *Local Histories/Global Designs* (2000), Walter Mignolo draws on the social-science work of Quijano and Wallerstein to criticize various recent desires for universalist theories among both neoliberals and neo-Marxists. Mignolo (2000b) argues that, parallel to the ethno-racialized classification of the Américas and the world (the embalming of identities), the colonial project in the Américas also classified languages and knowledge. The epistemology of the European Renaissance therefore was assumed to be the natural perspective from which knowledge could be described and suppressed. This same process, Mignolo suggests, was resituated after the Enlightenment, when the concept of reason opened up a new description, and reason became associated with northern Europe and indirectly with whiteness (Hegel and Kant).

What are we to make of Mohanty's and Moya's use of an apparently idealist Kantian "universalism" in their post-positivist realist project? Should a realist view of identity not severely criticize the abstract hegemonic universalisms in Kant and the Enlightenment? Is it possible to imagine an "epistemic diversality or pluriversality," as Mignolo (drawing on the work of Édouard Glissant), suggests in his work on Zapatismo? For Mignolo (2002c, 264–65), diversality is not "the rejection of universal claims, but the rejection of universality understood as an abstract universal grounded in a monologic." Further, he writes, a "universal principle grounded on the idea of the di-versal is not a contradiction in terms but rather a displacement of conceptual structures."

As an alternative to the Kantian universalism in Moya's and Hames-García's post-positivist realist project, I propose that Gloria Anzaldúa's, Victor Martínez's, and Arundhati Roy's imaginative works belong to a "diversalist" cross-genealogical field that I term (after Quijano) the coloniality of border and diaspora power: "coloniality" because of the many structural and ethno-racial similarities about identity formations binding them to a colonizing past, but "border and diaspora power" because there are certainly many discontinuities —the outernational dimension of represented space—to dictate the cognitive metaphor of the "world-system" text, which, as I have been suggesting, recalls the world political economy of Wallerstein and Quijano.

The category of the coloniality of power is not, of course, without its defects.[7] But it has fewer than others, and it has some local and global advantages. So let Quijano's coloniality of power be taken in this book for what it is: a hypothesis designed to grapple with hierarchy based on what he terms the "social classification of the world's population around the idea of race" (2000, 533). The racial and gender axis of *mestizaje* in Anzaldúa's *Borderlands/La Frontera*, of peasants in Martínez's poem "Shoes," and of caste in Roy's *The God of Small Things* have colonial origins in the Américas and South Asia, but Anzaldúa, Martínez, and Roy suggest that race, peasantry, and caste have proved to be more durable in our so-called postcolonial world.

By cobbling together Quijano's concept of the coloniality of power and Wallerstein's world-systems analysis—as well as their theorizing of Americanity—we can argue that the coloniality of power has survived in the Américas and South Asia (the Portuguese brought the idea of caste with them to India) for more than five hundred years, yet they have not come to be transformed into a world empire. The secret strength of the coloniality of power and the world-system is the political side of economic organization called capitalism. Capitalism, Wallerstein (1974, 348) astutely argues, has flourished precisely because the world-economy "has had within its bounds not one but a multiplicity of political systems."

The Borderlands of Chicano/a Narrative and Subaltern Studies

Over the past decade, an awareness has begun to develop of the affinities between the imaginative work of recent Chicano/a imaginative writers and the thought of U.S. migratory postcolonial thinkers. Indeed, what is remarkable is that it should have taken so long for the interlocking of concerns between Chicano/a writers and postcolonial thinkers to be properly appreciated. Among the most prominent of such common concerns are the location of knowledge from the perspective of the U.S. empire's borderland contact zones; the critique of dominant Occidentalist perspectives in the current practices of U.S. social sciences, humanities, and area studies; and the grappling with localized geopolitics of knowledge and what Mignolo calls "border epistemologies."[8] Furthermore, these affinities have not only been observed by scholars from the Global South (Latin America and South Asia), for example; they are also becoming part of the self-consciousness in what Spivak (1995, 179) has called the "emerging dominant" in American studies.

This section is a study of the interplay between the performative, border epistemologies of two Chicano/a imaginative writers and the changing discourses of American vernacular literatures and cultures. Gloria Anzaldúa's and Victor Martínez's writings about U.S. Latino/a life explore, among other things, the linguistic intermixture of ethnic and mainstream languages (English, Spanish, and Spanglish) to illustrate the changing languages of America. What vernacular varieties of English or Spanish will dominate in twenty-first-century America? Which *lingua rustica* will the some 30 million U.S. Latinos/as (with more than 10 million in California) hegemonize in their testimonios, novels, essays, and poetry? What new literary genres, produced by Chicanos/as, will emerge in American literature? If the "dialect novel" was all the rage in late-nineteenth-century vernacular America (Mark Twain, George W. Cable, Abraham Cahan, W. E. B. Du Bois),[9] is there a borderlands English or Spanglish already under way in U.S. Latino/a-dominant California, Arizona, Florida, Texas, Illinois, and New York? On another level, I want to investigate the enabling condition of some recent Chicano/a narrative and poetry and the various ways in which they seek to create an epistemological ground on which versions of the world may be produced. As many U.S. Latino/a writers themselves suggest, to read is to question and to understand the (bilingual) texture and the rhetorical resources of language. If Anzaldúa sees the aesthetic structure of knowledge as a form of nepantilism, Martínez sees minority writing as a form of the California borderlands of subaltern studies informing mass youth U.S. Latino/a culture.[10]

To begin, I juxtapose Anzaldúa's key concept of U.S.-Mexican border nepantilism against the U.S. historian Frederick Jackson Turner's well-known nineteenth-century idea of the frontier. I do so to emphasize that while Turner and Anzaldúa may share some affinities of narrative and subaltern conventions and self-locations in the United States—each writer locates stories in a tradition of border historiography—their contrasts, I think, run far deeper, for Turner's paradigms of the "frontier" and Anzaldúa's *frontera* are not equivalent.

One of the most imperial images of the American West, Turner's so-called Frontier Thesis helped shape the study of Americanization both domestically and, after the War of 1898, globally. William Cronin (1995, 692) suggests that "few historical arguments [about the significance of the frontier in American history] have risen so high and fallen so far in [U.S.] scholarly reception." In a more recent overview, Kerwin Klein (1997, 13) put Turner's significance this way: "[Turner] introduced a new vocabulary into history by using old words in a new way, borrowing terms from other disciplines, and mixing these elements." In other words, Turner had flair for mixing what social scientists call "nomothetic" and "idiographic" epistemologies and discourses.

Turner famously opens "The Significance of the Frontier in American History" (1893) by quoting from the census report of the 1890s that described empirically the disappearance of the frontier. Moreover, in a nomothetic vein, Turner theorized that U.S. modernity and modernization were caused by the frontier, for "free land and its continuous recession and the advance of American settlement westward, explain American development" (Turner 1920, 1). By emphasizing the movement westward, northeastern Euro-Americans not only encountered peoples and cultures that were "less civilized" than they had experienced, but through this very contact, Turner argued, they left behind their Old World civilization and invented a new, North American one.

As Klein (1997, 183) suggests, Turner's essay "narrates a dramatic struggle between past and present." Turner's compositional mode of emplotment rolls out from East to West; from the Puritan's errand into the wilderness to San Francisco of the Gilded Age. Turner starts off quoting social-science data (census reports), then quickly moves into the mythos of romance. His invocations of colonial frontier heroes (Daniel Boone, Andrew Jackson, and Abraham Lincoln) are, as Klein notes, perfect "synecdoches for the American frontier spirit."

All of the familiar themes of the U.S. cultures of imperialism are cobbled together in "The Significance of the Frontier in American History": the advancing of the frontier; the free land, or the nineteenth century's equivalent of the twentieth-century U.S. food stamp program; and the conquering of and errand into the wilderness. Throughout, Turner is gracefully straightforward: "The frontier prompted the formation of a composite nationality for the American people" (Turner 1920, 40). One of my favorite lines reveals Turner's poetic flair: "In the crucible of the frontier, the immigrants were Americanized, liberated, and fused into one mixed race, English in neither nationality nor characteristics" (Turner 1920, 40).

Klein sees Turner's essay moving in the direction of an Emersonian and Hegelian universalism. Other U.S. historians, such as Richard White (1994), locate it as part of an emerging incantatory imperialism. By strategically using frontier iconography in his essay—log cabins, covered wagons, canoes, and the like—Turner argued for a Jeffersonian "empire for liberty," surely one of the most interesting nationalist oxymorons for the cultures of U.S. imperialism. Like

White, George Sánchez (1993, 38) chastises Turner for constructing "a myopic vision" in his essay—"that of the East looking West, civilization looking toward chaos, Europe looking toward the rest of the world." Conversely, against Turner's hegemonic vision, Sánchez (1993, 38) suggests that the concept of the transnational frontera developed in postcolonial Chicano/a studies works against Turner's myopic imperialism; the transnational frontera, he argues, suggests "limitations, boundaries over which American power might have little or no control. It implies a dual vision, that of two nations looking at each other over a strip of land they hold in common." U.S. Latino/a border thinking therefore enacts a powerful contrapuntal corrective for mainline American studies.

In thinking about the emplotments of Turner's frontier essay and Anzaldúa's frontera thinking, it might be productive to consider what James Clifford has astutely noted about the diaspora emplotments of Paul Gilroy's postcolonial *There Ain't No Black in the Union Jack* (1987). Diaspora cultures, Clifford (1997, 265) writes, are "produced by regimes of political domination and economic inequality." These cultures, moreover, "cannot claim an oppositional or primary purity. Fundamentally ambivalent, they grapple with the entanglement of subversion and the law, of invention and subversion—the complicity of dystopia and utopia."

Does Anzaldúa's Chicana paradigm of the U.S.-Mexican borderlands share in expressing diaspora culture's dystopic–utopian tensions? Are both bad news and good news built into the text? Can Anzaldúa's re-codification of the utopian otherwise as nepantilism help us better ground or grapple with the tensions and ambivalences that Clifford theorizes in his reading of Gilroy's work? What are we to make of Anzaldúa's deportation stories, of her invocation of the U.S.-Mexican War of 1846–48, of the post–Jim Crow ethno-racial hierarchies in South Texas, of the international division of labor with undocumented women at the center of the maquiladoras, and of her dramatic swerve to nepantilism and new mestiza consciousness in *Borderlands/La Frontera*?

Border thinking, for Anzaldúa, is a site of crisscrossed experience, language, and identity. Mignolo's de-colonial reading of Anzaldúa is especially helpful in this context. She draws, Mignolo (2000b, 237) insists, "a different map: that of reverse migration, the migration from colonial territories relabeled the Third World (after 1945), toward the

First." This reverse U.S. Latino/a migratoriness, in Mignolo's view, helps explain Anzaldúa's powerful "languaging practices," which "fracture the colonial language" (Mignolo 2000b, 237).

If *Borderlands/La Frontera* thematizes not the hegemonic Hegelian–Emersonian universalism of Turner's Frontier Thesis but the epistemic diversal reason of the multiple broken tongues of Greater Mexico's local nepantilism, "such fractures," Mignolo (2000b, 237) argues, "occur due to the languaging practices of two displaced linguistic communities" in Anzaldúa's work: "Nahuatl, displaced by the Spanish expansion and Spanish displaced by the increasing hegemony of the colonial languages of the modern period (English, German, and French)."

This fracturing and braiding of colonial and postcolonial languages explain why *Borderlands/La Frontera* has the power to elicit such critical emphasis from Mignolo, one of the most innovative critics of de-colonial literatures of the Américas. Reading Anzaldúa as a Chicana feminist philosopher of fractured and braided languages is precisely what I address later as one of the major issues in *Borderlands/La Frontera* and, indeed, for U.S. Latino/a studies in particular and for the future of minority studies in general.

Rather than a unified subject representing a folk border culture in any holistic sense, we meet in Anzaldúa's Chicana neologism *autohistoriateoría*,[11] a braided, mestiza consciousness, and a feminist writer fundamentally caught between various hegemonic colonial and postcolonial languages and subaltern dialects and vernacular expressions. Her lament that "wild tongues" such as her own "can not be tamed" for "they can only be cut out" (Anzaldúa 1987, 76) might as well be addressed to her complex postcolonial audience of radical women and (feminist) men of color. Throughout *Borderlands/La Frontera*, Anzaldúa expresses regret that even her bilingual mother in Hargill has been partially complicit in valuing the English language of the hegemonic: "I want you to speak English. Pa' hallar buen trabajo tienes que saber hablar el inglés bien. Que vale toda tu educación si todavía hablas inglés con un 'accent,' my mother would say, mortified that I spoke English like a Mexican. At Pan American University, I, and all Chicano students were required to take two speech classes. Their purpose: to get rid of our accents" (Anzaldúa 1987, 54–55).

In *Borderlands/La Frontera*, Anzaldúa not only self-consciously speaks English with an "accent," she also writes in multiply accented, vernacular tongues. Read with its marked accentuation, Anzaldúa's work can be reinterpreted as expressing a North American situation of multi-dialectism. Her negative dialectical answers to her earlier meditations that she will not "tame a wild tongue," or "train it to be quiet," or "make it lie down" (Anzaldúa 1987, 53) are her feminist philosophical dictums of border language and de-colonial thinking. At the very heart of Anzaldúa's Chicana feminist autohistoriateoría is her claim that a braided "tongue" is centrally and dramatically at war with (internal) colonialism, U.S. Empire, patriarchy, and androcentrism's project to silence women: "Ser habladora was to be a gossip or a liar" (Anzaldúa 1987, 54).

Anzaldúa's response to being preoccupied with "the unique positioning consciousness takes at these confluent streams" (Anzaldúa 1987, i) is apprehended linguistically in the text in the juxtaposition of multiple dialects or tongues—Tex-Mex, *caló*, *choteo*, Spanish, and English—with their dominant and subaltern varieties. Moreover, this linguistic juxtaposition allows us to see Anzaldúa's attempts to reflect post–Jim Crow ethno-racial practices in South Texas, as well as attempts at nepantilism—however incomplete—to merge, transculturate, and braid different ethno-racial formations and languages in a single text. As she puts it, she struggles with an "almost instinctive urge to communicate, to speak, to write about life on the borders, life in the shadows" (Anzaldúa 1987, i). In this regard, Anzaldúa's *conciencia de la nueva mestiza* seems to be a respectful and gendered updating of W. E. B. Du Bois's famous insights of the early twentieth century about the cross-linguistic foundations of double consciousness and the shadows of the color line:

> One ever feels a two-ness, an American, a Negro; two souls, two thoughts, two unreconciled strivings; two warring ideals in one dark body, whose dogged strength alone keeps it from being torn asunder. The history of the Negro is the history of this strife . . . to merge his double self into a better and truer self. In this merging he wishes neither of the older selves to be lost . . . He would not bleach his Negro soul in a flood of *white Americanism*, for he knows that Negro blood has a *message* for the world. (Du Bois 1986 [1903], 364–65; emphasis added)

My point is that Anzaldúa, like Du Bois, sees her Chicana consciousness as a fractured, cracked, and braided construction, an effort to merge new cultural formations and ethno-racial subjectivities. Like

Du Bois, she highlights the inherent U.S. linguistic wars both inside the body of the nation and in the body of her soul, for like the U.S.-Mexican border itself, it is "an open wound, dividing a *pueblo*, a culture, / running down the length of my body, / [it] splits me, splits me / me raja, me raja" (Anzaldúa 1987, 2). Both Du Bois and Anzaldúa call for new ethnic, linguistic, and cultural exchanges between the Global South and Global North. If for Du Bois at the beginning of the twentieth century, blackness and whiteness were inextricably woven together, then for Anzaldúa at the century's end, Chicana, Latina, African American, and Euro-American vernacular English and Spanish have been knitted together into what Du Bois called "the very warp and woof of this nation" (1986, 545). This "colonial difference" is crucial to emphasize for those of us tracking Chicano/a studies' shifting and shifty cross-genealogy from the matrix of globalization's coloniality.

In arguing for the centrality of human language rights in *Borderlands/La Frontera*, I mean to support the astute and bold de-colonial evaluations of Anzaldúa's "border gnosis," without losing sight of the importance of her multiple renaming processes and radical re-codifications of womanhood. As Chicana feminist scholars such as Norma Alarcón, Chela Sandoval, Yvonne Yarbro-Bejarano, Angie Chabram-Dernersesian, Sonia Saldívar-Hull, and Paula Moya have rigorously and gracefully argued, *Borderlands/La Frontera* is fundamentally a Chicana feminist text; a first-rate *historia* of post–Jim Crow South Texas; a jolting new positioning of the native woman in Chicana studies; a terrific study in comparative whiteness and brownness; and a post-positivist realist call for identity and social justice.[12] Yet what is perhaps an equally powerful feature of Anzaldúa's text has also been one of its least analyzed: her discussion of nepantilism as a braided U.S. Latino/a linguistic consciousness. La conciencia de la nueva mestiza, for Anzaldúa (1987, 55), is "neither español ni inglés, but both"; it is a consciousness of *nepantla*, a Mexica term that signifies de-colonial in-betweenness and that is "capable of communicating the real values" of the U.S.-Mexican borderlands to others.

In arguing for the centrality of her "forked," "wild," and active feminist tongues, Anzaldúa (1987, 56) emphasizes that these tongues are informed with other, border-crossing tongues: "los recién llegados, Mexican immigrants, north from Mexico," and the older tongues of the "braceros." Into these vernacular tongues she merges the Tex-Mex dialects that she uses with her brothers and sisters and the "secret language of *pachuco*, a language of rebellion" to create a foundational consciousness of the new mestiza.

Read against recent legal attempts in California and Florida (states with large U.S. Latino/a populations) to force English-only linguistic absolutism, Anzaldúa's *Borderlands/La Frontera* offers readers a dialect-centered anti-absolutism, for there "is no one Chicano language just as there is no one Chicano experience" (Anzaldúa 1987, 58). In her own testimonial theorization of experience, she notes that in high school she was "encouraged to take French classes because French [was] considered more 'cultured,'" but ends by noting that "Spanish speakers [by 2005] will comprise the biggest [minority] group in the USA" (Anzaldúa 1987, 59). However, she also argues that by the end of the twentieth century, a braided "Chicana/o" English "will be the mother tongue of most" Chicanas/os (Anzaldúa 1987, 59).

I have focused on what may seem to be one of many issues: what Anzaldúa terms the practices and resistances of "tam[ing] a wild tongue" (Anzaldúa 1987, 54). My goal has been to highlight various things at once: to agree with Anzaldúa's insistence on the centrality of nepantilism as a minoritized and postcolonial linguistic project and to explore nepantilism as her attempt to merge multiple subaltern and vernacular "serpent tongues—my woman's voice, my sexual voice, my poet's voice" (Anzaldúa 1987, 59).

The souls of the outernational new mestizas, Anzaldúa (1987, 62) argues, have "nothing to do with which country one lives in"; they are "neither eagle or serpent, but both." It is precisely this going beyond the two-ness of national consciousness to which Anzaldúa aspires in *Borderlands/La Frontera*. If Gavin Jones (1999, 39) is right that at the heart of nineteenth-century American literature was "the cult of the vernacular," with real "political and cultural functions," Anzaldúa's autohistoriateoría grounds her late-twentieth-century work in the differential vernacular serpent's tongue, a catechristic subalternist tongue that is capable of cracking, fracturing, and braiding the very authority of the master's English-only tongue. In her rich post-new mestiza writings, Anzaldúa expanded the de-colonial theoretical concepts I have analyzed in provocative and creative ways. *La frontera* morphed into *nepantla, nueva mestizas* became *nepantleras*, and those interested in mestiza consciousness had to grapple with her iconic notion of *conocimiento*.[13] As AnaLouise Keating (2009, x) suggests, "Because scholars, publishers, students, and others [have] focused so much of their attention on *Borderlands/La Frontera*," these new decolonial theorizings have not yet fully "received the attention they deserve."

Anzaldúa's deep awareness of an interstitial *nepantla conocimiento*, however, empowers new, understudied Chicano/a narratives and transmodernist poetry. Victor Martínez's novel *Parrot in the Oven* is a splendid case in point. To better locate Martínez's double-voiced vernacular novel, I begin by exploring his poem "Shoes" (1992), an everyday symbol that reappears in the novel about gangs, *klikas*, and youth cultures in California:

Out of all of our enemies, all the catastrophes of nations
scattered to rubble, plowed over with salt, we still have
the warm friendliness, the unrelenting spirit
of our shoes to console us.
Two bubbles chopped square out of shapeless emptiness
how this invention hisses in a hurry to correct time
pumping little sneezes of sympathy for our tardiness.
Although they owe us nothing, they walk
in many of our dreams, conjuring music
from a vaporous sidewalk or standing
as pure reverence
over the peaceful herds of our dead.
They, who always return back to us faithfully
from every tropic, every desert,
to take us their jobs as stealth for the burglar,
spring under the killer's crouch, courage
for the guerrilla. They guard us
against thistles and thorns, protect us from stone
and unseen disasters of glass.
Wheels mean nothing to the shoe. They are the first
of peasants and would never think to kneel
before any god, or suck up to whatever tablet of the Law.
Ravenous for distance, they supply whole lives
with the loss of a mere heel
yet wear death, only once. (Martínez 1992, 12)

"Shoes" allows Martínez to represent everyday things in the world, especially what he describes lyrically as "the unrelenting spirit of our shoes" and how they often function "to console us." A flood of questions appears on the screen of transmodernist U.S. "border thinking": for what, specifically, do Martínez's shoes console us? For the "elements of San Joaquin"; for the pesticides of California agribusiness? For the worldliness of the documented and undocumented farm worker? For the nepantilism of our dwellings, the unhomeliness of mass youth culture?

In an intertextual and transcultural frame of reference, "Shoes" positions itself to comment audaciously on discussions of modernity and aesthetics, specifically by alluding to such discussions embedded in Vincent van Gogh's painting *A Pair of Boots*. Why is Martínez interested in the debates surrounding modernist art? Does his poem grasp the structural and socially symbolic meanings of peasants' "shoes" and farmworkers' "boots"? In his landmark *Postmodernism, or, the Logic of Late Capitalism*, Fredric Jameson (1991, 7) argues that van Gogh's painting unleashes the "whole object of agricultural misery, of stark rural poverty." In his poem, Martínez, an experienced former farm wage worker himself, thematizes "epistemic privilege," for "Shoes" apprehends the brutalizing world of agribusiness growers and their tussle with the wage earners, who, after 1965, were able to organize themselves through César Chávez's United Farm Workers Committee.

If, as Jameson suggests, van Gogh's painting can only evoke the alienated labor of peasants, who themselves are worn down like a pair of boots, the modernist painter can only represent this through his "hallucinatory surface of color," sometimes "garishly overlaid with hues of red and green" (Jameson 1991, 7). In other words, *A Pair of Boots*, like "Shoes," embodies deep dystopian and utopian tensions and ambivalences that we saw earlier in Anzaldúa's narratives of the U.S.-Mexican borderlands and Gilroy's narratives of the black Atlantic diaspora. I am even tempted to argue, after Jameson, that the works of art by both Martínez and van Gogh can be rewritten "acts of compensation which end up producing a new Utopian realm of the senses" (Jameson 1991, 7)—especially through the visual in van Gogh's painting and the figurative and tropological in Martínez's writing.

In this way, Martínez suggests, "shoes" always return to us; they form the very in-betweenness in our post-bracero North–South global division of labor in California. On another level, if, as Martin Heidegger (quoted in Jameson 1991, 8) once put it, van Gogh's painting "vibrates the silent call of the earth . . . its enigmatic self-refusal in the fallow desolation of the wintry field," "Shoes" is Martínez's attempt to represent the very Heideggerian "equipment" migrant farm workers in California need to make do. "They are," Martínez writes, "the first / of peasants and would never think to kneel / before any God, or suck up to whatever tablets of the Law."

Before moving on to a figural reading of *Parrot in the Oven*, I want to underline Martínez's use of the word "peasant" in his poem. What is he trying to link up in his meditation on Mexican American farm workers and peasants? Is Martínez, like the South Asian subaltern historians, trying to democratize U.S. poetry by looking on subordinate social groups—farm workers and campesinos—as the makers of their own minoritized destiny? My own sense is that, by looking at farm workers'/campesinos' shoes, Martínez is attempting to stretch the very category of the political far beyond the borders assigned to them in European and American political thought. Farm workers are not pre-political or pre-modern in any senses of the terms. Like Ranajit Guha (1988, 1997) before him, Martínez insists that farm workers are real contemporaries of the coloniality of power in the modern Américas (not pre-modern or primitive rebels) and that they are a fundamental part of the modernity that coloniality brought to the Américas some five hundred years earlier.

Martínez's *Parrot in the Oven: Mi Vida* was initially marketed by its publisher in New York as a young adult novel. Can we contrapuntally read this young adult novel against the apparently more mature, modern, adult philosophical poem "Shoes"? Do these works have anything in common? Do they inform each other and help us do away with false dichotomies, such as the "young adult" and "adult" classifications of literature? Why do mainline U.S. publishers insist on infantilizing U.S. Latino/a writers? Can a minoritized reading based on U.S. Latino/a mass youth culture help us better ground Martínez's epistemological obsession with the gaps between the farm worker's earth and a post-developed California world? My firm sense is that Martínez's novel opens up fresh vistas on the relationship between mass culture and the social by transforming radically the genre of the so-called young adult novel itself.

This emergent genre, like children's literature, is marginalized in the institutions of the academy. Martínez cross-cuts this subalternized form, however, by focusing precisely on the ethno-racialized subalterns in California, especially the young *vatos firmes*, the klikas, youth gangs, and their ritual initiations—what the Chicano hip-hop artist Kid Frost (1992) describes as the poetics of "las chavas, las balas, and the Chevy Impalas." If Robin Kelley (1997, 37) is right that "most rap music is not about a nihilistic street life but about rocking the mike," *Parrot in the Oven* takes its inventive linguistic lessons from the very youth culture it explores. What counts for Martínez is not just the tussles in the barrio but the wild storytelling riffs and figures of speech of the young Chicano/a characters—especially Manny's ability to make comparisons in his world; his often hilarious facility in seeing likenesses between unlike things; and, as Kelley (1997, 37) argues is fundamental to most urban rap music, his "ability to kick some serious . . . linguistic inventiveness." This is what Martínez's rich *Parrot in the Oven* is fundamentally "about."

As in "Shoes," we can discern or discover the hermeneutical horizon of at least two levels or symptoms of reading. To begin with, *Parrot in the Oven* focuses on Manny Hernández, a young homey from the barrio projects who is determined to discover for himself what it means (existentially and cognitively) to be a vato firme (a guy to respect). The male hero's coming of age is the *bildung* of the young adult novel. Moreover, Martínez continually meditates on the related spaces of home and leisure and, à la Gilroy and Kelley, sees the male body as an instrument not only of labor but also of pleasure. Manny, as we will see, draws a lot of pleasure through his intense labor of producing whirling figurative play.

At the beginning of *Parrot in the Oven*, Manny lives in the barrio 'hood, somewhere in the projects of Sal Si Puedes, and attends J. Edgar Hoover High School in the San Joaquin Valley. Like the farm workers in "Shoes," he has to make do and grapple with his working-class family life: an alcoholic father, Manny Sr.; an abused mother, Rebecca, who daily puts on a pair of worn-out boots and mops the barrio casita's floors; and his brothers and sisters. Manny comes of age in Sal Si Puedes in a poetic series of fast-paced chapter vignettes. Stylistically and rhetorically, Martínez maintains the specificity of his setting and mass youth characterization through artful everyday vernacular dialogues and through the use of intense language, what I discussed earlier as Martínez's startling elegant poetic imagery in "Shoes." Some of my favorite tropes include the following from Manny's consciousness:

> He could duck trouble better than a champion boxer could duck a right cross. (3)
>
> Dad is always "cursing," "simmering," and "ready to boil over." (5)
>
> Migrant farm workers are like "whirlwinds." (13)
>
> She was just trying to blossom herself up. (59)
>
> I had a face Dad said would look handsome on a horse. (80)
>
> She worked hard for beauty, teasing her hair as an ocean wave. (92)
>
> Her shadow will be erased, and her soul will drift to heaven like a fluff of a dandelion in the wind. And then it will blossom in another garden, so bright the colors will hurt your eyes. (89)

Against the tussles of everyday misery in Manny's barrio life, the world opens up its worldliness through Martínez's poetic transpositions and metaphoric exchanges.

Martínez's narrative focuses on the underside of the Hernández family romance, but *Parrot in the Oven* never lacks compassion. Throughout, Manny wonders how his sisters and mother "were able to stand it" (Martínez 1996, 12). Incredibly, perhaps, Manny even makes fun of the profound alienation and pain of his father's abusive patriarchy by saying to himself, "Deep down Dad liked me." This has to be read contrapuntally, I suppose, against all of the hard smacks given to him by his father, for even the title of the novel, *Parrot in the Oven: Mi Vida*, evokes a male folk patriarchal bruising. "Perico, or parrot, was what Dad called me sometimes. It was from a Mexican saying about a parrot that complains how hot it is in the shade, while all along he's sitting inside an oven. People usually say this when talking about ignorant people who don't know where they're at in the world" (Martínez 1996, 51–52), In other words, Manny's dad thinks his son is a *pendejo*, pure and simple.

Manny, the protagonist of the young adult novel, however, survives and even triumphs over his father's awkward love; California's underendowed, ugly Proposition 13 public schools; and countless barrio feuds by working himself through a final climactic gang-initiation beating. He is punched and whacked with storms of claps, kicks, and bites. When it is over, Manny's young body swells all over, and Martínez writes, "I could smell the acidy stink of the dirt, but strangely enough, there was no fear. Nor could I feel those blows, which felt, like instead of me, they were hitting a slab of meat on a table. . . . When they finally let me up, I sat there . . . swelling fast, flaring alive with throbs" (Martínez 1996, 194).

Parrot in the Oven ends by thinking not only about the body's pains and pleasures from the "sonic" forces surrounding it, but also by narrating the body's place, pursuing barrio spaces into some of its jolting corners and subtle surfaces. For Martínez, place is intriguing, valuable, pleasurable, and indispensable. At the novel's end, Manny forces us to face place, to confront it and take off its masks:

> When I opened the door to our house, the sun, out again, came rushing into the living room. Shadows lifted from the floor like a flock of birds rising into the horizon, and light guttered through the room, slapping away the dark for good. . . . Magda and Pedi were lying asleep. . . . Magda's hair was fanned out on a pillow, unteased. . . . Then I sat down on Dad's cushioned chair and watched them . . . and the room. . . . And it was a wondrous place. . . . My home. The light in the room was closing in around me. (Martínez 1996, 214–15)

Declaring Oneself a "Mobile Republic": South Asian Kinship and Identity

To conclude this chapter, I stay with the thematizations of minoritized identities and the coloniality matrix of power I outlined in a broad trans-Americanity mapping of sorts and examine briefly how post-contemporary South Asian writings in English of the memories of violence and identity may also help us think through the "colonial difference" in a more global framework. I do not approach this question as a specialist in the history of the English novel in India. My relation to a globalized matrix of power is clearly at an early stage of thinking. However, what I have found in preliminary readings of some of the most important English novels in India is this: at their center are histories and memories of violence and the coloniality of power—how humans produce absolutist "others" out of others. In this sense, narratives of the violence of colonialism in the English novel in India—

Salman Rushdie's *Midnight's Children* or Amitav Ghosh's *The Hungry Tide*, for example—are also narratological studies of the politics of identity and the colonial difference. What animates many South Asian novels in English of the memories of violence of British coloniality, of the Partition of 1947, and beyond is the question of how to live within the context of global coloniality. At another level, South Asian (Indian) writers working in English (like the double or mestiza/o consciousness of Du Bois, Anzaldúa, and Martínez) must continually grapple with the colonial histories that form the very English language they and their characters use.[14]

The complexities of South Asian identities and kinship are at the heart of Arundhati Roy's novel *The God of Small Things* (1997). Central to the novel is a vision of the continuity between knowing the world through experience and struggle and changing the central relations of the coloniality of power that sustain and make the world what it is. In addition, subalternized characters in the novel, especially children, divorced women, and peasants, defy bloodlines of kinship and caste to condemn the bloodshed of their everyday world in Kerala. In so doing, they defy the gods of both dominance and kinship to remember what they experienced and shared with the god of small things.

The radicalized sense of kinship sought in *The God of Small Things* involves an expanded standpoint positionality of oneself—in particular, the ability to enlarge and enrich one's ability to experience.[15] Thus envisaged, readers can better understand the political terms of the debate over the coloniality of power, caste, and the normative principles of kinship within postcolonial Kerala that inform and shape the narrative: the debate between Ammu and the twins Rahel and Estha, on the one hand, and Mammachi, Baby Kochamma, and the local police, on the other, about the (archaic) nature of so-called Untouchables in postcolonial Kerala. Did Velutha, that "cheerful man without footprints . . . count?," Ammu asks her children (Roy 1997, 208). Was it possible for Ammu, Rahel, and Estha, "bounded by the certain, separate knowledge," to have really "loved a man [Velutha] to death" (Roy 1997, 307)? "How could [Ammu] stand the smell? . . . They have a particular smell, these Paravans" (Roy 1997, 243), Baby Kochamma asks when she hears from the peasant Vallya Paapen what Ammu and Velutha have done. How we evaluate this debate over the global coloniality of power, the love laws, kinship, and the politics of the erotic depends on how we interpret Rahel's and Estha's remarkable transformation and defiance at the novel's end and how we see the melancholic relationship between their ability to experience and understand, their capacity to grieve for their mother and Velutha, and even, perhaps, how in their grieving they de-institute kinship.

Ammu's defiant response to her family's insistence on maintaining caste rules coherent in Keralan culture and society is to make the twins Rahel and Estha "promise" that they will "always love each other"—especially in the face of what Roy (1997, 168) refers to as the local "love laws," which pin down "who should be loved. And how. And how much." With this straightforward speech act of promising, Ammu tampers throughout the novel with the stable heteronormative issues of family, bloodlines, and the bourgeois nation. The political vision of the subaltern that *The God of Small Things* seeks primarily through the standpoint positionality of women, children, and peasants provides the context in which support of caste and the coloniality of power by family members such as Mammachi, by Baby Kochamma, and by the state police can be challenged, made specific, and given meaning. These are the many idioms of dominance and subordination that Roy thematizes in the novel.

Ammu's capacity to know herself is directly related to her ability to feel with others and tussle with the normative rules of kinship in Kerala: "It was what she had battling inside her. An unmixable mix. The infinite tenderness of motherhood and the reckless rage of a suicide bomber. It was this that grew inside her, and eventually led her to love by night the man her children loved by day" (Roy 1997, 44). When Ammu disgraces her bourgeois family by divorcing an alcoholic and abusive husband and returning with her young twins to her parents' home in Ayemenem, she intensely feels "that there [will] be no more chances. There was only . . . a front verandah and a back verandah. A hot river and a pickle factory. . . . And in the background, the constant, high, whining mewl of local disapproval" (Roy 1997, 42). It is Ammu's braided, "unmixable mix[ed]" subaltern consciousness of "tenderness" and "rage" that drives her feelings toward her children, the Untouchable Velutha, and her disapproving, mewling family and local culture and society. The urgent assurances that the peasant and card-carrying communist Velutha provides to Ammu profoundly change her and her children. Velutha, I sustain, makes possible a qualitative cognitive reorientation through his "beauty" and his labor and the gifts he gives her, the children, and the family's business. "As she watched him she understood the quality of his beauty. How his labor had shaped him.... Had left its stamp on him. Had given him his strength, his supple grace" (Roy 1997, 316). Interestingly, Velutha is important not only because he is the god of small things in Kerala but also because of the qualitative joy he produces in others with his magician-like "facility with his hands." Since he was eleven, Roy emphasizes, Velutha "could make intricate toys—tiny windmills, rattles, minute jewel boxes out of dried palm reeds; he could carve perfect boats of tapioca stems and figurines on cashew nuts. He would bring them for Ammu, holding them on his palm (as he had been taught) so she wouldn't have to touch him to take them" (Roy 1997, 71–72).

In addition to his graceful carpentry and toy-making skills, Velutha "mended radios, clocks, water pumps. He looked after the plumbing and all the electrical gadgets in the house" (Roy 1997, 72). Years later, Velutha's creative engineering skills are used at Ammu's family's business, where he reassembles "bottle-sealing machines" and maintains "new cannery machines" and automatic fruit and vegetable slicers (Roy 1997, 72). Indeed, one of the main reasons for seeing Velutha as a pivotal character in the political debate about "who counts" in Kerala and the world that *The God of Small Things* stages is that he reveals an enormous ability to create culture and society for everyone around him. He has an enormous imaginative and cognitive life of experiences that the coloniality of power in Kerala has denied him as a Paravan.

Although there are several tragic deaths in *The God of Small Things* (the novel opens with the memories of the Mol family grieving around the coffin of the Anglo-Indian Sophie Mol, who has drowned, and Ammu dies alone in a grimy room at the Bharat Lodge in Alleppey at the viable—and die-able—age of thirty-one), the novel revolves around the brutal death of Velutha and the postcolonial nation's inability to count him as one of its own.[16] After a forbidden sexual encounter between Ammu and Velutha is uncovered by Ammu's family, Baby Kochamma files a complaint with the local police on false charges and, with the approval of the local Marxist party hierarchy, Velutha is hunted down, beaten, and tortured to death at the police station. "His skull was fractured in three places. His nose and both his cheekbones were smashed, leaving his face pulpy, undefined. The blow to his mouth had split open his upper lip and broken six teeth.... Four of his ribs were splintered . . . [t]he blood on his breath bright red. Fresh. Frothy" (Roy 1997, 294).

The God of Small Things circles around Velutha's, Sophie Mol's, and Ammu's deaths and the subsequent "social deaths" of Rahel and Estha.[17] After the twins are forced by Baby Kochamma to "save" Ammu's sexual and caste reputation by condemning Velutha on false charges of kidnapping and child abuse, Roy shows how dominance (without hegemony) intrudes into the smallest spaces in Kerala. What Rahel and Estha experience, Roy writes, is "a clinical demonstration in controlled conditions . . . of human nature's pursuit of ascendancy. Structure. Order. Complete monopoly . . . If [the police] hurt Velutha more than they intended to, it was only because any *kinship*, any connection between themselves and him, any implication that if nothing else, at least biologically he was a fellow creature—had been severed long ago. [T]he posse of Touchable Policemen acted with economy, not frenzy. Efficiency, not anarchy. Responsibility, not hysteria" (Roy 1997, 293; emphasis added).

Velutha's life and brutal death force Rahel and Estha to tamper with the incoherencies of "kinship" and biology. Kinship therefore is not just a situation in which Rahel and Estha, Ammu and Velutha, find themselves but a set of practices in postcolonial Kerala that, as Roy suggests, are controlled, performed, ritualized, and monopolized by those in power. Kinship trouble, we might say, is what Roy seeks to de-institute in *The God of Small Things*.

In political and psychoanalytical terms, *The God of Small Things* traces Estha's and Rahel's struggles to "work through" the implications of their complex cathectic relations with postcolonial Kerala and the Ayemenem House (see LaCapra 1996). Estha never fully recovers; he stops talking altogether. Occupying as little space as possible in Kerala, he walks "along the banks of the river that smelled like shit and pesticides bought with World Bank loans" (Roy 1997, 14). Rahel, too, returns from a self-imposed diaspora of sorts in the United States, where she suffers a bad marriage in Boston, divorces, and labors at an ethnic restaurant in New York City. When she learns that Estha has returned to Ayemenem (they have been apart for twenty-five years, since December 1969), she comes home.

Surviving the brutal past in Kerala for Rahel is partly predicated on her identity of diaspora; her attempt to form a coherent present also involves a transgressive "acting out" with her twin brother, Estha. The adult twins do so by making the love laws and their rules incoherent. Interestingly, Roy cannot directly represent Rahel's and Estha's sexual transgression; after all, Roy explains, there was "very little that anyone could say to clarify what happened" to Rahel and Estha. "Nothing that . . . would separate Sex from Love. Or Needs from Feelings" (Roy 1997, 310). What can be narrated is that Estha and Rahel had held each other closely, long after making love, and that "that night was not happiness, but hideous grief" (Roy 1997, 311).

Hideous grieving, intimate loving, working through the coloniality of melancholia—all of these idioms are woven together in *The God of Small Things* through Rahel and Estha, suggesting the complexity involved in coming to know oneself and expanding one's capacity to experience with others. The figures of Rahel and Estha may well compel a reading that tampers with the normative spheres of kinship, bloodlines that sustain and monopolize the society and the nation by exposing the socially contingent character of kinship.[18]

Roy ends her postcolonial novel by suggesting how much theoretical and historical knowledge is involved in Ammu's, Estha's, and Rahel's learning to experience in Kerala. Their changing relationship with Velutha is based on an understanding of the brutality of caste, the love laws, and the necessity (and urgency) to de-institute them. *The God of Small Things* is one of the most intriguing postcolonial texts precisely because of the ways it indicates the extent to which subaltern identity and experience depend on a minor (or small) historiography. We cannot claim a political identification, Roy suggests, until we have reconstituted our small collective identities and re-examined who counts in our cultures and societies.

In conclusion, I suggest that Anzaldúa's iconic pensamiento fronterizo is linked to a realist view of U.S. minoritized studies. I suggest further that the recent directions in minoritized studies—subaltern studies, the coloniality of power, and post-positivist realist studies— could be taken as the most significant movements in U.S. postcolonial studies rather than as blueprints or master discourses to be imposed worldwide. Thus, pensamiento fronterizo in minoritized studies demands a different conceptualization of the self, of power, and of cultural citizenship. I have also assumed a framework in which the minoritized and subalternized designs in Anzaldúa's, Martínez's, and Roy's narratives are linked to different stages of the modern world-system: the coloniality of power from the Renaissance to the present in Anzaldúa's and Martínez's narratives and the love laws and British imperial difference in Roy's novel. All three minoritized designs in these Chicano/a and South Asian works argue for a border and diasporic thinking as a necessary epistemology on which a diversalist knowledge can be articulated in a transmodernist world governed by global capitalism and new forms of coloniality. Finally, this chapter is an argument for a critical and comparative cosmopolitanism from below; at the same time, I see in Anzaldúa's, Martínez's, and Roy's imaginative writings a plea for a new politics of nepantla's conocimiento—one that conceives border and diasporic thinking as a critical project.

2 ⊱

Migratory Locations:
Subaltern Modernity and José Martí's
Trans-American Cultural Criticism

If we see the formation of the modern world as a unitary global process that has entailed the mutual constitution of cores and peripheries, the project of provincializing Western modernity involves as well recognizing the periphery as the site of subaltern modernities.—FERNANDO CORONIL, *The Magical State*

The task of subaltern studies [is] to conceptualize multiple possibilities of creative political action rather that requiring a more "mature" political type of formation.—JOSÉ RABASA, "Of Zapatismo"

How is the migratory subaltern subject, in a trans-American politics of location, to be conceptualized as revolutionary and antimilitaristic, Latin American and North American, at one and the same time? What are the limits of our modern notions of citizenship, identity, and residence for activist intellectuals involved in intense processes of de-territorialization?[1] How does José Martí's exile and residence in New York City and the United States (1880–95) map out the boundaries of a "transnationally local" genealogy of modernist discursive practices?[2] It is with these questions about subaltern modernity that my study of trans-American cultural criticism begins through a rhetorical reading of Martí's Latinamericanism and Julio Ramos's classic study of Martí in the United States, *Divergent Modernities: Culture and Politics in Nineteenth-Century Latin America* (2001).[3]

Modernity, as Martí reminds us, not only involved him in "a superficial, vulgar, and uproarious intimacy" with U.S. mass culture and racial formations (as he critically put it in his chronicle "Coney Island" [1881]), but also embedded him in an "uneven modernizing" constellation of forces that compelled him to reflect on his mutual participation in and alienation from what Jürgen Habermas has called the public sphere.[4] Further, Martí's multivocal chronicles from the urban Global North (where he represented what Ramos characterizes as the "encounter and conflict with the technological and massified discourses of modernity" (44), telegraphed to Nuestra América's Global South, allowed him to explore and exploit what Ramos posits as "the changing, displaced situation of the writer in the capitalist city, in a society governed by new principles of organization that problematized the relation between literature and the predominant institutions of the public sphere" (281)—that is, the sphere in which political life is discussed openly by all citizens.

Martí's ruminations on modern cultures in this trans-American context took many forms, including his hybrid and experimental chronicles of daily North American life in *Escenas norteamericanas* (*North American Scenes*); his magisterial prologues, such as the one to *El Poema del Niágara* (*Poem of Niagara*), by Juan Antonio Pérez Bonalde, the Venezuelan poet in New York; his splendid cartographic poetry written in exile in New York City ("Domingo triste" and "Dos Patrias," among others, from *Versos libres* [Free Verses]); his classic anti-imperialist essays, such as "Nuestra América (Our America)"; and his moving translations of American sentimental literature for Appelton House (Helen Hunt Jackson's *Ramona*, for example), as well as his sober *testimonio* (testimony) on war and violence, the *Diario de campaña* (*War Diaries*).[5] As an émigré in an alien Anglo-Saxon environment, Martí often took the role of cultural anthropologist engaged in what James Clifford and George Marcus (1986) call the production of "writing culture." His scores of modern chronicles, prologues, and essays, what Ramos refers to as Martí's "minor writings" from this point of view,[6] thematized, among other things, the unfamiliar rituals, ceremonies, and daily practices of his host country.

While it is undeniable that Ramos's superb text on Martí's minoritized writings has received exceptional attention and critical praise over the past decade among Latin American studies scholars from all over the Américas, including Puerto Rico, Mexico, Argentina, Colombia, and the United States, his text's timely translation from Spanish into English allows me the opportunity to begin my own book, on transnationalizing critical U.S. studies, with a contrapuntal reading of selected sections of the text so that readers in mainline (North) American studies can better understand the historical significance and critical potential Ramos's Martí has to develop a new, comparative, trans-American cultural criticism.[7] As Fernando Coronil puts it in his powerful introduction to Fernando Ortiz's classic *Cuban Counterpoint: Tobacco and Sugar* (1995), the introduction to a celebrated book must ensure "a perspective that, while respecting the integrity of a cultural text, recognizes its provisionality and inconclusiveness, the contrapuntal play of text against text and of reader against reader" (Coronil 1995, xi). This chapter follows Coronil's sage advice by paying tribute to Ramos's critical Latinamericanism and by engaging in a transnational *contestación* (contestation) of sorts. It explores the ways in which Martí's vernacular knowledge produced in metropolitan New York City and its proto–Puerto Rican and Cuban barrioscapes influenced constructions of modern Latinamericanism. My emphasis of Martí's subaltern modernity and his resistance to the modern rationality of the enlightened *letrados* (lettered elites), as well as to the commodification and racialization of U.S. mass culture, might also be labeled what I call "the Martí differential"—calling for an unevenly developed trans-American cultural critique appropriate to an uneven aesthetic modernity.

Subaltern Modernities

The philosophical problem of modernity, or what Habermas (1983, 3) terms "aesthetics modernity," is the point of departure for both Ramos's rigorous exegesis of the nineteenth-century "enlightened letrado" tradition—from Domingo S. Sarmiento and Andrés Bello to José Martí—and his probing diagnosis of the beginnings of a Latinamericanist cultural criticism. To better see why this is so, I begin this chapter by situating the problem of modernity as both a chronological and a qualitative concept.

"Modernity," as Habermas reminds us, "has a long history" (1983, 3). Although there is a lot of room for debating modernity's origins and its celebrated (postmodernist) endings, Habermas starts off his view of modernity as "an incomplete project" by looking at the historical contrasts between the words "the ancients" and "the moderns." "Modern in its Latin form '*modernus*' was used for the first time," he writes, "in the late 5th-century in order to distinguish the present, which had become officially Christian, from the Roman and pagan past" (1983, 3). For Habermas (1983, 3), modernity and the modern conjure up "the consciousness of an epoch that relates itself to the past of antiquity, in order to view itself as the result of a transition from the old to the new." Raymond Williams (1983, 208) emphasizes something similar, writing that, in the English context, "a conventional contrast between ancient and modern was established before the Renaissance.... Modernism, modernist, and modernity [followed] in the 17th and 18th centuries, and the majority of pre-19th-century uses were unfavorable."

If, since the nineteenth century, "the emphatically modern document no longer borrows [the] power of being a classic from the authority of a past epoch," as Habermas (1983, 4) suggests, for modernity "creates its own self-enclosed canons of being classics," has the relation between the ancients (the classics) and the moderns lost its "fixed historical reference"? What happens when we no longer focus exclusively on iconic Western art in our understanding of modernity's project? In *Divergent Modernities*, Ramos, like Habermas before him, asks us to recall Max Weber's foundational analysis of cultural modernity as the separation of reason expressed in religion and metaphysics into the three autonomous spheres of science, morality, and art.[8] In other words, as the homogenous worldviews of religion and metaphysics broke down, scientific discourse, paradigms of morality and jurisprudence, and the production of art, in turn, became "unevenly" institutionalized.[9] Consequently, with the specialists controlling cultural symbologies and capital, a gap grew between the culture of the experts and that of the larger public. In the Latin American context, with its uneven division of labor, urbanization, and incorporation of its markets into the capitalist world-system or global economy, Ramos argues, "New regimes of specializations . . . at once relieved the *letrados* of their traditional tasks in state administration and forced writers to become professionalized" (xl). Ramos therefore is interested in analyzing what "the effects of a dependent and uneven modernization [were] on the [Latinamericanist] literary field" (xl). To begin such an institutional analysis, he rigorously pursues what he calls a post-contemporary "double articulation," examining literature "as a discourse that seeks autonomization" and undertaking "an analysis of the conditions that made the institutionalization of literature impossible" (xli).

Few trans-American intellectuals, Ramos demonstrates, have been as sensitive to modernity's "uneven development" and its contradictory implications as Martí, who moved from the apparent enlightened ambience of Nuestra América's "republic of letters" to Anglo-America's massified culture industry, while most of the time feeling deeply estranged from both versions. As Martí revealingly put it in a letter to an editor in Mexico, "The mail leaves from New York to a country of ours. I cover everything noteworthy that has happened: political cases, social studies, theater bills, literary announcements, novelties, and particular aspects of this land. . . . In sum, a Review done in New York on all the things that might interest our impatient and imaginative cultural readers, but done in such a way that it could be published in the daily presses" (Martí 1946, 111). Martí's work in New York as a foreign correspondent for *La Nación* of Buenos Aires, *El Partido Liberal* of Mexico City, and *La Opinion Nacional* of Caracas, and as a journalist for the *New York Sun*, was, in Ramos's words, "conflictive," opposed to the "highest" and "most subjective" value of "poetic discourse" (86).

Ramos begins his iconic genealogy of an emergent Latinamericanism with an examination of what he calls the "enlightened letrados," such as the Argentinean Domingo F. Sarmiento and the Venezuelan Andrés Bello, and contrasts them with the divergent subalternity of the exiled Cuban journalist, revolutionary, and poet José Martí, who, he suggests, inaugurates "the constitution of a new kind of intellectual subject" for the Américas (Ramos 2001, xliii). Part 1 of *Divergent Modernities* explores in detail how Sarmiento's classic *Facundo: Civilization and Barbarism* (1845) and Bello's modern notion of "*saber decir* (knowledge as eloquence)" brought on the destruction of what Ramos (after Angel Rama [quoted in Ramos 2001, 29]) describes as the republic of letters—that is, the intimate formation of national literatures and the founding of the modern nation-state. In other words, as Ramos suggests, after independence from Spain, "a new homogeneity, a national homogeneity that was linguistic and political" (3) took hold in Latin America.

From the start, modern nationalist discourse and culture turned not only toward Europe and the West, but also toward the Global North and the United States, and were used by intellectual elites such as Sarmiento to "legitimize [their] claims to authority." Especially in *Facundo*, Sarmiento's writing "represents history as progress, as a modernizing process interrupted by the catastrophe of local *caudillos*," for to write in this Latin American enlightened context is, as Ramos states, "to order; to modernize" (11). Throughout *Facundo*, Sarmiento "positions himself," according to Ramos, "between two competing modes of knowledge" (15)—what he characterizes as "proper" (civilized written discourse) and "foreign" (barbaric orality).

In contradistinction to Sarmiento, Bello did not privilege in his cultural criticism a romantic and undisciplined scholarship. Instead, he grounded his views of modernity in the humanist university institution itself, where scholarship was orderly and rationally separated into specializations. That is to say, in its division of the sciences from the social to the humanities, "the structure of the Western university is thoroughly modern and Occidental"[10]—for it divides a "universal reason" into "faculties." In Ramos's view, Bello's "constant reflections of the task of the university and the place of knowledge in society underline[ed] the relative autonomy of knowledge" (28). Yet like his fellow "enlightened letrado," Sarmiento, Bello envisioned writing "as a machine of action, as a device that transforms the chaotic 'nature' of barbarism [in Latin America]." Thus, for Ramos, in Bello "we find . . . the concept of *belles lettres*, which postulated 'literary' writing as a paradigm of knowledge" (29)—and, we might add, as a paradigm of rationality (where writing and grammar are associated with a will to reason).

As David Lloyd (1991, 19) has offered in a related context about the modern university, idealist theorists (such as Sarmiento and Bello) used theory to "furnish transcendental grounds to its concepts, and after this fashion the university divides the objects of knowledge into the quasi-permanent or canonical form of the disciplines." It is precisely in Bello's movement toward what we might term a "universalist rationality"—that is, his attempt to subsume local particulars into Western universals—that we can begin to understand Martí's subaltern (and trans-American) cultural critique against this universalist idealism. From this perspective, Martí's foundational essay "Our América" of 1891, with its hypothesis that "the European university must give way to the American university," can be seen as a prescient calling for "differential studies"—not the exhaustion of difference—of the Américas, and not Bello's integrated formation of the disciplines, affecting the production of knowledge in the university. As Ramos correctly puts it, Martí "speak[s] from the periphery" (212). His exile in New York City's barrioscapes not only "radicalized his situation" (83) but, as a journalist chronicling everyday life, also embedded him in a new institutional site where he could examine "the conditions of heterogeneity in the literary subject," as opposed to Bello's "Kantian-like unity of the manifold" (Lloyd 1991, 3). As a result, Martí's "critique from outside the institutional power spectrum, against the modernizing project" (234) separated him from the tradition of the enlightened letrados in the Américas.

Thus envisaged, Ramos's Martí is well situated to oppose what he calls the "will to rationalization"—that is, what his future fellow émigrés to the United States, Theodor Adorno and Max Horkheimer (1972), would describe as the Enlightenment's dialectical totalitarianism, with its well-known instrumentalized reasoning.[11] Ramos's Martí gives back, we might say, a "migratory mobility" to the enlightened letrados "unity of the manifold," reformulating the constituent parts of the body of knowledge so that its content functions "differentially."[12] Martí as a subaltern modernist in New York City is, therefore, almost in spite of himself, a "properly modern hero precisely because his effort to synthesize discursive roles and functions presuppose the antitheses governed by the division of labor and the fragmentation of the relatively integrated public sphere in which writing of the [enlightened] letrados had operated," according to Ramos (2001, xliii). The spirit and discipline of this subaltern modernity assumes clear contours, Ramos emphasizes, in Martí's trans-American boundary-crossing cultural work—the lateral minor writings he called *North American Scenes*.

If modernity "revolts" and "lives on the experience of rebelling against all that is normative," as Habermas believes was characteristic of the aesthetic modernity of, say, Charles Baudelaire, Martí emerges as one of the first proto–U.S. Latino anti-imperialist intellectuals in the barrios of New York City who in Ramos's view was both "heroic" and a melancholy "subject profoundly divided" (269). Ramos's startling exploration of this "profoundly divided" Martí, exiled, racialized, and estranged in New York City, takes up the bulk of part 2 of *Diver-*

gent Modernities. There, Ramos gives readers not the usual monumentalized and "maestro" Martí (championed by the letrado "vocational"
canon in the universities of the Américas), but the struggling revolutionary, journalist, modernist poet, and translator of sentimentalized
romances by Helen Hunt Jackson trying to make do in the major
capitalist city of the Global North (see Gillman 2008). Martí's critical
meditations on U.S. national literary and cultural icons (Ralph Waldo
Emerson, Walt Whitman, Mark Twain, Harriet Beecher Stowe, and
George Bancroft); his horror and amazement at the emergent mass
culture industry ("Coney Island" and "Jesse James") and at the sheer
technological power, engineering, and art of the United States ("The
Brooklyn Bridge"); and his critiques of the cultures of U.S. imperialism ("Our America"), as well as his nuanced testimony on war and
violence (*War Diaries*), as Ramos writes, were all "enmeshed in a complex and intense reflection on the crisis and reconfiguration of modern
literature" (270). If Martí's trans-American cultural work in general,
and in "Our America" in particular, "invert[s] the relation of subordination between intellectuals and people, writing and orality, making
the indigenous and subaltern the basis of Latin American identity,"
does Martí's own stylistic will to power also denounce "a sense of the
literary as both the adequate and necessary form of expression of Latin
Americanism," as John Beverley (1993, 11) writes? I return to this
question when I examine Martí's linking the War of 1898 and "Our
America" at the end of this chapter, but first I turn to Martí's earlier
writings: the prologue to Pérez Bonalde's *Poem of Niágara* and "The
Brooklyn Bridge" and "Coney Island" from *North American Scenes*.

For Ramos, Martí's prologue to *Poem of Niágara* is at once a profound and symptomatic manifesto on the emergence of "modern
poetry" in the Américas, with the "nostalgia of the great deed," as well
as the breakdown and erasure of the social conditions that "had made
possible the normative . . . contents of an epic authority in literature"
(270). In such a modernist and modernizing lifeworld, Martí suggests,
modernization entails "the suffering of modern man" in the face of a
"new social state," in which "all the images that were once revered are
found stripped of their prestige, while the images of the future are yet
unknown." Further, for Martí, modernity inaugurates an epoch or
consciousness characterized by what he lyrically calls the "building of
the sources and the obfuscating of the gods." For Ramos, Martí's

minoritized discourse (so reminiscent of Friedrich Nietzsche's notion of the "twilight of the gods" and Gabriel García Márquez's celebrated *el otoño del patriarca*) "explicitly relates the new social state [in the Américas]—linked to what Max Weber later called the 'disenchantment of the world' as an effect of modern rationalization—to the dissolution of a discursive and institutional fabric of belief that, until the moment, guaranteed the central authority of literary forms in the articulation of the constitutive nomos of the social order" (270).

Consequently, the trans-American poet in aesthetic modernity, for Martí, can only have "broken wings"—a melancholic figure caged in the cruel theater of solitude who can merely "present himself," in Martí's words, "armed with all his weapons in an arena where he sees neither combatants nor spectators; nor [sees] any prize" (270). Martí here demonstrates how the lifeworld has become infected by modernization. All cultural representatives (even Martí's cherished poet) have become "rationalized" under the brutal pressures of economic power and globalized and instrumentalized administered forces.

If one had to conjure the most likely source of Ramos's insistence on Martí's claiming our critical aesthetic attention, it would be his view of Martí's "opening salvo [in his prologue to *Poem of Niágara*] to any reflection of the relative disengagement of literature from the private sphere, given his reputation as a political writer" (xlii). Indeed, Ramos argues throughout part 2 of *Divergent Modernities* that "Martí spoke of politics and life from a specific kind of perspective or gaze, from a locus of [an uneven] literary speech" (xliii). Martí's gaze, as a subaltern analyst of the emergent hegemonic mass culture in the United States, for Ramos implies varied "mechanisms of authorization" and a set of socially symbolic "solutions to the emergent literary field."

What was to become Martí's magisterial *North American Scenes* recounted, in Ramos's words, "the multiple aspects of urban daily life [for] they ... serve[d] as a continual reflection on the place of the one who writes—in Martí's case, the Latin American—in the face of modernity" (Ramos 2001, xliv). Indeed, Ramos indicated that it is possible to say that much of Martí's trans-American cultural criticism itself aspired to "the defense of the 'aesthetic' and cultural values of Latin America by placing them in opposition to [North] American capitalist modernity ... and the economic power of the North American other" (xlv). As Martí bluntly put it in "Coney Island," "Such people [of the United States] eat quantity; we, quality" (205). It is precisely Martí's insistence on a ethno-national articulation of "Latin-americanism" that Ramos wishes to deconstruct.

In contact "with the regime of the political market" and with "labor" and "urban fragmentation" in New York City, however, Martí's idealist views on aesthetics and what Ramos refers to as his "concept of the aesthetic interior" underwent a sea change. On occasion, as in his letter to his friend and editor in Mexico City, Manuel Mercado, dated 1882, Martí reveals his arduous existential struggle with exile, modernization, and urban drudgery. "I now, live by means of commercial jobs keeping secretly to myself, so that no one will see, the terrors hidden in the soul" (quoted at 84). Elsewhere, in his poem "Hierro," Martí adds: "I have earned the bread: let us make poetry" (84).

If Martí writes with the self-consciousness that Foucault (1984, 38), associated with modernity (an insistence that the present represents a clear break with the past and that the role of both the poet and the cultural critic is to reflect on the "contemporary status of his own enterprise"), Martí, like Emerson and Whitman, as Ramos noted, articulates a self-consciously new domain "in which the poet encounters the city as the outside" (85).

Because Martí's writings on art and his defense of Latin American cultural values are connected to his career as a trans-American journalist (indeed, in Ramos's view, Martí "promoted himself" as an intermediary between the United States and various Latin American groups in Mexico, Venezuela, and Argentina), Ramos turns in part 2 of *Divergent Modernities* to a fascinating institutional history between 1870 and 1895 of Buenos Aires's major newspaper, *La Nación*, founded in 1870 by Bartolomé Mitre, just two years after he had completed his presidential term in Argentina. As Ramos emphasizes, *La Nación*, employed scores of news correspondents abroad, but no two were more important than José Martí and Rubén Darío, "who were key figures in the development of the early *modernista* chronicle" (79). Among other things, part 2 of Ramos's book explores how an uneven aesthetic modernity became dependent on newspapers, and how such dependence limited what he refers to as "literature's autonomy" (79). Ramos's hypothesis is that the Latin Americanist critique of modernity was itself "incorporated and promoted by the emergent cultural industry based on the new journalism of the epoch" (Ramos 2001,

80). If newspapers, as Benedict Anderson (1983, 88–89) famously argues in *Imagined Communities*, were key institutional sites "for the formation of new national subjects" and helped "subject orality to the law of writing," they also, paradoxically, helped initiate a new literary genre "tied to the modernist chronicle."

When *La Nación* inaugurated telegraphic service affiliated with the Havas Agency of Paris in 1877, it at once enabled Latin America's "community of readers to represent themselves as a nation inserted into a 'universe,' articulated by means of a communication network" (96), as Ramos describes it. To be sure, the telegraph in Latin America "stimulated the specialization," Ramos writes, "of a new kind of writer, the reporter, delegated to a new linguistic and commercial object, the news bulletin" (96). As Martí observes in the prologue to *Poem of Niágara*, "It is as though we are witnessing a decentralization of the intellect. The beautiful has come to the realm of all people."

If, as Darío noted in his *Autobiography*, *La Nación* "was a workshop for experimentation," for Martí, it was also a unique institutional location for examining what Ramos calls "the conditions of literary modernity," especially its relation with new writers and "contact and cultivation of a new readership" (102). While it is undeniable that Martí (like Darío) honed his "craft of style" in newspapers like *La Nación*, the newspaper, in Ramos's view, was more importantly a site where "organic intellectuals" (see Gramsci 1971) in the new culture industry could begin analyzing "the irreducible aporias of the will to autonomy and the hybridity of the literary subject in Latin America" (102).[13] Beginning with Martí in 1882, according to Ramos, *La Nación* "establishe[d] a clear precedent, transforming correspondence into the site not only for informative discourse on foreign lands and peoples, but formal and literary experimentation as well" (103). Martí's colleague, Sarmiento, was one of the first to recognize and champion uncritically Martí's journalistic writing as a place where the Cuban let "loose his howls." More conventional readers, however, like F. T. de Aldrey, editor of *La Opinión Nacional*, chastised Martí for his propensity to experiment freely in his reportage: "Readers of this country want news brief and political anecdotes and as little literature as possible" (105).

In contradistinction to the more "refined" and "bourgeois" fin de siècle chroniclers—such as Gómez Carillo, who in his narrative of strolling the streets of Buenos Aires, *El encanto de Buenos Aires* (The Enchantment of Buenos Aires), sang the praises of fashion and "the charm of merchandise" (116), or Sarmiento, who in *Travels in the United States* (1847) saw the urban modern city, again in Ramos's words, "as a utopic space" (118)—Martí's representation of the cities of the United States of the North, as he called them, rejects what Ramos refers to as "the logic of the fetish." Thus, Martí's capitalist city in the Global North was explicitly linked, Ramos tells us, "to the representation of disaster, of catastrophe, as distinctive metaphors for modernity" (118). Further, for Martí, the urban city spatialized "the fragmentation of the traditional order of discourse that the city has brought in its wake" (118). As Martí characteristically put it, "Everything [in New York City] is mixed [and] melts away," no doubt a reference to what Marx saw in *The Communist Manifesto* as the catastrophic process of capitalist modernization, for "All that is solid," he wrote, "melts into air" (Marx 1978, 476).[14] Against "enlightened letrados" such as Sarmiento, Martí's *North American Scenes* resists "producing a decorative image of the city" and instead "record[s] the misery and exploitation generated by the most advanced forms of modernity . . . in the United States" (141).

Martí's remarkable chronicle "The Brooklyn Bridge," one of the most celebrated engineering accomplishments of the nineteenth century, is emblematic of his attempt to "coexist with and among" North American technology. Washington Roebling's monumental bridge, the first one to use steel in its construction, palpitates, "throb[bing]," Martí writes, "a blood so magnanimously in our day" (166). Almost a hinge between two epochs, the bridge's cables are also "like the teeth of a mammoth that in one bite would be capable of decimating a mountain" (168). Although Martí sensitively "interprets the apparatus," he also sees this modern engineering event in North America as an allegory of modernity, quantification, and modernization. The bridge's arches, Martí notes, are "like the doors to a grandiose world which uplifts the spirit," and its half-stone and half-steel construction metaphorically concretizes history's progress: "No longer will deep moats open up around walled fortresses; cities instead will be embraced with arms of steel" (168). If, as Emerson insisted in his essay *Nature* (1836), technology itself is an extension of nature, then Martí's illuminating "The Brooklyn Bridge" follows this insight by thematizing engineering and technology as instruments to better serve culture and society.

On a more formal and rhetorical level, however, "The Brooklyn Bridge" contrapuntally reveals what Ramos refers to as "an anxiety . . . concerning the implications of modernization" (170). Insofar as Martí's chronicle "works with emblems, with cultural landscape," Ramos asks, what are the readers of "The Brooklyn Bridge" to make of Martí's allusions to the bridge as an "aerial serpent," its towers seeming "like slenderized Egyptian pyramids," and to its masses of ethno-racialized workers, "the link [of] which can be found neither in Thebes nor the Acropolis"? Are these iconic Western cultural emblems precisely the symbologies that have been "displaced by modernization"? What exactly does Martí (writing in and from the technological languages of the newspaper) "see" in his allegory? He, of course, sees many things—"the resounding dredges"; "heroic feverish workers clean-[ing] the base" of the bridge—and activates a deconstructive illusion of presence for his readers: "By the hand we will take our readers . . . and lead them to see up front" (173) the bridge itself.

In Ramos's view, "The Brooklyn Bridge" allegorizes not only the trans-American chronicler's "relationship with technology," but also the subject of "quantification," a "corollary to [the] gaze that attempts to geometrically rationalize space" (Ramos 2001, 174). On this strictly formal level, explains Ramos, Martí allegorizes "the asymmetry between the discourses tied to technology and literature"; as a result, "The Brooklyn Bridge" uses the "struggle of literary discourse" to push "its way through the 'strong' signs of modernity" (175).

In the process of "overwriting" this chronicle (Martí's writing was based on the journalist William Conant's essay on the Brooklyn Bridge, published in *Harper's* in 1883), Ramos suggests that Martí's chronicle put him "in the position of translator,"(175), for Martí, Ramos writes, "literally seizes a metaphor from Conant [a flying serpent], translates it literally as [*sierpe aerea*], and uses it to describe a different object" (185, n. 36). Beyond this literal translation project, Ramos maintains that "The Brooklyn Bridge" works "as a strategy of legitimation that takes into account the 'idealized' and 'mechanical' languages of modernity as obliterated matter for the supposed 'exceptionality' of style" (176). In other words, Martí's literary modernist chronicle ascends (like the bridge itself) "towards apotheosis," Ramos lyrically writes, "articulat[ing] a spatial hierarchization." (177). Hence, Martí fantastically explains, "Seeing them conglomerate to swarm quickly over the aerial serpent, squeezed together, the vast, clean, ever-growing crowd—one imagines seeing seated in the middle of the sky, with her radiant head appearing over the summit and with white hands, as large as eagles, open, in a sign of peace over the land—Liberty" (177). Martí's gaze is no longer that of the traditional positivist journalist. Rather, Martí's hybrid, modern text verges on what Ramos rightly calls "a hallucination" (177), where the chronicler sees a "swarm," a "crowd," and an "aerial serpent" and then immediately imagines seeing in "the middle of the sky" a "summit" and "eagles . . . over the land," culminating in a vision of "Liberty." This epiphanic writing is of great significance, Ramos argues, for Martí's "overwriting" is founded on a model of literary discourse as a dramatic deviation from the linguistic norm(s) in operation and hence resists the logic of what I earlier called the "enlightened letrados" universal rationality, a rationality that "imposes the value of exchange" (178) and a new statistical reason.

Responding to critics of his overwrought prose style, Martí insisted in 1881 that writers, like painters, work with concrete material (words) and that this intellectual process of labor distinguishes the writer's production from other kinds of intellectual work. Thus, Martí claimed that "there is no reason that one [writer] would avail of diverse colors, and not another. The atmosphere changes with different zones, as does language with different themes" (180). Put differently, language, too, Ramos writes, is "stratified by the division of labor." Style, for Martí, "is the medium of labor that differentiates the writer (as the use of color does for a painter) from the social, institutional practices that also use language as a medium," Ramos writes. Literature, in Martí's words, is itself an act of "concretizing. . . . Each paragraph must be organized as an excellent machine, and each one of its parts must be adjusted, inserted with such perfection among others, so that if any one part is taken from among the ensemble, it would be as a bird without wing[s], and the parts would not function . . . The complexity of the machine indicates the perfection of its make" (182). Briefly, Martí's "The Brooklyn Bridge" not only allegorizes "a literary will to style"; it does so precisely in a machinelike discourse that "coexists" and "struggles" (as Ramos wryly insists) "against discursive, antiaesthetic functions tied to the technologized medium of journalism." It is, therefore, "the incongruencies and contradictions" (concretized in *North American Scenes*) that "distinguish Martí's modernity" (183) from the more famous modernists of the period. Martí reshapes "fragments" and "remains" and refunctionalizes his "uneven" trans-American modernity as a kind of schizophrenic and capitalist "desiring machine" (see Deleuze and Guattari 1977).

While "The Brooklyn Bridge" summarizes Martí's multiple responses to North American modernization, "Coney Island" (1881) reveals his relentless animus toward North American mass culture, which, I think, has often led to charges (especially among his monotopical North American readers) that he was a snob or, worse, an arrogant mandarin. These glib criticisms of Martí in my view are entirely wrong, for Martí's pointed attacks on the emergent nineteenth-century mass culture were directed just as often against Latin American elitists and their "enlightened letrado" cultures. Both North American mass culture (and what Adorno and Horkheimer [1972] more precisely termed the "culture industry")[15] and the letrados' culture in Latin America, it bears repeating, deserve a thorough critique.

In contrast to the canonical letrados' view of Martí as a *clásico*, above the fray of the intense historical and political debates of his own time, and the more hagiographic view of Martí as a "granitelike" hero, Ramos's analysis of Martí and "Coney Island" documents precisely the historical contradictions and social conflicts that *North American Scenes* opened in the domain of modern, trans-American cultural criticism in the nineteenth century. Ramos first reconstructs the entire *North American Scenes* as "an immense urban cartography" (191), where the capitalist North American city not only is "a decentered space" (193), but also, at the same time, is gendered as a "sleeping woman," where women are either "masculinized" by modernization or take on the role of "solitary mothers." Tellingly, Ramos writes, the figure of the father "stands out by [his] very absence; he is nowhere to be found in Martí's modern landscape" (Ramos 2001, 193).

Modernization, the very process that Ramos has been tracing transnationally throughout *Divergent Modernities* (via Weber and Rama), is his shorthand for a variety of processes and concepts that require further elaboration. Habermas (1987, 2) is especially helpful here, for modernization, he explains, is "a concept . . . that refers to a bundle of

processes that are cumulative and mutually reinforcing; to the formation of capital and the mobilization of resources; to the development
of the forces of production and the increase in the production of
labor; to the establishment of centralized political power and the
formation of national identities . . . [and] to the secularization of
values and norms." As Ramos sees it, Martí's "Coney Island" thematizes many of the "bundle[s] of processes" that Habermas explains are
cumulative and constitutive of modernization. To begin with, the
chronicler and cultural thinker in "Coney Island" is, in Ramos's words,
"a displaced subject" who also happens to be simultaneously "exter-
nally exiled" (as a Cuban anticolonial subject working in New York
City) and "internally exiled" (as a "nostalgic" critical thinker from "a
higher spiritual world" in a base lifeworld motivated by "the flow of
money") (206).

One of the earliest results of the nineteenth-century culture industry in the United States, Coney Island, was its "annihilating and in-
comparable expansiveness," with its "colossal houses, as high as mountains," where coarse "peasants" and the "genteel" wealthy mix and
drink "distasteful mineral water," also gives Martí a place where he can
begin to look at the historical break between high culture and low
culture. Increasingly, the realm of high culture is associated with what
Martí calls the "we" (Latin Americans), and the low belongs to the
"they" (the people of the United States). But "Coney Island," at the
same time, reveals the emergent and thrilling U.S. culture industry to
be a place where the dispossessed and *damnés* are routinely com-
modified, ridiculed, and physically abused. As Martí writes, Coney
Island is the place where crowds "applaud the skill with which a ball
thrower has managed to hit the nose of a misfortunate man of color,
who in exchange for a measly day's wage, stands day and night with his
frightened head stuck through a hole made in the canvas, avoiding the
pitched of the ball throwers with ridiculous movements and exaggerated faces" (2002, 93).

This ridiculing of a "misfortunate man of color" by the socially and
hierarchically constructed "white," massified audiences of the culture
industry is more than just popular entertainment for Martí. It is also a
form closely associated with the thriller, minstrelsy (Lott 1996), and
white supremacy, where even leisure and entertainment are embedded in a struggle over the politics of popular culture, race, and nation.

In other words, for Martí, a radical critic of modern scientific racism (as Roberto Fernández Retamar emphasizes),[16] the incorporation of art and entertainment into the marketplace implies, in Ramos's view, "a sense of the degradation" illustrated for Martí in "the figure of the abused black performer" at Coney Island (Ramos 2001, 222).

That Martí felt especially unsympathetic toward urban mass culture of the Global North is undeniable. Indeed, as Ramos consistently points out, Martí clearly misjudges mass culture, privileging and "ideologizing" terms such as "culture" to mean an "abstract sense of a process of becoming cultivated," while simultaneously criticizing "culture's" abstract rationalism. Martí preaches, "In vain do men of foresight attempt, by means of culture and religious sentiment, to direct this driven mass that heedlessly seeks the quick and full satisfaction of its appetites" (219). The sources of Martí's concept of culture, Ramos suggests, are to be found in the author's own experiences with the anonymous mass culture in New York and its surroundings, such as Coney Island, where, Martí writes, "the marvelous prosperity of the United States of the North" and its "jovial and frenetic" crowds extend themselves "with a more tumultuous order" (222).

It is from his lofty aestheticizing position above the crowds that Martí "gazes with unfamiliarity at the material baseness of the masses in North America." More significantly for Ramos, Martí in his role as a cultural critic "in effect help[s] to formulate one of the grand narratives of legitimation for the wide-open field of the literary enterprise (which continued to function at least until the centennials of the Latin American Wars of Independence)" (222). By asserting in "Coney Island" the pitfalls of modernization in the capitalist United States of the Global North and proposing the superiority "of the aesthetic sphere" as a socially symbolic response, Martí's discourses (as well as those of Sarmiento, José Enrique Rodó, and, after the Porfiriato, the Mexican cultural critics Alfonso Reyes and José Vasconcelos and the Dominican Pedro Henríquez Ureña) "from the start [were] compromised by the project to legitimize the cultural sphere" (225). In other words, the modernist's uneven rhetoric of crises (what Ramos later calls their Lyotardean "narratives of legitimation" [Lyotard 1984, 1; Ramos 2001, 225]) contributed to producing the "bundle of processes" of modernization itself.

Ramos's analysis of "The Brooklyn Bridge," "Coney Island," and

North American Scenes leads him to ask whether it was a "coincidence that in the first decades of this century the proliferation of essays" by both trans-American intellectuals such as Martí and traditional Latin American letrados were "concomitant to the culturalist" project itself? Did the very "form of the (modernist) essay represent the ambiguous place of the modern writer faced with the disciplinarian will distinctive of modernity" (232)? If the essay form, as Ramos theorizes, "mediates between the interior of the beautiful (poetry) and the demands of society" (233), was this how modern chronicles "extended [their social territory as interpreters and public announcers] of the beautiful, first in the chronicle, but later in the essay, as a privileged form of the 'maestro' at the turn of the century" (233) and beyond?

Divergent Modernities concludes with a sophisticated exegesis of Martí's classic modern essay "Our America" (1891) and with two new supplementary chapters on Martí's proto–U.S. Latino migratory poetry written in New York City and on his lyrical *War Diaries* (1895). As in his earlier chapters, Ramos continues to analyze the formation of Latinamericanism, for "behind every assertion of what is Latinamericanism, there lies a will to power exercised from different positions on the map of social contradictions." Ramos therefore is troubled with Martí's attempts in "Our America" to defend "us" from a "they" who "would divest us of our self-representation" (253). Because Martí, among other things, interpellates his Latin American (and, one might add, his U.S. Latino/a) readers within an andocentric discourse of essentializing "familial homogeneity" and a "discourse of identity" (254), his critique of the cultures of U.S. imperialism and everything imported to "our" America (especially the colonizing discourse or the "tigers within" Latin America) necessarily entails, for Ramos, an ideology of the aesthetic and "the gaze of an aesthetic Latin Americanist subject" (259).

In its "intensely overwritten prose," and with its saturation of "telluric" figures of speech or tropes, Martí's "Our America" ends up, in Ramos's view, being the exiled Cuban's "reflection on the discourses that could legitimize and effectively represent the conflicting field of identity" (260). As an object of struggle over the field representation, however, Martí's trans-American gaze in the process produces a powerful defense of what we now call "subjugated knowledge," after Foucault, and what Walter Mignolo terms "subaltern border gnosis"

(Foucault 1980, 78–108; see also Mignolo 2000b). In other words, Martí offers us in "Our America" a rich defense of everything "excluded by the *letrados*," as Ramos emphasizes. From this perspective, Martí's bundle of "minor writings" constitutes for Ramos an alternative "Latinamericanist archive" that is capable not only of intervening in "the enigma of identity" but also of investigating "the conditions of possibility for good governance" in the Américas. Consequently, "Our America" involves itself in an analysis of the cultural politics of race, nation, and culture, for cultures that are marginalized (relegated to "underdevelopment") can also contain the grounds for a sober critique of the hegemonic Western norms by which they are judged. Further, "Our America" operates within what Ramos sees as "the critical intensity of a root knowledge—a knowledge of roots"—and we might add, as Paul Gilroy (1993) suggests of black British root work, as an intercultural knowledge of "routes."

Migratory Routes

Routes begins with [an] assumption of movement, arguing that travels and contacts are crucial sites for an unfinished modernity. The general topic, if it can be called one, is vast: a view of human location as constituted by displacement as much as by stasis.—JAMES CLIFFORD, *Routes* (1997)

From my position as a critical U.S. studies teacher, in a comparative literature department at Stanford, I wish to conclude this chapter by approaching *Divergent Modernities* as a valuable critical text for contributing to and expanding our emergent comparative American cultural criticism. Ramos's work opens up other spaces (as *The Black Atlantic* has accomplished for diaspora studies) and, in the process, develops and brings new problems, methods, and idioms to the forefront of cultural criticism in the Américas. To say this is to claim that Ramos's remarkable *Divergent Modernities* does for José Martí and critical Latinamericanism what Gilroy's great *The Black Atlantic* has done for nineteenth-century and twentieth-century African American modernists like Fredrick Douglass, W. E. B. Du Bois, and Richard Wright and for Pan-Africanist (Ethiopianist) discourses. Of course, Ramos wrote and published his book many years before Gilroy's ap-

peared in print, but my point in this penultimate section is to bring
Ramos's and Gilroy's outernational literary and cultural works closer
together as examples of the new, stunning mapping out of diasporic
and migratory black British and Puerto Rican/U.S. Latino scholarship. Indeed, it is undeniable that Gilroy's and Ramos's works suggest
some notable methodological parallels in their philosophically nuanced studies of the "countercultures" of subaltern modernity, and
they do so by focusing on specific diasporic and migratory intellectuals within an outernationalist framework.

More important, Gilroy and Ramos link together some cultural
conversations that have been kept separated in Europe, Latin America, and North America by their respective specialist and nationalist
gazes. The most crucial conversation, as Gilroy acutely puts it, is
about the long and often "bitter dialogue on the significance of slavery
and emancipation in the Western Hemisphere. It was very seldom
that these two sets of interest were able to touch one another" (Lott
1994, 46). That is, Gilroy contends that, before books such as C.L.R.
James's *The Black Jacobins* and Frantz Fanon's *The Wretched of the
Earth* appeared, slavery and modernity had very little to do with each
other, for the cultural conversation was "configured in a very Eurocentric way, [and] in a . . . dubious way, because it appealed to some
innocent essence of Europe" (Lott 1994, 46).

In writing *The Black Atlantic*, Gilroy attempts to show how there
was, indeed, "a common set of problems" (slavery, the Middle Passage, and trans-Atlantic modernity), and that these problems had
been articulated by African American intellectuals and travelers, such
as Du Bois, who had studied in the United States and Germany;
Wright, who lived in the United States, yet wrote many of his books
about African Americans from Paris, where he was engaged in conversations with Simone de Beauvoir and other intellectuals; and those
who founded the *Présence Africaine*, a panafrican magazine founded in
Paris by Alaine Diop in 1947, thus dissolving the rigid borders between Francophone and Anglophone worlds. Consequently, as Gilroy
astutely explains, a set of philosophical problems "was being articulated across intellectual and scholarly as well as linguistic and political borders." These subaltern modernities, in Gilroy's view, "defied
the boundaries that the nation-state puts in its place." Further, they
"marked out the cracks that the nation-state introduces into our

thinking of our history, and I wanted to address that fracture" (Gilroy 1993, 47). Briefly, for Gilroy, the black Atlantic in its political and cultural formations, involved a "desire to transcend both the structures of the nation state and the constraints of ethnicity and national particularity. These desires are relevant to understanding political organizing and cultural criticism. They have always sat uneasily alongside the strategic choices forced on black movements and individuals embedded in national and political cultures and nation states in America, the Caribbean, and Europe" (1993, 19).

Modernity, for Gilroy, thus is both a qualitative and a chronological category "that gets generated through and from the systematic and hemispheric trade in African slaves." Further ("where that becomes a modern experience"), Gilroy (1993, 76) adds, "it's not something that belongs exclusively to the blacks involved or to their contemporary heirs. It belongs to an expanded understanding of what the modern world is and how it worked . . . It's not anybody's special ethnic property. The experience of catastrophic terror does not become something that its victims can own."

Similarly, throughout *Divergent Modernities* (and especially in his new chapters on Martí, "Migratories," and "The Repose of Heroes: On Poetry and War in José Martí"), Ramos is interested in examining what it meant for Martí, a migratory, outernationalist intellectual, to be one of the first proto–U.S. Latinos confronting modernity and the cultures of U.S. imperialism. As Ramos asks of Martí's posthumous collection *Free Verses*, written during the 1880s in New York, "What house can writing found and firmly ground beyond its emphatic promise to do so?" (281). Does modern, trans-American writing for Martí "guarantee the residence and home of the subject"? (283).

Here, Ramos's study focuses on the melancholic text "Domingo Triste (Sad Sunday)," a poem about Martí's "biographical exile" that also marks the larger sense of modernity, when a society is now "governed by the new principles of organization" (281). Martí therefore can represent the late-nineteenth-century migratory proto–U.S. Latino/a subject as a kind of "residue," Ramos writes, "displaced and contained in a receptacle, the shell"—or, as Ramos quotes Martí, "A friend came to see me, and he asked myself! about me; . . . I am the shell of myself, which on a foreign soil / turns at the wish of a wild wind, / vain, fruitless, shattered, broken" (283). For Ramos,

Martí's poem thematizes melancholy displacement, inter-American routes, and "the experience of migratory flux" (283), where the transnational ethno-racial subject possibly loses itself, becoming "the shell of myself."

But this nineteenth-century proto–U.S. Latino migratory subject, to Ramos's mind, is also "the bearer of traces" (283). Martí's "*here* of plenitude" (in the capitalist city of New York) is "the there of the subject that writes" (Cuba), and vice versa. The emergent proto–U.S. Latino/a subject, in other words, wrote as early as the 1880s about that edge delineated by separation and fracture, and as Martí himself complexly put it in the lyrical "Sad Sunday," "I bear the pain which the whole world observes / a rebellious pain which the verse breaks land that is, oh sea! the fleeting gull I passing on its way to Cuba on your waves!" (283).

Martí's figural insistence on rupture and fractures is key to understanding the slippery signifying chain in "Sad Sunday." Exile and migration break the subaltern modern poet's verse. But Martí's poetic verse (as Ramos acutely phrases it) may at the same time "break the pain," for poetry is metaphorized here as a "gull" and hence can extend "a lasso, a meeting with the absent land" (284). Briefly, "Sad Sunday" can only repeat "something" of the migratory poet's "originary plenitude" in Cuba, for it inscribes in New York "an image, an echo of experience" (285). Proto–U.S. Latino/a writing in the late 1880s, thus envisaged by Martí, is a creature "of the wind, of echoes," and an echo that is also a result of local, hemispheric, and global forces of terror and empire.[17]

It is against the grain of this domestic and planetary terror that we can better locate Martí's subaltern modernity, for his "minor writing" is about our (trans)modern world and our place in it. Martí's subaltern modernity—and here *Divergent Modernities* is especially instructive—is not that of the enlightened letrados, with their rhetorical emphasis on "reason" and "rationality." Martí does not express the nineteenth-century view of Latin American intellectuals (such as Sarmiento or Rodó) who revealed the continent's barbarism, its "backwaterness" to its habitat. Rather, through exile, he is forced to become more specialized—first as a news correspondent, then as a translator for Appleton House and a kind of cultural diplomat, and finally as a founder of the Cuban Revolutionary Party in 1892. Fernández Retamar (2009, 6) suggests that Martí was the "giant voice of another world" and, further, that the "not quite fifteen years he lived in New York permitted him a deep understanding of [the United States], its virtues and dangers and an identification with its radical thinkers." Fernández Retamar is absolutely right: Martí not only identified with U.S. dissenters such as John Brown and the abolitionist Wendell Phillips, but he also contributed to making known in Latin America the radical imaginative works by Helen Hunt Jackson, Harriet Beecher Stowe, and Mark Twain, among others.

Subaltern modernity embeds Martí in a powerful political system (what he famously referred to as being inside "the belly of the beast"), where by necessity he worked through and against the various imperial centers (Spain, Cuba, and the United States)—modern centers governing their subaltern peripheries (colonies and neo-colonies) primarily for economic reasons. While the imperialism of Spain and the United States were never equivalent for Martí, he nevertheless saw the U.S. Empire as implying, for Nuestra América, direct and indirect political and military control. And, of course, in his battle against Spain's imperialism, he gave his life on May 19, 1895, at Dos Ríos, Cuba.

For Martí, the "American empire" was "not a contradiction in terms," as Amy Kaplan (1995, 328) suggests it has usually been seen in U.S. popular perception and mainline scholarly analyses. In *North American Scenes*, Martí was particularly sensitive to the terrors and catastrophes of modernity wrought by slavery, the American Civil War, the U.S.-Mexican War of 1846–48, and the conquests by the United States of the territories and indigenous peoples of North America. If, as Kaplan (1995, 328) writes, the 1890s mark "a turning point in the history of American imperialism," it was precisely at this time that Martí joined the public debate of his epoch between "self-avowed imperialists and anti-imperialists." Were the acquisitions (in the aftermath of the Spanish–American War of 1898) of Cuba, the Philippines, Puerto Rico, and Guam, Kaplan asks, merely "aberrations" of U.S. history and foreign policy?

"Our America," read some one hundred years later, indeed challenges the idealist and narrow Anglocentric definition of U.S. imperialism, especially as it was proposed by realists such as George F. Kennan (1950), who, in Kaplan's words, saw "imperialism as only the formal annexation of colonies" (Kaplan 1995, 328). Further, Martí's writings anticipate a more cultural approach to his and our own age of

U.S. Empire, for like, say, the views of Richard Drinnon (1980), Martí closely links continental and transoceanic expansion. Through belief in the racial superiority of Anglo-Saxons, the superiority of Occidentalism, and the desirability of subjugating non-whites, the ideologies of empire, as Kaplan (1995, 328) contends, brought together "U.S. manifest destiny with a transoceanic passage to India."

At a time that we are pondering our some one hundred years of the cultures of U.S. imperialism (1898–present), we may wish to read Martí's subaltern modernity as a chronological and relational concept in which, in Coronil's dramatic terms, "heterogeneous social actors . . . appear on history's stage as subaltern [subjects], just as there are times or place in which they play dominant roles." "Subalternity," as I have been using the term in this chapter, "defines not the being of a subject," as Coronil (1997, 6) theorizes, "but a subjected state of being . . . , a double vision that recognizes at one level a common ground among diverse forms of subjection and, at another, the intractable identity of subjects formed within uniquely constraining worlds" (see also Saldívar 1997). Martí's "double subaltern vision" is nowhere more visible and moving than in his cogent account of the formation of the Cuban's "soldier-subject" in *War Diaries*, which he kept on his routes from the United States to the Dominican Republic and Haiti on his way to fight for Cuba's liberation from the Spanish Empire in 1895. While *War Diaries* has been a significant "literary" document for twentieth-century Cubans associated with José Lezama Lima's Orígenes group ("celebrated," Ramos writes, for its "fragmentary, intense prose" [279, n. 331]), we should also read *War Diaries* primarily for its devastating "critique of violence." It is precisely through "aesthetic mediation" that Martí believes one can begin to contain what Ramos refers to as "the ineluctably aggressive energy of the revolutionary forces" (277). Hence, Martí writes,

> The spirit I have sown is that which has spread, across the island; with it, and guided in accordance with it, we will soon triumph, and with the greatest victory, and for the greatest peace. I foresee that, for a little while at least, the force and will of the revolution will be divorced from this spirit—it will be deprived of its enchantment and taste . . . and of its ability to prevail from this natural consortium; [it] will be robbed of the benefit of this conjunction between the activity of the revolutionary forces and the spirit that animates them. (277)

The double drives of war and enchantment, for Martí, have to be mediated, separated, and finally integrated. This revolutionary conjunction is the only possibility for survival, dignity, and victory and for what Martí called the "greatest peace." It is from this subaltern double perspective that we can also end this section with Fernández Retamar's contrapuntal insight that *"el moderismo es el primer período de la época histórica del imperialismo y de la liberación* (modernism is the first historical periodization of the epoch of imperialism and liberation)" (Fernández Retamar 1995c, 41).[18] Ramos's *Divergent Modernities* contrapuntally celebrates the vitality, melancholic struggle, and the double subaltern vision that Martí wrought as a chronicler, soldier-revolutionary-subject, and radical critic of empire, terror, and violence in the face of the cultures of European and U.S. imperialism. I end this chapter on the politics and poetics of subaltern modernity by examining Martí's critique of the cultures of imperialism of Spain and the United States through his iconic formulation of critical Latinamericanism.

Latinamericanism and 1898

As the chronicles from *North American Scenes* remind us, the antagonism between the local and the global is not new to Martí's critical Latinamericanist discourse.[19] At least since his magisterial "Our America" of 1891, Martí's Latinamericanism has been mobilized as a defense of both the local and the hemispheric in the face of an emerging U.S. globalization of the world. The year 1898 and Latinamericanism are, therefore, related formulations for Martí. As we saw earlier, many of Martí's poems and chronicles written in New York can be read as early responses to the reconfiguration and displacement of border contact zones and oceanic boundaries, enacted by U.S. military expansion in the "splendid little war" of 1898 and by what we now call the cultures of U.S. imperialism.

"Our America" links the proto–U.S. Latino's revolutionary condition of modernity with the internationalization of capital and hegemonic cultural flows. Martí's work, thus envisaged, is a profound critique of the hemisphere's condensation of spaces and borders produced by the War of 1898's intense re-worlding of the Caribbean, the Américas, and the Pacific. However, Martí's keyword "Latinamericanism" bears a boa-deconstructionist-like ambivalence. A double meaning is structured into its name, for "Latinamericanism," as *Divergent Modernities* showcases, both refers to the field-imaginary located in the metropolitan centers of the Américas (Havana, New York City, Mexico City, Buenos Aires, Santiago) and names a vernacular knowledge and imaginary in the longstanding tradition of subalternist discourses of the Américas, of the colonial world upside down described by Waman Poma as *Pachakuti* and, more recently, by Subcomandante Marcos and the Zapatistas' dictum "A world in which many worlds can co-exist."[20]

3 ❧

Looking Awry at the War of 1898:
Theodore Roosevelt versus Miguel Barnet
and Esteban Montejo

Subaltern Studies in/of the Américas should bring to the forum the diversity of colonial and imperial expansions in the past five hundred years, and the postmodern and postcolonial as a complementary critique of modernity; it should also contribute to erasing the borders between cultures of scholarship in the North and cultures to be studied in the South.
—WALTER MIGNOLO, *Local Histories, Global Designs*

American exceptionalism is the name of the much-coveted form of nationality that provided U.S. citizens with a representative form of self-recognition across the history of war. As a discourse, American exceptionalism includes a complex assemblage of theological and secular assumptions out of which Americans have developed the lasting belief in America as the fulfillment of the national ideal to which others nations aspire.
—DONALD PEASE, *The New American Exceptionalism*

In an essay published in *American Literary History* on the new trans-American studies of the twenty-first century, Cyrus Patell (1999, 182) suggested that this post-exceptionalist, comparative work may have a crucial role to play in developing what he termed a "cosmopolitanism that will expose and defeat imperialism wherever it exists, a cosmopolitanism that can reject the old, Bad History and begin to write anew." Parts of this chapter can be read as a response to Patell's New Historicist remarks, but I have a more limited focus. How do we go about "defeating" the cultures of U.S. imperialism in our literary histories, and how, at the same time, do we encourage a critical discussion of some of the New Historicism's inheritances, including the legacies of consensus, Gramscian Marxism, and hegemony? That is why inciting such questions, Patell's call for such a discussion of U.S. literary history is timely. To facilitate a focused comparative discussion, and for reasons of familiarity, I stick in my opening comments to the emergent critical work of the South Asian Subaltern Studies Group and the Latin American Subaltern Studies Group. But I hope that the arguments I develop in the chapter around Amy Kaplan's iconic reading of Theodore Roosevelt's *The Rough Riders* (1999 [1899]) and my own explorations of the *novela testimonial Biografía de un cimarrón* (1966) by the Cubans Miguel Barnet and Esteban Montejo, and George Mariscal's *Aztlán and Viet Nam* (1999) will have a more general import for helping us continue writing a subaltern and post-exceptionalist history of the United States and of the Américas.

My chapter uses some of the examples and epistemic experiences of the South Asian and Latin American subaltern studies groups because their rigorous work, I think, can help us situate the question of subaltern history and literary history within a broader postcolonial critique of modernity and of history itself. Dipesh Chakrabarty (1997, 35) puts it this way: "Writing subaltern history, documenting resistance to oppression and exploitation, must be part of a larger effort to make the world more just. To wrench subaltern studies away from the keen sense of social justice that gave rise to the project would be to violate the spirit that gives the project its sense of commitment and intellectual energy."

Whether we like it or not, the production of South Asian and Latin American subaltern studies is transnational. Their editorships are from North America, Australia, India, Mexico, Cuba, and the Américas. Lately, important links have been formed between Ranajit Guha's and Chakrabarty's South Asian group and John Beverley's, Ileana Rodríguez's, and Walter Mignolo's Latin American group, and one can visualize a similar forging of links with scholars in Chicano/a studies, U.S. Latino/a studies, ethnic studies, African American studies, Native American studies, and women's studies in the United States. Perhaps it is this very linking that Gayatri Chakravorty Spivak (1995, 188) had in mind when she proposed that in "the struggles against internal colonialism," African Americans, Chicanos/as, and Native Americans are the "postcolonials in the United States."

Can the South Asian Subaltern Studies Group's imperative to itself to "think through the specificities of Indian history" help us in the United States to think through the specificities of our nation and make that archive central to our work? Can the conceptualization of "the nation and its fragments" (Chatterjee 1995) help us continue critiquing U.S. nationalism and its nationalist historiography? As Chakrabarty (1998, 463) explains, "If the old nationalism imagined the nation as a political body with an identifiable center to it, the primary task of Subaltern Studies is to challenge this center and to try and examine Indian history to see how the picture of a variegated many-centered India might emerge—and, indeed, how each of these centers could in turn be destabilized." This is what I initially tried to propose in *Border Matters* (Saldívar 1997), for it is by examining the contact zones of the U.S.-Mexican borderlands, the spaces where the nation ends or begins, that we can begin destabilizing U.S. nationalism, its nationalist historiography, and its various centers. I challenged this stable and naturalized status of the nation and its *intersticios* by looking at the assumed equivalence we make between the national and the cultural (Saldívar 1997, 14). In what follows, Roosevelt's classic American text *The Rough Riders* and Barnet's and Montejo's *Biografía de un cimarrón* (published in translation as *Biography of a Runaway Slave* [1994]), I suggest, are intensely involved in a struggle of dominance and subordination over the history of the Spanish–American–Cuban–Philippine War of 1898.

When I teach undergraduate and graduate seminars on the War of 1898, I do not take a straightforward view of the dominant U.S. historiographies of the war. That metropolitan view sees only an indistinct confusion or, at best, as Ivan Musicant characteristically put it in *Empire by Default* (1997), the title of his mainline book on the War of 1898, an "empire by default."[1] Rather, I begin by looking awry. That is, I look from a subalternist angle and see the War of 1898 in its distinct form in contrast to the dominant and metropolitan Anglocentric view. My approach to some of these problems is to pick our way through two of the foundational memoirs and *testimonios* of the war in Cuba by Roosevelt and Barnet and Montejo and ask: who writes or tells the history of the subordinate? In the case of Barnet and Montejo, the question resonates with a response directed to Roosevelt's pen. Did the conquest of Cuba by Roosevelt and the United States empower them to impose on the conquered a past written from a metropolitan point of view? Were Roosevelt's representations of "Spain" and

"Spaniards" at the center of what María DeGuzmán (2005, 142) calls "the development of U.S. national identity as an Anglo-American imperial power"? Did Roosevelt's gun confer a right on his pen, as well?[2]

I agree with the dissident U.S. historian Louis Pérez Jr. that, in looking at the historiography of the War of 1898, we have for the most part two realities, two substances, and two *historias*. U.S. histories, like Musicant's *Empire by Default*, for instance, asks us to look at 1898 straight on, matter-of-factly, and using only U.S.-centered documents, artifacts, and sources and see the war as it really was. The point I suggest is less idealistic. If we look at the War of 1898 straight on and from only U.S. and English-language sources, we will see nothing but a formless point or spot. Pérez (1998, 111) says, "The [U.S.] historiography of 1898 [has been] self-contained and self-validating, inferring larger meanings often by way of metaphysical meanings." Destiny, chance, forces, and empires by default all served as "popular explanatory" ideological devices to negate the responsibility of the United States as a modern empire.[3] In other words, the accumulated metropolitan historiography of the War of 1898 in the United States over, say, the past one hundred years, "has flourished primarily as the reworking and refining of old themes, mostly from old sources, reformulating old conclusions, restating old arguments. Advances have been more in the form of style than substance" (Pérez 1998, 109).

It is only by looking at the War of 1898 within an "interested framework," permeated and "distorted" by dominant U.S. histories, that the object 1898 can assume clear and distinctive features. Slavoj Žižek's phantasmatic paradox of desire and Donald Pease's political notion of the U.S.'s disparate "state fantasies" that emerged to organize U.S. citizens to its many wars of imperialism are, I think, useful here as beginning frameworks: "The paradox of desire is that it posits retroactively its own cause" (Žižek 1992, 12). Thus envisaged, the War of 1898 is an object that can be perceived only by a gaze "distorted" by desire in Žižek's terms, and the War of 1898 can be seen as a U.S. state fantasy of American exceptionalism that developed into what Pease (2009a, 1) calls a "dominant structure of desire out of which U.S. citizens imagined their national identity."

What Harold Bloom once wrote of poets—"how one poet helps form another" (Bloom 1997, 5)—can also be said of U.S. wars of imperialism: wars continue each other. In her classic essay "Black and Blue on San Juan Hill" (1993, 219), on Roosevelt's *The Rough Riders*, Kaplan suggests something similar: "The Spanish–American War of 1898 can be understood to have continued the Civil War in an imperial national discourse of the United States at the turn of the century."

Like most great essays, "Black and Blue on San Juan Hill" is by no means what it appears to be—that is, a rhetorical New Historicist reading of Roosevelt's attempt in Cuba to recuperate the gallant strenuous life of the Civil War and to heal the wounds and divisiveness of the war and attain its goal of national recuperation. Kaplan's essay achieves a corrective gaze to mainline views of the War of 1898 in at least two significant ways: by debunking John Hays's popular view of the Spanish-American War as a "splendid little war" and by contributing, through a refinement of the techniques of reading the ethno-racial national body, to a more substantial reading of the cultures of U.S. imperialism.

Kaplan suggests a nationalist motive for the U.S. imperial adventure in Cuba and, by extension, in Puerto Rico and the Philippines. As a war of empire directed against an external enemy, Spain, the War of 1898 reunified the United States as a nation. Roosevelt and his Rough Riders did battle on at least two fronts for Kaplan: nationally against African American soldiers, the so-called Smoked Yankees,[4] and internationally against Spain in their colonies' struggle for national independence.

Under the aegis of a general theory of imperialism,[5] this large order brings together textual, gender, and ideological criticism in a combination that is unusual in essays on Americanist writing. Kaplan has been "corrective" in the best sense, not out of a desire to assert a strong influence, but because she has tended to be more attuned to the multiple ways in which "the study of American culture has traditionally been cut off from the study of foreign relations" (Kaplan 1992, 11). Even with regard to the materialist critics of American imperialism to whom she was indebted—Edward W. Said, William Appleman Williams, and Michael Paul Rogin—she is not paralyzed by their presence. In fact, she gracefully corrects their readings by focusing on how imperialism cognitively maps the relation of the "domestic" and the "foreign" in largely gendered terms. More recently, in her erudite "Manifest Domesticity" (1998, 581–82), Kaplan explains that, within the structures of feeling of the United States, the "domestic has a double meaning that not only links the familial household to the nation but also imagines both in opposition to everything outside the geographical and conceptual border of the home. . . . The idea of foreign policy depends on the sense of the nation as a domestic space imbued with a sense of at-homeness, in contrast to an external world perceived as alien and threatening. Reciprocally, a sense of the foreign is necessary to erect the boundaries that enclose the nation as home."

Yet Kaplan does more than provide techniques and the know-how to read the cultures of U.S. imperialism. She provides a larger understanding of the notion in American culture and society of how the American empire can be seen historically as "a contradiction in terms."[6] Kaplan does not see U.S. foreign policy, from its founding American Revolution to what Zapatista Subcomandante Marcos calls its Fourth World War in Chiapas, as wars of "anti-imperialism" or as "acts of liberation." From Kaplan's perspective, the global dominance of the United States, its anarchy of empire, has enlisted popular support, undergirded political practices, and provided American exceptionalist master narratives and fantasies of the nation.

Roosevelt's personal narrative *The Rough Riders* is emblematic for Kaplan, for Roosevelt remaps the nation by imagining a community through both its margins and centers. As we know, Roosevelt wrote *The Rough Riders* when he was the governor of New York, for, after his Cuban military adventure, as his recent biographer H. W. Brands (1997, 372) explains, he sought "to have his heroism ratified by an act of Congress." In this light, *The Rough Riders* is Roosevelt's rhetorical plea for a Medal of Honor.[7] His gaze—heroic, boastful, nationalist, and narcissistic—is a delicate literary negotiation, to be sure. As a war narrative, *The Rough Riders* tells the (tall) tale of the regiment: its recruitment and training in San Antonio, Texas, near the Alamo, and its dramatic fighting in Cuba. Typically, Roosevelt adopts a dominant metropolitan point of view and, in the process of the story, erases the cast of thousands from the military fighting. In Kaplan's reading of *The Rough Riders*, Roosevelt phantasmatically imagines at the Loma de San Juan an interracial community of white and black soldiers fighting on distant shores. In his new frontier of U.S. imperialism, he reimagines the nation, with white "natural fighters" and commanders like himself in charge, dominating inferior African American soldiers. African American soldiers, as Roosevelt argues, are incapable of having black commissioned officers as their leaders; Cubans, Puerto Ricans, and Filipinos, too, are incapable of self-governance. (In his address "The Strenuous Life," delivered in Chicago in 1899, Roosevelt stated his views this way: "[The Philippine] population includes half-caste and native Christians, warlike Moslims, and wild pagans. Many of their people are utterly unfit for self-governance" [Roosevelt 1994, 188].)

All of this is dramatically thematized in *The Rough Riders* when Roosevelt's mixed black and blue regiment has all but taken the Loma and the island. "On the hill around me I had a mixed force composed of members of most of the cavalry regiments, and a few infantrymen," he writes. "No troops could have behaved better so far; but they are, of course, peculiarly dependent upon their white officers" (Roosevelt 1999 [1899], 147). Later, in the chapter titled "The Cavalry at Santiago," Roosevelt (1999, 149) relates how "the colored infantrymen who had none of their officers began to get a little uneasy and to drift to the rear, . . . or saying that they wished to find their own regiment."

Conjuring this scene as African American soldiers on the verge of mutiny, or as an out-of-control form of black insurrection, Roosevelt (1999, 149), in his inimically manly tone, writes: "This I could not allow . . . so I jumped up, and . . . drew my revolver, halted the retreating soldiers, and called out to them that . . . I would shoot the first man who, on any pretense whatever, went to the rear."

Kaplan focuses on this remarkable scene in *The Rough Riders*, noting how Roosevelt's narrative symptomatically shifts gears and how it provides a startling counter-narrative. "Why," she asks, "is this scene so startlingly violent?" (Kaplan 1993, 222). To be sure, Roosevelt's confrontation with the African American soldiers underscores what she calls the "domestic color line in a foreign terrain." Further, the scene "compensates for the occluded vision of the political landscape" (Kaplan 1993, 222). That is, Roosevelt manages not only to subordinate African American soldiers at gunpoint but also to erase General Máximo Gómez's and General Antonio Maceo's Cuban revolutionary army of approximately fifty thousand soldiers, 60 percent of whom, according to Ada Ferrer (1999), were *mambises insurrectos*.[8] In fact, even when Roosevelt acknowledges the Cuban insurrectos in his narrative, he describes them as "utter tatterdemalions as human eyes ever looked on. . . . It was obvious, at a glance, that they would be of no use in serious fighting" (Roosevelt 1999, 94). For Kaplan, *The Rough Riders* shifts from representing "conflict with an external enemy, Spain, to internal struggles with African American soldiers" (Kaplan 1993, 222). In other words, Roosevelt (unconsciously) uses discourses drawn from the shadow of the Black Legend to reinforce a racially encoded gaze that served to metamorphose the rival imperial power "Spain" into the colonizer and the Anglo-Saxon colonizer—Theodore Roosevelt and the U.S. Rough Riders—into the superior, virile civilizer.[9]

Kaplan concludes her whirling essay by suggesting that *The Rough Riders* symbolically "confront[ed] and subordinat[ed] African Americans within the national body" while simultaneously making a place for new colonized subjects in the disembodied American empire" (Kaplan 1993, 229). Roosevelt's imperial battlefield, Cuba, in other words, "mirrored . . . the domestic urban sites" of the U.S. ethno-racial sites Roosevelt himself knew firsthand as the former police commissioner of New York City. In disciplining and punishing the African American troops on the Loma de San Juan, Kaplan (1993, 231) argues, "Roosevelt was exercising the regulatory power of Americanization that eluded his grasp on the [mean] streets of New York." The African American soldiers in Cuba hence were "forced into the body politic at gun point" by Roosevelt and "Americanized by keeping their place in the line of force and [in what W. E. B. Du Bois called] the color line."[10]

If Roosevelt abandoned any ethno-racial strivings in New York, he rediscovered the ethno-racial frontier in the borderlands of Cuba, with his largely *pinche rinches* Rough Riders confronting new Indians, Mexicanos, Chicanos, and African American soldiers threatening to undo the white-supremacist nation-state. It was thus only after putting down the seeming revolt of the "Smoked Yankees" that Roosevelt gained a better position as a metropolitan chronicler to complete his Occidentalist story of "the winning of the west" and, as a kind of final antidote to Reconstruction, begin healing "the conflicts of the Civil War" by bringing together what Kaplan (1993, 232) calls " blue and gray on distant shores."[11] In other words, Roosevelt's master narrative of the War of 1898 played a constitutive role within U.S. political culture by inciting within the multitudes who took them up what Pease (2009, 5), alluding to a later U.S. war of imperialism, called the state's "desire to organize their identities out of the political antagonisms within the national culture." Roosevelt as a legislator inaugurated his compact of the white-supremacist "strenuous life" as a response to traumatic events in Cuba, Puerto Rico, and the Philippines.

One of the Cuban mambí insurrectos operating in the region of Cuba where Roosevelt and his Rough Riders fought was Esteban Montejo. After the War of 1898 and, in fact, seven years after the Cuban Revolution of 1959, Montejo produced, with Barnet, an anthropologist and novelist, one of the most striking novelas testimonial of the War of 1898 and, significantly, one that has been little used by trans-American historians and literary scholars of the Spanish–American War. Testimonios, as we know, are of great interest in inter-American cultural and literary studies because of the way they incorporate real historical time and space—what Mikhail Bakhtin (1981, 84) called the "chronotope." Further, they usually advance critical subalternist attitudes toward metropolitan institutions,[12] turning what seems to be a private "life history" to the public sphere. Montejo's novela testimonial (straight out of Havana) produces rich evidence of how thousands of Cuban mambises helped clear the landing ground of Spanish colonial forces, thus allowing Roosevelt and the U.S. Cavalry relative safe landing at Daiquirí and military operations at Santiago de Cuba and its environs. While throughout *The Rough Riders* Roosevelt suggests that Cuban insurrectos were invisible or "of no use in serious fighting" (Roosevelt 1999, 94), Montejo disrupts this dominant history by recalling the following *memorias*:

> Siempre que veo a un negro [mambí] de éstos en mi memoria, lo veo fajado. . . . Nada más se fajaban. Para defender la vida, claro. Cuando alguien les pregunataba que cómo se sentían, ellos decían: "Cuba Libre, yo son un liberá." (Barnet and Montejo 1966, 157)

> Whenever I see one of those black [mambises] in my memory, I see him fighting. . . . They just fought. To defend their lives, of course. When someone asked them how they felt, they would say, "Cuba Libre," "Me's a liberator." (Barnet and Montejo 1994, 153)

Montejo's signifyin[g] vernacular testimonio,[13] titled by Barnet *Biografía de un cimarrón* (*Biography of a Runaway Slave*), is not a slave narrative or a war memoir in the conventional sense. Rather, as one of the foundational testimonios of Cuba, it is co-produced and cobbled together by Barnet and the 105-year-old Montejo, who lived as a slave on a sugar plantation, as a fugitive in the Cuban jungle, and as a masculinist, machete-bearing mambí soldier in the Cuban War of Independence.

Montejo gives us specific reasons for his decision to join the Cuban Revolutionary Forces. He joined because he desired to be a liberator and to defend himself and to fight for "Cuba libre." Montejo joined up in December 1895, fighting initially under the command of General Antonio Maceo: "Los españoles desde que nos vieron se enfriaron de pies a cabeza. . . . Los españoles eran unos cagados para los machetes (From the moment they saw us [mambises], the Spaniards went stiff all over. They were scared shitless of the machetes" (Barnet and Montejo 1966, 165; 1994, 161).

While Montejo readily agrees that "a la verdad que los cubanos nos portamos bien [we Cubans acquitted ourselves well)" (Barnet and Montejo 1966, 167; 1994, 162)—a direct rebuttal to Roosevelt's mendacious charges in *The Rough Riders*—and thus freely identifies himself as a Cuban nationalist, like, say, José Martí, he consciously "interpellates" himself in ethno-racialized terms as a subaltern *mambí*.[14] "Yo mismo vide a muchos mambises que iban para arriba de las balas (I myself seen many mambises who rose above the bullets)" (Barnet and Montejo 1966, 167; 1994, 162). From the beginning of the section entitled "La Guerra de Independencia," Montejo distinguishes himself from both mainline and Creole modernist chroniclers of the War of 1898 by documenting his participation in combat.

What Montejo expected to correct as a subaltern chronicler is linked explicitly in the novela testimonial to his subject positionality as a mambí: "Llegaron a pensar que nosotros éramos animales y no hombres. De ahí que nos llamaran mambises (Of course, [the Spaniards] thought we were animals, not men—that's how they came to call us Mambises)" (Barnet and Montejo 1966, 163; 1994, 163). While Montejo does not provide a technical explication of the larger geocultural meanings of 1898 as a specifically Cuban date designating what Roberto Fernández Retamar (1995b, 120) would call the beginning of "modernismo," he clearly envisions his ethno-racial formation in starkly subaltern terms: "Mambí quiere decir hijo de mono y de aura. Era una frase molesta, pero nosotros la usábamos para cortarles la cabeza (*Mambí* means the child of a monkey and a buzzard. It was a taunting phrase, but we used it in order to cut off [the Spaniards'] heads" (Barnet and Montejo 1966, 167; 1994, 163).

Some five years before Fernández Retamar proposed "Calibán as our symbol" in his classic, anticolonial essay "Calibán: Notes toward a Discussion of Culture in Our America" (1971; in Fernández Retamar 1989), where he simultaneously analyzed the term *"mambí"* as "the most venerated word in Cuba" because it "was despairingly imposed on us by our enemies at the time of the war of independence," he almost forgets Montejo's subalternist knowledge, insisting that "we still have not totally deciphered its meaning" (Fernández Retamar 1989, 16). But Fernández Retamar meticulously captures Montejo's transcultural sense and sound by writing that *"mambí" "seems to have an African root, and in the mouth of the Spanish colonists implied the idea that all *independistas* were so many black slaves . . . who of course constituted the bulk of the liberation army" (Fernández Retamar 1989, 16). (As an aside, Roosevelt fantastically seems to compound this insight, writing in *The Rough Riders* that "it was impossible to tell the Cubans from the Spaniards" [Roosevelt 1999, 119]). My point is not to correct Fernández Retamar in a schoolmarmish sense for leaving Montejo's text out of his celebrated genealogy of Calibán in Cuba but to stress the importance of Montejo's *choteo*, his vernacular and signifyin[g] *memorias* for trans-Americanist scholars working on the War of 1898.

At any rate, Montejo's vivid *memorias* of black mambises and white creole Cuban insurrectos fighting together complicates and supplements the dominant histories by Roosevelt and those scores of U.S. historians who have followed him. Montejo summons up more than what Gail Bederman (1996) terms the discourses of "manliness and civilization" when he says, "We were brave and put the [1898] revolution above everything else" (Barnet and Montejo 1994, 183). He directly addresses the corrosive "possessive investment in whiteness"[15]—to use George Lipsitz's remarkable phrase and theory—in discussing Roosevelt's "dashing" and "gallant" cavalry (Barnet and Montejo 1994, 146): "Con los negros no se metía mucho. Les decián, 'Nigre, nigre.' Y entonces se echaban a reir (The Americans didn't care much for the blacks. They called them Nigger, nigger. . . . And they laughed" (Barnet and Montejo 1966, 200, 1994, 194).

Thus envisaged, Montejo's subaltern testimonio confronts the very legitimacy and authority in metropolitan narratives like Roosevelt's *The Rough Riders:* "Y nada de cuentos de camino.... Una vez me puse a decir que los americanos en Santiago de Cuba eran un *paquete* y que ellos no habían tomado aquello de por sí. . . . Y la verdad es que en Santiago el que se fajó fue Calixto García (Don't believe any cock and bull stories . . . , he warns. One time I started to say that the story of the American intervention in Santiago was poppycock—that [the U.S. cavalry] couldn't have taken the town by themselves. And the truth is that in Santiago the one who really fought was Calixto García)" (Barnet and Montejo 1966, 202; 1994, 196). Near his novela testimonial's end, Montejo concludes by remarking that "Wood, Teodoro Roosevelt, el otro, . . . la partida de degenerados . . . hundieron este país (Wood, Roosevelt, the other one . . . the whole bunch of degenerates . . . sank this country)" (Barnet and Montejo 1966, 203; 1994, 197). Some seven years earlier, Fidel Castro had articulated similar sentiments, saying in a radio broadcast on January 24, 1959, "When after thirty years of struggle, our people, our liberation army had already virtually defeated the Spanish army, then the United States intervened in Cuba. It declared the Cuban republic would be independent, but when the time came to turn the island over to the Cubans they occupied it. The [U.S.] Congress came up with an amendment— imposed by force—to our constitution giving the United States the right to intervene in Cuban internal affairs. There was no justice. When one country reserves the right to intervene in another, that country is not independent."[16] Montejo, Fernández Retamar, and Castro might indeed concur with Guha's claim that, in a land under foreign occupation (under colonialism and imperialism), only a "spurious hegemony" exists (Guha 1997, xiii), or better still, what Guha famously calls a "dominance without hegemony" (Guha 1997, xii), where coercion outweighs persuasion.

Montejo's *memorias* on the War of 1898 are, therefore, important for several reasons. First, although produced after the War of 1898, and from the largely masculinist vantage point of the Cuban Revolution, they are one of the most significant testimonies of a mambí insurrecto during the struggle for independence. Second, Montejo's subaltern memories demonstrate how mainline U.S. histories and metropolitan memoirs of the war (like Roosevelt's) have erased the crucial importance of the mambises in defeating Spain's imperial army. Last, it corroborates Pérez's argument that "a comparably large and rich body of records in Cuba" and I would add in Puerto Rico and the Philippines "seems to have hardly mattered" for U.S. historians and chroniclers of the war (Pérez 1998, 109). I agree, too, with Fernández Retamar's contention in *Cuba Defendida* (1996, 71) that history seems to have gone awry for Cubans in 1898: "En más de un aspecto somos hijos e hijas de aquel 1898 que significó un giro violento (in more than one respect, we are the sons and daughters of the violent turning point in 1898)."

Unlike Roosevelt's *The Rough Riders* or Barnet's and Montejo's testimonio, the action of the Chicano antiwar narratives, stories, plays, and poems about the Vietnam War in George Mariscal's anthology *Aztlán and Viet Nam* (1999) takes place not solely on distant shores but also domestically on the mean U.S.-Mexican borderlands of California, Texas, and New Mexico and Greater Mexico.

This awareness of an entangled, fragmented, and discrepant response to the cultures of U.S. imperialism empowers new, alternative histories of its wars of empire. Mariscal's *Aztlán and Viet Nam* is a brilliant case in point. Mariscal (1999, 2) departs from "middle-class, Euro-American" accounts of the war by bringing together "writings from Chicano veterans who fought the war in Vietnam and from Chicano and Chicana activists who fought the war at home." His text is a mixed-genre overlay of testimonios, critical essays, songs, speeches, letters, *cuentos* (stories), poetry, and art. *Aztlán and Viet Nam* links historically the experiences of the Chicano/U.S. Latino "grunt" in Vietnam and the new social antiwar student movements. Mariscal, who served in Vietnam in 1968–69, argues that he put the anthology together because mainline histories of the war have erased how Chicanos gave themselves to the U.S. Armed Forces more than any other ethno-racial group: "More enlistments, more casualties, [and] more medals. . . . The first thing that struck me was how we [Chicanos] had been left out of the history books. There was absolutely nothing in Mexican Americans fighting the war" (quoted in Beitiks C-8).

Almost all of the entries in part 1 of *Aztlán and Viet Nam* thematize the space and speed of what we now (after Michael Herr and Fredric Jameson) can call the experiences of postmodern technological warfare.[17] The texts Mariscal includes dramatize extraordinary linguistic innovations, especially in the materially braided ways in which the Chicano soldiers' discourse fuses a range of vernacular speeches such as *caló* and choteo. In fact, many of these Chicano and Chicana war texts break down almost all of the traditional paradigms of war narrative and speak to the difficulty of finding any shared language through which soldiers can convey their experiences in Vietnam. Jameson's account of Herr's *Dispatches* (1977) is singularly relevant here, for Herr's pronouncements on *la vida loca* owe much to the ordinary experiences of the Chicano soldiers and their profound sense of technological alienation.

Ignacio García's epistolary account of Román's physical and psychological wounding in "Unfinished Letter to Terry" (García 1999, 133–35) is an example of this new, mysterious technological reification of the Vietnam War: "I am writing while riding on a trembling helicopter. . . . I received shrapnel wounds and will be sore for several weeks. . . . Psychological scars will be another thing. . . . I have seen human bodies torn apart by bullets, shrapnel, bombs and bayonets, machine guns, and powerful rockets. . . . Split heads, decapitated bodies, gaping stomach holes." In Román's space and speed of the chopper and in his new letter-writing machine (which can be represented only in motion), he gives us something of this new techno-spatialized warfare of Vietnam. How do we read for space and speed? As Jameson (1991) suggests in his iconic "cognitive mapping" vision, the subject is a figure in movement at a new velocity who rejects the modern "cartographic" gaze. It is the trajectory of the Vietnam-era chopper that Román needs somehow to measure, without turning into a self-deluding (Althusserian) subject. Space and movement are central in García's narrative.

In part 2, Mariscal leaves us with a moving historical account of essays that call for a moratorium on the war by Henry "Hank" López, Rubén Salazar, and Luis Valdéz; *corridos* about Vietnam by Daniel Valdez; and riveting antiwar poems by María Herrera-Sobek, including her rousing critique of the cost of machismo to the cultures of U.S. imperialism in "Silver Medals": "The silver medals / Purple hearts / medals of conquering heroes / Hung on Chicano homes / Another Mexican American hero / Brought home / Under the Stars and Stripes / Long gone the need / To prove his manhood / Long gone the need / To prove his red-blooded / American genealogy / And only the stars / Twinkle at our foolish pride" (Herrera-Sobek 1999, 232–33).

Aztlán and Viet Nam includes a haunting poem, "The Viet Nam Wall," in which the poet Alberto Ríos portrays some of the ruptures brought on by the war and bears witness to images of war, grieving, and violence that were constitutive to the American exceptionalist narrative. I quote from most of the poem herein:

I
Have seen it . . .
The way like cutting onions
It brings water out of nowhere
Invisible from one side, a scar
Into the skin of the ground
From the other, a black winding
Appendix line. . . .
Names, long lines, lines of names until
They are the shape of the U.N. building
Taller than I am: I have walked
Into a grave. . . .
The names are not alphabetized.
They are in the order of the dying,
An alphabet of—somewhere—screaming?
I start to walk out. I almost leave
But stop to look up names of friends,
My own name. . . .
Flowers are forced
Into the cracks
Between sections.
Men have cried
At this wall,
I have
seen them. (Mariscal 1999, 280–81)

Ríos's poem, like Maya Ying Lin's modernist anti-memorial itself, reminds us that the representational project of remembering (who may mourn, when is life grievable, who died in Vietnam, why the ethnic U.S. names Rodríguez and Johnson outnumber all other names

on the wall) is a crucial site where our national imaginaries are contested, redefined, and re-visioned. Moreover, Ríos's poem highlights
the view that the Vietnam memorial was anti-heroic—a "scar" in the
skin of the ground, a monument of U.S. violence suffered and wielded
not in the service of a heroic military cause, like other mainline U.S.
war memorials. As Ríos suggests, the V-shaped memorial wall de-
scends into the space of the political by taking us underground,
"like walk[ing] into a grave" and thus representing a "scar" that will
never heal or fade away. Its legibility is not alphabetical but a mind-
numbingly chronological naming of violence, death, and loss on black
marble walls—what Ríos sees as some fifty-eight thousand names or
"an alphabet of screaming." The only other legibility Ríos finds are the
names of his many dead friends and, uncannily, even his own name,
carved into the wall of death that seems so overly determined. What do
the V-shaped "appendix lines" stand for? What is the office of the
Vietnam wall for? Does Ríos's "alphabet of somewhere screaming"
stand for all the violence of all of the U.S. wars of empire? Ríos's poem,
like Mariscal's critical anthology, draws attention to the difference
between the ethno-racialized names that the wall memorializes and
their failed incorporation into the national narrative of American
exceptionalism.[18]

In juxtaposing mainline personal memoirs (*The Rough Riders*)
against the grain of Cuban subaltern *memorias* (*Biografía de un cimarrón*) and Mariscal's critical anthology on the Vietnam War, I have been
attempting to continue to expand the expression "subaltern studies"
and post-exceptionalist American studies. As Chakrabarty suggests,
" 'Subaltern studies,' once the name of a series of publications in Indian history, now stands as a general designation for a field of studies
often seen as a close cognate of postcolonialism." In this chapter, I
have been using subaltern studies freely, as Beverley, Chakrabarty,
Guha, Mignolo, and Spivak taught us, as a historiographic project that
raises questions about postcolonial ways to write history and, as
Rosaura Sánchez (1995) demonstrates in her archival work on testimonios from California in the nineteenth century, as alternative ways
to write American literary history. In particular, I have been sensitive
to Guha's suggestion that, in recovering the specificities of insurrec-
tions against colonialism and imperialism, we need not only to read
backward from the historical archive—for, as Guha (1983, 333) writes,

"The historical phenomenon of insurgency meets the eye for the first time as an image framed in the prose, hence the outlook, of counter-insurgency—an image caught in a distorting mirror"—but also to practice writing in reverse.

I cannot end without noting that hegemonic mainline U.S. foreign policies and histories of Vietnam are beautifully countered by minoritized anthologies such as *Aztlán and Viet Nam*. For instance, we know that President Lyndon Baines Johnson, like Theodore Roosevelt before him, was fixated on the mythic exceptionalist history of the Alamo, where, as James T. Patterson (1996, 593) put it, "Brave men had fought to the death to resist attack." According to William Chafe (1991, 274–75), Johnson lectured to his advisers on the National Security Council that Vietnam was "just like the Alamo." Are the contiguities between Roosevelt's account of an American empire and the War of 1898 similar to those accounts of Johnson? Like Roosevelt, Johnson was imperious, quick on the trigger, and mendacious.[19] For many U.S. historians, then and later, the imperial struggle in Vietnam was simply "Johnson's War," as Larry Berman (1989) coined it, just as Roosevelt's war memoir *The Rough Riders* might easily have been baptized, as Roosevelt himself once fantasized, "Alone in Cuba." What might it mean for those of us in critical U.S. studies to attempt for the first time to trenchantly tie the efforts of the Chicano antiwar activist and scholar Mariscal and the writers he anthologizes in *Aztlán and Viet Nam* to the anticolonial struggles of José Martí, W. E. B. Du Bois, and C. L. R. James, all of whom worked assiduously to reveal the interanimating relationships between colony and metropole, the color line and the anarchy of U.S. imperialism—relationships often only made visible by writers such as Charley Trujillo, Alberto Ríos, and María Hererra-Sobek, who moved among so many aspects of the peripheralized globe and studied in the very centers of intellectual power? What writers such as García, Ríos, and Sobek reveal in their work is how much mainline Americans believed in the modernist omnipotence of U.S. (war) technology. And they often thematized how the (silent) majority of Americans presumed the cultural and military superiority of white, Euro-American ways. As Patterson (1996, 606) writes, Southeast Asians, Americans thought, "could not stand up for long against Western civilization."

What *Aztlán and Viet Nam* shows is how misplaced and racially absolutist U.S. thinking had badly misinterpreted the situation in Vietnam. Short of perhaps dropping nuclear bombs on civilian centers the way Truman obliterated Hiroshima and Nagasaki in the Second World War, Mariscal opines, it is hard to see how greater military aggression could have achieved victory for the United States. Many of the testimonial narratives in his book pointedly suggest that Johnson's military problems in Vietnam stemmed from one simple fact: the North Vietnamese were always willing to fight the U.S. invaders for however long it took to defeat them. As Frank Delgado tells Charley Trujillo in the *soldados'* oral history section of the anthology, "We were brainwashed into thinking we had a noble cause, which I don't think [we Chicano *soldados* had]. The Pentagon underestimated the North Vietnamese capacity, determinism, and willingness to sacrifice. I had a hell of a lot of respect for them because they knew what they were doing" (Mariscal 1999, 154). In addition, Ho Chi Minh's commanders were very good at infiltrating and motivating their army: the frontiers they guarded were estimated to extend more than one thousand miles, and behind the border, Ho had a reserve army of five hundred thousand or so troops. By 1964, revolutionary subalternity that had ignited the North Vietnamese could not be stopped by U.S. military arms. Neither Johnson nor his advisers understood this. Some, like Mariscal's Chicano and Chicana combatants in *Aztlán and Viet Nam*, did.

Can we view heterogeneous subaltern groups as the subjects of their own history? Can we begin interrogating the relationship between, say, "subjugated knowledges" (Foucault's term) and "border gnosis" (Mignolo's term) and hence examine the archive itself and history and literary history as forms of the power–knowledge couplet? Subaltern studies reminds us of the fundamental inadequacy of metropolitan knowledges and of the institutions that contain them.[20]

4 ⤺

In Search of the "Mexican Elvis": *Border Matters*, Americanity, and Post-State-centric Thinking

How can we begin suturing a new set of contingent relationships to democratize an emerging trans-American studies? How can we begin mapping out a space that situates the Américas in our age of globalization as a cohesive but complexly differentiated space? Can a trans-American literary and cultural studies help us to be less state-centric in our scholarly work? In this chapter, I center my thoughts on an attempt to identify and characterize a shift that has been going on in Chicano/a cultural politics. This shift is not definitive, but it is framed in the cultural semiotics of antiracism and the critique by mass cultural producers of dominant state-centric thinking. Border thinkers such as El Vez, the Mexican Elvis, and the Chicano novelist John Rechy, among others, have responded in their work to the challenge that the rising awareness of trans-state phenomena has presented to the analytic frameworks of cultural studies. Cultural and musical performances from Los Tigres del Norte of Silicon Valley to the border performances of El Vez from San Diego attracted me immediately because their songs (in Spanish, English, and Spanglish) thematized the distinctly significant geo-cultural locations of California in our network society.[1]

Fueled by a combination of foreign and domestic production, California's economy—before the global recession of 2008—was ranked among the top five in the world. As a result, population shifts have dramatically reshaped the recent history of the state, spurred by migrations from different parts of the country, as well as immigration.[2] As George J. Sánchez emphasized in *Becoming Mexican American* (1993), Los Angeles International Airport is now the single largest port of entry for immigrants to the United States, and since 1965, workers

from all of the world have nourished Silicon Valley's high-tech informational modes of production and the state's agricultural valleys. By
beginning and ending *Border Matters* (Saldívar 1997) with the migratory music of Los Tigres del Norte and El Vez, the Mexican Elvis, I was
emphasizing that both undocumented and documented Mexican and
Chicano migrants and immigrants have contributed to the economic
and cultural flows emanating from California to the world. The sheer
magnitude of these border crossing and diasporic migrations not only
have altered and complicated the boundaries of ethno-racial formations;[3] they have also disrupted the traditional terrain of U.S. area
studies in the context of globalization. In the music of Los Tigres del
Norte and El Vez, was a power and structure of ethno-racial feeling
that many of my students, and others, directly experienced and that
could attract interest to neglected questions of the border (thinking)
subject, cultural citizenship, transculturation, and language rights in
the United States.[4] Los Tigres del Norte and El Vez, the Mexican Elvis,
name a "collective will" (undocumented and subaltern), an experience (post–North American Free Trade Agreement), and, perhaps, a
new pedagogy (a coalition of learning). *Border Matters* holds dialogues with these ideas and other recent debates in what Walter Mignolo (2000b, 11) has called the formation of "border *gnosis*"—that is,
the debate on the universals and particulars—and with Michel Foucault's notion of the "insurrection of subjugated knowledges" (Foucault 1980, 81). *Border Matters* offers a study of this particular U.S.-
Mexican "border thinking" from a diverse assortment of texts and
socio-cultural practices—*corridos* by Tish Hinojosa; funky Chicano
alternativo by El Chicano; hip hop by Frost; punk sonics by Los
Illegals; novels, poems, and short stories by John Rechy, Helena Viramontes, and Américo Paredes; paintings by Carmen Lomas Garza;
and post-contemporary writings on social science by the anthropologists Renato Rosaldo and Leo Chávez and by the historians Vicki Ruiz
and George Sánchez—that challenge the national homogeneity of the
U.S. public sphere.

Thus envisaged, *Border Matters* makes a link between Foucault's
idea of "subjugated knowledges" and what we can now confidently
call "subaltern knowledges" in and of the borders of the Américas.
As Foucault (1980, 81–82) famously put it, "By subjugated knowledges I mean two things: on the one hand, I am referring to the

historical contents that have been buried and disguised in a func-
tionalist coherence or formal systematization. . . . On the other hand,
I believe that by subjugated knowledges one should understand . . .
something which in a sense is altogether different, namely, a whole set
of knowledges that have been disqualified as inadequate to their task
or insufficiently elaborated; naive knowledges, located low down on
the hierarchy, beneath the required level of cognition." In other words,
"subjugated knowledge" is that which is buried behind the formation
and production of knowledges in the West and what is considered to
be too way out and behind the mainline public sphere. (As we say in
Berkeley, way-out people know the way out.) Foucault (1980, 82), we
might say, turns precisely to the way-out subjugated knowledges, for
"these unqualified . . . knowledges" involve us on "the . . . particular,
local, [differential], and regional knowledge . . . which owes its force
only to the harshness with which it is opposed by everything surrounding it."

My cross-genealogical work follows the lead of both Foucault's genealogy (what he defines as a "union" of "erudite knowledge" and
"local memories" [Foucault 1980, 83]) and that of Mignolo's "border
gnosis" (what he defines as a subaltern "knowledge conceived from the
exterior borders of the modern/colonial system, and border gnosel-
ogy as a discourse about colonial knowledge . . . conceived at the conflictive intersection of the knowledge produced from the perspective
of modern colonialisms (rhetoric, philosophy, science) and knowledge produced from the perspective of colonial modernities in Asia,
Africa, and the Américas/Caribbean" [Mignolo 2000b, 11]). But what
happens when we move the production of knowledge to a different
intersticio—say, the spaces of the cultures of U.S. imperialism or of the
militarized U.S.-Mexican border, where the question is no longer one
of subjugated knowledges but one of subaltern knowledges? What
happens to identity, epistemic experience, and the border-thinking
subject when we locate them within the structures of U.S. (internal)
colonialism and what Aníbal Quijano and Immanuel Wallerstein call
the production of "Americanity" in the modern (colonial) world-
system?[5] If identities are produced by a supplying and enforcing of
an "Americanity" of power that thoroughly invades, embalms, and
renders stable the individual, how can we begin to situate El Vez's
resignifications of the "raced" Elvis Presley subject? Do his massified

cultural performances offer us the possibility to mobilize the "sign chains" of identity, gender, and identifications in new ways? What does his transculturation of Elvis demonstrate about ethnicity and identity in the United States?

My firm sense is that El Vez's performances allow us to consider what Eric Lott (1996, 4) terms becoming "more aware of the uneven and contradictory character of popular life and culture, the ambiguities or contradictions that may characterize the pleasures of the masses." By transculturating the already braided and "raced" subject of Elvis Presley, El Vez signifies on one of the central "counterfeits" of our times and on what Lott (1996, 52) sees as the "complex affair[s] of manly mimicry." In addition, El Vez's performances remind us that a subject remains a subject only through what Judith Butler (1997, 99) sees as "a reiteration or a rearticulation of itself as a subject." El Vez thus calls for a radical making of subjectivity, of "multiple interpellations" in and against the internal and external global borders of power.[6] His point, as Foucault (1982, 212) put it, is "not to discover what we are but to refuse what we are."

My reflections for this chapter start where I ended *Border Matters*. In that book's conclusion, I explored the border thinking in the performance art of El Vez in songs from *Graciasland* and *GI Ay, Ay! Blues*. I supplement those meditations by examining El Vez's songs "Never Been to Spain," "Taking Care of Business," and "Immigration Time." In the middle of the chapter, I add new reflections on John Rechy's magical urbanist fable of Los Angeles, *The Miraculous Day of Amalia Gómez*, in the context of gender, subjectification, and globalization. I then conclude by returning to El Vez's transculturation of two of Elvis Presley's songs from the 1950s: "Trying to Get to You" and "Mystery Train."

El Vez (Robert López) is one of the most dynamic Elvis performance artists from East Los Angeles to Memphis and Viva Las Vegas. He has toured extensively in the United States and Europe with his band the Memphis Mariachis. Backed by the Beautiful Elvettes, he has opened for the B-52s, Elvis Costello, Carlos Santana, and, most recently, David Bowie. (As a parenthetical personal note, in August 1997 I participated in a workshop with El Vez on the aesthetics, politics, and philosophy of staging Elvis in the 1990s at the Third Annual International Conference on Elvis Presley at the Memphis College of

Art.[7] On May 5, 1998, I contributed to a film documentary on El Vez shot at the American Music Hall in San Francisco, where he performed his iconic Gospel show, with its religiously poetic slogan, "This ain't no church picnic.") "El Vez," *Newsweek* writes, "is a multiethnic, multicultural, multicostumed revolutionary who reinvents art from a [Chicano/Latino] perspective."[8]

Those of us who teach El Vez in ethnic studies university classes love him because he has what we want in the 2000s: swagger, attitude, and groove. El Vez is big on "el groove," for he casts himself as "el groover" lowriding low and slow on MTV. Serious. *Malo*—Bad. El Vez is the Subcomandante Marcos of attitude; the big bang of minoritized U.S. Latino/a pop performance. His voice is as tight as a fist, playing with the Elvis Presley break beats, splitting and cross-cutting them.

My education in Elvis Presley studies owes much to, and has been shaped by, what El Vez/Robert López has demonstrated in his performance art. I agree completely with his observation (gleaned from Phil Ochs) that "if there's any hope for América it lies in a revolution. If there's any hope for a revolution, it lies in Elvis . . . becoming Che Guevara" (quoted in Habell-Pallan forthcoming, 207). In other words, El Vez, complete with gold lamé suit à la Elvis and "Elvisizing" the crowd, clues us in to how ethno-racialized minorities reach a mass audience; how if you really want to be like Che or like Che's fan way down past Louisiana in Chiapas—the Zapatista Marcos—the best way to do it is to try to communicate as completely and radically as Elvis Presley once did. Again, I agree with Lott (1996, 103) that we must not forget that even in his "cultural conquests," Elvis Presley explicitly "dismantl[ed] . . . racial music" in the South and thus bent the color bar of radio and mass culture. El Vez believes in giving the people the showbiz and the glitter, but he also aspires to give us something solid to chew on.

What unites many of us today in critical U.S. studies is a shared experience with space and tradition (those cultural things that deal with continuity, genealogy, and convergence) and an appreciation of cultural translation and the displacements of border crossings and diasporas of the early 2000s. "Getting lost in translation," as El Vez explained in one of his numerous interviews, is "what the Chicano/ U.S. Latino/a experience in America is all about" (Habell-Pallan forthcoming). His performance art is therefore shaped, I believe, by tradition and translation. His Elvis Presley performances pay tribute to El Rey's (the King's) working-class migratory roots and routes, from Tupelo to Memphis—what brings the discrepant American experiences together as a culture. But El Vez's performance art also entails cross-ethnic translation and geopolitical displacement. American ethnic cultures, El Vez suggests, always negotiate between tradition and translation, convergence and displacement.⁹ As El Vez preaches in his cover of Elvis Presley's hit "Never Been to Spain" (1968), "I'm not Hispanic from across the Atlantic, Soy de Mexico / Yo soy Chicano." Here El Vez is not interested in what anthropologists and sociologists à la Robert Park's Chicago school have theorized as assimilation and acculturation. He is fascinated more by issues of what the Cuban cultural theorist Fernando Ortiz called transculturation (the hurricane-like contact of cultures) and the dangerous American crossroads and balancing acts between cultures we know all too well.¹⁰

On another level, El Vez's "Never Been to Spain" allegorizes his concern with colonial legacies in the Américas (both North and South) and with what we might call "transnational localism." According to Mignolo (2000b, 21), transnational localism reveals "the local histories from which global designs emerge in their universal drive"—the long history where the European Renaissance and modernity and rationality, as well as the ineradicable traces of local culture meet. " 'Cause," as El Vez sings, Columbus "thinks he discovered us in 14 ninety-two / who discovered who . . . / I'm not Hispanic from across the Atlantic . . . / I'm a mechanic from across Atlantic [Boulevard, in East Los Angeles]." It is El Vez's tracing of colonial and de-colonial legacies in translocal cultures in Mexico and in California that helps him begin to reverse and resignify the cognitive maps of domination and desire, precisely by using Elvis Presley's iconic pop song almost against itself.

El Vez does not pretend in "Never Been to Spain" that his transnational localism (what he puts positively as "I've been to Chichén Itza [where] Mayan Culture [in Yucatán, Mexico], man, it thrived boy / before Columbus had a teacher") will replace the more entrenched disciplinary knowledges of Europe and the area studies of the United States. By the same token, he suggests that we cannot expect from the European Renaissance and modernity's aftermath the knowledges that the Amerindian Mayans have: "You can't discover what's been uncovered." El Vez uses Elvis Presley's song to go beyond the subalternization of knowledge and to map for us the occupation of new cultural spaces, new public spheres, and alternative musical soundings. The song announces at the start of his performance career that he will take on multiple identifications to tell us about the legacy of European modernity encountering its limits as it is taken over by and in local histories embedded in global colonial roots and routes.

To continue illustrating some of the broad themes of *Border Matters*, I now consider the effects of gender and globalization on the recent literatures of California. John Rechy's Los Angeles *fábula* (fable) *The Miraculous Day of Amalia Gómez* (1992), like El Vez's music, portrays documented and undocumented U.S. Latina women who provide labor for the consumer in the world-system in which they are unequal participants and who often bring home work and solicit the work of their children, making the domestic space of the home a site of labor: "To keep afloat—and as the children grew it became more and more difficult—[Amalia Gómez] occasionally took in piecework to do at home. Her children would help. Gloria would adjust the expensive labels, Juan would glue them on the garments, and Amalia would sew them. When Manny was home [and not in the juvie], he would fold the items with exact care, sometimes making them all laugh by creating a grotesque face out of one of the garments" (Rechy 1992, 56). The everyday lives of Amalia and her children, Rechy suggests, are fraught, "stamped," and "linked" by the conditions of the globalization of Amalia's work as a U.S. Latina sewing woman, from her sewing machine to the vulnerability of the subaltern in capitalist transmodernity and to the contrast of what must be seen as nirvana by the dominant and as a border-patrolled state and as a "spurious hegemony" for the subordinate—what Ranajit Guha (1998, xii) calls a "dominance without hegemony."[11] That is, Rechy maps out a California world where coercion (the juvenile hall, the prison-industrial complex, La Migra or the Border Patrol, the LAPD) outweighs persuasion.

Family relations in *The Miraculous Day of Amalia Gómez* thematize, among other things, the conditions of everyday life within the contradictions of the nation-state as capitalism extends globally. As Lisa Lowe (1996, 169) suggests in a related context on California Asian American literature, "The immigrant's lack of civil rights promised to citizens of the nation permits the 'private space' of the . . . home to become a workplace that prioritizes the relations of production . . . over family relations." *The Miraculous Day of Amalia Gómez* tells us about the radical constricting of the private or domestic sphere under the pressures of ethno-racialized and gendered relations of production. From the breakdowns in communication between Amalia and her border-crossing mother; between Amalia and her *telenovela*-embedded *comadres* at various sweatshops in Los Angeles; between Amalia and her children; and, perhaps, between Amalia and La Virgen de Guadalupe, who appears to her at the tony Beverly Center mall at the end of the novel, Rechy's fable allegorizes how cultural ties often bear the weight of immigration laws, of chauvinist state propositions, and of treaties (the Bracero Program and NAFTA).

In talking about a post-contemporary California literary fable like Rechy's with the cultures of globalization, we can also contrapuntally turn to other evidentiary forms of narrative, such as the cross-disciplinary book *Behind the Label*, by Edna Bonacich and Richard Appelbaum. *Behind the Label* is a rich social history of the apparel industry in Los Angeles. According to Bonacich and Appelbaum (2000, 20), that industry provides "a good example of how our society works, and how the system [within the context of globalization] produces and reproduces an intensifying polarization by class and race." By examining corporations and manufacturers such as Guess (founded by the Marciano brothers in 1981) and how they eventually moved 40 percent of their production to Mexico, they are able to show how movement "offshore ratchets down wages in the industrial world" and how workers in poor countries must operate in "political regimes . . . that have restricted [their] ability to organize and demand change" (Bonacich and Appelbaum 2000, 7).

Los Angeles may be the cultural capital of fashion and design in the United States, but it is no longer, Bonacich and Appelbaum emphasize, the site where in-house production takes place. In-house production by manufacturers such as Guess and Wal-Mart, among others, have virtually disappeared from Los Angeles and the United States. What has replaced in-house production (as *The Miraculous Day of Amalia Gómez* demonstrates) are sweatshops where immigrant workers are oppressed by contractors. Young U.S. Latina and Asian American workers usually put in fifteen-hour days for a few dollars to make designer-label clothes.

Behind the Label looks at what life is really like for U.S. Latina and Asian American women immigrant workers; it is quite good in exploring what Bonacich and Appelbaum (2000, 41) call the new "ethnic distribution of the [apparel] industry" in California. "Largely white-owned manufacturers," they claim, "employ primarily Asian contractors to control and exploit [U.S.] Latino labor" (Bonacich and Appelbaum 2000, 141). Thus, when riots broke out in Los Angeles in 1992, the rioters did not attack white-owned manufacturers and corporations. Bonacich and Appelbaum (2000, 20) argue that many African American and U.S. Latino/a rioters burned Korean immigrants' shops and blamed these "mom and pop operations" as their "direct oppressors." For Rechy and Bonacich and Appelbaum it is the subaltern woman who is the paradigmatic subject of the current configuration of the international division of labor.[12] Questions of the heterogeneous subject-constitution of the subaltern for these California writers and researchers gain monumental importance. I have focused on their work as a sign of our times.

The cultural emergence of El Vez, the Mexican Elvis, I would add, is surely another sign of the times, for he provides a remarkable example of how California immigrants are remaking mass popular culture. Mixing the multiple realities of the U.S.-Mexican border-crossing experience to California with classic rock-and-roll sounds by mainline pop bands such as Bachman Turner Overdrive and the Oakland-based Sly Stone and Larry Graham, El Vez performs a frenzied revisioning of what it means for documented and undocumented workers to be "taking care of business" in California:

> for an easy addition you get workers for the kitchen
> paid under table, they won't tell-o
> if you need a handyman, you can go to the standard brands
> and get one of those stand around fellows
> you see us slaving in the sun, from la migra we must run
> you tell us you like it this way
> Taking Care of Business
> blowing leaves, no green card up our sleeves
> Orale.[13]

The texture of El Vez's "Taking Care of Business" is, of course, one of unifying forms. "Taking Care of Business," conceived through jagged contours of rage, satire, and symbolic contradiction, unites itself stylistically with hard-driving rhythmic structures of feelings and a tight groove. On a different register, El Vez's "Taking Care of Business" presents the hegemonic push–pull view of documented and undocumented Mexican and Central American workers' migration to California and the United States. The song sums up a complex view of the border-crossing experience for workers in historical terms, reminding listeners to ponder the following: Have millions of undocumented laborers not built up expectations that their employment as fieldworkers, dishwashers, gardeners, and nannies (and being underpaid) will continue? Should residency be the only route to legal and cultural citizenship?

Although El Vez does not use U.S.-Mexican corridos (border ballads of intercultural conflict) to do his cultural work, his performance art displays the same intense negotiations with identity that characterize the artists and writers from the U.S.-Mexican borderlands. His declarations of multiple interpellations imaginatively use rockabilly riffs, signs, and symbols to testify to George Lipsitz's proposition that popular culture "enables people to rehearse identities, stances, and social situations not yet permissible in politics" (Lipsitz 1994, 137). Indeed, El Vez's "borderization" of the North American pop icon Elvis serves as a concrete site where social relations are not only constructed but also envisioned. El Vez's songs, we might say after Louis Althusser, Ernesto Laclau, and Judith Butler, do not merely reflect reality in the *frontera*; they help construct and interpellate it.

Admittedly, if it is true that El Vez's music (like the original El Rey's music) can be all things to all people, his U.S.-Mexican border sound inevitably cuts both ways. His art has been honed within late capitalism's culturally dominant modes of spectacle and pastiche. "There's been a resurgence of younger Elvises," he notes, "but I like all Elvises" (quoted in Masuo 1995, 84). Thus, on one level, López's music can function as a highly de-centered tribute to what Greil Marcus (1991, 26) describes as Elvis "the polite rocker, the country boy in Hollywood[,] true folk artist and commodity fetish." Like Guillermo Gómez-Peña's performance art, El Vez's borderization of Elvis Presley (complete with extravagant attire—mariachi pants, penciled mustache, and gelled pompadour), however, uses the economy of commodity circulation—compact disks—as a vehicle to protest against California's Proposition 187, the English-only movement, and the like.

"Rather than an impersonation of Elvis," Masuo (1995, 85) writes, "El Vez is a translation—or, as López's business card proclaims—an incredible stimulation."

If López is correct that "Elvis impersonators are almost like the court jesters of our time" (quoted in Masuo 1995, 85), then to be El Vez, he reasons, is to be a borderlands trickster to the second power. At his best, this is what López accomplishes in songs such as "Immigration Time," which blends Elvis's "Suspicious Minds" with the Rolling Stones' "Sympathy for the Devil." Here he addresses directly the moral hypocrisy of California's and the U.S. government's immigration policy against undocumented workers:

> I'm caught in a trap, I can't walk out
> Because my foot's caught in the border fence
> Why can't you see, Statue of Liberty
> I am your homeless, tired, and weary.
> We can go on together, it's Immigration Time. . . .
> And we can build our dreams, it's Immigration Time.
> Yes I'm trying to go, get out of Mexico
> The promised land waits on the other side.
> Here they come again, they're trying to fence me in
> Wanting to live with the brave and the home of the free. (*Graciasland*)

López's "Immigration Time" appropriates the major cultural tropes of U.S. immigration writing, a national writing understood in terms of what recent commentators have described as a ritual practice enacting Americanization. Rather than vilify the shared dilemmas of other ethno-racial groups whose icons and narratives have transformed U.S. immigrant writing into national archetypes, El Vez aligns the plight of undocumented Mexican workers with those archetypes and symbologies that scholars such as Werner Sollors and Thomas J. Ferraro have shown to be part and parcel of the national imaginary. White Anglo-Saxon Protestants, after all, "fled religious persecutions," and ethno-racial minorities "were forcibly removed, incorporated, enslaved, and interned" (Ferraro 1993, 7).

"Immigration Time," in my view, thematizes undocumented Mexican border crossers' desire to move out of the margins (the Immigration and Nationalization Service's and Department of Homeland Security's border fences notwithstanding) into the larger world where other groups elaborated their representations of America as "the home of the brave" and of the "tired" and the "weary." It is, to be sure, a long walk from the patrolled fences of the Tijuana and San Diego borderlands to New York's Statue of Liberty, but El Vez's song speaks to the profound degree of cultural self-distancing it takes to be in a position to write protest songs in English for undocumented migrant workers.

To conclude, I turn to two early Elvis songs—"Trying to Get to You" and "Mystery Train"—which López transforms into twenty-first-century transcultural *descargas*. With "Trying to Get to You," El Vez, the San Diego groover who always seems ready to escape into the Memphis Beale Street blues, now has his eyes turned toward de-constructing América as the de-colonial site of the home, the home country, and the unhomely. In a powerful montage as richly braided as anything in our cut-and-mix culture and society, El Vez crosscuts Presley's "I got your letter and I came running" mode of emplotment with an enlarged idea of the subaltern (a term now meant to include a range of *campesino/a* groups and ethno-racialized minority border crossers),[14] multiplying border thinking in their travels North from Mexico:

> I've been traveling over borders
> over hills and barbed wire too
> I've been traveling night and day
> I've been trying to get to you
> (USA).
> There's a lady in the harbor
> bring me your homeless, weary too
> on the darkest, dreary nights
> toward the shining shining bright
> O baby trying to get to you.[15]

Just as in Elvis Presley's beautifully sung rendition of the 1950s, Robert López's border song contains elegance, passion, *coraje* (anger), and an evangelical (born-again in East L.A.) humility. He does not forget to thank his "Lordy, Lordy" for helping him along on his migrations North from Mexico. But what is also interesting here is the strong, strict arrangement, with López singing and submitting to a blues realism and to what Houston Baker Jr. (1987, 3) has called "blues matrix." While he never takes it over, he carries over the restrained emotions to his shining bright love object, that "lady in the harbor." The song is evocative in its floating sense of harmony mixed with the hunger of libidinal desire and the desperate American double striv- ings (as W. E. B. Du Bois once put it), linked to a pure outpouring of joy that tumbles out of his rock-and-roll *rola*.

But it is in his Global South rockabilly-in-Spanglish anthem "Misery Tren" that El Vez poses the history of the subaltern against the histori- cal unity of the ruling classes realized in the neoliberal state. Here El Vez hijacks the mystery train, jumps on the ghostly mystery sonics that Junior Parker and, later, Elvis preached about at Sun Studios in the 1950s. Parker's, Presley's, and López's songs all rely on odd chop- ping beats, the inevitable train whistles in all their glory, technological alienation, and flair, mixed together with a stark blues realism. Parker and Presley ride that long black train, sixteen coaches long, for that train "carry my baby and be gone"; López submits to a James Brown and Public Enemy phat Night Train and exploits and takes it as far south as he can go—all the way to Mexico's *frontera sur*:

> Train, train de la Revolución
> Train, train de la revolución
> este tren toma me baby
> pero it will never again . . .
> tierra y libertad
> tierra y libertad . . .
> Pancho Villa y los Zapatistas
> Pancho Villa y los Zapatistas
> Adelita es la mujer to destroy los capitalistas.[16]

López's "Misery Tren" is his minimalist ode to revolution and to Zapatismo. It is also his popular striving and calling for an expanded sense of subalternity, with its project of "tierra y libertad (land and liberty)." For López, the Zapatismo's "border thinking" is something to sing about,[17] for it is not only a social uprising but also an uprising that proposes a new way of knowing. ("Tierra y libertad" is not cast within a universal history or as a cry from the universal spirit. It is referenced from five hundred years of the coloniality of power in the Américas.) "Misery Tren" forces us not only to reappraise the politics of pop but also to derail the state and the types of individualization that are linked to the state and the coloniality of power, even when the subaltern cannot be represented by or in the state formation. The choppy break beats in "Misery Tren" and its fragmentary rhythms can be read only as the sign of another mode of a translocalized vernacular emplotment and *pensamiento fronterizo* rather than as an incomplete Gramscian metropolitan project.

In this chapter, I have taken a cluster of different social songs and texts (primarily from California) and discussed how they operate in terms of the overlapping subaltern codes and conventions with which they engage. Like other entho-racialized pop artists (Elvis Presley and Prince, for instance), El Vez develops his performance style far from the centers of cultural dominance. Like Elvis and Prince, he, too, acquires much of his braided musical semiosis through recording and mass radio. El Vez's music therefore draws on and reinscribes a Southern and Southwestern American sound. Nowhere is this braided transculturation more evident than in El Vez's bilingual "JC, Sí, I Am a Lowrider," a song that ends most of his marathon live performances. In it he not only signifies on Broadway musicals (*Jesus Christ Superstar*) and Aretha Franklin's rendition of "C.C. Rider" but also takes on Prince's gender-bending erotics (what the feminist musicologist Susan McClary [2000, 154] terms the artist's deliberately pitched "vulnerable falsetto"). A veritable rock opera about the Chicano lowrider's structures of "lowness," the song constructs a world in which Southern, Midwestern, and Southwestern soulful soundings moan, groan, and caress the song's foreground, while its familiar chords bring coherence as a backdrop of Americana pop:

> Lowrider superstar, are you as cool as they
> say you are?
> lowrider superstar where do you go on that big
> fine [Chevy Impala] car?[18]

I conclude with one last Robert López slogan: "Act locally, think Elvisly." What does it mean for those of us doing critical U.S. studies that López deliberately leaves out the state? Does his sloganeering represent what many social scientists see as a lack of faith in the state as the mechanism of reform in our everyday lives? Would it have been impossible to think this way, say, some thirty years ago, when everyone seemed to be thinking and acting at the state level?

The translocal performance art of El Vez, the Mexican Elvis, thematizes a remarkable shift from acting and thinking at the state level to thinking and acting at the ethnic Elvis (global) level. This shift, moreover, parallels a larger shift in the unit of analysis in U.S. Latino/a studies—a new study of hemispheric and world cities, transnational studies, and renewed focus on regions (why the South has new Mexican immigrants in the poultry zones of Arkansas and the agricultural fields of North Carolina). All of these movements help us address the limits of state-centered thinking. It remains to be seen how far El Vez's logic critiquing the state will help us restructure an emerging trans-American studies.

Making U.S. Democracy Surreal:
Political Race, Transmodern Realism,
and the Miner's Canary

Some of my initial critical thoughts on Lani Guinier's and Gerald Tor-res's *The Miner's Canary: Enlisting Race, Resisting Power, Transforming Democracy* (2002) were first cobbled together in a University of Cali-fornia, Berkeley graduate seminar on cultural studies and on social structure that I co-taught a few years ago with the sociologist Michael Omi. In our seminar's discussion of *The Miner's Canary*, I confessed that as an undergraduate literature major at Yale I had met and collab-orated on an experimental Spanglished literary journal with Gerald Torres, who was then completing his law degree at the Yale Law School. Preparing this chapter had stirred up memories of my discus-sions with Gerald about approaching the problems of Chicano/a multiculture and *mestizaje* from a different angle, about "bare life" and the structuring of law and violence, and about our divergent readings of our favorite imaginative writers at the time from the Global South, especially Gabriel García Márquez and Toni Morrison. My Berkeley transdiciplinary graduate students, hearing again that elusive sound-ings Gerald and I heard many years ago down the mean streets of New Haven about Chicano/a multiculture, tended to dislike my literary (figural) reading of this legal and activist book, for instance, my claims concerning Torres's dystopian melancholic take on *mestizaje* and his utopian faith in *lo real maravilloso* and *magical realism*. In the differ-ence between my reading and theirs, I now see that Guinier and Torres's book on political race still interests me deeply for the reasons I will discuss below.

In *The Miner's Canary: Enlisting Race, Resisting Power, Transforming Democracy* (2002), Lani Guinier, a professor of law at Harvard University, and Gerald Torres, a professor of law at the University of Texas, Austin, demonstrate the enormous complexity of what they call "political race" in the United States today.[1] By exploring the relationships among race, class, law, and nation as they have evolved over, say, the past one hundred years in the United States, they highlight racist attitudes that transcend the left–right political divide. Moreover, they challenge current, mainline sociological and critical race theory's approaches to race, raciology, and racism, as well as to the ethnic absolutism and bias of American legal studies.

Let me also highlight that *The Miner's Canary* enters our political debates about "political race" at a particularly stark moment for progressive scholars and activists. Given the political defeats in California, Texas, and Michigan, and the rest of the country, around affirmative-action policy, and given the hegemonic ascendancy of the new network-power empire building of Bush–Cheney, Guinier and Torres imaginatively respond to our neoliberal epoch with an avowedly "aspirational project" rooted and routed in a field-imaginary from the Global South (*lo real maravilloso*) that they suggest can destabilize the limits of the real in the Global North.

As Guinier and Torres see it, their aspirational project has crossed into the Global North from the Global South because U.S. law and legal strategies have not been effective means to pursue social justice in this country. "Legal institutions," they argue from within the belly of the beast, "construct a form of social solidarity that . . . inhibits the development of robust democratic counterweights to the agglomeration of private power" (36). More specifically, Guinier and Torres seek to deconstruct and critique the ascendancy of colorblindness in the United States with evidence of the continued salience of race color-consciousness. They want to resuscitate race color-consciousness in the legal and political environment that endeavors to embalm it as a matter of normative and hegemonic principle.[2]

Thus envisaged, *The Miner's Canary* is both a timely and a robustly provocative exercise in *contestación* (contestation), one that is compelling and persuasive in its breadth, depth, and cross-disciplinariness. I intend to use the term "*contestación*" throughout this chapter as an interlingual pun that draws on the Spanish and English meanings of the word. As I see it, "to contest" is to answer but, "to contest" is also to dispute, to provide alternative paradigms or explanations. The subject of contestation here is "political race"; more narrowly, what is being contested in *The Miner's Canary* is the political arena for the future of African American and U.S. Latino/a political alliances. Rather than hoping for change from a hostile court, Guinier and Torres argue for a different strategy that they believe can get us through the current impasse. While *The Miner's Canary* attracted considerable attention from reviewers at scores of U.S. newspapers and magazines interested in ideas about political race and racial formation, it was little commented on by those of us interested in trans-American literary and cultural studies. *The Miner's Canary*, indeed, should interest those of us who teach American literature because its activist scope accommodates, in a profoundly original formulation, a subalternist critique of the "dominance without hegemony" (see Guha 1997) of the United States, where coercion outweighs persuasion.

Early in *The Miner's Canary*, Guinier and Torres begin to rewrite their near-contra-dictionary of keywords. "Race," for them, "is . . . the miner's canary" (11). From the very start, the book institutionalizes the latent similarity between "race" and "the miner's canary" into the radical new identity that races *are* miners' canaries. Our incredulous, Sancho-like question—"What races?"—cannot dispel the quixotic activist vision of Guinier and Torres because, while we Sanchos might attempt to explain away the similarities, for Guinier and Torres the process of transposition has already surpassed analysis. The sense of the word "race," instead of designating the thing, which the word should normally designate (a sense that for this particular word is already in the realm of metaphor), goes elsewhere. (As an aside, I should also note that the assimilation of differences into similarities is for rhetoricians the figural basis of all rational discourse; it is also one of the characteristics the late Jacques Derrida ascribed to metaphor in his classic essay "White Mythology" [1982].)[3]

Eschewing notions of race either as biological or, as we used to say in the 1990s, as a social construction, Guinier and Torres articulate race as the miner's canary. "Miners," they write, "often carried a canary into the mine alongside them. The canary's fragile respiratory system would cause it to collapse from noxious gases long before humans were affected, thus alerting the miner's to danger" (11). Continuing their rather extended figural understanding of race in the United States—that is, as an extended metaphor or allegory—Guinier and

Torres argue "those who are racially marginalized" are the miner's canary, and their distress is the first sign of a danger that threatens us all. "It is easy enough to think that when we sacrifice this canary, the harm is to communities of color. Yet others ignore problems that converge around racial minorities at their own peril, for the problems are symptoms warning us that we are all at risk" (11).

Given that the continuing and largely unwelcome presence of millions of so-called illegal aliens in the United States has also been explained in racial terms as America's new "brown menace" and what Mike Davis (2000, 75) sees as "the moral equivalent of the obsolete red menace," Guinier's and Torres's project of linking up the metaphor of the canary with a progressive global project of "political race" is all the more urgent. The brown-menaced anarchy of workers from the Global South (primarily Mexico and Central America) has recently been described as the result of the demands placed on the "legal" working classes and the so-called underclasses, which were required to bear the responsibility of Americanizing all incoming undocumented workers into the hegemonic U.S. way of life. Today, U.S. mainline society's antipathy toward "illegal' aliens" cannot be tidily hidden away, but the idea that this antipathy has anything to do with violent racism—the noxious poison in the mine's air that kills the canary—remains a discomfiting revelation.

Samuel Huntington—a onetime policy wonk for John F. Kennedy and not a reactionary knave—whose latest work on social science from Harvard, *Who Are We?: The Challenges to America's National Identity* (2004b, 243), presents the "corrosive" influx of a too fertile "brown menace" from the Global South as the single most immediate and serious "threat to the cultural and possibly political integrity of the United States" and articulates a link between immigration and multiculturalism. This connection has now moved on to discussions and debates about how this U.S. multiculture should be governed. Although *Who Are We?* tends to turn complicated matters such as identity and culture into a cartoon world where Popeye blasts Speedy González mercilessly, Huntington presumes to speak for a whole American civilization. The challenge for American policymakers, he says, is to make sure that the United States gets stronger and purer by draconically closing off its border with Mexico. Is Huntington simply an ideologue? Is he someone who desires to make civilizations and identities what they are not—shut down, sealed-off entities that have been purged of the myriad currents and crosscurrents that animate human history? Against Huntington's linking of geopolitical problems to the prospect of the diversity of the U.S. multiculture we can place Guinier's and Torres's call for the construction of a new "language to discuss race" in America and hence build "progressive democratic movements led by people of color but joined by others" (12). By reconnecting "individual experiences to democratic faith," like magical realist novelists, "to social critique, and to meaningful action that improves the lives of the canary and the miners by ameliorating the air quality in the mines" (12), Guinier and Torres propose a shift in the way that we think about race and put political race to use.

If race in America is "the miner's canary," it follows metonymically, synecdochically, and catachrestically throughout this book that race is also "diagnostic" for Torres and Guinier, "signaling the need for more systematic critique." Race, for them, thus "continues to be salient" (12) in our culture and society. This chapter aims to articulate Guinier's and Torres's diagnostic, figural conception of race for those interested in ruthlessly modernizing class analysis and to chart how political race expresses itself in a variety of transmodern literary texts. As Paul Gilroy elegantly argued in *There Ain't No Black in Union Jack* (1987), the place of black labor in processes that transform workers into a class and distribute surplus labor power in society raises a series of fundamental doubts about the degree of homogeneity that can be ascribed to the making of the English working class. "Conflicts around 'race,' nation and ethnicity," Gilroy (1987, 20) argued, had to "be examined in the light of these other divisions [not only between those in and out of work but also between those in the various sectors of waged employment, between men and women, and between older and younger people] where the unity of a single 'working class' [could] not be assumed but [remained] to be created."

As adept practitioners of the critical race theory (CRT) project,[4] Guinier and Torres see racism as "constitutive" of our culture and society. Not surprisingly, they begin *The Miner's Canary* with American New Historicist–like anecdotes and *historias* about race. Through their own framing stories, they attempt to "thematize" the difficulties of theorizing race outside the dyadic constraints of colorblindness, on the one hand, and color-consciousness, on the other. The limitations of these existing American dyads, they argue, demonstrate the need for an alternative conception of race—a way out that they call "political race," for "way-out" people know the way out.

Guinier begins her story about race by recalling how she once tried to explain to her son Niko, who was then eight years old, why she used the word "black" to describe a woman about whom she was writing. Niko, who was educated at a Quaker school, protested that "black" did not really add anything to her sentence about the woman, because "it didn't matter" (1). Guinier responded to Niko with the dialectics of difference: it makes a world of difference that the subject she was writing about was a woman and not, willy-nilly, a person. Niko may have been blind to race, but at eight he already had insights about gender. But why, Guinier asked, had Niko not grappled enough with the idea that race was a category that could not be erased?

Guinier's opening story helps her begin to illustrate a crucial argument in *The Miner's Canary*—namely, that the culture and society in which Niko and the rest of us live is not a colorblind, race-free world. Rather, it is a culture and society in which, when older Nikos and Josés "walk down" the mean streets, "cops" may stop them, or young men of color may resent them, in both cases "because of a potentially deadly combination of racism and machismo" (3). Guinier agonizes over whether, in having to school Niko for the racist hard knocks that may lie ahead, she created a story about racial identity in America that was entirely too negative. Are all black and brown (racially profiled) men and women, as Ralph Ellison (1995 [1952], 94) dramatically put it in *Invisible Man* "walking personification[s] of the Negative"? Guinier worried that she had failed Niko as a parent and had gone overboard in suggesting that race is always negative and a stigma. "What was missing from my conversation with my son was recognition that being forced to identify with a group of people can be an unexpected blessing. Those who are racialized by society may miss out on a specific kind of liberty, but they gain a perspective on wholeness and its relationship to freedom. . . . They also learn from a place at the bottom . . . to be skeptical of authority, to distrust hierarchy, to find comfort in community" (4).

Guinier's story captures something about the particular "negative dialectics" of black–white racial formations.[5] Gerald Torres's opening story shifts the politics of location from the urban streets of the U.S.

Northeast to the "magical urbanism" and the U.S.-Mexican borderlands of San Bernardino, California.[6] Here we find Torres engaged in
his *autohistoriateoría* of sorts (like the late Gloria Anzaldúa) attending
an inner-city, multicultural public school—a barrioscaped school con-
sisting of Asian Americans, African Americans, and Chicanos/as. Torres recalls that he and his friend Steve, a Chinese American, dated
white girls (as Ritchie Valens did), earned straight A's in their college
preparatory courses, and believed that they were the "vanguard" of a
brave new multicultural world that one day would make "color" obsolete. "We would be the agents of a race-less society" (7). However,
looming all around them, like the curse of breeding children with a
pig's tail, were brutal race riots between whites and blacks, whites and
Latinos, and blacks and Chicanos. "What we did not understand,"
Torres notes, "was that transcendence would eliminate the positive
content of race as well as the negative" (7). Against the Southern
Hotel California pull of colorblindness, Torres felt the racial structural
ties of the feelings and *conocimiento* of his Chicano/a community—
what Anzaldúa theorized in *Borderlands/La Frontera* as "*la conciencia
de la nueva mestiza*" (1987, 99). Had the coloniality of power in the
Américas spawned a "new race"?

In the magical urbanism of San Bernardino high school; later, at
Stanford University, where he attended college; and perhaps even at
the Yale Law School, Torres grappled with the harsh choices about his
colonially wounded identity. Would he follow a hard Chicano culturalist line that—until very recently—deemed Chicanos free from Afro-
Latinidad "blackness," or would he adopt the pan-ethnic categoriza-
tion of *hispanidad* (Hispanicity) that "would separate [him] from
[his] own Mexican culture" (8)?

Torres's brisk narrative, which, like Guinier's opening story, mixes
reminiscence with *autohistoria* reflection, contains a small sub-story
on the experiences of Chicano *mestizaje*: "We who are neither black
nor white are now seduced with a simple two-part offer. In the first
step, we can trade in our Mexican culture and our local connection
with black people and [Native American] Indians"; in exchange, "we
get a chance to share a language and national identity with others
across the country who have also grasped the name Hispanic. Then, if
we agree to become Hispanic, as a second step we are promised a
chance to trade up. We are offered the possibility of joining a new
paradoxical category: Hispanic whiteness" (8–9).

Through these small autohistorias, Guinier and Torres illustrate their own hesitations about the usefulness of the American conceptualizations of colorblindness and color-consciousness. This Manichaean conceptualization of race leads them to imagine a "third way [of thinking that] navigates the shoals of identity politics and the fantasies of colorblindness. It is a political project that does not ask who you married, or what your daddy was. At its core it does not ask what you call yourself but with whom do you link your fate. It is a fundamentally creative political project that begins from the ground up, starting with race and all its complexity, and then builds cross-racial relationships through race and with race to issues of class and gender in order to make democracy real. We call this project political race" (9–10). One of the major interventions *The Miner's Canary* stages is precisely a shifting of the paradigm of race from a focus on identities embedded in bodies to theorizing race as a race politics from below. Thus envisaged, race is powerful precisely because it provides a foundational grounding of the natural hierarchy on which other social and political conflicts have come to rely.[7]

I now turn briefly to Guinier's and Torres's cross-genealogical methodology to continue examining their materialist critique of idealist high theory. While they emphasize that *The Miner's Canary* is a "work in critical race theory," they also suggest that the book is "not about critical race theory" (36–37). In other words, although they are ideologically sympathetic as law professors to the CRT movement, *The Miner's Canary* is their critique of what they see as "both legal doctrine and theory's [inability] to address the condition of racialized groups in our culture" (36). Although struggles of social justice and race have been raging within law schools, they argue, the debate too often has "been disconnected from the material reality of being raced in the United States" (36). That is not to say that critical works such as Walter Benjamin's essay, "Critique of Violence" (1996 [1978]) and Jacques Derrida's "late" work on deconstruction and justice, human rights and wrongs, and the multiple ways the force of law embeds itself through violence, as he argued in the classic essay "Force of Law: The 'Mystical' Foundation of Authority" (1992), are antithetical to Guinier's and Torres's project of watching the canary. Derrida's canaries, after all, included European ethnocentrism and phallogocentrism as defining characteristics of Europe's inherited tradition. Rather, Benjamin's and Derrida's leftist critical theory and insights need to be deployed in what Guinier and Torres term the political terrain of "political race"—that is, into political theory and democratic practice "at the level of social movements" (37). Derrida argued that deconstruction of the political field occurs in the becoming of the world and that critical thinking is the thinking of "the to-come (à-venir)." What, then, is the role of praxis in works such as *Specters of Marx: The State of Debt, the Work of Mourning, and the New International* (1994)? How might have Derrida's deconstruction grappled with the reconstruction of citizenship, political incorporation, and rights in an epoch of the decline of sovereignty, the configuration of the post-national in Germany, the critique of ethnic absolutism in multicultural Europe, and what he called the "hospitality" that should be shown to migrants *sans papiers*? If deconstruction happens in the world, how was hospitality called for by events such as globalization? (As an aside, I would also suggest, aligning myself with Guinier's and Torres's critique, that we need not conflate Derrida's ethics with something we might call Derrida's politics. Did Derrida sacrifice politics to ethics?) By advancing CRT's analytics and metrics into making democracy a praxis of *lo real maravilloso*, Guinier and Torres "hope to go beyond the efforts of critical race theory to reformulate legal doctrine, in order to explore the critical meaning of race for progressive politics" (36). "Can race," they ask, "work as a political instrument for social change" (37)?

"Political race" is thus Guinier's and Torres's attempt to reconceptualize both politics and race, first, by advancing a concept of race not as "identity" (but as an anti-anti-essentialist prism to frame political praxis) and second, by going beyond defining race as a social construction. If race is not only socially constructed, as we used to say in the 1990s, for Guinier and Torres race also involves us in the "relationships to power within the conflicts of . . . political history" (15). "Race," as U.S. progressive sociologists and historians such as Dalton Conley, George Lipsitz, Melvin Oliver, Thomas Shapiro, and W. E. B. Du Bois himself theorized, is "tied to many socioeconomic factors such as life expectancy, health, [bank loans], accumulating wealth, likelihood of completing a number of years of education or likelihood of spending a significant amount of time incarcerated" (15).[8]

"Political race" insists on the centrality of the symbolic and material wages of race as a point of departure for Guinier's and Torres's radically democratic projects because racially minoritized people (the subaltern in the United States) are often "among the first to see the pernicious effects of normalized inequality" and hence are "more motivated to understand those problems of access to social power" (17). Throughout *The Miner's Canary*, Guinier and Torres argue that race is not only a riveting category of analysis, but also insist that "race as a miner's canary" can animate political praxis. Thus envisaged, political race is "diagnostic," "aspirational," and "activist," "signaling the need to rebuild a social movement for social change informed by the canary's critique" (12).

If colorblindness obfuscates our entrenched racial inequality in America, political race can help us unpack and explain the dynamics of racial stratification in the economy that produce barriers to attaining a radical democracy and a social equality. By championing "reform from below" through public policy movements—reforms led by racially minoritized people themselves—and moving beyond racial issues, Guinier and Torres believe (and the magical realists from the Global South insist on believing in the politics of the [im]possible), political race movements in the United States can address the broader needs of other groups (such as poor whites, housewives, workers, and citizens overtaxed so the state can build new prisons at the expense of new schools) in a wider dominance without hegemony. Guinier and Torres thus turn in *The Miner's Canary* to a series of autohistorias and case studies featuring City Council races in Chicago; union campaigns led by black workers, preachers, and ethnic Mexican workers at a Super Kmart in Greensboro, North Carolina; and the aftermath of Cheryl Hopwood's successful reverse-discrimination suit over law-school admissions at the University of Texas, Austin. All of these *historias* allegorize for the canary watchers how racialized minority activists formed cross-racial coalitions to remake a new radical democracy of sorts.

These new social movements with political race at the center challenge the mode of production and struggle for control of the ways in which culture and society appropriate scarce resources, but, as Guinier and Torres suggest, this is not their primary orientation. They are struggling not only for the reappropriation of the material structure of power and production, but also for broader and more democratic control over socioeconomic development as a whole. Guinier's and Torres's goals in *The Miner's Canary* involve the radical transformation of new modes of subordination (within a system of dominance) located outside the immediate processes of power and production and that consequently require the reappropriation of space, time, and relationships between individuals in their day-to-day lives. All of these are perceived to be the results of social action. The struggles over race in America are broadened and spread into new areas, for the defense of raced identities begin to constitute the substance of new conflicts. Guinier and Torres argue that our culture and society should be understood as a self-creating process rather than as a finished edifice or structure. The distinctive feature of the case *historias* that Torres and Guinier map out in *The Miner's Canary*, diverse as they are, rest on their potential for worlding the issues of freedom and liberation beyond the particularistic interests of globalized workers employed full time. The distinctive feature of *The Miner's Canary* is located in the common struggle for sociopolitical control of American historicity.

Transmodern Marvelous Realism

While we do not need another definition of what (transmodern) marvelous realism, introduced more than a half-century ago by Alejo Carpentier, really is, it seems clear to me that the iconic and minoritized trans-American narratives that I discuss by Alejo Carpentier, Gabriel García Márquez, Toni Morrison, Arturo Islas, Maxine Hong Kingston, Helena María Viramontes, Robert Stone, E. L. Doctorow, and the Hernández Brothers, among others, are empathetically implicated in any attempt to map out the specificity of transnational Americanity's culture and literature and, thus, to gauge this culture's distance from what might be called "high modernism." Whether or not one uses the neologism "transmodernism"—most recently theorized by Enrique Dussel—there can be no doubt about the fact that the position of women and men of color, and so on, in post-contemporary society and their effect on the planet is fundamentally different from what it was in the period of high modernism and the historical avant-garde.

Seen in this light, transmodernity is an attempt to think historically; it either expresses what Fredric Jameson (1991, ix) calls "some deeper irrepressible historical impulse"—in however "de-realized" and "distorted" a fashion as imaginative writers from the Américas might have it—or represses it. Dussel, moreover, suggests that transmodernist *historias* are closely related to the Global South's "philosophies of liberation." According to Dussel, the concept of transmodernity (as opposed to Europe's and North America's iconic notion of postmodernity) may be a better way to understand Latin America's critical response to Europe's so-called unfinished project of the Enlightenment and to Europe's and North America's skepticism of reason. As Nelson Maldonado-Torres (2008, 235), Dussel's best interpreter and former student, suggests, Dussel's concept of transmodernity "serves as an orienting idea in furthering—not the unfinished project of the Enlightenment but the unfinished project of decolonization." What follows is my attempt not only to link Torres's and Guinier's notion of "political race" with Dussel's transmodernity and Carpentier's *lo real maravilloso*, but also to revisit Louis Althusser's late Marxism and its rejection of postulates of realism and Judith Butler's feminist deconstruction of the real.

Like many post-realists, Althusser reminds us that "realism" is not a style that gives an undistorted reflection of the world. Realism, in his formation, represents the ideologically hegemonic way to conceive and express our relationship to the natural and social worlds around us. In other words, as Althusser suggested in his classic "Ideology and Ideological State Apparatuses" (1971, 162–63), realism functions ideologically: it offers itself a neutral reflection of the world when it is but one way to *conjure* the world. In her essay "The Force of Fantasy: Feminism, Mapplethorpe, and Discursive Excess" (1990, 110), Judith Butler argues that fantasy is to be equated not with what is not real but, rather, "with what is not *yet* real, or what belongs to a different version of the real." In any case, this chapter on political race, critical canary watching, and transmodern marvelous realist narratives is not intended as a full survey of the marvelous realist writers from the Américas, for the transmodern condition cannot account without strain for all the literary productions that follow.

It is generally accepted that, in addition to influencing Guinier's and Torres's theory of political race, as I have discussed, the marvelous realist movement in the Global South led by Alejo Carpentier, Gabriel García Márquez, and Juan Rulfo had a powerful influence on a diverse group of post-contemporary minoritized writers of color in the

United States. They include Toni Morrison, the author of *Sula, Beloved,* and *A Mercy,* among others; Arturo Islas, the author of *The Rain God* and *Migrant Souls;* Maxine Hong Kingston, the author of *The Woman Warrior, China Men,* and *Tripmaster Monkey;* Helena María Viramontes, the author of *The Moths and Other Stories, Under the Feet of Jesus,* and *Their Dogs Came With Them;* and E. L Doctorow's *Book of Daniel* to *Ragtime.* While these works have been widely praised for their oppositional, feminist, Jewish, gay, and minority discourse poetics, and for their powerful supernatural lyricism, their use of (transmodern) marvelous realism has received little attention in our largely Anglophone and Eurocentric English and American literature departments, owing to an inadequate understanding of a vast and rich literary and cultural movement in the Américas that began over some sixty years ago. The provocative Hispanist William Childers (2006), suggests that traditional scholars of Spain could also profit from seeing Cervantes's fiction as grappling not only with Europe's coloniality of power and internal colonialism but also with Americanity's *lo real maravilloso.* As he puts it, "There is a common ground between Cervantine fiction and magical realism, and that the basis for that common ground is their shared confrontation with coloniality of power" (Childers 2007, 45). Both Anglophone and Hispanaphone literature departments, then, might wish to grapple more with Americanity's coloniality and with its *lo real maravilloso.*

To be sure, the concept of (transmodern) marvelous realism raises many problems, both theoretical and historical. I will not retrace the rich polemical debate among Latin Americanist and U.S. scholars over the concept "magical realism," for Fernando Alegría (1986), Roberto González Echevarría (1977), Faris and Zamora (1995), and Amaryll Beatrice Chanady (1995) have written the most cogent and useful critical surveys of the debate. Instead, my task in this section is to make the very demanding arguments about (transmodern) marvelous realism available to readers primarily in the United States who have heard about its importance but so far have been baffled by it. To simplify matters and to save some space, I will focus first only on Carpentier's prologue to his revolutionary novel *El reino de deste mundo* (The Kingdom of This World; 1949), arguably, the first marvelous realist text in the Américas, and then on Gabriel García Márquez's *The General in His Labyrinth* (1990), one of his less commented-on novels but perhaps his best example of a (transmodern) magical realist novel. Then I will switch gears and examine some of the U.S. minoritized writers who use the Global South's *lo real maravilloso* in their works. At the chapter's end, I will conclude my thoughts on the miner's canary, political race, and (transmodern) magical realism by commenting briefly on Guinier's and Torres's conceptualization of political race in Morrison's iconic *Beloved.*

For many scholars, (transmodern) marvelous realism as a concept appears in four different moments in the twentieth century and the twenty-first century. The first appears during the avant-garde years in Europe when the term was used in Franz Roh's *Nach-Expressionismus: Magischer Realismus* (1925), and when the surrealist André Breton proclaimed "the marvelous" an aesthetic concept and part of everyday life. The second moment was in the late 1940s when the related concepts *el realismo mágico* (magical realism) and *lo real maravilloso* (marvelous realism) traveled, as they say, from Europe to the Américas and were appropriated by the other trans-Americanists—Arturo Uslar Pietri and Alejo Carpentier—as a yardstick to measure, compare, and evaluate indigenous cultural art forms in the American grain. Whereas Pietri adopted Roh's term "marvelous realism," Carpentier, the more influential novelist and theorist, used Breton's version of *le merveilleux* and theorized in the prologue to *The Kingdom of This World* his famous concept of the "marvelous American reality."

A third period of (transmodern) magical realism can be said to have begun in 1955 when the literary scholar Ángel Flores published his influential essay "Magical Realism in Spanish American Fiction" (Flores 1995). This third phase, as González Echevarría suggests, continued through the long 1960s, when criticism searched for the roots and routes of *latinidad* in some of the novels produced during the "boom." As we shall see, there is probably an additional fourth phase, or "crack," as Morrison, Islas, Kingston, Viramontes, the Hernández brothers, and Junot Díaz, among others, expanded the marvelous realist tradition in transmodernist and often "signifyin[g]" ways.

Flores (1995 [1955], 1) argued that what distinguishes magical realism from other realisms is that it attempts to transform "the common and the everyday into the awesome and the unreal." Moreover, Flores emphasized the connections between magical realism and examples of European modernist aesthetics practices by Franz Kafka in his novels and Giorgio de Chirico in his paintings. In 1967, Luis Leal joined the growing debates by critically responding to Flores's essay. In "Magical Realism in Spanish American Literature" (Leal 1995 [1967]), he argued that magical realism was an exclusively New World literary movement. Included in his school of magical realist writers were Arturo Uslar Pietri, Miguel Ángel Asturias, Félix Pita Rodriguez, Alejo Carpentier, Juan Rulfo, and Nicolás Guillén. According to Leal, the basic difference between the competing schools of "magical realism," "realism," and "surrealism" is that "the magical realist does not attempt to copy (like the realists) or make the real vulnerable (like the surrealists), but attempts to capture the mystery which palpitates in things" (1995, 123). But Leal's essay ignored the profound impact European surrealism, modernism, and ethnography had on the generation of writers he analyzed, especially Carpentier.

Born in Paris and raised in Cuba, Alejo Carpentier made these connections in the iconic "Prólogo" in his Caribbean novel *The Kingdom of This World*. In the question "Pero qué es la historia," Carpentier asks, "de América toda sino una crónica de lo real maravilloso? (What is the history of the Americas but the chronicle of *lo real maravilloso*? [Carpentier 1949, xv]), Carpentier suggests the ideology that lies at the center of his marvelous realist narrative: how to write in a European language—with its Western systems of thought—about realities and thought structures never before seen in Europe. Carpentier asked for the first time in 1949 the following questions that would influence generations of writers from the Américas: what is the African, Amerindian, and mestizo/a heritage of the Américas, and how can it function as a stylistic, an ideology, and a point of view? While Carpentier learned much from the surrealists' experiments to explore a kind of second reality hidden within the world of dreams and the unconscious, political tensions that arose among the surrealists themselves caused him to break away from them. Carpentier probably also went his own way, as González Echevarría (1977, 123) astutely suggested, because European surrealism clashed with his "Spenglerian conception of man and history he had absorbed through avant-garde journals like the *Revista de Occidente.*"

Thus, despite his early fascination with surrealism, Carpentier never became a committed disciple of Breton. Unlike Breton and his followers, Carpentier argued in *The Kingdom of This World, The Lost*

Years (1953) and *Explosion in a Cathedral* (1962) that the "second reality" the surrealists explored in automatic writing is merely part of everyday life in Latin America. Furthermore, as a follower of Oswald Spengler's *Decline of the West* (in Spengler's universal history there is no fixed "center"), Carpentier eschewed the surrealists' Eurocentric doctrine of the marvelous and argued that all things of a truly magical nature are, in fact, found within the reality of the Américas—not in the "boring" cities of Europe. According to Carpentier's revised essay "De lo real maravilloso americano" (1967, 114), the "discovery," conquest, and colonization of the New World are magical events in themselves: "open Bernal Díaz del Castillo's great chronicle [*True History of the Conquest of New Spain* (1552)] and one will encounter the only real and authentic book of chivalry ever written: a book of dust and grime chivalry where the genies who cast evil spells were the visible and palpable *teules*, where the unknown beasts were real, where one actually gazes on unimagined cities and saw dragons in their native rivers and strange mountains swirling with snow and smoke." For Carpentier, then, Bernal Díaz de Castillo's chronicle of the Spanish conquest of Mexico is an exemplary marvelous realist narrative because the hegemonic foot soldier (unwittingly) had written about the clash of cultures—Old World and New World—and described in detail the superimposition of one layer of reality on another.

Forming a background for Carpentier's theory and thematized in *The Kingdom of This World* is what he sees as the "fecundity" of the New World landscape. Carpentier's concept of *lo real maravilloso* can therefore be summarized in his own words: "due to the untouched nature of its landscape, its ontology, the Faustian presence of the Indian and the Black, the revolution inherent in the continent's recent discovery and the fruitful cross-breeding this discovery engendered, America is still very far from exhausting its wealth of mythologies. Indeed, what is the history of America if not the chronicle of the marvelous of the real?" (Carpentier 1964, xiv–xv).

In short, Carpentier set up an antithesis between Eurocentric surrealism, on the one hand, and the Global South's *lo real maravilloso*, on the other. As is clear from the "Prólogo," Carpentier unfavorably compared surrealism with a privileged New World aesthetic grounded in a reality that is inherently magical (voodoo, Santería, and so on). To be sure, Carpentier's thesis rests on the claims that New World artists and people experience the marvelous in their everyday lives—what Raymond Williams, the Marxist theorist from the Welsh borderlands, in a different context called "structures of feeling"—and therefore have no need to invent a domain of fantasy. Thus, on the basis of local New World privilege, Carpentier rejected surrealism as sterile and legitimized, in near-transmodern marvelous realist fashion, the mode of writing he elected: a "chronicle of the marvelous of the real." *The Kingdom of This World*, therefore, is emblematic of the kind of narrative experimentation we now take for granted in (transmodernist) trans-American fiction: historical events move backward; characters die before they are born; and "green" tropical winds destroy the landscape.

Although Gabriel García Márquez's use of (transmodern) marvelous realism includes Carpentier's familiar tropes of the supernatural—one of the foundation concepts of magical realism—his version differs significantly from Carpentier's and inaugurates the rise of the Global South's (transmodern) marvelous realist movements. As is well known, García Márquez's concept of (transmodern) marvelous realism in *Leafstorm* (1955), "Big Mama's Funeral" (1962), *One Hundred Years of Solitude* (1967), and *The Autumn of the Patriarch* (1976), all in *Collected Stories* (1984), presupposes an identification by the narrator with the oral expression of popular cultures in the Latin American pueblo. In other words, as I argued in *The Dialectics of Our America* (Saldívar 1991), García Márquez's thematization of (transmodern) marvelous realism and the politics of the possible are usually expressed in his early stories about the rise and fall of Macondo through a collective voice, inverting, in a jesting manner, the values of the official Latin American culture. When García Márquez wrote his (transmodern) magical realist novel *The General in His Labyrinth*, he brilliantly reversed his past attempts as a novelist to transform the ordinary into the mythical and magical, for in this controversial text he deconstructed the saintly image of Simón Bolívar, the Great Liberator of the Américas, by rendering this national hero as a man of ordinary, even crude, attributes.

In *The General in His Labyrinth* the (transmodern) marvelous real is at the center: it focuses on a real historical personage, Simón Bolívar, and is based, according to García Márquez (1990, 272), on two years of "sinking into the quicksand of voluminous, contradictory, and often uncertain documentation." In other words, if Bolívar went out at night prowling the mean streets of Bogotá when the moon was full, then we can be assured that García Márquez, with the assistance of the Cuban geographer Gladstone Oliva and the astronomer Jorge Doval, has made an inventory of nights when there was "a full moon during the first 30 years of the last century" (García Márquez 1990, 51).

Of course, García Márquez avoids, like the plague, a conventional chronological narrative of Bolívar's life. Rather, in transmodernist fashion, he begins his narrative *in medias res* when Bolívar is forty-six years old, shrunken by an unnamed illness that will surely kill him. Rejected as president by the elite and the campesinos of Colombia— the new country he helped to liberate—Bolívar leaves Bogotá for a wild, whirling journey by boat down the Magdalena River, eventually hoping to sail to London.

But the general never gets out of his "labyrinth." In the fierce light of death's shadows, Bolívar is defeated by the "backwater" elements, by the chicanery of his enemies (especially General Santander), by the rancor of his ambitious colleagues, by his "chronic constipation" or by his "farting stony, foul-smelling gas" (García Márquez 1990, 9, 11, 45) and by his own solitary nostalgia for his former revolutionary self. Embarking with his noisy groupies from port to port, city to city, safe house to safe house, the general endures either celebrations and fiestas in his honor or is hounded by an army of widows who follow him everywhere, hoping to hear his proclamations of consolation.

Although Bolívar "wrested" from the Spanish colonists an empire five times more vast than all of Europe, and although he had led twenty years of war "to keep it free and united" (García Márquez 1990, 37), he is at the end of his life as a solitary man, praying for the right moment that he might make a political comeback.

Like the labyrinthine journey down the Magdalena River, the structure of the transmodernist novel is full of currents, crosscurrents, and serpentine emplotments. Deconstructing its own "return to storytelling," *The General in His Labyrinth* twists and disrupts historical time and space until not only Bolívar but the reader cannot tell where he is. Like the transmodern arts of memory themselves, full of traumas and resistances of all sorts, are scenes from the general's earlier triumphant life: his utopian geo-social proposal to "extend the war into the south in order to realize the fantastic dream of creating the largest country in

the world: one nation, free and united, from Mexico to Cape Horn";
his eternal temptations by the enigma and "furtive loves" of beautiful
women; and his latent same-sex desires for the Baron Alexander von
Humboldt, who had "opened his eyes" and "astonish[ed]" him in
Paris by the "splendor of his beauty the likes of which he had never
seen in any woman" (García Márquez 1990, 48, 96–97, 154).

Just before he dies in December 1830, Bolívar proclaims that (Latin)
América is "ungovernable," for the nation will fall inevitably into the
hands of the unruly mob and then will pass into the hands of almost
indistinguishable petty tyrants: "either unity or anarchy" (García
Márquez 1990,105). He prophesies, moreover, the post-contemporary
perils of what Andre Gunder Frank called "the development of underdevelopment": "I warned Santander that whatever good we had done
for the nation would be worthless if we took on debt because we
would go on paying interest till the end of time" (García Márquez
1990, 221). In any case, the United States, in Bolívar's eyes, is "omnipo-
tent and terrible, and its tale of liberty will end in a plague of miseries
for us all" (García Márquez 1990, 223).

Arguably the most important of the Global South's imaginative
writers, García Márquez takes up the slack of Carpentier's *lo real
maravilloso* and the traditional historical novel in his transmodern marvelous realism and combines them into a genuine post-
contemporary dialectical aesthetic. In *The General in His Labyrinth*,
García Márquez presents the reader with a semblance of historical
verisimilitude and shatters it into alternative patterns, as though the
form of historiography was retained (at least in its traditional versions) but now, for some reason, seems to offer him a remarkable
movement of invention. As Toni Morrison first noted in her astute
and understudied master's thesis at Cornell University on Virginia
Woolf and William Faulkner (see Wofford 1955), the alienation of the
central consciousness in the modernist novel (like the serious writer)
is enormous. But, as García Márquez suggests in *The General in
His Labyrinth*, the solitude of the great political leader—Bolívar
and then, perhaps, Fidel Castro—is another thing entirely. "Nevertheless, here in this novel," Gerald Martin (2009, 461), García Márquez's official biographer, argues, "although Bolívar's character is, undoubtedly, based factually on that of the Liberator, many of his foibles
and vulnerabilites are a combination of Bolívar's, Castro's and García

Márquez's own." García Márquez's subject is power, not tyranny, in the Américas.

If it makes sense to evoke a certain "return to storytelling" in the transmodern period, the return can be found in the wild genealogies and speculative minoritized U.S. texts of Toni Morrison, Arturo Islas, and Maxine Hong Kingston. In their novels and experimental memoirs, they shuffle, like Petra Cotes in *Cien años de soledad* (García Márquez 1967), historical figures and names like so many cards from a finite deck. Recovering alternative critical U.S. histories in the unwritten texts of history (songs, *cuentos*, and talk story), these transmodernist marvelous realists' texts resemble the dynastic annals of "small-power kingdoms," as Jameson (1991) puts it, and realms very far removed from the traditional white, male American novel.

Morrison's *Sula*, originally published in 1973, like most of the (transmodern) marvelous narratives under discussion, is embedded in the historical. For example, no mild apocalypse is the total destruction of the black neighborhood at the beginning of *Sula*: "in that place, where they tore the neighborhood and blackberry patches from their roots to make room for the Medallion City Golf course, there was once a neighborhood" (Morrison 2004, 3). The Bottom's segregated history in Ohio—cut across, contested, and obliterated—is written in a single sentence whose content extends from the dialectics of underdevelopment to the glossy transmodern projects of magical urban renewal. Thus, the "blackberry patches"—Morrison's imagery of nature—have to be "uprooted" to make way for what Marx referred to as capitalism's modernization.

After describing the leveling of the Bottom, Morrison focuses on the other hurts wrought by capitalism's (late) modernizations: Shadrack's unforgettable imagined bodily deformation as a part of the post-traumatic stress disorder resulting from his experience in the First World War and Eva Peace's radical act of self-mutilation. Abandoned by her husband Boy Boy around 1921, Eva (Big Mama) sets out to keep her family together and financially sound: "eighteen months later, she swept down from a wagon with two crutches, a new black pocketbook, and one leg" (Morrison 2004, 34). Big Mama's self-mutilation allows her then to build a new life and an enormous *casa grande* (big house) on 7 Carpenter Road.

As in the case of *One Hundred Years of Solitude*, *Sula* is a black vernacular chronicle of *lo real maravilloso* with a difference, but it is entirely accessible to the reader because no real boundaries are created by difficult narrative techniques. Moreover, like the chronicles of Carpentier and García Márquez, *Sula* covers the Bottom's history (which seems to move in reverse), from its apocalyptic endings to its rich beginning. The sense of de-reality in *Sula* has nothing to do with magic; it is created by Morrison's mind-blowing events. Who really doubts Big Mama's self-mutilation, Plum's attempt to return to Big Mama's womb, the plague of robins heralding Sula's return to the Bottom, and Ajax's command of yellow butterflies?

Arturo Islas is fascinated in his work by the liminal U.S.-Mexican borderlands, a post-contemporary "laboratory" where we can see culture of the First World imploding its transmodernist strategies into the Third World. Islas's last installment, however—planned as a trilogy about the Ángel family, with sprawling narratives and genealogical trees as convoluted as Faulkner's and García Márquez's—was never completed, for Islas died from complications of AIDS in February 1991.

The first novel in the trilogy, *The Rain God* (1984), was published by Alexandrian, a small press in Palo Alto, California. Although rejected and censored by more than twenty mainstream presses and editors in New York (who decide what counts as culture for the rest of the United States), *The Rain God* was named one of the three best novels of 1984 by the California Bay Area Reviewers' Association. Telling his story from the point of view of a Faulknerian Quentin-like narrator with a radical difference—"I don't hate Mexicans! I don't hate Anglos! I don't hate Gays! I don't hate [the Global] South!"[9]—Miguel Chico is a bookish English professor living the epistemologies of the closet in San Francisco. A two-toned narrative about Greater Mexico, written at times in the trans-American styles of Henry James, William Faulkner, Juan Rulfo, and García Márquez, *The Rain God* covers three generations of Ángels—from just before the Mexican Revolution (1910–17) to the 1980s—who migrated North from Mexico.

Despite this large chronotope, imaginative geography—Greater Mexico—and complex genealogy, *The Rain God* is a high minimalist novel of subtlety and psychological nuance: "he, Miguel Chico, was the family analyst, interested in the past for psychological, not historical, reasons. Like Mama Chona, he preferred to ignore facts in favor of motives, which were always and endlessly open to question and interpretation" (Islas 1984, 23). Islas's transmodern "open text" thus offers the reader a poetic landscape that, like the borderlands themselves, is both over-determined and profound. The narrative, too, moves in electric *telenovela* chapters from one family crisis to another. Miguel Chico visits the cemetery on the Day of the Dead; Mama Chona, the family matriarch, puritanically controls her family's values; Miguel Grande cannot resist the soap-operatic passions of Lola, his wife's best friend; Miguel Chico's uncle, Félix Ángel (the Rain Dancer), is murdered in the desert by a homophobic white soldier.

One of the most significant features of transmodern magical narratives is their attempt to negotiate forms of high art with certain forms and genres of mass culture and the cultural practices of everyday life. Islas's second installment, *Migrant Souls* (1990), exploits this post-contemporary impulse by bringing together the impact of the classic Puritan rhetoric on our culture, what Clifford Geertz, among others, calls the shaping influence of religious or quasi-religious symbols of society (book 1 of *Migrant Souls* is appropriately entitled "Flight from Egypt"), with references to the 1950s through mambo, doo-wop, Elvis, and mass-culture magazines such as *Popular Romance*.

Most significantly, Islas re-conceives literary and cultural practices in *Migrant Souls*. What happens, Islas asks, when American culture and literature are understood in terms of "migration," not imagination? How is the imagined community of the nation—to use Benedict Anderson's term—disrupted by hybrid, mestizo/a U.S.-Mexican borderland subjectivities? Caught between the postcolonial border zones of the past and present, Spanish and Indian cultures (Doña Marina's tamales and Miguel Chico's "Tlaloc"), Josie Salazar and her cousin Miguel Chico attempt to cross over the borderland contradictions of their everyday lives in Del Sapo, Texas. Like Ernesto Galarza in *Barrio Boy* (1972), Islas in book 1 of *Migrant Souls* allows us to witness the Ángel family's migration North from Mexico. This change from one culture to another corresponds to the actual course of travel the founding Ángel clan undertakes: "the Rio Grande—shallow, muddy, ugly in those places where the bridges spanned it—was a constant disappointment and hardly a symbol of the promised land to families like Mama Chona's. They had not sailed across an ocean or ridden in wagons and trains across half a continent in search of a new life. They were migrant, not immigrating, souls" (Islas 1990, 41).

Within this simple form, however, are subsumed the transmodern

themes of transformation, hybridity, and multiple subject positions—
what Gloria Anzaldúa in her border-defying writing *Borderlands/La
Frontera* called the "new mestiza/o consciousness." If Islas's narrative
had focused exclusively on this literal border-crossing story, he would
have written, perhaps, a fairly conventional ethnic tale about acculturation and imagination. But he did not. Instead, Islas also examined
the border zones of sexuality, gender, ethnicity, nationality, and so on.
In fact, Islas's only other border-crossing tale in book 1 is the hilarious
scene of Josie's father smuggling an illegal turkey across the U.S.-
Mexican border (after he had made it clear that he prefers enchiladas
for Thanksgiving dinner). After a humiliating border check at the
International Del Sapo bridge, he treats his family to menudo and
homemade tortillas.

Just as the founding Ángels crossed the "bloody river" in search of
their city upon a hill, the younger Ángel generation migrates to Chicago, Washington, D.C., and California. Book 2, entitled "Feliz Navidad," thus looks ahead to Vietnam and the Chicano Student Movement, where Miguel Chico's cousin Rudy appropriates and recodifies
the term "Chicano" from borderland oral culture and unsettles all of
the conservative Hispanic identities conferred on the Ángel family by
Mama Chona. More important, "Feliz Navidad" looks ahead to the
publication of Miguel Chico's first novel, *Tlaloc* (*The Rain God*):
"Miguel Chico's novel had been written during a sabbatical leave
when he decided to make a fiction instead of criticize it. A modest
semi-autobiographical work, it was published by a small California
press that quickly went out of business. *Tlaloc* was an academic, if
not commercial, success and its author became known as an ethnic
writer" (Islas 1990, 160). For Islas, the point is not to declare that *The
Rain God* and *Migrant Souls* are (transmodern) marvelous texts and
stop there but to show in hybrid perspectives how ethnicity was invented and with what consequences.

Such nontraditional and critical views of the acculturation and political incorporation of the United States are readily apparent in the
blurred genre works of the Asian American feminist Maxine Hong
Kingston. In *The Woman Warrior* (1976) and *China Men* (1980), Kingston's texts are developed as transmodern fragments of traditional
"talk story," myths, and the draconian rules imposed by Chinese parents. "No Name Woman," a talk story about the father's sister who is

forced to have an illegitimate child in the pigsty and who then commits suicide, is used by MaMa to caution the author about transgressing the family's rigid sexual codes. "Shaman," another talk story written by the author, exemplifies MaMa's attempts to tell her children "chilling" ghost stories to cool off the unbearable heat in the family's laundry in Stockton, California. In both cases, these oral tales are powerful stories of survival migrant cultures used by Chinese Americans to fight discriminatory U.S. government policies against Asians.

When Kingston declares that *China Men* is a book about "claiming America,"[10] her declaration characterizes the mood of a new generation of U.S. (transmodern) marvelous realist writers of color. Like Carpentier's and García Márquez's speculative chronicles, *China Men* (at times, also written in the oppositional poetic style of William Carlos Williams's *In the American Grain*) is a highly inventive history of Gold Mountain (the United States). Kingston's earliest episodes begin in fact where Williams's leave off—around 1850—and the book ends with visions of American violence and the Vietnam War. At the same time, Kingston documents in vivid detail the various racist Exclusion Acts the U.S. government passed against Asians.

Against the American grain, *China Men* not only challenges white, male constructions of American history but also aligns itself with the discovery by professional historians that "all is fiction" and that there can never be a correct version of history. Because the narrator's father does not talk story—only the women do ("You say with a few words and the silences" [Kingston 1980, 14])—Kingston invents different versions of the father's migration from China to America. In one of her most speculative and magical versions, she describes how, perhaps, he sailed first to Cuba, where the sky dropped rain the size of long squash, or to Hawaii, where papayas grew to the size of jack-o'-lanterns. Another version imagines how a smuggler brought him to New York by ship, locked in a crate, and how he rocked and dozed in the dark, feeling "the ocean's variety—the peaked waves that must have looked like pines; the rolling waves, round like shrubs, the occasional icy mountains; and for stretches, lulling grasslands" (Kingston 1980, 50). Still another version has BaBa coming to America, not illegally, but "legally"—he arrives in San Francisco to endure incarceration at the Immigration and Naturalization Service (INS) prison on Angel Island.

The ultimate goal of Kingston's *China Men* is thus to elaborate a logic of transmodern possibility, divergence, and the politics of the possible through a rhetoric of speculative historiography. Like Islas, Kingston explores the dialectics of the differential to emphasize cross-cultural interpretation and transculturation rather than assimilation. In order words, Kingston offers alternatives to mythologies predicted on the lingering white-supremacist "master narratives" of Anglocentric cultural centrality. In sum, all of the transmodern American precursors fall into place in our new marvelous realist genealogy of the Global South: canary watchers of political race such as Carpentier and García Márquez and their heirs, the U.S. minoritized writers of color, recover alternative histories in the unrecorded texts of history (songs, cuentos, and talk story) at the very moment that historical alternatives are in the process of being systemically expunged—CIA and FBI archives notwithstanding. Unlike the historical fantasies of other epochs, the transmodern marvelous narratives by these writers do not seek to diminish the historical event by celebrating the so-called death of the referent or of the subject.

These transmodern marvelous narratives, however, can be seen as entertaining a more active relationship to resistance and the politics of the possible, for they construct a speculative history that is simply their substitute for making the real kind. Transmodern cuento, fabulation, or talk story is no doubt the reaction to social and historical bankruptcy, to the blocking of possibilities that—as Jameson (1991, x) stresses—leaves little option but the "prodigious exhilaration of things." Their very invention and contagious inventiveness, however, privileges a creative politics by the sheer act of multiplying events they cannot control. Transmodern magical realist invention thus, by way of its very speculation, becomes the figure of a larger politics of the possible and of resistance.

Another form of transmodern marvelous realism in the United States is in some ways more quotidian than the previous ones. Here a new Kmart/mass-culture realism, minimalized and self-examining, has grown up in the various writings of Helena María Viramontes, Robert Stone, and others. If, as Malcolm Bradbury (1988) noted, there has been "warfare in the Empire of Signs" for our post-contemporary generation, there is "also every sign . . . that the Empire can indeed strike back." While these writers hardly share a homogenous ideological sensibility, they do share a common sense that a crisis in representation is clearly at hand. Our old-fashioned and socially constructed American realism (William Dean Howells, Theodore Dreiser, and Frank Norris) is now increasingly combined with a minimalism that deals with the new underclass of silenced peoples in our cities of quartz (workers, women, and so-called ethnic minorities) who typically feel adrift, or who feel that their histories have been systematically erased by urban planners and INS death squads, or who feel "controlled" by their access to controlled substances.

Raymond Carver, for example, addresses the local, urban vernaculars and blends them by focusing on slight plots and eliptically structured dramatic conflicts in *What We Talk about When We Talk about Love* (1981). Minimalist in form, perhaps symptomatic of the reading public's dwindling attention span, as John Barth (1986) suggests, Carver's texts dramatize "the most impressive phenomenon of the current (North American, especially the United States) literary scene (the *gringo* equivalent of *el boom* in the Latin American novel): the new flowering of the (North American) short story." While Barth's comments on the "flowering" of the post-contemporary short-story scene are on target, I am distressed by his Anglophonic mapping of the hemisphere. Like that of many mainstream writers in the United States, Barth's criticism remains largely confined to well-established and longstanding disciplinary and geopolitical borders, with the result that our American (using the adjective in its genuine, hemispheric sense) literary history remains largely provincial. For Barth, there is no real dialogue between Latin American writers and "gringo" transmodern minimalists. In any case, America, for him, becomes a synonym for the United States.

In the more pertinent and glossy essay "The Short Story: The Long and the Short of It" (1981), Mary Louise Pratt suggests that the formal marginality of short-story cycles enables them to become arenas for the development of alternative visions and resistances and often introduces women and children as protagonists. Marginal genres such as the short story thus are often the site of political, geographical, and cultural contestation. Likewise, the anthropologist Renato Rosaldo in his transmodernist essay "Fables of the Fallen Guy" (Calderón and Saldívar 1991, 93), on the narratives of Alberto Ríos's *The Iguana Killer* (1984), Sandra Cisneros's *The House on Mango Street* (1991), and

Denise Chávez's *The Last of the Menu Girls* (1986), argues that these writers' worlds are "fraught with unpredictability and dangers, and yet their central figures have enormous capacities for responding to the unexpected." Deconstructing disciplinary and generic borders of all sorts (unlike Barth and the INS), these Chicana/o writers collectively move toward liminal terrains and border zones that readily include newly arrived migrant workers from south of the border, Anglos, African Americans, and heterogeneous neighborhoods.

Similarly, Helena María Viramontes's short-story cycle *The Moths and Other Stories* (1985) focuses on the internal and external urban borders that often disrupt the neighborhoods of East Los Angeles. These borders, Viramontes suggests, are reproduced in our ethnic neighborhoods by urban planners who provide the maps for the hegemonic discourse of boundaries. Such glossy, transmodern designs, from Portman's Westin Bonaventure Hotel to the sprawling freeways, thus serve to erase and displace the old ethnic neighborhoods. In "Neighbors," for example, transmodern urban planners destroy the Chicano barrios in East Los Angeles: "the neighborhood had slowly metamorphosed into a graveyard. . . . As a result, the children gathered near in small groups to drink, to lose themselves in the abyss of defeat, to find temporary solace among each other" (Viramontes 1985, 109).

Like Islas's and Viramontes's narratives, Robert Stone's work, which we may call transmodernist *meditative* realism, concentrates on stories that are already embedded in an inter-American, hemispheric, and global dimension. *Dog Soldiers* (1975), a novel about heroin and drug dealers, for instance, travels globally between Saigon, San Francisco, and a middle-class retreat near the U.S.-Mexican borderlands. Stone's hardnosed language and lurid scenes of sexual violence bring him clearly within the orbits of Kmart realism. *A Flag for Sunrise* (1981), however, places itself at the intersection between North America and Central America. Stone's archaeology of the Américas allegorizes for us the persistence of an antithetical geographical space in the New World landscape. His novel, indeed, uncovers many layers of American identity by demonstrating how the U.S. government tries constantly to project its structures outward, creating and re-creating its North–South dichotomy to render the South as "primitive" and victim.

In *A Flag for Sunrise*, Frank Holliwell, a burned-out anthropologist, travels to the mythical Central American country Tenecan at the request of his Vietnam army friends who are now running the CIA to spy on the Catholic liberation theologist Justin Feeney, who is suspected of Marxist revolutionary activities. The transmodern ethnographer soon becomes a double-agent who falls madly in love with a nun and is caught in Stone's post-contemporary dialects of romance: Marxist revolutionaries are depicted as "children of light," and the Central American death squads are described as being farted out of the devil's ass. At worst, Stone's transmodern romance appropriates Central America by turning it into a sexual and religious playground for the hip *norteamericanos*; at best, he can be seen, through the wondrous dialectical transformation of romance, to be breaking hold of a "real" that seems unshakably set in place.

In contrast, E. L. Doctorow's narratives—from his award-winning *The Book of Daniel*, originally published in 1971, to his most recent novel, *The Long March*, published in 2006—in some ways do the inverse of what I have been arguing. More precisely, the ragged edges of the real entirely disappear. Doctorow's work thus reveals a new spatial historiography that has unique things to tell us about what has happened to the sense of history in the United States.

Read collectively, Doctorow's major novels map out generational "moments" in the epic of American history: *Ragtime*, published in 1975, with its collage-like production of real-life characters and events among whom appear imaginary WASP and ethnic characters (Morgan, Ford, Younger Brother, Coalhouse Walker, and so on), like *World's Fair* (1985), is set in the first three decades of the twentieth century. *Billy Bathgate* (1989), like *Loon Lake* (1980), reconstructs the Great Depression, and *The Book of Daniel* juxtaposes, without apologies, Old Left and New Left Marxism in America—communism of the 1930s and student radicalism of the 1960s.

In a blistering review of Doctorow's American "epic," Jameson (1991, 23) argues that his novels not only resist our political interpretations but also are precisely organized to "short-circuit an older type of social and historical interpretation which [they] perpetually hold out and withdraw." Jameson is, of course, absolutely right in his reading of Doctorow's simple, declarative sentences (especially in *Ragtime*), for unlike, say, the dialectical sentences of García Márquez or Kingston, Doctorow allows himself to write only in the digestible, bestseller style. While Doctorow's novels are splendid in their own right and, perhaps, the author has merely decided to convey his great theme—the disappearance of our homemade radical past—formally, through the glossy surface of late capitalism's cultural dominance itself, the sharp edges of the real have almost entirely disappeared, substituted by pop images and the simulacra of that history.

One of the most hybridized interventions in our post-contemporary narrative traditions comes from Jaime and Gilbert Hernández, whose graphic *fotonovela* magical realist Chicano writings are a transmodern blend of comic books, science fiction, Southern California *cholo/a* (Chicano youth culture), signifyin[g] magical realist storytelling, and subaltern theorizing. In the late 1970s, the Hernández brothers became deeply involved in the musical signifiers of punk, and this transmodern phenomenon opened their eyes to the possibilities of expressing themselves in the fotonovela realist novel. Their literary productions are in many ways aligned with the incorporation of habits of "futurology" into our everyday life and the magical realism of García Márquez's Macondo, but they also repeat the de-territorializing gestures of borderland theorists such as Rosaldo, Anzaldúa, and Néstor García Canclini, who see in their transmodern ethnographies and feminist theories of the U.S.-Mexican border a laboratory for the transmodern condition, where migrant workers smuggle into their baroque new homelands regional art and medicinal herbs from the South and send back from the North contraband VCRs and CD players.

In *Love and Rockets* (1982–2009), Jaime and Gilbert Hernández extend the borderlands to Los Angeles by interspersing in their work tongue-in-cheek science fiction stories (the "Mechanics" series) with transmodern realist tales set in a barrio they call "Hoppers 13." Gilbert Hernández, like Robert Stone, has moved his texts in utopian directions by creating a series of stories based in the mythical Central American town of Palomar.

Love and Rockets was the first U.S. graphic fotonovela to adopt the European method of "album collection" after magazine serialization. Although they are represented only in a bimonthly magazine of relatively modest circulation (it sells between 18,000 and 19,000 copies) on the West Coast, the Hernández brothers are arguably the most widely read Chicano writers in America today. Since 1982, the Hernández brothers have produced thirty issues of the regular magazine and several album collections of their work, including *Music for Mechanics* (book 1), *Chili's Burden* (book 2), *Las mujeres perdidas* (book 3), *House of Raging Women* (book 4), *Heartbreak Soup* (book 5), *The Reticent Heart* (book 6), and *Locas* (book 7). Their texts, read collectively, are a dizzying mix of polyglot love comics and reckless superhero adventure; their virtuoso drawings, moreover, represent derealized characters of intelligence, wit, and human frailty. For Jaime and Gilbert Hernández, white, male superiority has had its chance, and they now see their (transmodern) magical realist graphic narratives as engaged with the dynamics of the articulate ascendance of others.

I conclude this chapter by returning to the earlier discussion of Lani Guinier's and Gerald Torres's CRT formulation of "political race" and see how it functions in their micro-critical reading of Toni Morrison's *Beloved.* Guinier and Torres begin their thrilling exegesis of *Beloved* by emphasizing that mainline U.S. "realism" was not possible for Morrison's project to "convey the experiences of an African-American runaway slave who chooses to slay her baby daughter rather than return her to slavery" (23). But by turning to the Global South's marvelous realism, they suggest, Morrison adeptly "destabilized" and "distorted" the spatial and temporal landscapes of Kentucky and Ohio, where most of the novel takes place, and was thus able to "carve a free space" (23) for her readers to re-conceptualize their assumptions about maternity, mother love, ethics, and history. By then re-introducing the slain child into the story first as a ghost and then as the dead child Beloved, they argue, Morrison "forces the reader to question her original reaction to the infanticide" (24). Could Morrison's *lo real maravilloso,* they ask, be used to help us to imagine the "racial past" of the United States?

For me, Morrison is the United States' epic poet of the Middle Passage, of the brutal trauma of the African diaspora to the Américas, where the black Atlantic is history. No one with radical sympathies can read any of Morrison's work—*The Bluest Eye, Sula,* or *Beloved* (and her splendid recent novels, including *A Mercy*)—without seeing her narratives written with great reverence for those millions of Africans (often weighed down with ball and chain) who suffered from the slave ships' "unspeakable" violence, terror, severing of limbs, and death in the making of global capitalism and coloniality. What is interesting culturally, however, is that Morrison conveys the spectral history of reversal and loss in the catastrophic Middle Passage through the very logic of a life-affirming unity in lo real maravilloso, where the black Atlantic is both submarine history and unity. If there is any American realism left in *Beloved,* it is an expanded, "thick," and outsize realism (like García Márquez's) that is meant to be derived from the shock of grasping Beloved's (the dead child's) confinement and en-slavement near the end of part 2 of the novel in what I call Morrison's voyage of the *damnés.* Does Morrison (like the great Caribbean poets and theorists Kamau Brathwaite and Édouard Glissant) use images of dystopian terror on the slave ship, then replace this image with uto-pian images of promise and solidarity and to what Ian Baucom (2005, 311) calls the "politics of the abysmal event"? What happens when Morrison temporally and geographically shifts the focus of her great drama from nineteenth-century Kentucky and Ohio to the earlier *longue durée* of the seventeenth-century and the eighteenth-century black Atlantic slave ship? Morrison condemns the black damnés to seek History by way of seeing the dead child Beloved now not "crouching" but "standing" on the mutilated and dying bodies on the slave ship. The subject's legs "are like my dead man's eyes I cannot fall because there is no room to the men without skin who are making loud noises. . . . If I had the teeth of the man who died on my face I would bite the circle around her neck" (Morrison 1987, 249).

I have found the human account of everyday life in Marcus Re-diker's *The Slave Ship* (2007) particularly useful here, because it seems to offer a suggestive historical and symptomatic reading of why Mor-rison moves her readers from Ohio to the black Atlantic's Middle Passage late in the novel. Very briefly, Rediker focuses his narrative on the "wooden world" of the slave ship that carried millions of Africans to the Américas. Like the dead child Beloved's unsublime experiences on the slave ship in Morrison's text, Rediker describes through diaries, letters, and confessions that the captains and sailors kept how the enslaved Africans lived in cramped quarters alongside a multitude of crew—mostly captained by British and U.S. men. Looming above the masters and the slaves (the guards and the prisoners) were sickening epidemics, shipwrecks, and the daily threats of mutiny and insurrec-tion. So it makes sense to see Morrison's moving the drama of *Beloved* from Ohio to the Black Atlantic slave ship as a way to expand the number and variety of historical actors surrounding Beloved, the dead child, on the multiethnic slave ship. The slave ship—for Morrison and for Rediker (2007, 9)—is simultaneously a "war machine," a "mobile prison," and a "factory."

Violence, torture, the severing of limbs, strangulation, and rape "cascade downward" from the hegemony of the captains to the dominance without hegemony of the subaltern slaves. A war *within* the slave ship as sailors (prison guards) tussled with the slaves (prisoners) could easily be turned outward, for the slave ship's enormous "war-making capacity," Rediker (2007, 9) suggests, could also be "turned against other [metropolitan] vessels." If the sailors produced slaves within the ship as factory (thus "doubling their value"), as Rediker calculates, the slave ship as factory as it moved from a market on the eastern Atlantic to the west also helped create "labor power" and the coloniality of power in the growing world economies of the seventeenth century, eighteenth century, and nineteenth century.

It is from this enlarged temporal and spatial shift from Sethe's, Baby Sugg's, Denver's, Paul D's, and the Garner and Bodwoin families' dramas in Ohio to the dead child's (Beloved's) "standing" on the Black Atlantic slave ship's multitude that we can also see why the slave ship produced not only slave workers for the plantations in the Américas but also what Guinier and Torres call "political race" on the slave ship itself. At the beginning of the voyage of the damnés, British or U.S. captains hired a crew of sailors who, on the coast of Africa, would become what Morrison describes as "men without skin," or white men. Then, at the beginning of the Middle Passage, British or U.S. captains loaded on the slave ship a multiethnic collection of Africans, who on arrival in the American port suddenly became "black." Political race and the coloniality of power were therefore made on the voyage of the damnés in the making of global capitalism.

Amid this ineffable terror, violence, and premature death on the slave ship, Guinier's and Torres's "political race," we might say, helped fashion a creative, life-affirming response to the politics of the abysmal event. If, as Guinier and Torres suggest, "some will say that political race is a ridiculously optimistic exercise of our imagination" (24), Morrison's and Rediker's expanded dramas on the Black Atlantic slave ship imagine how slaves inaugurated an imagined (fictive) kinship, often by calling one another brother and sister to replace the natal alienation of what had been violently and brutally broken by their abduction. Political race, thus envisaged, emerged not only among the slaves/damnés on their voyage but also in what Rediker (2007, 8) describes as "civil society in Britain and America as abolitionists drew one horrifying portrait after another of the Middle Passage for a metropolitan reading public." Political race is thus—as Guinier and Torres freely admit—"ridiculously optimistic," for those who are raced "white" can join in solidarity in newer social movements with people of color and "disrupt common assumptions about movements for social change" (24). Morrison's voyage of the damnés, too, begins with a radical claim on the imagination, a demand that we see and imagine the stories of those who were not able to record their stories, or whose stories were not recorded by the captains and sailors of the slave ships. She asks us to see Beloved standing on the slave ship with ball and chain, surrounded by others, "the iron circle is around our neck," going into the abyss—in the submarine, alluvial "water with my face" (Morrison 1987, 250–51). The catastrophic history of Middle Passage's voyage of the damnés is the sea, and it is not *terminal*—as it was for the British and U.S. abolitionists—but a ghostly anti-Enlightenment middle passage into an experience of political race, interculturality, transmodernity, and global coloniality.[11]

6 ❦

The Outernational Origins of
Chicano/a Literature: Paredes's Asian-Pacific Routes
and Hinojosa's Cuban Casa de las Américas Roots

What does Asia have to do with Américo [Paredes], and with the U.S. Mexico borderlands, the crossing of which represents such a volatile issue in the contemporary cultural politics of the U.S.? What is the Asian connection to the U.S. borderlands? To race and gender on the border? To matters of class structures in the U.S.? I claim that the history of Asian immigration and American interventions in the Asia Pacific global region is related to each of these questions and to the history of the U.S.-Mexico borderlands, but not in simple-minded ways.—RAMÓN SALDÍVAR, "Asian Américo: Paredes in Asia and the Borderlands"

It is always risky to try to account for the canonical success of U.S. minoritized writers. In my previous work on Américo Paredes and Rolando Hinojosa as figures of trans-American literary and cultural studies, I tried to focus on the intriguing examples of Paredes's and Hinojosa's extraordinary history writing of Greater Mexico in their subaltern texts.[1] So far, I have chosen to concentrate on their outpouring of minor novels, short stories, poetry, and criticism as a way to rethink a potential divide between their early literary successes and prizes and the later (middle-age) so-called lapses, flaws, and failures. It is a periodization that is gaining monumental status in recent Chicano/a literary and cultural histories. For example, to speak of Paredes's middle-age writing career exclusively in terms of recalcitrant nostalgia and of his mythic rendering of Greater Mexico's patriarchal culture and Mexican Americans (after 1848) as somehow having fallen from a once "stable" and "egalitarian" pastoral state in the opening chapters of *"With His Pistol in His Hand"* (1958), as Renato Rosaldo did so strikingly, is, of course, not wrong. But Rosaldo's dominant portrait of the middle-aged border ethnographer stuck in the conservative mode of pastoralism seems to me an unfinished painting of Paredes's life and work. That image erases the rest of Paredes's life and the earlier Asian-Pacific journalistic writings of his Second World War years, the rich production of his outernationalist writings from Tokyo, when he witnessed, as a young, proto-Chicano reporter for *Pacific Stars and Stripes*, the American military and cultural hegemony beginning to take over the planet (see Rosaldo in Calderón-Saldívar 1991, 87).

In following Ramón Saldívar's magisterial arguments that Paredes's Asian-Pacific journalistic writings foreshadow the subject of global coloniality and modernity in the later writings, I am also suggesting that we need to re-examine this outernantional literary and journalistic terrain that U.S.-Mexican borderland scholars are only now beginning to take into account in their understanding of Paredes's minor and iconic literary and cultural texts. How were Paredes's years in Asia, from 1945 to 1950, generative for his outernational idea of "Greater Mexico"? What postwar idea of other Asia(s) did he bring back to the U.S.-Mexican borderlands for understanding U.S. racial formations? Was there a laboring of borderlands' culture? With Rolando Hinojosa's iconic South Texas novel *Klail City y sus alrededores*, I will go back over the literary and ideological terrain of this work's winning the prestigious Cuban Casa de las Américas Prize in 1976 that I described in previous work (via the dialectics of Roberto Fernández Retamar's school of Calibán). But *Klail City y sus alrededores* deals more directly with Cuba's vernacular culture (via the roots of the Cuban vernacular aesthetic of the *choteo*) than I first recognized. It wasn't until I visited Cuba and Casa de las Américas as a judge of the inaugural *premio extraordinario* in U.S. Latino/a literature that I was able to better understand the history of the Cuban vernacular choteo and to begin formulating its impact on Rolando Hinojosa's novels about Greater Mexico. Instead of viewing Paredes and Hinojosa as local South Texas writers, I propose to take an alternative route here and attempt to read the planetary Asian-Pacific and Cuban-Gulf of Mexico roots and routes that helped form these great writers.

Despite having published scores of journalistic chronicles exploring how U.S. military occupation had transformed Japan in *Pacific Stars and Stripes*, poems about the cultures of U.S. imperialism and the military occupation of Japan, and short stories that take us from the social spaces of twentieth-century Greater Mexico and into the Pacific theater of the Second World War and the opening days of the Korean War, Américo Paredes is usually viewed by U.S. scholars as only a local-color writer and folklorist.[2] However, Paredes, as we will see, is one of the earliest proto-Chicano writers responsible for putting transnational culture at the center of his cultural studies project and for theorizing the relationship of folk ballads on intercultural conflict (*corridos*) to Mexican American belles-lettres.[3] His vernacular aesthetic is most usefully approached within this historical and formal ethno-musicological framework of corridos. The particular qualities of Greater Mexico's border folksongs, which had a profound influence on at least three other Chicano and Chicana writers—Rolando Hinojosa, Gloria Anzaldúa, and Tomás Rivera—provide a key for reading Paredes in an outernational frame and confronting his critical perspective.

Paredes's interaction with what he topo-spatially baptized "Greater Mexico's" border folksongs is considerable. From his middle-age study of border folksongs in his master's thesis, "Ballads of the Lower Border" (1953) at the University of Texas, Austin, to his interdisciplinary study of the border hero Gregorio Cortez, "*With His Pistol in His Hand*" (1958), Paredes began to de-essentialize the border cultures of South Texas on which his text focused. Paredes's study inaugurated not only the multicultural discipline of Mexican American studies at the University of Texas but also the proto-Chicano studies interest in border studies in general. Both of these cultural histories of border music emphasize his ongoing relationship with the folksongs of *danzas* and corridos. Moreover, the structure of the border folksong provides an understanding of the hybrid and transcultural quality that is the hallmark of Paredes's prose style. Greater Mexico's folk music, as we know, as a form of *norteño* cultural semiosis, is by nature intertextual and amalgamated, but Greater Mexico's danzas and corridos are particularly so. In *A Texas-Mexican Cancionero* (1976), Paredes describes the nature of how the border folksong as the *décimas* and *romances* originally from Spain migrated to Mexico and then north to Greater Mexico to mix with its more or less indigenous border musical styles—family music, *cantina-parranda* music, music sung on horseback, *conjunto* music, and so on. As a young boy growing up on the *ranchos* of South Texas and Tamaulipas, Mexico, Paredes (1995, xviii) recalls feeling no shame in listening to these songs, for the folksongs not only recorded the "long struggle to preserve an identity and affirm [one's] rights as a human being," but also focused on the long history of Greater Mexico's "intercultural conflict" and the borderer's resolve *de no ser dejado* (not to be refused). Thus envisaged, it was, for Paredes (1995, xxi), "quite an experience to sit outside on a still, dark night and hear [the] distant lonely music." Paredes is best understood as a border-crossing intellectual, equally at home as a folklorist, a cultural anthropologist-ethnomusicologist, a creative imaginative writer, and a social historian of Greater Mexico.

Like the amalgamation of Greater Mexico's border folk music, Paredes's first great novel, *George Washington Gómez: A Mexicotexan Novel* (1990), written between 1936 and 1940, invokes and revises U.S.-Mexican border songs of intercultural conflict such as "Los Sedicio-sos" and "Ignacio Treviño." The novel, like the corridos of the early twentieth century, commemorates the proto–Mexican American up-rising of 1915 that took place in the brush country of South Texas. Although it was similar to the famous West Coast uprisings of Watts and Los Angeles of some fifty years later, the uprising of 1915 dif-fered because *los sediciosos* (the seditionists) acted in accordance with a declaration of grievances and intentions—what in Spanish was called a *plan*. In his novel, Paredes explores how the *plan* de San Diego, Texas, was called many things at the time both locally and nationally—a conspiracy hatched by communists, a machination of the German Kaiser, a utopian scheme on the part of local intellectuals such as Venustiano Carranza, or simply a wild and unruly plot by rancheros and campesinos on both sides of the U.S.-Mexican border.[4] As *George Washington Gómez* suggests, however, there was indeed a great deal of the improbable about the *plan*, too—especially as the novel's central protagonists Gualinto; his mother, María; his sisters Carmen and Maruca; and his uncle Feliciano looked back to the uprising and the execution of Gumersindo (María's husband) by the devious Texas Rangers with the clarity of historical hindsight. And like the corrido "Los Sediciosos," Paredes's novel had a tone of ambiva-lence to it, for like the corrido "Los Sediciosos" itself, *George Wash-ington Gómez* was partly an epic ballad celebration of those Mexican

1. Photograph of Américo Paredes and Japanese friends, Tokyo, 1943. *Courtesy of Nettie Lee Benson Latin American Collection, University of Texas Libraries.*

Americans with the "resolve *de no ser dejado*" and partly a lyrical lament for the many thousands of victims of South Texas who, in Paredes's own words, were "executed" by the Texas Rangers (Paredes 1995, 33), who helped the U.S. military put down Greater Mexico's uprising.

As Gualinto—improbably named George Washington Gómez—grows up, he cannot help but admire the epic-like, male heroism of los sediciosos (since their acts of violence and resistance were directed at the hated death squads of *rinches* and their allies). His mother, María, and his Uncle Feliciano (along with the larger Mexican American community), however, largely know that they are victims of the repression because of the *plan*'s utopian and revolutionary dream of founding a multicultural Spanish-speaking Republic of the Southwest. (The *plan* had called for a union of Mexicans and Native American Indians, African Americans, and Asian Americans.) In counterpoint to Gualinto's largely masculinist view of the corrido's historia of "Los

Sediciosos," Feliciano poses early in the novel the contrapuntal alternative corrido "Ignacio Treviño" by singing the opening lines of the
ballad in which the protagonist, a policeman in Brownsville, Texas,
around 1911 finds himself caught up in local machine politics of the
region, and the Texas Rangers try to assassinate him. Treviño, however, survives the hit and barricades himself in a saloon, and, as the
corrido suggests, there are no casualties when the Texas Rangers show
up, just so many shot-up *juíscle* (whiskey) bottles. Feliciano sings part
of "Ignacio Treviño" to the Gómez clan to emphasize his rather realist
views that the border troubles of the times only encouraged the Texas
Rangers—to quote from the corrido again—"a puro matar (to kill and
kill)" Mexican Americans. Thus, like the corridos "Los Sediciosos"
and "Ignacio Treviño," Paredes's dialectical *George Washington Gómez*
is not all praise-song of the leadership of the *plan* de San Deigo—
Aniceto Pizaña and Luis de la Rosa—and their followers. While there
is grieving, mourning, and melancholia for the victims of the Texas
Rangers' brutal executions, Paredes's novel commemorates how there
was also a "bloody swath" for which Greater Mexico's los sediciosos
would be partly remembered.[5]

In his iconic *"With his Pistol in His Hand,"* a study of the legends,
cuentos, and corridos of Gregorio Cortez, a campesino, Paredes begins with a geographically astute chapter on the border cultures of
Nuevo Santander and on the musical aesthetics of South Texas and
the borderlands—what he called Greater Mexico. For Paredes (1995,
xiv), Greater Mexico incorporated "all the areas inhabited by people
of Mexican culture—not only within the present limits of the Republic
of Mexico but in the United States as well—in a cultural rather than a
political sense." He then switched gears in the next chapters and
produced an intellectual biography of Gregorio Cortez, a hero of the
U.S.-Mexican borderlands who was falsely accused of horse stealing
and murdering an Anglo-American sheriff in 1901. Cortez, however,
outsmarted a posse of local death squads (the Texas Rangers) across
half the State of Texas. Paredes ends this portion of the book by
delving into a rigorous, rhetorical analysis of the corrido proper,
which, he argues, broke down the normative, white-supremacist hierarchies of race and class in Texas. The Texas Rangers—the rinches—
were not brave and invincible, as liberal historians such as Walter
Prescott Webb and Frank Dobie and Hollywood movies starring the

dashing Gary Cooper memorialized, but foolish and cowardly ("All the rangers of the county / Were flying, they rode so hard . . . But trying to catch Cortez / Was like following a star"). The writing of Paredes's text, like the corrido itself, as José Limón (1992) first demonstrated, was itself as a "new corrido" of sorts. Indeed, Paredes's scholarly book was wildly creative, a decided alternative to conventional academic discourse and a self-conscious critique of it.

In the book's final words about corridos—Paredes's self-fashioning *despedida* (farewell) about how the border ballad of intercultural conflict had developed in South Texas in the decades between the manifest annexation of Texas by the United States in 1846–48 and the U.S. colonization of the Philippines in 1898, he noted that although the "traditions and musical patterns [in Greater Mexico's corridos] are Castilian," their "social and physical conditions . . . were more like those of [medieval] Scotland" (Paredes 1958, 243). This comparative, transnational move by Paredes some fifty years ago—where he connected socio-cultures divided by idiom (*lengua, idioma*), space, and time—was politically courageous and refreshingly anti-essentialist, as well as intellectually provocative.

The questions U.S.-Mexican borderlands scholars of Paredes's career have been grappling with for decades are many and complex: Where and how did Paredes's conceptualization of (trans)national culture come from? Did he simply pick it up as an undergraduate and graduate student in the English and anthropology departments at the University of Texas in the late 1950s, after he had returned from the Pacific theater and started studying corridos? Had he imbibed Greater Mexico's hybrid cultures of intercultural conflict in his native borderlands of Brownsville, where he was born and raised? Or had he conceptualized transnational cultures by paying attention to the local sonic danzas and corridos he grew up singing on the local radio stations with the Queen of the Boleros, Consuelo "Chelo" Silva, one of the first female Mexican American recording artists, whom he had married in 1939?[6] How had his Second World War experiences as a reporter for *Pacific Stars and Stripes* in Japan and, later, his experiences working for the American Red Cross in China helped him better understand his border multiculture? Until recently, these questions had not been fully comprehended or answered adequately by Paredes scholars of the U.S.-Mexican borderlands.

2. Américo
Paredes's front-
cover collage for
Ramón Saldívar's
*The Borderlands of
Culture.*

In his nuanced and award-winning *The Borderlands of Culture* (2006), Ramón Saldívar demonstrates convincingly and movingly how Paredes began to de-essentialize his sense of U.S.-Mexican border culture when he arrived in Japan in late 1945 as a thirty-year-old U.S. Latino soldier, and began to write chronicles for *Pacific Stars and Stripes* and *El Universal,* a mainline newspaper in Mexico City. Paredes composed seventy-four major articles and feature columns over a five-year period. In Tokyo, Saldívar astutely argues, Paredes experienced forms of the cultures and politics of U.S. imperialism; stark nationalism; and class, sexual, and ethno-racial domination on a scale quite different from the one he had already experienced growing up on the bloody borders of the United States and Mexico. His newspaper chronicles noted the melancholy despair of the exhausted Japanese and their dystopian anguish and regret mixed with the birth of the utopian hope that came with the end of the global war. Paredes asked what postwar Japan might feel and look like under the new U.S. military occupation. Would Japan's language, mass media, and arts also evolve? What would it be like to live in a homeland inundated with Anglo-Americans in tight hegemonic control?

In Tokyo, Paredes also witnessed and reported on the opening day of the war crime trials of various Japanese military leaders, especially the highly demonized Hideki Tojo, commander of the Japanese Army and prime minister of Japan. Chronicling these legal and military tribunals for both *Pacific Stars and Stripes* and *El Universal*, Paredes cast the conduct of the hegemonic Military Tribunal of the Far East as an alternating sequence of tragic-comic dialectics and as comic-cosmopolitan moments. He critiqued the poor organization of the tribunals by the United States, the difficulties of meting out justice in languages as dissimilar as Japanese and English, noting that the proceedings were becoming what he described in Spanish as a "tragedia de errores" (Saldívar 2006, 387).

At the center of the court drama, seated in front of the tribunal's president, William F. Webb, was the Japanese icon Hideki Tojo, who, according to Paredes, was the "very symbol and personification of Japanese aggression, in whose person was concentrated all the crimes of the Japanese forces."[7] While the other war crime defendants displayed a wide range of emotions and postures, for Paredes Tojo remained a "dignified representative of a bloody era." Paredes concludes his chronicle by offering an insight that—Saldívar (2006, 387) explains —was rare for this moment in history: that as a symbol and personification of Japanese aggression and as the "representative [man] of a bloody era," Tojo is very much the scapegoat and whipping boy for the Emperor Hirohito himself.

Thus envisaged, Paredes not only dissected in his chronicles from Tokyo the comedy of errors of the war crimes Military Tribunal of the Far East but also memorialized them in his little-analyzed anti-imperialist poem "Westward the Course of Empire," which he wrote from Tokyo on December 24, 1948 (Paredes 1991):

Favored by Rome's solicitude
Hannibal drank his potion
While Cauhtéhmoc swung from a ceiba
Without benefit of a trial

You, Hideki, had your day in court
People believe in being civilized
where we are from.
Through the quickening twilight bayonets
gleam
the warheads are at the ready
Carthage, city of tirenes
Tenochitlitán, city of lakes
your time will come.

In a wry footnote to that poem, which was not published until 1991 in a collection of his poems entitled *Between Two Worlds*, Paredes explained to his U.S. readers: "Hideki Tojo and his fellow 'war criminals' were hanged on December 23, 1948, earlier than scheduled, we were told, so that our Christmas holidays would not be spoiled" (Paredes 1991, 140).

Paredes's anti-imperialist poem surely adds another literary dimension to his conceptualization of how social transformations may be effected in a situation of complexly imbricated cultural strata. As Saldívar (2006, 389) suggests, the poem reflects on the newly globalized achievements of the "expansionist ideology" of the United States and its hegemony of global coloniality. Perhaps a near-elegy, the poem also focuses on memory, geographically mapping the course of imperial movements from the Global South to the Global East, from Tenochititlán to Tokyo. Saldívar (2006, 289) even notes that the poem reverberates "with pathos" in its accentuation of Tojo's iconic "gravitas and dignity" played out under the bright lights of history's judgment that seemed to reflect "off of Tojo's cranium" and the glowing nuclear sublime of U.S. atomic warheads.

Through his modern journalistic chronicles from Tokyo, Saldívar argues, Paredes witnessed how Asian writers, filmmakers, artists, and everyday citizens struggled to render American imperial modernity into their own equivalents—their own subaltern modernity. Did those very transnational experiences, Saldívar (2006, 390) asks, prove "crucial in the development" of Paredes's ideas linking up national (multi)culture, citizenship, race, and "the discursive understandings of their interrelationships under the twin terms of *history* and *folklore*" in his mature work?

It was precisely in Tokyo and in the late 1940s in China (where he worked for the American Red Cross), Saldívar (2006, 390) demonstrates that Paredes "explored the conditions of [the couplet] of border/power knowledge"—and, I might add, Greater Mexico's *pensamiento fronterizo*. Also in Tokyo, Paredes gazed on a new, globalized dominance for the first time from his transmodern Greater Mexican perspective across a hemispheric horizon, from the Global North to the Global South, but also from a manifest westward movement to the East. Last, it was in Japan and Asia that Paredes saw up close both a dominating U.S. occupying army and an emergent subaltern Japanese "hybridity" that came into being with its contact with the emerging American empire. From the dung heaps of disastrous military defeat, a new national identity was being self-fashioned and produced that, in the words of Yoshikuni Igarashi (2000, 12–13), "could encompass the memories of loss and devastation through the realm of everyday culture rather than through abstract political discourse."

Almost immediately, the combination of Paredes's inborn writing talent and the professional zeal of Miguel Lance Duret, his editor at *El Universal*, and his military editors at *Pacific Stars and Stripes* produced short chronicles about Tokyo that were readable, provocative, and unique. One of the articles that stands out some sixty years later is a political (allegorical) piece about the U.S. military hegemonic occupation of Tokyo and its totalizing underdevelopment of food such as rice for the average citizen—a piece originally published in Spanish in *El Universal* and simply entitled "Desde Tokio (From Tokyo)."[8] The article highlights how "toda clase de articulos de primera necessidad (the basic supplies of everyday necessity)" had fallen short because of the lack of coal. Japan's coal miners, Paredes reports, often "do not eat enough" to have the human strength to "produce the required extraction." Food for the Japanese was exorbitantly expensive, because the fertilizers needed to produce it were hardly available due to the lack of "*carbón* (coal)" needed in the potassium and nitrogen industries. The young newspaperman sees an emergent "circulo diabólico de la economía japonesa (diabolic circle of the Japanese economy)" and wonders whether the U.S. occupying forces and the Japanese government are doing everything possible to "romper esta cadena que estrangula todas las actividas (break the chain suffocating all activity)" in Japan. He asks prophetically how, in the era we today call globalization or Americanization, the local Japanese have solved their biggest problem of scarcity—"el de cómo y cuando de llenar el estómago (how and when to fill the empty stomach)."

The first half of "Desde Tokio" is political in the military sense of the everyday effects of the U.S. Armed Forces' occupation of Japan. The second half, though, is almost a manifesto about the cultural politics of an emergent U.S.-backed culture of consumption and spectacle at the Ginza: "No hay cosas que no se puede comprar en la Ginza de Tokio (There is nothing one cannot find at the Ginza in Tokyo)," Parades writes. "La Ginza," whose name Paredes says means "the silver chair," is in fact a street or, better still, a commercialized section of Tokyo. Although the urban locals baptized the Ginza "el Broadway del Oriente," Paredes can only compare it more skeptically to Greater Mexico's *tercer mundo*: "[La Ginza] tiene más parecido al San Luisito de Monterrey que a la calle de las luces de Nueva York (The Ginza looks more like San Luisito of Monterrey, Mexico, than the street of bright lights of New York)."

Paredes is awed by the sheer spectacle and business scale of the "black market" and the more than 1,200 stores of the Ginza. He is also struck by Tokyo's multitude—the more than four hundred thousand weekend flaneurs who enjoy "the evening's breeze," theaters, cinema, cabarets, and an emergent nightlife sex industry "along the Ginza sidewalks." Paredes sees in Americanized Tokyo what he calls a *renaciemiento*, or rebirth, of cabaret, where the doors of clubs named "Ginza's Oasis," "Eden," "Marigold," and "Manhattan" are open to the scores of occupying Allied soldiers, "entre los cuales se encuetran muchos mexicanos. El mexicano en el Japón ha creado gran fama en el baile (among whom there are many ethnic Mexican Americans. The Mexican American in Japan is famous for being an expert dancer)."

Before Tokyo's Americanization and military occupation, young women mainly worked as "office administrators," "telephone operators," "waitresses," "actresses," and "geishas"; in the moment of Tokyo's culture industry of cabarets and dancehalls, Paredes writes, young women turn to earning a living "*bailando* (dancing)," where they market sexual desire to avoid starvation. What, then, is the appeal of this thrilling and "silvery" urban space of commercial and entertainment nightlife culture in the face of Tokyo's "ruins" of wartime bombardment?

Paredes concludes "Desde Tokio" by looking hard at the eeriness all around him to see "más alla del triste presente comericiantes de la

Ginza (beyond the sad commercial present of the Ginza)" and by phantasmatically imagining with the vendors' and businessmen's future hope of a fully cosmopolitanized Japan and Tokyo: "en lugar de las ruinas de los bombarderos ven jardines, hotels modernos y grandes tiendas (instead of the bombed ruins, they see gardens, modern hotels, and big stores)." In chronicles like "Desde Tokio," Paredes articulates, as noted earlier, what Saldívar (2006, 355) calls his thematization "of postwar global structures of recreational commerce."[9] On the Ginza, Tokyoites simultaneously learn to labor under domination in American-style dance clubs and unlearn the hegemonic Japanese wartime stifling of the body and desire. With the historical veracity of his newspapers chronicles, Paredes captures the feelings not only of the Japanese businessmen but also of the many Japanese artists and intellectuals he meets in Tokyo, who focus on their own iconic wartime images of ruin and distress, the unspeakable and unthinkable nuclear-bombing defeat and destruction unleashed by Harry Truman and the U.S. military forces on Japan.

In Tokyo, Paredes also imagines how he might begin approaching the narrative strategies he would use to create the continuities that masked the historical disjunctures of defeat of his own Greater Mexican border culture and that might transcend the imperial loss it endured at an earlier epoch of empire, with the Alamo, Davy Crockett, and the death squads of rinches unleashed in 1915 during the revolt of los sediciosos.

Paredes's postwar *"With His Pistol in His Hand"*—on border ballads of intercultural conflict, on the tragedy of errors and terror unleashed by the Texas Rangers and their inability to capture Cortez, then the State's inability to prove Cortez's alleged murder of the local sheriffs after putting him on trial in eleven different Texas counties—offers scores of ironic parallels between the U.S. government's execution of Japanese war criminals, Nazi Germany's terrorization of ethno-racial others in its occupied territories during the Second World War, and the criminalization of Gregorio Cortez and the Greater Mexico's border communities by the United States. For example, Paredes (1958, 26) pointedly asks what motives "must have been involved" in the Texas Rangers' "practice of killing innocent Mexicans"—whose number Walter Webb put at between five hundred and five thousand. In listing all of the Texas Rangers' possible motives for executing innocent Mexican Americans, he wryly includes the following Second

World War analogy, which made historical sense to his readers: "A more practical motive was the fact that terror makes an occupied country submissive, *something the Germans knew* when they executed hostages in the occupied territories of Europe during World War II" (Paredes 1958, 26; emphasis added).

We can now convincingly insist that, in Paredes's experiences in the late 1940s in Asia, the American empire and social conflict played out in ways different from but inevitably comparable to the history generated by the control of Greater Mexico by the United States since the 1840s. On the new U.S. frontier in the Asian-Pacific theater of the Second World War, Paredes witnessed a new temporal borderlands in which the logic of U.S. foreign policy metamorphosed from Franklin Delano Roosevelt's "antifascism" into Harry Truman's "anticommunism."[10] In writing about the borderlands of Greater Mexico in his academic text, *"With His Pistol in His Hand,"* Paredes rhetorically relied on his Cold War geopolitics, his experiences with Asian-Pacific cultural and racial conflicts, and the contradictions of Anglo-American Cold War democracy to help him begin to theorize his new global imaginary of Greater Mexico where Gregorio Cortez's grandson, the Mexican American Louis, years later was drafted into an air unit that dropped an atomic bomb on Japan. The heroic deeds of Louis Cortez's grandfather once could be passed down orally through heroic border corridos, Paredes emphasized; Louis's heroic deeds, however, now could only be "absorbed" into a new American exceptionalist celebration of "festivities and parades." "Theirs," Paredes (1958, 106), concludes, "[was] a different world."

Hinojosa's Cuban Roots

The sense of solidarity, which is the same as what Catholics call the Communion of Saints, has a very straightforward meaning for me. It means that in every one of our acts each one is responsible for the whole of humanity. When a person discovers this it's because his political consciousness has reached its highest level. Modesty apart, this is my case. For me there is no act in my life which is not a political act.
—GABRIEL GARCÍA MÁRQUEZ in Suárez (1978)

In 1991 I asserted that U.S. minoritized writers such as Rolando Hino-josa, Ntozake Shange, and Arturo Islas from the Global North increas-ingly had turned to the Global South's prose style and epistemology of *lo real maravilloso* monumentalized by Gabriel García Márquez and the Cuban Revolution to transform their visions of history writing in the novel.[11] I emphasized that I would not attempt to situate their writings and trans-American cultural conversations in isolation. Rather, in my work I located what heterogeneous literatures of the Américas had in common by examining some of the institutional dialogues in the 1960s, 1970s, and 1980s in Havana, an alternative artistic and cultural (not only political) capital of the Américas, where an international group of literary and cultural judges annually since 1959 has selected Latin America's premiere literary prize" the Casa de las Américas award (Saldívar 1991).[12] My view was that the constructing of alternative ver-sions of (literary) history for these minoritized U.S. writers related to a desire to transform a narrow Anglo-American-centric concept of liter-ary tradition and the linear view of history on which it was predicated.

I arrived in Havana via Mexico City for the first time in January 1997, a Chicano studies' *ensayista* (essayist) and scholar from Berkeley in-vited by Roberto Fernández Retamar, president of the Casa de las Américas and one of Cuba's greatest poets and critical theorists, to serve as a *jurado* (jurist) for its inaugural premio extraordinario in U.S. Latino/a literature. Although I landed at Havana's sprawling José Martí airport (with two fellow literary judges from Mexico City, Bár-bara Jacobs and her *compañero*, the celebrated Guatemalan novelist Agusto Monterroso), we spent most of the first week in the classical port town of Matazanas—what my Cuban colleagues affectionately referred to as the Athens of Cuba—poring over the short story col-lections, volumes of poetry, and experimental hybrid combinations that U.S. Latino/a writers had submitted for the trans-American and Cuban prize. Meanwhile, the world outside this literary institution was convulsed by political events continuing the relentless tightening of the three-decade blockade of Cuba by the United States (a blockade my Cuban comrades estimated had cost Cuba some $45 billion), especially with the pernicious Helms–Burton Act. Because Helms–Burton outlawed, among other things, the free travel of U.S. citizens to Cuba (for we would be trading with the enemy), I had traveled some-what clandestinely to Havana—I say "somewhat" because, to my great

3. Photograph of José Martí monument, Havana, 2010.
Courtesy of Mónica González García.

surprise, on the day I arrived at the Hotel Nacional, a young female diplomat with the Clinton administration based at the Swiss Embassy knocked on my door and welcomed me to Havana. First, I flew directly (via Mexicana Airlines) to Mexico City; then I flew (via Cubana Airlines) to Havana—without having my U.S. passport officially stamped. In 1992, the U.S. government had passed the so-called

Cuban Democracy Act, which attempted to crush Cuba's revolutionary processes through economic suffocation—something the U.S. government for the most part had succeeded in accomplishing through disinformation campaigns led by the CIA, sabotage, terrorism, invasion at the Bay of Pigs, and so on.

In Mantanzas, I saw up close the comings and goings of my fellow jurados, almost all of them celebrated literary writers and activist intellectuals from the Caribbean, Latin America, and Europe. Many of us did not know one another when we were officially and ritually sworn in at the Casa de las Américas on the evening of January 13, 1997, and we kept it that way out of habit initially by staying put in our small groups (*focos*) that had been assigned to us. I was the sole jurado representing Chicanos that year (and hoped to be sworn in under two symbolic flags: the U.S. Stars and Stripes and César Chávez's United Farm Workers flag), and I met daily and talked with the other two judges of the premio extraordinario: the young Cuban American imaginative writer and literary scholar Emilio Bejel, who had left Cuba for the United States when he was a young boy, and the iconic Pablo Armando Fernández, the acclaimed Cuban poet and activist-intellectual who often spoke fondly to us about his best friends, Fidel Castro and Gabriel García Márquez, whose portraits hung in his beautiful home in Havana. So how would a Chicano ensayista, a Cuban American imaginative writer, and a Cuban revolutionary poet select a winning manuscript in the new U.S. Latino/a category? Would we help Casa de las Américas in the process of continuing to build bridges to Cuba?

What I recall most was that the judges for *narrativa*, *cuento*, and *poesia* occasionally eyed the judges for newer and more protean genres such as testimonio—and for our premio extraordinario—with what I took to be a mix of skepticism and resentment. Was the testimonio, they wondered, not a hipper, more revolutionary genre, made all the more so when Che won the inaugural prize for his testimonio *Episodes of the Cuban Revolutionary War, 1956–58*, and more recently when Rigoberta Menchú, the Guatemalan Mayan activist, won it with her riveting and provocative *Me llamo Rigoberta Menchú: Y así me nació mi consciencia*? Likewise, were we U.S. Latinos and Latinas not all the rage—like J-Lo, whom we heard singing on Cuban radio?

Allow me to briefly recount how we spent our days as jurados in

Mantanzas. Many of us usually started early in the morning, entering the gracefully declining Hotel Valle's restaurant assured that we did not really need anyone else's company, for as critical readers of texts we were used to extended periods of solitude doing what many of us did best: silently read books. All of us looked a bit ridiculous lugging our manuscripts around, trying the best we could also to avoid the professional Casa de las Américas staff, who reminded us that we needed to complete all of the manuscript reading in a timely manner. However, our silence at the breakfast tables did not seem to last for long: we began to join one another at the breakfast tables to talk about the many manuscripts we were reading and to garner a sense of what next breakthrough text we might have in our hands. One judge introduced himself as a first-time novelist from Costa Rica; another, a dedicated poet from El Salvador, politely asked whether I would be interested in setting up an exchange program at Berkeley with him; and still another volunteered that she was in exile in Germany, fleeing narco-trafficking violence in Bogotá. At one of the breakfast meetings in Matanzas, I also met the humble Cuban writer and testimonio producer Víctor Casaus, author of *Girón en la memoria* (1982). And earlier, at a formal reception in Havana, I was excited to meet and talk with the renowned Cuban writer and anthropologist Miguel Barnet, who with Esteban Montejo, his 105-year-old *mambise* informant, had cobbled together the foundational *novela testimonial Biografía de un cimarrón* (1966). We excitedly talked about the upper-division course on the War of 1898 I was preparing to teach at Berkeley when I returned to campus for the spring semester.

Over the next several mornings, our solitary demeanor as readers quickly disappeared. Nevertheless, starting off the early mornings by tanking up on the rich Cuban *café con azúcar* helped the conversing and the inevitable and infectious Cuban choteo and signifying. For instance, I enjoyed telling some of my Cuban hosts that when I first arrived in San Francisco to attend Stanford University as a graduate student in 1977, I took off immediately to the Castro District looking for the *contrapunteo* of rice and beans. Many years later, my mentor at Stanford, Arturo Islas, confessed to his hipster graduate students that he often ran into Michel Foucault in the Castro environs.

When we first arrived at the Hotel Valle (after sightseeing for the first three days in cosmopolitan and revolutionary Havana), we were jolted by the endless *palmeras*, tobacco fields, and sugar mills that surrounded the colonial port city, and many of us encountered the severe measures Cuba had been forced to take when Fidel Castro officially declared the commencement of Cuba's "Special Period for Times of Peace." That is, Castro had implemented a new series of austerity measures for the Cubans that seemed to me to be typical of wartime maneuvers. After our many breakfast rituals of Cuban choteo and signifying were over, I saw the judges speedily leafing through their vast tomes, quickly getting through a short-story cycle or moving through volumes of testimonios. Other jurados attempted (as I tried to do) to read through the stacks of manuscripts more systematically. But all was for naught, for as soon as we finished closely reading the *ladrillo* we were reading, another jurado would urge us to reconsider the text we had just banished to the reject pile, so by the end of the afternoon, many of us ended up with the same number of manuscripts we had started the day with.

What I found odd during the long hours of reading was that none of the jurados ever was tempted enough to put down his or her reading assignments and jump in for a swim in the Hotel Valle's Olympic-sized pool. January in Cuba was supposed to be warm and tropical; as our luck had it, though, winter cold fronts from Alaska and the North had transformed Cuba into a cold island, with temperatures below freezing. The locals laughed at us *fuereños* who had imagined free time for sunbathing in the wintry Cuban tropics. Our senior Cuban mentor, Pablo Armando Fernández, told Emilio Bejel and me that this was why the Casa de las Américas always met to select the prizes in January and not, say, in April, which was not the cruelest month in Havana or Matanzas.

Many of us were not surprised to see minor culture-war tussles among Cuba's gathering of the tricontinental left. Bárbara, my near-*paisana* from Mexico City, and I, for instance, wanted little to do with the flashy Parisian French translator of Jorge Luis Borges, Julio Cortázar, and Gabriel García Márquez, among others. One morning, she interrupted a conversation we were engaged in about the state of Greater Mexico's imaginative writing by coolly asking whether any U.S.-Mexican border writers had written anything worthy of French translation. I stalled a bit and then asked, if none had, why were scores of French, Spanish, and German graduate students in Europe's lead-ing American studies programs writing so many doctoral dissertations on Chicana and Chicano writers and topics such as Ana Castillo, Rolando Hinojosa, Alurista, métissage, Nepantla, and Atzlán?

But there were, of course, many more "right-on" exchanges of solidarity than culture-war jostlings like the one Bárbara and I atypically encountered that January morning in Cuba. The Casa de las Américas had guaranteed some structured dialogues by having the jurados sit on roundtables to discuss our regional, national, and outernational literary specialties and our vernacular tongues. I remember being interviewed live on Cuban television in Havana discussing the iconic and minoritized literary works of the Chicano/a writers Rolando Hinojosa and Gloria Anzaldúa. And by this time I was immersed not only in the task of manuscript reading I had been assigned to complete for the premio extraordinario but was also sketching my notes of traveling theory I would write up once I had returned to Berkeley.

One magical evening we were invited as guests of Casa de las Américas to hear a special performance for the jurados by Los Muñequitos de Matanzas, one of Cuba's premiere rumba groups, but our unruly group of writers, performers, and teachers kept the performers waiting for two hours. Our highly organized international consultant, Gonzalo, had taken us on a wonderful detour that late afternoon to visit the independent cultural artists and writers Alfredo Zaldívar and Rolando Estévez and the publication offices of the ultra-hip *Vigía*, an avant-garde literary magazine run by a group of very young Cuban artists and poets. The wonderful Cuban American poet and anthropologist Ruth Behar (1996, 137) has aptly described the breakthroughs of *Vigía* this way: "*Vigía* draws on an aesthetic that is self-consciously about material scarcity, its curators use scraps of paper, carton, and cardboard, and drawings and calligraphy done by hand to produce books that are mimeographed in editions of 200, each numbered and unique. The desire to make beautiful books, not just functional mass-produced texts—at a moment when the merchandising of socialist Cuba is so rampant that even images of Fidel Castro and Che Guevara are on sale as tourist souvenirs—is not simply daring; it is an act of faith in the utter necessity of the cultural arts. Lately, *Vigía* has been reaching out to Cubans in the diaspora." All of us took home beautifully handmade *Vigía* books. I purchased a copy of my *tocayo* (namesake) Zaldívar's remarkable *Soy un tauro perdido y otros poemas* and a stunning children's book for my son, David Xavier, who was then ten and was busy learning Spanish at his public school in Oakland. I also found and purchased an unpretentious Che pin at the *Vigía* bookstore, which I wore without apology back in Berkeley.

It was well past 11 P.M. when we arrived to listen to Los Muñequitos (straight out of Mantanzas). A rumba group originally formed in 1952, Los Muñequitos had steadily moved from playing *guaguancó rumba* to an even more transculturated mambí inflected sonic noise, expertly mixing bembé, batá, and yambú African-Cuban sounds. Singing to the funky beats of their hourglass-shaped batá drums and cha-chá timbales, Los Muñequitos that night produced a resonant and whirling creolized symphony in songs such as "Tata se ha vuelto loco!" Cuban hip hoppers jumped on the small dance floor, producing a solid performance *rito*.

My remaining days in Cuba were packed with official and everyday prosaic events. On my daily trips walking around Havana—after we had selected the premio extraordinario in Matanazas—from the famous Hotel Nacional (where parts of Francis Ford Coppola's film *The Godfather II* had been filmed), I walked past the forlorn ice-cream parlor where the Cuban filmmakers Alea and Tabio had shot *Fresa y Chocolate*. Havana was in what our local hosts politely called "gentle decline," but in places the beautiful revolutionary city was falling tragically apart. I was continually inspired by the surrounding political iconography of Havana, an insistent presence I recall some ten years later, with Che's slogan "Socialismo o Muerte" on the barrioscaped walls and my favorite graffiti spray-painted on gigantic billboards— "Revolución en cada barrio!" All of these semiotic monuments of the revolutionary Cuban public sphere seemed to bear witness to the fact that, in my barrios of Oakland, Berkeley, and San Francisco, there were no *revoluciones* of any kind anymore. Alas, even Berkeley's infamous Telegraph Avenue was no longer a "happening"; it had, as one of my colleagues at Berkeley ironically put it, turned into a "bazaar." Where else but in twenty-first-century Berkeley could a social movement called the Free Speech Movement become a sanitized University of California café?

Our group of judges eventually narrowed the field for the premio extraordinario in U.S. Latino/a literature to two well-wrought collections of experimental stories. Later, we unanimously awarded the first

4. Photograph of classic car and Cuban youths, Havana, 2010.
Courtesy of Mónica González García.

prize to the Cuban American Sonia Rivera-Valdés for her blistering, lesbo-erotic *Cinco ventanas del mismo lado: Las historias prohibidas de Marta Veneranda* (1977), set in New York City.[13] An honorable-mention prize was given to the Nicaraguan American writer Alejandro Murguia for his short-story collection *Tropics of Desire* (1997), set in Mexico City, Los Angeles, and the Mission District of San Francisco.[14] Then I felt perfectly free to use my remaining days in Havana to begin researching the fever of materials housed at the Centro Casa de las Américas and its nearby *bibliotecas* at the University of Havana. In addition, I made sure to interview the brilliant group of editors at Casa de las Américas, including Jorge Fornet and Luisa Campuzano. Conversely, I found myself responding to probing questions about the Chicano/a social movements in the United States from Marcia Leiseca, the co-founder of Casa de las Américas and one of its best theorists of ideology. Leiseca emphasized what many Cuban Marxist comrades had been saying during my fifteen-day travels in Cuba: that we Chicanos/as were bridges over the pernicious U.S. blockade of Cuba. I told my host, Roberto Fernández Retamar,

5. Photograph of Cuban storefront with images of Che Guevara and Fidel Castro, Havana, 2010. *Courtesy of Mónica González García.*

that I did not want to leave Cuba without his reflections on why in 1976 the jurists had awarded the Casa de las Américas prize for the best Latin American novel to the Chicano writer Rolando Hinojosa for *Klail City y sus alrededores* and how the 1960s had impinged on his revolutionary thinking about minoritized writers. Why had the transcontinental group of jurists selected Hinojosa's U.S. minoritized novel (written in the Spanish vernacular spoken by Mexican Americans of South Texas) as a Cuban and Latin American text? Although Fernández Retamar gracefully deferred answering my initial questions about Hinojosa's literary text and the Cuban roots and routes of this monumental prize, he offered me the services of his great staff of archivists, philologists, and literary critics to help me begin formulating a possible answer.

Early the next day, Jorge Fornet, the literary critic and editor of Casa de las Américas, and I began our initial discussion of Hinojosa's prize by going over the original *Acta* of February 5, 1976, that the novelists and literary scholars Juan Carlos Onetti (Uruguay), Domingo Milani (Venezuela), Lincoln Silva (Paraguay), and Lisandro Otero (Cuba) had written in their award statement: in *Klail City y sus alrededores*, Rolando Hinojosa, "with a fine humor" and embedded in a internal "colonial prose," had represented a familiar "historia" of the Chicano pueblo.

Moreover, the Cuban and Latin American judges praised Hinojosa's Greater Mexican–American novel as a virtual "handbook of folkloric techniques" and suggested that its high modernist form displayed all of the Chicano author's talents as *Klail City y sus alrededores* edged itself to the limits of the narrative form. I then said to Fornet that Hinojosa's virtuoso handling of the Cuban vernacular aesthetic and performative tradition of the choteo—what the Casa de las Américas jurists had called the novel's "fine humor"—surely had something to do with his endearing himself to the Casa de las Américas jurados by making his text a narrative of both higher and lower aesthetic frequencies. Was Hinojosa's infectious use of the vernacular Tex-Mex-Cuban *humor*, via the Black and Brown Gulf of Mexico, one of the central reasons that, some twenty years later, one could still purchase a new Cuban edition of Hinojosa's novel at the Librería Rayuela?

In one of my informal presentations, I noted that *Klail City y sus alrededores* was obsessively concerned with the problematics of the power–coloniality couplet and with disjunctive class and ethno-racial formations in Greater Mexico's borderlands. At one extreme of the contrapunteo of Greater Mexico's intercultural conflict, Esteban Echevarría's oral historias at El Oasis Cantina (a chronotopic patriarchal center of the novel, where the knots of Hinojosa's chronicle are tied and untied) lead to one of the text's most socially symbolic sections—

6. Photograph of Rolando Hinojosa, Julio Cortázar, Carola Duncopt, and Fernando Urrea; Pasa Caballos, Cuba, 1988.
Courtesy of Rolando Hinojosa.

"Echevarría tiene la palabra"—and to one of the central cultural critiques of the entire Klail City Death Trip series:[15] the death-squad-like executions by the Texas Rangers of the pueblo Chicano. That is, Echevarría's listeners at the cantina-parranda performance are, in effect, a composite of the largely male-centered audience that Hinojosa visualized as his readers. Through the presence of Echevarría's living, melancholic voice and those of his companions at the cantina, a friendly and unruly commerce of storytelling and listeners is restored in our transmodernizing planet. An intimacy of oral communication, Echevarría's living *lengua* (tongue) and the parranda setting that awakens his colonially wounded words profoundly affect the entire tragicomic atmosphere of the novel.

In "Echevarría tiene la palabra," we are given not only transcultural Cuban-Chicano-Spanish choteo lessons but also a historical response by the Greater Mexican pueblo to the iconic view of the "quiet, deliberate [and] gentle view" of the Rangers in Walter Prescott Webb's bestselling *The Texas Rangers* (1935):

Amigo de la raza, ya quieran, raza! Choche Markham es bollilo y rinche. Qué va ser amigo de la raza! No me anden ustedes a mí con eso. Si fuera amigo no le hubiera rajado la cabeza a Olegario Gámez con las cachas de la .45. . . . Choche Markham está casado con mujer Mexicana y deje usted de contra: la trata peor que a una perra y Dios sabrá por qué vive con ella. Choche Markham es un aprovechado y montonero. Flacocabrónde-huesoscolrao, a mí no me lo dá. . . . Eh? Que chingaos pasa cuando viene aquí don Manuel? Se acaba todo el pedo, verdá? (Hinojosa 1976, 18)

Our friend, is he? A champion of the *raza*, you say? A friend? Choche Markham? Ha! My Gawd. *Raza*! Is there no such thing as memory? Was splitting Olegario Gamez's skull with a Colt.45 the action of a friend? Well? Go on, Somebody: explain that piece of business to me, goddamit! The man's a coward. To the core. . . . Piece of Texas *rinche* shit . . . And listen to this: he's married to a Mexicana, did-you-know-that? And how does he treat her? Well, Ha! *Qué chingaos*! (Hinojosa 1987, 16–17)

This turn from Hinojosa's carnivalesque atmosphere of *"maromas"* in the inaugural text of the Klail City Death Trip series, *Estampas de Valle y otras obras* (1973) to the Texas *rinche* excremental shit in *Klail City y sus alrededores* is quite revealing, for Hinojosa apparently agreed with the pre-revolutionary Cuban philosopher Jorge Mañach's multiple insights about the aesthetics of the Cuban vernacular choteo. The Cuban choteo, as the Cuban American literary scholar Gustavo Pérez-Firmat interprets Mañach's humor, is not a form of rhetorical wit, for he reads the Cuban's text, *Indagación del choteo* (1928), as always displacing figurative language upward.[16] Echevarría, as one of Greater Mexico's *choteadores* of the borderlands—is anything but subtle in *Klail City y sus alrededores*. In fact, he has no time at the cantina-parranda performances for clever and respectful subtlety; as the Cuban and Latin American jurists in fact testified, invective seems more his speed. It has since been my view that Hinojosa's *gran cronicón* of Belken County, Texas, thematizes not the refined folkloric irony of, say, Américo Paredes but the scatological assaulting of the great Cuban American writer and critic Gustavo Pérez-Firmat or of the U.S. Pulitzer Prize–winning Dominican American novelist Junot Díaz. In other words, Esteban Echevarría's perorations at the Oasis Cantina are more interested in Texas rinche shit than in Greater Mexico's wit. Mañach (1928, 47), of course, expressed the epistemological border thinking of Echevarría's choteo more plainly by defining the Cuban variety of the choteo as "so unintellectual that, confronted by an ingenious sally, it can only answer with another exasperating jeer. It is not a variety of dialectics, but of assault." Thus envisaged, the Cuban roots and routes of the Tex-Mex choteo, in Hinojosa's hands, is a vernacular signifying that seemingly opposes all iconic authority. Anything is fair game for the choteador in Belken County.

It is here in the Cuban vernacular aesthetics of unruly and unkempt linguistic *lenguaje* and humor that Hinojosa's text crossed the Black and Brown Gulf of Mexico and was baptized by the Casa de las Américas jurists as an example of Cuban vernacular Latinamericanism. *Chistes* (jokes) may have structured Hinojosa's Greater Mexican *Estampas del Valle*, but the choteo's "assault against authority" and against the Texas Rangers took hold in Hinojosa's novel of Greater Mexico. Echevarría's monologues performed at the Oasis Cantina demonstrate the choteo's lowness: it is a low, Greater Mexican ethnopoetics that, like a Chevy lowrider, lowers its intended victims. This emphasis on aesthetic gravitational movement downward in *Klail City y sus alrededores* is highlighted when Echevarría freely admits, "Me cago en los rinches y en sus pinches fundas contoy pistolas" ("The whole mess of the rangers and their guns and holsters are full of shit" (Hinojosa 1976, 19). Echevarría does not consider lowness in only the aesthetic vernacular sense, and he certainly does not sublimate the Texas Rangers' devious low-downness in his monologues. Rather, Hinojosa's performances of Greater Mexican choteo through Ecehvarría, like the Cuban choteo, keep our noses—as Mañach and Pérez-Firmat might claim—in the dirt, and he does so by means of improper words and total disrespect for the Texas Rangers.

This rhetorical descent from the angelic Texas Ranger heavens (as Webb portrayed them) to the dung heap of Greater Mexico's history of border troubles describes precisely Hinojosa's understanding of the choteo's rhetorical trajectory. Choteo is the Antillean–Greater Mexican vernacular that transculturates *Klail City y sus alrededores* into a Latin American text otherwise, for the choteo, as Mañach (1928, 11; emphasis added) definitively characterized his keyword, is a "familiar, slight, and festive thing—*una forma de relación* that we Cubans consider typically ours." Hinojosa thus demonstrated in *Klail City y sus alrededores* that scores of Greater Mexicans considered the choteo "typically ours," too.

On my penultimate day in Havana, after Fernández Retamar had

7. Ministry of Interior Defense Building, Havana, with image of
Che Guevara. *Courtesy of Ambroise Tézenas.*

listened politely to my improvisational rap about the oceanic (Gulf
of Mexico) roots and routes of the Cuban–Tex-Mex choteo in *Klail
City y sus alrededores* over a Caribbean lunch and I was on my way
back to my hotel, I found a copy of *Glosario de afronegrimos* (1924),
in which the social scientist Fernando Ortiz suggested that the Cuban word "choteo" derives from an African root meaning "to speak."
This etymology is corroborated, he noted, by the Cuban word *"chota*
(snitch)." When I returned to Berkeley, I looked up the Greater Mexican word "chota" in the Chicano studies library's copy of the *El Libro
de Caló* (Polkinhorn et al. 1983) and found it translated into English as
"the police." It was then that I realized that my trip to Cuba and to its
premier literary and cultural institution, Casa de las Américas, had
been nothing short of a miraculous traveling theory tale embedded in
the revolutionary history of Cuba's and Greater Mexico's transculturations.[17] Furthermore, I learned firsthand of the many challenges that
arose after the Cuban Revolution that confronted intellectuals such as
my great host, Roberto Fernández Retamar. Those challenges, which

Fernández Retamar had painted for me in Havana and on a meandering bus trip to Matanzas, had multiplied for him when his superiors sent him to Paris as a cultural attaché. He lived in Paris for almost all of 1960. From that vantage point, he not only meditated on Che's tricontinentalist thinking that was alive at the time in Cuba and the underdevelopment of the under-industrialization of the Global South; he also contemplated the decolonization of Africa, the emergence of the African independence leader Patrice Lumumba, Fidel Castro's interventions at the United Nations, and the beginnings of the French journal *Tiers Monde*. All of these experiences, Fernández Retamar told me, had impressed on him the theme of planetary underdevelopment. He also told me about his thrilling chance encounter with Che Guevara many years later, in 1965, in Europe. They had exchanged texts: Che had given him a manuscript entitled "Socialism and Man in Cuba," and Fernández Retamar had given Che a version of his brilliant essay "Martí in His (Third) World," which had recently appeared in the Cuban journal *Cuba Socialista*, alerting Che that the article contained many ideas influenced by his countryman, the Argentine Martin Estrada. Later, they shared impressions. Che, Fernández Retamar recalled, was generous with his arguments about Martí in his *tercer mundo* but told him not only that he could see Estrada's ideas percolating in the work, but, more importantly, Frantz Fanon's. As it turned out, both Che and Fernández Retamar were correct: Estrada, Che, and Fernández Retamar all had read Fanon's work rigorously. I returned to Berkeley ready to teach my course on the War of 1898 with Fernández Retamar's Fanonian and Che's tricontinentalist thinking and to a department of ethnic studies that had been founded in 1968–69 with an outernationalist ideology very similar to the anticolonial philosophy of praxis of Estrada, Che, Fanon, and Fernández Retamar. I thank Roberto Fernández Retamar for passing on to me his Cuban, Greater Antillean, and planetary registers that frame our wars at home and abroad.

Transnationalism Contested:
On Sandra Cisneros's *The House on Mango Street* and *Caramelo or Puro Cuento*

The universe a cloth, and all humanity interwoven. Each and every person connected to me, and me connected to them, like the strands of a *rebozo*. Pull one string and the whole thing comes undone.
—SANDRA CISNEROS, *Caramelo or Puro Cuento*

Near the border *figurality rises*.
—FRANCO MORETTI, *Atlas of the European Novel 1800–1900*

Although she has been publishing poems, short stories, essays, and novels of the highest quality since the late 1980s, Sandra Cisneros, author of the transnational bestselling novels *The House on Mango Street* (1991) and *Caramelo or Puro Cuento* (2003), is still much better known in minoritized U.S. Latino/a literature circles than in mainline American, Latin American, and comparative literature seminars and institutions. This neglect in traditional American literary matters is somewhat unfair.[1] There are signs, however, that Cisneros's work is being read in the U.S. public sphere with the same enthusiasm that has greeted her in U.S. public middle schools, where *The House on Mango Street* has received major attention as an iconic text in the classroom, and in Mexico, where it has been very well translated into Spanish by the feminist Mexican novelist Elena Poniatowska (see Cisneros 1994a). While some first-rate U.S. Latino/a literary and cultural critics have focused their criticism either on Cisneros's first novel, *The House on Mango Street*, or on short stories from *Woman Hollering Creek and Other Stories* (1992), there have not yet been—as far as I know—any substantial contributions to the interpretation of her works as a whole.[2] There are good reasons for this delay. Sandra Cisneros is a complex transnational novelist, poet, and short-story writer who is particularly difficult to place. Commentators cast about in vain for suitable points of comparison. *The House on Mango Street*, for example, like most imaginative literature written by U.S. Latinos/as, has been infantilized by U.S. marketers as a paradigm of "young adult" literature or as an experimental book of short stories.[3] Why not consider a more serious reading of Cisneros's *The House on Mango Street* as her attempt to write the great (transnational) American novel? Or as her attempt to paint her idea of the *convivencia* of Mango Street's multiculture and the primacy of the domestic and political economy of the house (the *oikos*) and thus combat the civilizational "common sense" and contentious (pathological) diagnosis of immigration from the Global South?[4]

Perhaps Cisneros's own avowed admiration for local writers from the multiculture of Chicago, her hometown, has added to this confusion. Like Carl Sandburg's and Gwendolyn Brooks's impassioned public oratory, Cisneros, as an experimental woman writer of color, finds it unusual to be drawn into and fascinated in her fictions with what she calls "a common-man poetics" (1985, 65), but this does not mean that her work, so full of references to the Pilsen neighborhood in Chicago's Lower West Side, makes her a local-color, vernacular writer in rebellion against the times. But it also true that her imaginative literature focuses primarily on Chicago's largest ethnic group, in which one out of five Chicagoland residents is a U.S. Latino or Latina.

While it is true that Cisneros writes about having had to confront what she characterizes as "the embarrassment of my poverty and to admit my distinctiveness" in her Iowa Creative Writing workshops (where she initially started writing her major poems and *The House on Mango Street*) (Cisneros 1985, 64), her early work is not imbued with a moralizing thematics. The novel *The House on Mango Street* indeed contains a gallery of impoverished colonial immigrant subjects from within and against the "anarchy" of U.S. Empire—namely, U.S. Latinos/as, ethnic Mexicans, Puerto Ricans, Dominicans, and well-rounded Anglo-American and African American characters.[5] But Cisneros does not consider Greater Mexico's beleaguered multiculture in the mean barrioscapes of Chicago as primary moral themes. Her novels *The House on Mango Street* and *Caramelo or Puro Cuento* do not indict La Providencia, Fortuna, or the many U.S.-Mexican border-crossing destinies and destinations in her fiction. Perhaps Cisneros's

8. Portrait
photograph of
Sandra Cisneros.
*Courtesy of Al
Rendon.*

admiration for the modern writer Jorge Luis Borges is provisionally relevant for an initial placing of her fiction, for, she, too, is interested in what Borges once described as *infamia* (infamy) in her poems, novels, and short stories as an aesthetic, formal principle of difference.[6] Many different worlds are therefore conjured up in Cisneros's fiction and poetry: displaced border brides like Cleófilas in "Woman Hollering Creek"; love poems of the greater San Francisco Bay Area in *Loose Woman* (1994b); stories of religious miracles from Tepeyac from *Woman Hollering Creek and Other Stories*; transmodern Mexican melodrama from the streets of Chicago, San Antonio, and Mexico City in *Caramelo or Puro Cuento*—all of which would probably be shapeless without the ordering presence of infamy.

A good illustration can be taken from one of the short stories that Cisneros published in *Woman Hollering Creek and Other Stories*. Borrowing from the transnational stylistic conventions of Mexican *tele-*

novelas (soap operas) and their metonymically articulated Televisa TV advertisements, Cisneros's stories often read like a hybrid combination of the work of the popular Mexican romance novelist Corín Tellado,[7] the Chicana feminist Gloria Anzaldúa, and the masterly dynamic duo of Borges and Gabriel García Márquez, except that they are a great deal more succinct and deviously more melodramatic.[8] In an allegorical rewriting of the Mexican myth of the star-crossed lovers Iztaccihuatl (the White Woman) and Popocateptl (the Smoking Mountain), the short story titled in Spanglish "Bien Pretty," Cisneros's central protagonist, Lupe Arrendondo, an aspiring painter from Berkeley, wants "to do an updated version of the Prince [Popo] and Princess [Izta] volcano myth," so well known to millions of urban Chilangos/as, "that tragic love story metamorphosed from *classic to kitsch calendar art*, like the ones you get at a La Carnicería Ximénez or Tortillería Guadalupana. Prince [Popo] half-naked warrior built like Johnny Weissmuller, crouched in grief beside his sleeping Princess [Izta] . . . buxom as Jane Mansfield. And behind them, echoing their silhouettes, their namesake volcanoes" (Cisneros 1992, 144; emphasis added). In "Bien Pretty," the star-crossed lovers are also U.S.-Mexican border-crossing lovers: Lupe is an aspiring Chicana artist from northern California, and Flavio Mungia is an undocumented Mexican immigrant turned cockroach exterminator, who has migrated North from Mexico. They are "destined" to meet, fall in love, and part in San Antonio. Lupe (Izta) falls romantically in love with the stud Flavio (Popo). However, in a Chicana feminist, *nueva mestiza* twist of sorts, Cisneros de-romanticizes the Mexican prince. With a cool, Sinatra-like structure of feeling, Lupe the painter gives us the punch line to the short story's climax this way: "Went back to the twin volcano painting. Got a good idea and redid the whole thing. Prince Popo and Prince Izta trade places. After all, who's to say the sleeping mountain isn't the prince, and the voyeur the princess, right? So I've done it my way. With Prince Popo lying on his back instead of the Princess. Of course, I had to make some anatomical adjustments in order to simulate the geographical silhouettes. I think I'm going to call it El Pipi del Papo. I kind of like it" (Cisneros 1992, 163). And in Cisneros's exemplary representation of the changing American dialect in her fiction, Flavio, who in "Bien Pretty" acts like the "vermin" he exterminates for a living, might also be seen as a U.S.-Mexico border-crossing "varmaint."[9]

As in all trans-American post-contemporary melodrama,[10] Lupe comes to understand herself and even invokes the title of a Venezuelan soap opera—"Amar es vivir" (To love is to live)—to thematize her passionate vocation, standpoint epistemology, and self-location. There is no happy ending, however, for Lupe, for she is devastated by Flavio's undocumented cockroach infamy.[11] At the story's end, she can only consol her new *mestiza* soul by "looking for old Mexican movies. María Félix, Jorge Negrete, Pedro Infante, anything, please, where's somebody's singing on a horse" (Cisneros 1992, 161). The portrait of the Chicana artist has to wear the mask of melodrama to create and contest (*contestar*) a transnational style.

Cisneros's characters are usually prototypes for the feminist border thinker, and her worlds are prototypes for a highly stylized form of transmodern fiction. For all their variety of tone, focalization, and setting, the different short stories that make up *Woman Hollering Creek and Other Stories* have a similar point of departure, a similar structure, a similar climax and "spaciness," and a similar outcome. The inner cogency that links these moments together constitutes Cisneros's distinctive transnational style (see De la Mora 2004). Her short stories and novels, as I demonstrate, are allegories about the geography and style in which they are often written. Before focusing on the geography of Greater Mexico's border style in *Caramelo or Puro Cuento*, I begin the chapter by discussing Cisneros's bestselling novel *The House on Mango Street* as exploring aspects of Greater Mexico's *cultura de convivencia* within the catastrophes of the urban, Global North.[12]

The first impression one receives of Cisneros's transnational novel *The House on Mango Street* is that of a prophetic pronouncement of cultural convivencia, remote from the cold spirit held up as Western modernity. Indeed, as one reads this text, one is struck by the prophetic (spiritualized) tone espoused by the central protagonist, Esperanza, as the minoritized allegorical figure of the poet, as a figure that echoes poetic language.[13] Posing the question of prophetic difference, as well as sexual difference from within the "bare life" and (legal) violence of the Global North's "magical urbanism,"[14] Cisneros's novel also dramatizes the crucial roles of material oppression. That is, as Mike Davis (2000, 54) suggests, U.S. Latinos/as immigrants are, in the most fundamental sense, struggling to reconfigure the "cold" frozen geometries of the old spatial orders in the Global North to accommodate a "hotter," more exuberant, and magical urbanism.

One of the penultimate chapters of the novel, "A House of My Own" (re-sounding the title of Virginia Woolf's iconic *A Room of One's Own*), summarizes the various standpoint epistemologies and locations of the young protagonist, Esperanza, in her narrativized space and time (the chronotope) of the streets in one of the barrios of the U.S. Global North, presumably Chicago's West Side barrio: "Not a flat. Not an apartment in back. Not a man's house. A house all of my own. With my . . . books and my stories . . . only a house quiet as snow, a space for myself to go to, *clean as paper before the poem*" (Cisneros 1991, 105; emphasis added). Like the novel's beginning chapter, "A House of My Own" fixes an identity for the central intelligence of the novel, Esperanza, by dialectically mapping her surroundings negatively. She emphasizes that she is not thinking about apartments and, certainly, not about a man's house. Cisneros thus uses the chronotope of the house and its metonymically linked Mango, Loomis, Paulina, and Keeler streets to get at the idea of her family's migratory roots and routes from the Global South to the city streets and houses of the Global North. What Esperanza remembers most about her past is "having moved around a lot" (Cisneros 1991, 3). Moreover, Cisneros foreshadows and highlights in the passage the unifying image of "empty space" in the novel—the house as "clean as paper before the poem."

Cisneros, therefore, is less interested in thematizing an existential poetics of space, it seems to me, than a prophetic consideration of the dialectically over-determining spheres of the private and the social,[15] for as Gayatri Chakravorty Spivak (1988, 252) and Ramón Saldívar (1990, 182) have noted in different contexts, "the oikos" is a "metaphor for the *polis*." Each of the 49 "lazy poem"-like chapters of *The House on Mango Street* in fact refers to these organizing private and social figures,[16] as Esperanza thinks about the nature of her barrio's multiculture, its convivencia, and its economy, especially the multiple ways other young U.S. Latinas' "bare life" in and around Mango Street are all domesticated in the "barred" economies of the patriarchal houses and apartments. That is, Cisneros focuses on how the house's *oikonomia* as domestic, sexual, and political economy weaves the spheres of the public and the private together. The economy, for Cisneros's characters Esperanza, Sally, Rafaela, Minerva, and Mamacita (Big Mama) and their families, as the Greek term "oikonomia" etymologically suggests, is "the one who manages the household." And Esperanza (Hope), as her name in Spanish suggests, continually points out the overlapping spaces of the domestic and political economy of the house on Mango Street in a spiritualized and prophetic language.

I have sketched out one of the ending chapters and the beginning chapter of *The House on Mango Street* (perhaps this may all be too familiar to you) to try to show the mood, method, tone, and atmosphere in which Cisneros's text was written as a response to a graduate discussion on creative writing at the University of Iowa. The notion of the poetic as a sacred figure (as well as the language of the oikos as the figure of the poet's house) is frequent and common throughout the text. As a near-redeemer and a gifted storyteller, Esperanza, as Walter Benjamin might have put it, fans "the sparks of hope" in the novel and espouses the view that within the "empty space" of the novel a revolutionary moment is possible when the past bursts into the present—as if rising from the grave to rectify the wrongs suffered at the hands of a banal progress called the American dream.[17]

This notion of the barrio house, the oikos, on Mango Street as the sacred, as the prophetic house "quiet as snow . . . clean as paper before the poem" (Cisneros 1991, 108), and as the house as ineffable language finds its extreme form in "A Room of My Own." Thus envisaged, one can praise Cisneros for establishing in her first transnational novel an idea of what had almost been forgotten in the novels of the U.S. Latino/a multiculture—the ideas of the sacred, of the prophetic, and of hope. But one would also have to note how Cisneros's *The House on Mango Street* complicates this tidy pattern. She uses a chiasmus of hope as well as that of the catastrophes and states of emergency that occur to the women, children, and families on Mango Street. The foundation of hope, Esperanza, thus becomes that of remembrances of the state of emergencies on Mango Street.

As one of Esperanza's many *comadres* tells her, "When you leave you must remember always" (Cisneros 1991, 105). So Esperanza, who likes "to tell stories," tells us a particular *historia* "about a girl who didn't want to belong" in the barrioscapes of the Global North. She did not belong on Loomis, Paulina, or Keeler street, and she did not belong to "the sad, red house" on Mango Street. "I put it down on paper," Esperanza explains, "and then [*el fantasma*] does not ache so much. I write it down and Mango [Street] says goodbye sometimes. She does not hold me with both arms. She sets me free" (Cisneros 1991, 110).

But why is the sad red house a *fantasma* for Esperanza? What kinds of specters haunt all of the barrio women, children, and men on Mango Street?

The foundation of hope for Esperanza becomes remembrance, becomes historia, which confirms the function, even the duty, of the poet and radical historian of Greater Mexico. To recall the past—as Esperanza puts it—for all "the ones who cannot" get out (*por los que no [salen]*)" (Cisneros 1991, 110) is Cisneros's political act, a remembrance that involves readers of her text with images of economic power and with images that claim the prophetic, the sacred powers of poetic language and empty space. These distinct constellations of images in *The House on Mango Street* split off from their fixed locations, undoing the concepts of a straight, homogeneous time "to flash up" into and reconstitute the present. Rewriting Marx, Benjamin (1969, 261) reminds us that "ancient Rome was a past charged with the time of the now which he blasted out of the continuum of history."

Benjamin's reference is to historical remembrance, to a concept of the historical that dovetails and injects itself into a prophetic and sacred concept, thus marrying history with the poetic and the sacred. So, too, Cisneros gives us in *The House on Mango Street* both the poetic languages of Esperanza's despair (she lives in a beleaguered house with "tight steps," with "windows so small you would think [they] were holding their breath," and with "bricks [that] are crumbling" [Cisneros 1991, 4])—that is, with the bare life of Greater Mexico's multiculture in the Global North: poverty, street violence, criminal injustice, the killing of undocumented workers, and the rigors of history that go with that. But at the same time, Cisneros provides readers with *esperanza*—hope.

So we have it all in *The House on Mango Street*: Esperanza's critical reflections on the oikos; the possibility of Esperanza writing Chicana historical barriology in sacred and apocalyptic tones;[18] and the particular eloquence that comes with this hope, historical rigor, and poetic revelation. The specialized temporalities of bare life in the barrios of the Global North thus also stand against the injection and infusion of the "subject" into the heterogeneity of Greater Mexico's urban multiculture. Moreover, Esperanza has a clear redemptive mission: the obligation to seize the moments of the past "moving around" within her emphatic loyalty across the generations "A las mujeres (To the Women)" announced at the novel's beginning. Hence, Esperanza (like Benjamin's desire to have empathy with the past) sketches out a philosophical perspective (opposed to mainline historicism) in which she proposes a notion of redemption that implies an emphatic relationship to the past and a version of obligation linking subjects across time. Rather than only fixed in the utopian future announced in her name—*Esperanza*—Cisneros's protagonist is backward-looking, too, thus gesturing an attempt to bridge the gap between the present and the past.

Beyond the cardinal turning points in the novel—Esperanza's move from the Loomis Street apartment to the phantasmatic house on Mango Street; her desire in the chapter titled "Sire" to be "all new and shiny" and gazing "back hard" at the barrio punks of Mango Street; and the beginning of Esperanza's "own quiet war" and rebellion against her ethnic Mexican immigrant father and patriarchy in the chapter "Beautiful and Cruel" (Cisneros 1991, 72, 89)—the narratological fillers of *The House on Mango Street* open up the interiorized spaces of the immigrant apartments and houses in the barrio and fill in how Esperanza's self is linked to Greater Mexico's multiculture of convivencia. Can Cisneros's poetic (sacred) language get at the realities that are largely unrepresentable in the barrioscapes— something like Althusser's absent cause? Are the absent causes unsettled, distorted, and phantasmatic in *The House on Mango Street*?

In one of the novel's early (postcolonial) chapter-fables, "The Family of Little Feet," for instance, Esperanza's mother gives her and the barrio *amigas* some pairs of used high-heeled shoes. Here the subject-self of convivencia that the girls create is one that must transact beyond the domestic oikos into the fully commercialized and fetishized *polis*. That is, the girls of Mango Street have to grapple with the forms of their gendered roles as agents in the trafficking of a sexual oikos. Wearing the fetishized red high heels (perhaps like Dorothy in *The Wizard of Oz*), the young girls find themselves almost spawned into fetishized body parts: "We have legs. Skinny and spotted with satin scars . . . good to look at, and long"; experimenting with their new roles, Esperanza and her friends "strut in their magic high heels," in their magical urbanist space, and learn how to properly "cross and uncross their legs" (Cisneros 1991, 38). The metamorphosis of the barrio girls is so alluring that Mr. Benny, the Mango Street grocer, lectures them about their "dangerous" red Oz-like shoes. "You girls too young to be wearing shoes like that," he says. So offended by the sexualized state of emergency in Mango Street that Esperanza and her friends seem to have initiated right before his eyes, Mr. Benny can only imagine putting down the girls' nearly sexualized riot and revolution by demanding that if they do not take off the red shoes, he will have to "call the cops." A passing street person then stops Esperanza near a Mango Street tavern, fetishizes her "little lemon shoes" and offers her a "dollar [for] a kiss" (Cisneros 1991, 38–39).

Aside from this spectacularized history of the many gendered women's experiences in the novel, *The House On Mango Street* concludes with the stories of the multitude of undocumented (largely Mexican and Central American) workers in the Global North—what Esperanza sees as the sad *Geraldos sin apellidos* (nameless Geraldos) who inhabit Mango Street's taverns and dancehalls. All the Geraldos who work in the service economy—"You know the ones," Marín explains to Esperanza. "Green pants [and] shiny . . . Saturday shirts" (Cisneros 1991, 65). Marín is the last to see Geraldo alive when she dances with him and shares some *convivencias* of *cumbias* and *rancheras*. Later that night, he is killed by a hit-and-run driver. "No address. No last name," Marín says to Esperanza. "Ain't it a shame. . . . Just another *brazer* who didn't speak English" (Cisneros 1991, 66). Geraldo *sin apellido* is nothing to Marín—not a boyfriend or a lover. For Esperanza, however, *Geraldo sin apellido* stands for the millions of unremembered day laborers without papers and hospitality in the Global North, the Geraldos whose houses are *en otros países* (in other countries). No local remembrances of Geraldo exist in Mexico anymore; the only surviving (spectral) memories of Geraldo in Mexico are noted by a local friend as Geraldo "*ése se fue al norte* (he went North)" (Cisneros 1991, 66).

But Esperanza recalls, too, the outsize and magical urbanist Mango Street story of Mamacita—really "Mamasota" because, Esperanza explains, Mamacita is a "huge, enormous" elegant woman (like a character in a Fernando Botero painting), with a "flutter[ing] of hips," who is imprisoned in her third-floor apartment by her husband because she is "too beautiful to look at" (Cisneros 1991, 76–77). Mamasota remains trapped in her husband's space and place and refuses to come out of her "third-floor front" either because, Esperanza ruminates, "she can't climb the stairs" because of her enormous weight or because as a woman recently moved from the Global South, Mamasota is "afraid of English" (Cisneros 1991, 76–77).

"All day," Esperanza says, Mamacita "sits by the window," singing "homesick songs about her *país* in a voice that sounds like a seagull." When she complains to her bilingual husband, "*Cuándo, cuándo, cuándo*" (77)—when might they return home to the Global South?— he icily responds, "Ay caray, we are home. This *is* home" (Cisneros 1991, 77–78). With this rather local response to Mamacita's transnational desire for her pink house in another country, "with lots of startled light," he turns a blind eye to his wife's suffering "as if he had torn [away] the only skinny thread that kept her alive, the only road out to that country" (Cisneros 1991, 78). As if this is not devastating enough, Esperanza concludes her barrio story by recalling how Mamacita's young baby boy broke her heart by singing to her not the "homesick songs about her country" that she loved hearing "on the local Spanish radio shows," but singing to her in "a language that sounded like tin," a coca-colonized "Pepsi commercial he heard on TV" (Cisneros 1991, 77–78). "No speak English, . . . No speak English," the Mango street crowd overhears Mamacita yelling at her startled boy.

Incapable of imagining "home" or a house in a "language that sounded like tin" to her ears, Mamacita *chilla* (cries) and can only turn to Greater Mexico's multiculture of songs of convivencia that resemble seagulls—songs that fly (like seagulls) across the oceanic diasporic spaces that connect the Global South to the Global North. Can there ever be a dynamic motion of transactional and transnational magic urbanism, a figuration of an oikonomia of trans-mutability for Mamacita, Esperanza asks? Esperanza empathizes with Mamacita's fate, saying, "Yo también lloraría (And then I think she cries. I would)." In each of these chapters about the *Geraldos sin apellidos*, about the multitude of immigrant Mamacitas and Big Mamas locked up in their domestic spaces and places, Esperanza negotiates with the beleaguered realities of Greater Mexico's multiculture. In the shared experiences with women such as Minerva and Mamacita, and in the nameless and faceless Geraldos, pre-eminently infused with the global oikos all, Cisneros helps to create in *The House on Mango Street* an alternative phantasmatic space for the subjects of Greater Mexico that is not subjected to or haunted by the mathematical homogeneity of post-contemporary America's stern civilizationalism.

Visual culture in the form of the iconic Colombian artists, painter Fernando Botero and the writer Gabriel García Márquez also stand at the center of *The House on Mango Street* in rounded, solid, and voluminous form. As we have seen, characters like Mamacita are laced with a new visual vocabulary from the Global South based on sensual human shapes. Like Botero's complex cubist-like paintings, Cisneros's text provides a visual polemic in the very form of Mamacita's fullness, solidity, and graceful "fluttering of hips." For Cisneros, as for Botero and García Márquez, the association of *hermosura* (beauty) with the roundness of a gigantic pear is part of the reason the husband keeps Mamacita locked up for himself. It is in this voluminous "scaling up" of the human body that Cisneros's distortion of the real is raised to the determining element of style. It dominates in every figure and in almost every object in the story about Mamacita; volumes inflated to bursting are omnipresent. If proportion is not an unvarying, eternally valid system, Cisneros turns here in sections of *The House* on *Mango Street* to begin painting an alternative style produced and circulated from the Global South through the distortion of Mamacita's proportion, with her abundance and formal fullness.

I conclude this section on *The House on Mango Street* and its aesthetic connections with Botero's and García Márquez's outsize realism by noting that in April 1960, a young García Márquez ended one of his most bombastic journalistic essays by arguing, "La literatura colombiana, en conclusión general, ha sido un fraude a la nación (Colombian literature in general has defrauded the nation)" (García Márquez 1992c, 667). With this startling critique of Colombian literature and its failure to paint a "national culture," García Márquez meditated on the Global South's and Colombia's theme of "*la violencia*" as a real problematic for Colombian writers. He also called attention to the underdeveloped literary genealogy that had retarded narratological production. Arguing that Colombian writers were right smack in the middle of the country's violent historical underdevelopment, and thus eyewitnesses to "*una gran novela*," García Márquez argued that the Colombian novelist did not yet have access to the narratological know-how needed to write Colombia's great novel.[19]

García Márquez offered readers of his journalistic essay a blunt cultural critique of the limits of the national imaginary. He also offered an explanation for a literary history that had failed readers in its ability to paint Colombia's violence: "In reality, Colombia was not culturally mature enough for the political and social tragedy of the last years to have left us with anything more than some fifty crude testimonies" (García Márquez 1992c, 665–66). He concluded that this Colombian narratological failure was also a condition of the nation's underdevelopment, because its imaginative literature mostly had been written by a generation of worn-out and bone-tired writers: "Since the conditions needed to produce a professional writer do not exist, literary creation has been relegated to the free time that is left over when we have finished our normal occupations. Literature is necessarily the craft of the tired" (García Márquez 1992c, 666). The journalist García Márquez ended his critique of the Colombian novel by calling for a new narratological aesthetic—that is, he ended by comparing and contrasting Colombia's failed literary practices with the cutting-edge, transnational practices of its painters, such as Botero.

In contrast with Colombia's novelists, who were underdeveloped by a history of violence, according to García Márquez, Colombian painters had succeeded by envisioning in their works an art of liberation. By working in that space, painters like Botero expressed "a new form of artistic expression" by starting "at the beginning, learning the hard way about their art and their role" and, in the process of laboring, "sustain[ing] vigorous pressure on their milieu" (García Márquez 1992b, 666). In other words, artists like Botero critiqued Colombia's national imaginary by painting an outernational consciousness, what García Márquez termed a "good wind from the North," where the circulation of their art was received with engaged criticism: "The best thing that could happen to [Colombia's] literature would be the appearance of similar criticism" (García Márquez 1992b, 667). Botero's paintings (in which art is an accusation) thus stand behind the outsize realism in both García Márquez's *Cien años de soledad* (1967) and Cisneros's *The House on Mango Street*; they provide both novelists with an inventive aesthetic of an outsize planetary volume and scale.

The center of the fictional universe in Cisneros's transnational novel *Caramelo or Puro Cuento* (2003) radically plays with Borgesian acts of dissimulation, impersonation, and infamy, where the creation of truth, error, and beauty for the narrator, Celaya, begins with acts of duplicity. *Caramelo or Puro Cuento*, Cisneros's second-bestselling border-crossing novel, in fact describes the totally imaginary world of Celaya Reyes, who stands in for Cisneros's desire to be an *anthropoeta*.[20] At the very beginning of Cisneros's eighty-six-chapter tour de force, Celaya (also known as Lala) insists in a "Disclaimer" to her readers that her "stories are nothing but string, bits of stray and ends found here and there, embroidered together to make something new. I have invented what I do not know, and exaggerated what I do *to continue the family tradition of telling healthy lies*" (Cisneros 2003, 1; emphasis added). *Caramelo's* novelistic world is from the very start filled with metaphor, dissimulation, and deceit—what the Reyes's family calls "healthy lies." Moreover, through the disclaimer we are encouraged to see the peculiar ways in which Cisneros's figural language of "stray" and "ends" of simple "string" begins to wrestle with its unresolvable problems of denomination as "knots" and "strands," so many distinct and specific embroideries or text formations that cannot be theorized or ordered into a law (although Cisneros seems to do just that through the writing of a novel). Last, the novel is rewritten as a ghost story in which Celaya's Mexican "Awful Grandmother," Soledad, spectrally haunts the Chicana Celaya and often debates with the ethnic granddaughter's transmodern choice to emplot the tale we are reading. In other words, masquerades, impersonations, family hoaxes, and infamy are also thematized throughout the novel.

Cast in the form of an imaginary disclaimer with a fictive reader or film spectator, the prologue to Cisneros's novel starts with an innocuous metaphor about the relationship the narrator bears to her text: "I have invented what I do not know and exaggerated what I do to continue the family tradition of telling healthy lies. If, in the course of my inventing, I have inadvertently stumbled on the truth, *perdónenme*. To write is to ask questions. It doesn't matter if the answers are true or *puro cuento*" (Cisneros 2003, 1). That is, the narrator renounces her will to truth in *Caramelo or Puro Cuento* and asks in advance for forgiveness if, in the course of telling us "healthy lies," a Reyes family tradition, she somehow "stumbles" on the truth. But as we read through this transnational novel, the narrator's humble and dispassionate renouncement is precisely what we are not allowed by Cisneros. Celaya first asks the reader to pardon her inadvert will to

9. Front cover of
Sandra Cisneros's
novel *Caramelo or
Puro Cuento*.

truth, then flatters the imaginative writer's critical vocation "to ask questions" as an inquisitor in a rather transparent attempt to gain the reader's trust, for in the writer's inquisition of the culture and society of her Greater Mexico, "it doesn't matter," Celaya argues, if the answers are true or not. Celaya's new metaphor of the writer-critical social theorist is underwritten by her claim that the will to truth, or what she calls *puro cuento*, are the same thing. In renouncing her will to truth and in casting herself as a critical imaginative writer whose job it is to question the truth and errors of Greater Mexico's culture and society, Celaya thus leaves readers with the exciting freedom to establish their own unconstrained reading of *Caramelo or Puro Cuento*.

But we are not as unconstrained as we might desire, as becomes apparent when Celaya's opening disclaimer continues with a consideration of the difficulty of representing memory and truth in the fabrication of historias: "After all and everything only the story is remembered, and the truth fades away like the pale blue ink on a cheap embroidery pattern: *Eres mi vida, Sueño contigo mi Amor, Suspiro por tí, Sólo tú"* (Cisneros 2003, 1). Although Celaya's voice as narrator speaks from the disclaimer directly to the reader as if from outside the fiction of the novel—the way a film spectator reads a disclaimer about the falsity of the events that she is about to witness on the screen— Celaya's voice, from the start of *Caramelo or Puro Cuento*, speaks from within the text's fabricating, dissimulating, deceitful fictions. The disclaimer's narrator has thus taken on a role that allows her to write words and ask questions that seemingly stand in solidarity with the epigraph in Spanish that precedes the disclaimer: "*Cuéntame algo, aunque sea una mentira* (Tell me a story, even if it's a lie)." If Sandra Cisneros the author has lent the words to the epigraph with considerable authority by virtue of the proper sign, Celaya insists in the disclaimer on maintaining the author's will to storytelling, for "healthy" *historias*, even if they are lies, are "all" and "everything."

This insistence on the primacy of artifice, dissimulation, and the dysfunctionality of language ("healthy lies" and *"puro cuento"*) in the disclaimer is, of course, but the first of many transformations in *Caramelo or Puro Cuento* of what is "real," "true," and "fictive," and of the utopian possibility of what is not yet real in the novel. Musing on the direction her disclaimer should take, Celaya ends by directing our attention to the narratological webs of string, "the odds and ends" she has found and stitched together (like a *rebozo*) in the novel we are about to read. These stringy bits of narrative not only "make something" new—a novel—but long after the "cheap" painting-like blue-ink patterns ("the truth") on the pillows on which her Mexican grandparents sleep have faded away, what remains are the mass-mediated *historias* with the film titles of Mexican melodramas and boleros: "Eres mi vida, Sueño contigo mi amor, Suspiro por tí, Sólo tú" (Cisneros 2003, 1).

Because Celaya adorns her text, *Caramelo or Puro Cuento*, not with intricate and refined webs of aesthetic erudition but just with some odds and ends of simple string, she decides to make do by embroidering a *historia* modeled broadly on the very mass-mediated Mexican melodramas and boleros whose titles are stitched on her Mexican grandparents' pillows, as well as on the family mestizo rebozo that has been passed down through the generations from Soledad to her. In other words, Celaya offers us a novel solution: Greater Mexico's fiction, its "puros cuentos" will be narrated in the form of aesthetic deceptions and dissimulations and in the vernacular aesthetic tradition of the Reyes family's "healthy lies," as well as in the form of the iconic mass-mediated *telenovelas* that allow her to empathize and link up her own somersaulting historia with that of her Mexican grandparents, who have witnessed and experienced a lifetime of astonishing historias in the Global South. In the epigraph and disclaimer, Celaya willingly accepts the author Cisneros's initial challenge in Spanish— "*Cuéntame algo, aunque sea una mentira* (Tell me a story, even if it's a lie)."[21] Further, Celaya accepts Cisneros's challenge to tell us her life history and accepts the author's challenge to reject the seduction of mimetic representation by freely inventing and "exaggerating" even if the requisite words that make up the story of *Caramelo or Puro Cuento* come from iconic Mexican soap operas, melodramas, and boleros. One of the issues that clearly underlies *Caramelo or Puro Cuento* is: can mass-mediated Mexican melodramas and telenovelas, with all of their plot twists and somersaults, underwrite Greater Mexico's new, transnational borderlands of Chicana fiction? Are Mexican and Venezuelan soap operas appropriate and proper models to invent an intricate Chicana novel? Or are Mexican telenovelas and boleros newer art forms, like the classical Mexican *caramelo rebozos* of Santa María del Río?[22] Almost in spite of itself, *Caramelo or Puro Cuento* ends up conjuring an impossible painting of what falls outside figurative language (perhaps the caramelo rebozo itself) and what figurative language cannot absorb or incorporate.

Traditionally, it has been the critical reader's role to pose these questions. In *Caramelo or Puro Cuento*, Cisneros, through the anthropoeta Celaya, usurps that role by dramatizing the question of authority.[23] Can we locate an anterior version of our own attempt as critical readers to demonstrate that authority is either a property of a coloniality and semiosis and not of writing, or that authority is an analytic construct and not an empirical presence in Cisneros's disclaimer? At stake in the prologue and in the novel is the possibility that, as Edward Said (1975, 23) long ago put it, "Within the discontinuous system of quotation, reference, duplication, parallel, and allusion which makes up writing, authority—or the specific power of a specific writing—can be thought of as something whole and as something invented—as something inclusive and made up . . . for the occasion."

If we now consider all of the possible metaphoric transformations and critical transculturations that occur in the disclaimer to describe the text of *Caramelo or Puro Cuento,* we are still left, I think, with a troubling residue of knots—namely, the narrator's explanation of the need for so many possible metaphors and metonymies for a single text: truth and error, historia and "puro cuento," "naively unbelievable stories" and "true witnessing of a lifetime of astonishments," caramelo rebozo and telenovela, melodrama and history, negation and paradigm. Celaya never allows a final, unequivocal description of the transnational text to emerge. In her disclaimer and in the novel, then, the ambiguous collapsing of authority is indicated by the failure of the text's own various statements to constrain the text within any one context. From the outset, the author and her fictional voices and anthropoeta establish this dialogue of contradictions concerning the nature of Greater Mexico's literary language, the nature of mass-mediated secondary orality, and the manner in which to create a proper language for the expression of the decolonial historia of Celaya's and the Reyes family's travels from Chicago's Global North down south to and across Greater Mexico's borderlands into Mexico City.

The theme of the quest for a proper and exemplary decolonial figural language of the Chicana novel announces itself within the tradition of Greater Mexico's radical critique of migration and incorporation. Celaya traces her family's history from her Mexican grandparents' time before the Mexican Revolution (1910–17) to their traveling journeys from Mexico City to Chicago and to San Antonio. Celaya is the youngest of the six Reyes children and the only daughter in the immigrant working-class family. *Caramelo or Puro Cuento* is centrally the story of Celaya's development and education—from her birth to young adulthood—and of those who accompany her, and her first focalizations are those that thematize the relationship between truth, lies, and storytelling. Early in the novel, when the Reyes clan has just driven straight from Chicago through Saint Louis to the South Texas borderlands, Celaya asks, "Did I dream it or did someone tell me the story? I can't remember where the truth ends and the talk [story] begins" (Cisneros 2003, 20).[24] Later, to pass the time on their astonishing annual car journey from Chicago to Mexico City, Lala asks her father why, years earlier, he had left his home of Mexico City for the Global North—"Philadelphia, Memphis, Little Rock, New York City"—and why he had not initially settled in these U.S. cities

"wip[ing] tables" and "wash[ing] dishes," as so many of his *paisans*
had, after the Mexican Revolution? He answers, "Because it wasn't my
destino" (Cisneros 2003, 247).

But as Celaya and her traveling cultural stories unfold, like a caramelo rebozo, she worries less about drawing the boundaries between
where her grandparents' and parents' astonishing histories end and
where their "[talk] stories" and the Mexican iconic movies begin.
Even the title *Caramelo or Puro Cuento*, as I have suggested, is multi-
layered and nuanced. Celaya's great-great-grandmother was a skilled
weaver of Mexican rebozos—caramelo rebozos (shawls) that ranged
from traditional black-and-white flecked cotton in which subaltern
poor women carry their babies to the most crafted and refined silk
rebozos, so well wrought that one can be pulled through a wedding
band. Like the puro cuentos Celaya textually and tactically learns
through her grandmother to weave together in the novel (in Latin,
"*texo*" means "to make" and "to weave"), the rebozo twists, turns, and
knots, like the rebozos worn in indigenous women's hair and with
silver ornaments. Cisneros's contested Greater Mexican rebozo, the
novel *Caramelo or Puro Cuento*, stands in as a kind of "cradle" and
repository of transnational memory and culture, as a red "flag" of
subaltern and transmodern Zapatista tradition, as an umbrella or
parasol, or as a basket when going to the market, or modestly covering
the blue-veined breast giving suck. "That world with its customs" that
Celaya's grandmothers witnessed in Mexico and passed on to her
(Cisneros 2003, 94). *Caramelo or Puro Cuento* describes the golden-
and-tan-flecked rebozos with black and white that also "[bring] to
mind the sweet candy of the same name" (Cisneros 2003, 94). But as
the novel unfolds before us, *Caramelo or Puro Cuento* takes on a series
of other meanings, standpoint epistemologies, and subject positions,
as well. It becomes a leitmotif for what is customary and customized,
like a Chevy lowrider, and custom-made by hand.

For Celaya, the careful and detailed study of the "language of knots
and rosettes" in her Mexican grandmother's rebozos becomes her
primary science, serving to establish as a base for the expression of her
will to truth (Cisneros 2003, 94).[25] The weaver's string, even its odds
and ends, as the disclaimer so aptly put it, are thus the future anthropoeta's instrument of truth. Her elegant statement that her poor
grandmother, Soledad, was destined not to become a "knotter of

fringes" herself because when she "was still too little to braid her own hair," her own mother died and thus left her bereft of the semiotics of "silk and *artisela*, of cotton and ikat-dyed secrets" (Cisneros 2003, 94) also provides an example of the rhetoric of exchanges and values that characterize Celaya's linguistic and rhetorical habits. On another level, by studying the mestizo caramelo rebozo's secret "language of knots," as she herself puts it, Celaya also hopes to interpret the "whole mystery" of what Karl Marx (1976, 139) called the "form of value" hidden in the exchange of one object for another. Celaya's analysis of the caramelo rebozo's value drives the exploration of "metaphoric identification" into fresh complexities. Part of the mystery for Celaya consists in trying to fathom what the caramelo rebozo could possibly have in common with objects like the "umbrellas or parasols"; the rebozo as a "basket when going to the market"; the rebozo as a "cradle" of culture and a "flag" for dissident groups that it conjures up for characters such as Inocencio and Lala. Here, too, Celaya's prescient analysis remains in the realm of metaphor—the identification of two distinct objects with one another. Is there a primal "metaphorical violence" in seeing two distinct commodities as the same?[26]

Still another important postcolonial and transnational way to see the caramelo rebozo's "metaphorical identity" and its mysterious, hidden foundation of value is to materialize the caramelo rebozo—as Soledad and Celaya do throughout the novel—as itself a tactile, decolonial text of métissage, a repository of memory, of colonial semiosis, and Americanity, like the Andean Inca *quipu*. For example, at the end of chapter 21, "So Begin for Your Good Understanding and My Poor Telling," Cisneros suggests this decolonial reading herself in a fascinating scholarly footnote in which she meticulously traces the roots and routes of the rebozo's planetary beginnings: "The *rebozo* was born in Mexico, but like all *mestizos*, it came from everywhere. It evolved from the cloths Indian women used to carry their babies, borrowed its knotted fringe from Spanish shawls, and was influenced by the silk embroideries from the imperial courts of China exported to Manila, then Acapulco via Spanish galleons. . . . The quintessential Mexican rebozo *is the rebozo de bolita*, whose spotted design imitates a snakeskin, an animal venerated by the Indians in pre-Columbian times" (Cisneros 2003, 96, fn.). What Cisneros almost forgets to write in the footnote is that the Amerindians in pre-Columbian times who wove their rebozos and their related Andean quipus to produce a different writing system and sign carriers did not go unnoticed by their Spanish conquerors. As Walter Mignolo (1995, 83) suggests, "The *quipu* certainly did not go unnoticed among those who were in Peru observing Amerindian cultures during the first century of the conquest." One Spanish renaissance commentator, José de Acosta—like Cisneros's worldly footnote about the pre-Columbian Mexican rebozo —even compared in his *Historia natural y moral de las Indias* (1590, 285) the Peruvian quipu (as a writing and as a recordkeeping system) to those of China and Mexico: "The Indians of Peru, before the Spaniards came, had no sort of writing, not letters nor characters nor ciphers nor figures, like those of China or Mexico; but in spite of this they conserved no less the memory of ancient lore, nor did they any less account of all their affairs of peace, war, and government."

The Andean quipu—resembling the tactile Mexican rebozo de bolita Cisneros describes in *Caramelo or Puro Cuento*—literally is a textile in which a bunch of knotted strings of different colors have semiotic meaning. Acosta (1590, 285) defined the Andean quipus as "a kind of record keeping or register made out of sets of branches in which a diversity of knots and a diversity of color [strings] mean different things." What should attract us to the Andean quipu and Mexican rebozo is not only their aesthetic appearance but also what the Incas, and what Soledad, Celaya's Mexican grandmother, did with them. Could their greater and lesser bundle of knots and fringes be arranged in different ways to draw forth a multitude of laws, rituals, and words of governmentality? My point is that Cisneros is asking us to consider the rebozo's pre-Columbian tactile aspect—like the Andean quipu's tactile aspect—for in the process of organizing and weaving strings and silk, the rebozo maker might have produced meaning and recorded memory.[27] But Soledad (the Awful Grandmother) and her granddaughter Celaya can only "chew on the fringes" of the caramelo rebozo. "Oh, if only [Soledad's] mother was alive," Cisneros writes. Could she "have told her how to speak with her *rebozos*?" Alas, no one is left who can instruct Soledad's daughters when she is dead and her body is wrapped in her rebozos to make sure that "it's the blue one on top, the black one beneath, because that's how it's done, my girl." But *Caramelo or Puro Cuento* continually asks the question of colonial semiosis, "Who was there to interpret the language of the *rebozo* to Soledad?" (Cisneros 2003, 105).

Through a process that rhetoricians term "metastasis," Celaya, throughout *Caramelo or Puro Cuento*, is able to bypass her grandmother's Mexican authority unproblematically from the literal statements about the family rebozo's "secrets" as a mother tongue of sorts to the figural notion of the caramelo rebozo as a transnational tongue (*lengua* and *idioma*) of the nueva mestiza's soul. This is the process by which Cisneros's novel operates.

Thus, when the Awful Grandmother, Soledad's own mother, Guillermina, suddenly dies, Celaya notes how her great-grandmother left "behind an unfinished Mexican *rebozo*, the design so complex no other woman was able to finish it without undoing the threads and starting over." One poor woman tries to finish the weaving, only to give up, sighing, "I'm sorry, I tried, but I can't. Just to do a few inches nearly cost me my eyesight." Soledad also fails to finish weaving the caramelo rebozo, allowing the granddaughter from Greater Mexico's North to quip, "Unfinished, like her life." Right in the middle of the novel, Cisneros's story about Soledad and Celaya seems undone, too, its narrative "fringes" hanging "like mermaid's hair" (94). Worse, the already begun caramelo rebozo, with its "astonishing fringe work resembling a cascade of fireworks on a field of sunflowers," has started to lose its use value "because of the unfinished *rapacejo*" (Cisneros 2003, 94). Almost forgotten and lost, Soledad's "plaything," the caramelo rebozo, is taken over by Celaya and her family in Greater Mexico.

At issue in *Caramelo or Puro Cuento*, as these discussions about the use value and symbolic capital of the grandmothers' Mexican caramelo rebozo thematize, is the series of questions of what constitutes a "pure" and "proper" "language of knots and rosettes." Is the language of the rebozo a negation of mainline literary figural language? And if a proper "language of knots" does exist, then who possesses it in *Caramelo or Puro Cuento*?[28] Soledad's mother leaves Celaya unschooled in the secret language of the Mexican rebozo; her father, Ambrosio, we learn in the long, meandering middle sections of the novel, also abandons poor Soledad by "tying the knot with the baker's widow" and thus leaving Soledad to make do in her "childhood without a childhood" (Cisneros 2003, 94–95). The Mexican rebozo's "black dye" somehow seeped into Soledad's father's unloving heart, for how else could Celaya explain "his dark ways"? Soledad had to grapple with "only the soft fringe of the unfinished shawl," and Soledad's fingers took "to combing this, plaiting, unplaiting, plaiting over and over, the language of the nervous hands—Stop that her [awful] stepmother would shout, but her hands never quit" (Cisneros 2003, 94–95). Thus does Soledad transform from a potential "weaver" of rebozos into "thirty-three kilos of grief" when Ambrosio Reyes gives her away to his cousin in Mexico City.

If Soledad loses the unquestioning faith of the Reyes' clans in the conventions of the language of caramelo rebozos, after her death she returns—an *alma en pena* (soul in pain)—to demand and sometime receive from her granddaughter Celaya unequivocal precision in the proper language of rebozos. Thus, when Celaya ignores the sentimental "dark, black dye" of the rebozo that seeped into Ambrosio, the course of Cisneros's narrative is sidetracked and becomes the competing tale of Soledad's and Celaya's search for an equivocal foundation for the telling of how Soledad became the "Awful Grandmother"; the search for a primary *logos* that might order Celaya's speech acts and allow the narrative of *Caramelo or Puro Cuento* to proceed naturally toward its proper conclusion. In "So Here My History Begins for Your Good Understanding and My Poor Telling," for example, after Celaya tells of how poor Soledad was unable to perfect her mother's art of "dividing the silk strands, of braiding . . . them into fastidious arcs, stars, diamonds, . . . as her own mother had learned it," Soledad's ghost retorts by saying, "*Puro cuento*. What a *mitotera* you are, [Celaya]" (Cisneros 2003, 93). In alluding to the possibility of entering into her historia with the possibility of Celaya's "puro cuento" of errors, Soledad's ghost contests the very transnational story we are being told by Celaya.

The constant interruption of the numerous interpolated tales of the "dark" actions of Soledad, the Awful Grandmother, offers another important aspect of Cisneros's narrative process of displacement, traveling cultures, and digression. Soledad's unfinished story of her "childhood without a childhood," like the unfinished Mexican rebozo itself, could well serve as an emblematic instance of the novel's entire pattern or design. To forestall the Awful Grandmother's ghost from another rush into "black inked" disaster, Celaya begins to tell Soledad's story, which requires the listeners to be familiar with Mexican melodramas and telenovelas: "So this part of the story if it were a *fotonovela* or *telenovela* could be called *Solamente Soledad* or *Solo en el mundo*" (Cisneros 2003, 95). When Soledad, the Awful Grandmother, continues to interrupt Celaya's digressive and low-brow narration of her life history as a telenovela—and, as a result, fails to keep an accurate account of her grandmother's story of loss, mourning, and melancholia—Celaya decides to keep the dialogical narrative going for the next one hundred or so pages. In other words, Celaya decides to tell her own crafted exemplary story—a story both firmly rooted, like the Mexican rebozo, in folk traditions of the *cuento sin fin* (tale without end) and as a post-contemporary, mass-mediated telenovela, with footnotes and *infamia*. If Soledad's interruptions of Celaya's stories displace the issue of the narrative from its thematic to its linguistic and generic concerns and delay the expression of the story's concluding terms, then, in the larger structural level of the novel as whole, the interpolated tales of *Caramelo or Puro Cuento* also divert the narrative from its apparent goal—namely, telling us the story of Soledad's descent into transnational melancholia and awfulness.

Between the beginning and the end of narration in *Caramelo or Puro Cuento*—the eighty-six chapters, with an extra *"pilón* (as a bonus gift)," to boot—lies the narrative *reticentia*, the rhetorical figure that interrupts, suspends, and braids and twists meaning aside. This rhetorical design (like the unfinished caramelo rebozo on which the novel is modeled and for which it is named) brings the entire narrative structure of Cisneros's novel closely in line with the structure of the interrupting sentences of Soledad, the Awful Grandmother. The dynamics of storytelling usually impel a narrative toward its conclusion. *Caramelo or Puro Cuento*, however, continually sets up delays, stoppages, and deviations in the flow of Celaya's discourse in an attempt to keep her story open, to delay the subject from predicating a definitive and restrictive end to the text's plurality, dialogism, and diversality. By deferring the end of the narration, Cisneros and her various narrators (especially Celaya and Soledad) dramatize the inability of any one of the narrators to tell the whole story of Greater Mexico and the Reyes family. Any movement toward such a completion is always displaced onto yet another track or genre in search of an authoritative end. Thus, on the level of individual cuentos, and even of the novel as a whole, the processes of displacement and deferral seem to form the essential characteristics of *Caramelo or Puro Cuento*'s meaning.

This "deferral" of *Caramelo or Puro Cuento*'s narrative is perhaps a clue to the most significant differences between Celaya and Soledad

Reyes. Soledad's speech acts continually reflect her will to structure, to provide definitive endings and mainline, highbrow, dependable meanings for events in the world.[29] "Nonsense," she insists to Celaya. "It wasn't like that at all. It was like this" (Cisneros 2003, 97). Instead of the Mexican and Venezuelan melodramas and telenovelas on which Celaya loves to model her narrative, Soledad prefers stories with marked allusions to Western modernist writers, such as Virginia Woolf: "Even with all those empty bedrooms, [she] found herself without a real room of her own" (Cisneros 2003, 114). In contrast, Celaya's speech acts present a will to unstructured high-art definitions and racialized structures of feeling. Celaya prefers the odds and ends of the unfinished caramelo rebozo—from its pre-Columbian tactile origins to its post-contemporary knotty endings. Soledad reacts quickly to interrupt what she considers misuses of popular and mass-mediated Mexican culture; Celaya, however, wants to embroider Soledad's life history as iconic Mexican filmic melodrama. "If this were a movie from Mexico's Golden Age of cinema," she tells Soledad's ghost, "it would be black-and-white and no doubt a musical" (Cisneros 2003, 98). Whereas Soledad's ghost abuses "what really happened," Celaya abuses "what truly happened." In both cases, the attempted expression of meaning is displaced.

In the last part of *Caramelo or Puro Cuento*, Soledad's favorite son, Inocencio, teaches Celaya to displace meaning at the level of figuration. The most fascinating instances of Inocencio's displacement of meaning occur in chapter 58, "Cielito Lindo," where Celaya incorporates her father's nuanced views on the borderlines of cuentos and history. "Tell me more *cuentos* of your life, Father," insists Celaya. "But I keep telling you, [Celaya], they're not *cuentos*. Lala, they're true. They're *historias*." "What's the difference between '*un cuento*' and '*una historia*'?," Celaya asks (Cisneros 2003, 246).

Inocencio Reyes's pivotal substitution of the words "true" and "historias" for Celaya's "*cuentos*" is, of course, a continuing interruption of the proper relationship that should hold between a word and its referent. It marks a pivotal instant in *Caramelo or Puro Cuento* of what will become a constant process of displacement and detour in his statements. From this point forward, Inocencio's language seems to develop sense of its own accord, detached from the object (fictional stories) to which his word is apparently pointed, liberated from the truth that could bring the word "cuentos" into harmony with its referent (history). We might say that Inocencio institutionalizes the latent similarity between stories and histories into the new radical identity that stories are true histories.

On another level, Celaya's question about the difference between cuentos and truth illustrates the tension between grammar and rhetoric in *Caramelo or Puro Cuento*. Asked by Celaya whether his cuentos are true, Inocencio might well have responded with a rhetorical question in which the figure is conveyed directly by a syntactical device. He might have answered Celaya with the question, "What's the difference?" In other words, Inocencio is not interested in asking for difference; instead, he means something like, "I don't give a damn what the difference is." The same grammatical pattern engenders—as Paul de Man once argued in a different context—two meanings that are mutually exclusive; the literal meaning asks for the concept (difference) whose existence is denied by the figurative meaning.[30]

The next major instance of this process of metaphoric displacement concerns Celaya's uses and abuses of what she learns from her grandfather is the critical difference between "lies" and what he calls "healthy lies." When the Awful Grandmother first chastises the young Chicana Celaya for not eating her rich chocolate *mole*, made with "a recipe as old as the Aztecs/Mexicas" (Cisneros 2003, 55) and then accuses her of being an inauthentic Mexican from Greater Mexico, Chicago, and forces her to remain at the table until she has finished eating an entire plate of the spicy Mexica food, the Little Grandfather rescues Celaya this way:

> What a silly you are, Lala! No need to cry because of a plate of *mole*. Come now, niña.
>
> But the Grandmother said. . . .
>
> Never mind what she said. Do you think she's the boss around here? Watch what I'm going to do. Oralia!
>
> Sí, señor.
>
> Give this to the neighbor's dog. And if my wife asks, say the child ate it. You see how easy that was?
>
> But it's a lie.
>
> Not a lie. A healthy lie. Which sometimes we have to tell so there won't be trouble. (Cisneros 2003, 56–57).

This passage describes a rather pragmatic and progressive transformation of perception. Celaya is given a lesson by the Reyes's patriarch on the critical difference between truth and lies.

Some thirty chapters later, the issue of "healthy lies" seems nearly too settled for Celaya. When the Awful Grandmother's ghost again interrupts her *historia* and admonishes her for telling "lies, lies. Nothing but lies from beginning to end," Celaya responds by reminding the ghost, "You don't realize what a tangled mess you've given me." Almost anticipating the terms of her own theory of the Chicana novel, Celaya insists, "They're not lies, they're healthy lies. So as to fill in the gaps" (Cisneros 2003, 188). In other words, like Roland Barthes before her, Celaya is not so much interested in, say, the turning points that make up the plot of *Caramelo or Puro Cuento*. Rather, she is fascinated with the *historias'* "fillers,"[31] the healthy lies, the will to *poesis*, fabrication, dissimulation, *infamia*, and exaggeration that make up the great bulk of the novel's chapters.

The readings described within the novel and the beginning instance that defines Celaya's writing as a kind of complex ethnic Mexican rebozo in the novel's disclaimer display an attempted process of critical interpretation. If the writing of *Caramelo or Puro Cuento*, like the reading and interpretation of a text or rebozo, involves a paring away of supplementary elements that get in the way of critical understanding, one must read the sense of mimesis in this text otherwise. At almost every point that the somersaulting and twisting narrative attempts to claim authority by reference to the truth of history (family history), the text also names the contradictory and negative moments of poetic fabrication, like the unfinished Mexican caramelo rebozo. For Celaya the feminist anthropoeta, then, the past is not just a temporal category, a valorized and patriarchal category as in, say, the world of the epic (the world of founders). Celaya is interested in the very distinctions between *historias/puros cuentos* (stories) and historical discourse, for they are distributed, as Émile Benveniste (1966, 238) put the distinction between *historia* and history as tenses "in two distinct and complementary systems [that] are the manifestations of two different planes of enunciation."

The history of *Caramelo or Puro Cuento*, then, can be reduced to a confrontation, a transnational *contestación* (contestation) of incongruent meanings and enunciations: puros cuentos–history, novel–

telenovela, proper–improper, ideal–real, and literal–figurative. At the same time, however, it is nearly impossible to define at any one instance in the novel any of these polarities and dyads in the precise terms of truth or error. Each element of the polarity shares in truth and error and thus eliminates its relationship to its opposite as a polarity. (Thus, in part 2, the Awful Grandmother's ghost seems to go on endlessly in a string of passages in which she affirms and denies the truth of Celaya's stories.) Whenever *Caramelo or Puro Cuento* is described in terms of the truthful expression of any of these polarities, it is always possible to point to the presence of the opposite inextricably tied to it, thus deconstructing its truth value. Does *Caramelo or Puro Cuento*'s narrative allegorize its own deconstruction?[32] At every point that the text speaks about history, poetry, the artistry of Mexican rebozos and telenovelas, imitation, value, and desire, is something else metaphorically signified? The signified concept is the flowing chain of the narrators' language and their metaphoric words.

The final elegy in which Celaya's anthropoeta pen acquires voice to praise the immigrant and transnational world of her father, Inocencio Reyes, also resurrects the system that defines the father as the "trace," the "graphism," the "residue," and archive of the conversion of Mexicans into Americans. If Inocencio's whole existence, first in Greater Mexico's Chicago and then in San Antonio, has been nothing but an English language that, according to Celaya, "has never been good," for when he is nervous, it seems to come out like a rebozo, all "folded and creased," worse than in those old grammar books, the "*Inglés Sin Stress* home course in English," when he first came to the United States, in chapter 78, "Someday My Prince Popocatépetl Will Come," Inocencio is first assimilated, translated, and transculturated into the very "papers" that make up the text (Cisneros 2003, 208, 375). This final metastasis is also like the pun in the novel's title: *Caramelo or Puro Cuento*, a space as a repository of contradictory *historias*, layers of dissimulation ("healthy lies"), and spheres of activities.

After "La Migra" (the INS) goes to Inocencio's upholstery shop on Nogalitos Street in San Antonio and accuses him of hiring so-called illegal aliens, he tells Celaya and the family, in his broken and folded English–Spanglish, that La Migra is demanding "proof that I'm a citizen." Hilariously, the Reyes clan turns the poor barrio house upside down, helping the distraught and tongue-tied Inocencio find the shoe box that contains Soledad's unfinished caramelo rebozo, as well his military discharge and U.S. citizenship papers. Celaya writes about how desperate her father became: "We find drawers stuffed with old bills, letters, class photos, drapery rings, birthday cards, food coupons, rubber bands, . . . but no shoebox" (Cisneros 2003, 375). Although Inocencio's upholstery shop is well organized, "with every tool, every bolt of fabric, every box of tacks in place, a scrap is in place" but at home, Celaya reports, "Mother's chaos rules" (Cisneros 2003, 375).

Almost by accident, the shoebox—Inocencio's barrio archive—turns up. But it is not enough that the box (the archive) is found. All of the Reyes family climb into Inocencio's van and accompany him to the upholstery shop, where the INS agents have promised to meet him after lunch. When the agents drive up in their infamous green vans, Inocencio confronts them in his broken, colonially wounded English. "Now you see. I *no lie*, Father says, waving his papers" (Cisneros 2003, 376; emphasis added). One of the papers is, in fact, a letter dated November 23, 1949, declaring that Inocencio has been "honorably discharged from the U.S. Armed Forces" after fighting against Europe's fascists in the Second World War. The second paper archived in the shoebox is a letter from the White House signed by the anticommunist President Harry Truman that says, "To you who answered the call of your country and served in its Armed Forces to bring about the total defeat of the enemy, I extend the heartfelt thanks of a grateful Nation. . . . Because you demonstrated the fortitude, resourcefulness and calm judgment necessary to carry out that task, we now look to you for leadership and example in further exalting our country in peace" (Cisneros 2003, 377). After listening to their commander-in-chief's lionizing of Inocencio, the INS agents shrug and mumble apologies. Inocencio can respond only in his broken, melancholy Spanglish: "For you I serving this country. For what, eh? Son of a mother . . . Make me sick!" (Cisneros 2003, 377). *Caramelo or Puro Cuento* thus moves from a language of imitation and desire to a transnational and decolonial language of broken wounds, metaphors, and melancholic loss.

Inocencio's shoebox of identity papers, however, is also the archival record and fever of the conversion and transculturation of ethnicity to paper that is required when he crosses the U.S.-Mexican border and, through U.S. military service against European fascism, incorporates an identity of legal citizenship in the United States. Contemplating the contents of the shoebox after the family returns home to find the house a mess, with drawers open, couch cushions on the floor, and, worse, Zoila's dinner "burnt and stinking," Inocencio opens a domino box stuffed with Celaya's childhood braids and Soledad's "toffee-striped caramelo rebozo, which he wraps around himself like a flag" (Cisneros 2003, 378). Inocencio's conversion from Greater Mexican infamy—from illegal Mexican to what Cisneros wryly calls ethnic "Merican"—can never be complete, and like the caramelo rebozo he wraps around himself "like a flag," it becomes an integral part of the post-contemporary present. The paper archive, like the rebozo that is passed down through the Reyes family, is figured finally by Celaya as the supplementary "trace" of early migratory (immigrant) life, an "outernational" trace that paradoxically stands in for a loss of history yet simultaneously marks the figurations of Greater Mexico—a Mexican community *de adentro* (from within) that commences with the investment through puros cuentos and memory, in that melancholic loss.

Like the U.S.-Mexican border-crossing experiences represented in *Caramelo or Puro Cuento*, the border-crossing puros cuentos and histories are in the last instance recalcitrant and liminal spaces that cannot be totally assimilated or translated. We might even say that *Caramelo or Puro Cuento* goes on to question our most basic assumptions about origins and their ends. Cisneros permits the introduction of a critical study of cuentos and discourse where space and rhetoric are entwined and where rhetoric depends on space. Can space act on style, producing a double enunciation (toward the novel and the telenovela)? Near the U.S.-Mexican borderlands, does figurality go up and across? Geography indeed acts on style in transnational novels about Greater Mexico such as Cisneros's *Caramelo or Puro Cuento*.

I began this chapter by wondering why the bestselling transnational novels written in English by Sandra Cisneros were not better known in the iconic literary establishments of the United States. Why are writers like Cisneros not seen as pillars of great critical U.S. literature? As I have shown in this chapter, Cisneros's novels about Greater Mexico have stronger ties to the mass-mediated telenovelas and racial melodrama tradition of the Global South (especially Mexico and Latin America) than to Euro-American realist novels, not only because of the heritage of internal colonialism and the coloniality of power that is part and parcel of Americanity, but ultimately because of the ways the writers of telenovela screenplays represent the primal scene of what Cisneros (2003, 409) has called "la Divina Providencia" who emplot the mass-mediated stories "with more plot twists and somersaults than anyone would ever think believable" because the Global South's "histories" confirm it. Cisneros raises the issue in *Caramelo or Puro Cuento* of how one specific immigrant ethnic Mexico community in Greater Mexico has seen its decolonial situation reflected in the mass-mediated works of Spanish language telenovelistas, as well as in that of the magical urban realists Jorge Luis Borges and Gabriel García Marquez, all writing on the cusp of interculturality and transmodernity. To conclude, I raise the much broader issue of the place of "Americanity" in our hemisphere and our planet. To get to the heart of the matter in the space of an appendix, I find that there is no better approach than to end with a dialogical conversation I had with an interlocutor, Mónica González García, from Americanity's South.

On the Borderlands of U.S. Empire:
The Limitations of Geography, Ideology,
and Disciplinarity

Interview by Mónica González García

Mónica González García is pleased to have had the opportunity to converse with Saldívar, a scholar whose trajectory in Chicano/a and Latino/a studies and literature was honored by the Modern Languages Association (MLA) in 2005. The conversation intends to encompass the American map in its entirety, embracing a variety of topics, such as his first book, *The Dialectics of Our America* (1991), already one of the formative texts in a fresh field called comparative American studies; the boundaries of imperial history; the role of Cuba's Casa de las Américas in modifying the geopolitics of knowledge; the recent manifestations of U.S. immigration law; and the drama *Fukú Americanus* (2009), based on the Pulitzer Prize–winning novel *The Brief Wondrous Life of Oscar Wao* (2007), by Junot Díaz. We hope that this interview will open the space for scholars, and especially graduate students, to continue thinking about the subaltern and hegemonic remappings of the idea of América.

"Our América" and the América That Is Not Ours

Mónica González García: Your first book, *The Dialectics of Our America* (1991), advances a crucial critique intended to remap the limits of American studies, a task that involved questioning additional boundary disciplines such as Latin American literature and Chicano/a studies. Among other assertions, your book interrogates the notion of "Our América" because you say it is a cultural system that traditionally has been articulated in relation only to itself and Europe. Furthermore, you state that it is necessary to rethink the term "América" to reach what you name a trans-geographic notion of the American culture. In your perspective, what are the benefits of reformulating the idea of América as a trans-geographic notion? In this context, why do you use the term "Our América" and not, say, "Latin America"?

José David Saldívar: Some twenty years ago, I completed the manuscript of *The Dialectics of Our America* and sent it to Duke University Press for review and publication. I did not know at the time that the book would have a scholarly audience both inside and outside the United States (in Cuba, Mexico, and elsewhere in Latin America, as well as in the European Union), as it has had; nor did I know that it would be cited as one of the early texts in what today is called the new comparative American studies. I was trying to move the mainline institution of American studies outside the United States, the América that is not (only) ours, and more in the direction of a fully globalized study of the Américas—that is, within a Wallersteinian world-system scale and unit of analysis. Today, I would have added the Peruvian historical sociologist Aníbal Quijano's analytical paradigm of the *patrón de poder* (coloniality of power) and Walter Mignolo's riffs on border gnosis to the book's theoretical mix.

As I wrote *The Dialectics of Our America*, I understood myself to be in an embattled relation to certain mainline area studies in the U.S. academy (especially our homemade exceptionalist American studies and some varieties of Latinamericanism in U.S. universities), even as I understood my text to be part of a more nuanced comparative American studies that was developing in the literary and critical work of, among others, Roberto Fernández Retamar, Gustavo Pérez-Firmat, Doris Sommer, and Vera Kutzinski. With its allusions to the history of the study of Hegelian–Marxist dialectic (and immanent critique) and the Cuban poet José Martí's anticolonial criticism, the title and the text pointed to a tradition of critique that sought to explicate the vocabulary of the trans-American (trans)modernities of thought to which it belonged—moving historically from Martí's Latinamericanist discourses framed by the long 1898 in "Nuestra América" to a newer, more scandalous, and yet unknown Cuban Marxist discourse in the U.S. academy theorized by Che Guevara and Fernández Retamar, and away from mainline American studies literary and cultural criticism. In the book's ending, I even baptized this dialectical Cuban–Caribbean political and cultural critique the "School of Calibán" in honor of Retamar's "Calibán," Aimé Césaire's *A Tempest*, and Houston Baker Jr.'s "Calibán's Triple Play," which I then felt, as a minoritized Chicano subject, to be an emerging part of.

Of course, I believe there remains today a warrant in comparative American studies for a more rigorous and continued trans-American critique—what I am proposing here as trans-Americanity—as well as what other trans-American scholars are critically producing in their work. For instance, Anna Brickhouse's *Transamerican Literary Relations and the Nineteenth Century* (2004) moves in new, exciting outernationalist directions by telling us about a history—the so-called American Renaissance— in which mainline American literature written by Nathaniel Hawthorne, James Fenimore Cooper, William Cullen Byrant, and Edgar Allan Poe was facilitated by "intertextual" exchanges across linguistic and political borders in the American hemisphere. Brickhouse begins by telling us about the Congress of Panama of 1826—the first inter-American conference to take place in the hemisphere—and ends in the 1850s with the failed attempts by the United States to incorporate Mexico and Nicaragua into its territory. One of the most powerful chapters of Brickhouse's text grapples with Hawthorne's "Rappaccini's Daughter" and Frances Calderón de la Barca's travel writing, *Life in Mexico*, an autoethnographic text that comments on the hemisphere's debates over coloniality, race, slavery, and U.S. political designs on Mexico. Brickhouse (2004, 13) wonderfully recovers what she calls the "Mexican genealogy" of Hawthorne's short story—both in its intertextual appropriations from *Life in Mexico* and in its post-contemporary afterlife in Octavio Paz's drama *La hija de Rappaccini* (1990 [1956]), a work that provides the spatial and political implications of Hawthorne's reading of Calderón's text. In the chapter's coda, Brickhouse turns to the feminist Gloria Anzaldúa's *Borderlands/La Frontera* to measure both Hawthorne's and Paz's hemispheric racial absolutisms in their representations of La Chingada–Malinche, a Mexica woman who served as Cortés's translator.

Likewise, Kirsten Silva Gruesz's *Ambassadors of Culture* aims to provide readers with a new, comparative framework for the study of a trans-American literary culture, what she calls "a communion between the Anglophone and Hispanophone worlds" (2002, 4). Throughout the text, Gruesz stretches "the silhouette of U.S. identity—in both its spatial and temporal dimensions" (2002, 4)—out of recognizable shape to explore a group of Anglo-American, Latin American, and U.S. Latino/a writers and intellectuals. The nationalist (ethnically absolutist) framework of traditional American literary studies is subjected here to an extensive critique. It is counterpoised to Gruesz's notion of a "'borderlands'" cultural history—a concept that frames the Anglophone, Hispanophone, and Latino/a experience in the United States in a different and excitingly original way. As Gruesz emphasizes, *Ambassadors of Culture* explores the almost "forgotten history of travels and translations" between U.S. and Latin American writers. More significantly, she makes a strong case for examining how the "presence of Spanish-language literary productions in the U.S. borderlands" from, say, 1823 to 1880, shapes and justifies the formation of a new inter-American literary tradition and canon where before none had been recognized (Gruesz 2002, 4).

I especially liked the way Gruesz looks at writers from the Global South (José Maria Heredia, Martí, Miguel Terube Tolón, Rafael Pombo, Isabel Prieto, among others) who are exiles, refugees, and expatriates in urban centers like New York, San Francisco, and New Orleans. Conversely, she also does a superb job in calling attention to canonical and minoritized writers from the North (Henry Wadsworth Longfellow,

Bryant, Maria Gowen Brooks, and William Henry Hulbert) who, in their imaginative works and essays, thematized their particular interest in the Caribbean and Latin American South. By rigorously examining these early-nineteenth-century inter-American roots and routes, she helps us "imagine a new form of cultural history" of the Américas, a new cultural and literary history that questions "the imperial conflation of the United States with America" (Gruesz 2002, 4). Thus envisaged, Gruesz's *Ambassadors of Culture* (like Brickhouse's book) is groundbreaking work.

In Gruesz's hands, Longfellow, for example, should be remembered and reread not only because he is the sole canonical white male poet to have been dropped from mainline American literary anthologies and canon, but because he was also one of the first trans-American ambassadors of culture. He was "an avid consumer and (re)-producer of the Hispanic cultural tradition" who translated Cervantes's *Novelas ejemplares* and addressed some of the most significant issues of his day in poems such as "Evangeline"—the ethics of imperial acquisition in the Américas, "the displacement of pastoral communities in the course of empire," and the "compatibility of Catholic and Protestant ways of life" (Gruesz 2002, 78, 99). Gruesz's Longfellow, in short, becomes one of the first and most important cultural mediators between the Anglophone and Hispanophone worlds.

Gruesz argues persuasively that Walt Whitman's literary career was significantly marked by his travels to polyglot New Orleans ("a Caribbean city") in 1848. While the New Orleans period "did not suddenly convert Whitman into a radically new writer," it offered him what Gruesz (2002, 128) describes as "substitute for the foreign travels he was never able to experience, and provided the leisure and the opportunity not only to play the flaneur . . . but to practice the work of rearranging random facts" into material pages that "contained multitudes." More significantly, New Orleans, Gruesz (2002, 122) emphasizes, put Whitman "in close proximity to a polyglot city, as close as he would ever come to Spanish America."

I should also mention one other aspect of Gruesz's exemplary text. In *Ambassadors of Culture* she demonstrates how former Mexican and Spanish American citizens became "local ambassadors of culture" through their roles as editors of Spanish-language newspapers and journals in the United States. As she eloquently puts it, "The translation practices of these new participants in the national compact ought to be revealing because of their positioning as marginal subjects within this representational economy" (Gruez 2002, 100). By studying the imaginative writing and translation practices in "borderlands periodicals" such as *El Clamor Público* (Los Angeles) and *El Bejareno* and *El Ranchero* (San Antonio), and by examining premier cultural organs such as *El Mundo Nuevo* (New York), Gruesz (2002, 100–107, 176–204) demonstrates how "print communities" enabled diverse "political affiliations" during the nineteenth century. For Gruesz, "recovered texts" from Spanish-language newspapers allow us to read trans-American writing as both cosmopolitan and local expressions.

So, yes, the late-nineteenth-century ideas of Martí's "Nuestra América" —the "América that is [not only] ours" and "European America" that are, in hindsight, like two sides of the same worn-out coin—have to be severely deconstructed and reconstructed, with the unit of our analysis, which, as Brickhouse and Gruesz demonstrate, is no longer the nation-state's phantasmatics. Fernández Retamar, too, had it exactly right in the 1960s when he theorized Martí's writings in his (Third) World. In the early 1990s, I was arguing that we needed to use the unit of analysis of the North Atlantic Treaty Organization and the state fantasies of the Cold War. Did the Cold War supply us with a horizon of intelligibility for an understanding of trans-American events? Today, Mónica, as you know from having grown up in the face of the totalitarian shadow of Augusto Pinochet and neoliberal Chile, the United States of America belongs—if I can put it this way—through its new imperialism to the whole world. To answer the last part of your question first, let me just say that I was using Martí's anticolonialist notion of "Nuestra América" of 1891 as shorthand for what I felt as a Chicano critic to be Martí's magisterial contribution to the debates on the formation of Latinamericanist ideology. Given that Martí had conceptualized his critique of the cultures of U.S. imperialism in exile from Cuba and, simultaneously, as the political founder of the Cuban Revolutionary Party from within the diasporic spaces of the modernized Puerto Rican barrioscapes of New York City—as Julio Ramos taught us in his great *Desencuentros de la modernidad en América Latina* (1989), I had always felt that Martí's comparative critiques of imperial América in the essays and chronicles of his *Escenas norteamericanas* (North American Scenes) were "right on" and indispensable for any beginning attempt to theorize a new, critical reading of América. But as I also noted in my essay "Las fronteras de Nuestra América," a text superbly translated into Spanish and published in the *Revista Casa de las Américas* (1996), I often wonder why Martí's critical readings of "Our América" and the "América that is not ours" stopped, territorially, so prematurely and abruptly at the national borders between the Global North and the Global South. Why did he accept the political and cultural borders of the Treaty of Guadalupe Hidalgo of 1848, which had ended a U.S. imperial war, this time with Mexico? What if Martí had thought of the borderlands of Greater Mexico—that is, both sides of the Rio Grande culturally going back to 1749, when parts of the U.S.-Mexican border were first colonized by Spain? Now, in having said this, I do not wish to be misunderstood: in the U.S. academy today, we desperately need to read Martí's *North American Scenes* to understand how his fifteen-year stay in the Global North turned into an occasion to record his critique of an exceptionalist Puritan and European America and its totalitarian dialectic of the American Enlightenment. That is, I would much rather keep on teaching and reading Martí's magisterial traveling theory (collected by Cuban editors in twenty-six volumes) than, say, the French aristocratic writer Alexis de Tocqueville's *Democracy in America*. Why U.S. historians and literary critics continue to privilege the French traveler's monarchist view and not the Cuban's critique of American democracy is something we should continue to ponder. Why do American intellectuals privilege French *Latinidad* (Latinity) in our political culture over, say, *Cubanidad*? Why have mainline Americanists sided with Tocqueville's search in the United States for a "limited" democracy that would facilitate what he fantasized as a restoration of French democracy? In his rich book *The New American Exceptionalism* (2009a, 148), Donald Pease suggests that Tocqueville studied U.S. democracy to discover the metalanguage and laws at work within a democracy that he found "lacking a revolutionary dimension."

When I was in Cuba at the invitation of the Cuban government and its cultural institution Casa de las Américas in 1997, Fernández Retamar and I had the great occasion to begin discussing some of these questions of American exceptionalism as we walked around Havana, and we both attempted to imagine a newer and, yes, more utopian possible inter-American space that Martí's "Nuestra América" had inaugurated in 1891 and that we could still use today. Of course, in my informal conversations with Fernández Retamar I mainly listened to him speak passionately and eloquently about Cuba's War of 1898 as a *desastre*, about the Cuban Revolution, about Martí in his (Third) World, about Che and his apprenticeship with the long 1960s, and about the terrible U.S. blockade we felt so painfully all around us, like an imperial wound. But as you note in your question, it has been awfully hard for anyone (the enormous efforts of the Casa de las Américas notwithstanding) to get around my government's unethical, mindless, and gross blockade of Cuba since 1959. To complete answering your question, then, I was using the scale of the modern world-system theory to understand what the Américas held politically and culturally in common. This, in the early 1990s, was the best way to go. Last, I was trying to answer a basic research question in that first text: Do the Américas have a common literature? It is a question I am still grappling with today in some of my work.

González García: The intellectual production of Cuba has an important place in your critique. Regarding this tradition, you analyze the critical work of José Martí and Roberto Fernández Retamar because, as you explain, both of them seek to establish a conversation between "Our América" and "North European" (Anglo) America. In a sense, Martí and Fernández Retamar represent two emblematic moments of a trans-

American interaction characterized by war, intervention, revolution, blockade, polarization, and so on. Do you believe it is possible to found a new literary, cultural, and critical "Americanism" that can deconstruct this traditional dynamics based on two mutually exclusive paradigms? In other words, is there any alternative in America to the Caliban-versus-Prospero model of interrelations?

Saldívar: Yes, you are absolutely right about those very powerful emblematic trans-American interactions of cultural critique inaugurated by Martí and continued by Fernández Retamar. In my work, I was most concerned at the time to criticize the pervasive Anglophone assumptions in post-contemporary American literary and cultural criticism. I sought to criticize those North American nationalist views of the Américas that made all kinds of presumptions about the limits of America and that restricted the meaning and romance of America to its well-known slogan of itself as "E pluribus unum (Out of the many, one)." I felt as a young Chicano (colonial and imperial) subject that there was way too much emphasis in the U.S. academy and culture at large on the hegemonic "unum" of this slogan about the horizons of America and not enough critical attention paid to the colonial difference of the "pluribus" in the meaning of America. In the 1990s, at the height of what some right-wing commentators called the "culture wars" in the U.S. academy, I was arguing against any theory of American literature and culture that restricted the meaning of America from within the nationalistic presumptions of its own practices and that therefore set up exclusionary norms within its theorizing about itself, often with racialist and imperialist consequences. By turning, for example, to some of Martí's cultural criticism—especially his essay "Nuestra América" and his stunning essay about the pop-culture "Wild West Show" he saw performed in New York City—we can now see clearly that he was "projecting," in political and psychoanalytic terms, from his melancholic colonial wound in New York City a direct response to what was to become Theodore Roosevelt's War of 1898 (the so-called Splendid Little War). The Wild West Show's painting of U.S. Manifest Destiny was displaced in Martí imagination from the United States to Cuba and therefore relocated in a new external position. The essays, indeed, tell us a lot about U.S. cultures of the spectacle. Therefore, as Martí saw the Wild West Show's tableau of violence right in front of his eyes—the killing of Native American Indians—he also "projected" the killing of Cuban *mambíses* and creoles by Roosevelt, the future U.S. Rough Rider, thus passing from the center to the periphery. By then turning from Martí's projections of 1898 to the Cold War critique of U.S. empire as a way of life in Fernández Retamar's celebrated reading of Martí in "Calibán," which was written almost at the same time that he had been theorizing a new ideological way to "read Che," I was attempting to ground my own emerging cultural criticism of the Américas from an outernational perspective—that is, from the barrioscapes of the U.S. Latino/a communities and from Che's praxis of tricontinentalism and Fernández Retamar's revolutionary Cuba.

Thus, from my first text to my most recent work, I continue to push in my comparative American studies work for an outernationalist study of American literatures, cultures, and ideologies. That is to say, I am not today, as a professor of comparative literature at Stanford, very interested in any new, New Historicist readings of Shakespeare's *The Tempest* that merely rewrite the political allegories of Ariel, Caliban, Miranda, Sycorax, and Prospero without addressing the cultures of the new imperialism of the United States. (As a parenthetical aside, this does not mean, however, that the New Historicist criticism by, say, my former Berkeley colleague Stephen Greenblatt is not still enlightening us, for in his rich biography of Shakespeare, *Will in the World: How Shakespeare Became Shakespeare* [2004], he suggests that before W. E. B. Du Bois and Ralph Waldo Emerson, Shakespeare's Protestant–Catholic family entanglements had allowed him to attain what Du Bois and Emerson had called a "double consciousness." This has many potential implications for readings of the School of Calibán.) So when I teach Fernández Retamar's manifesto "Calibán" in my seminar on the War of 1898, I find that the essay is not "really" about Shakespeare's last play, *The Tempest*, but in fact about Martí's anticolonial criticism and struggle.

González García: Still regarding your first book (and the logic of binary models of interaction), one of the theses you propose has to do with the limitations of the paradigm "center–periphery" because it "cannot entirely account for the hybrid appropriations and resistances that characterize the travel of theories and theorists who migrate between places in our 'First' World and 'Third' World" (Saldívar 1991, xvii). You suggest going beyond that paradigm and exploring hybridity and in-betweenness. In this context, the Chicano writer Rolando Hinojosa, as you argue, would represent that in-betweenness as an author who portrays the culture of contact and conflict developed on the U.S.-Mexican border. You affirm that Hinojosa's Casa de las Américas prize in 1976 for *Klail City y sus alrededores* may be considered a model for a broader literary and cultural American history. It seems that you propose an alliance between "heterodox" American sectors. What is the current status of these conversations between Casa and Chicano/a literature? Has the (Latin American) canon been modified since 1976 due to this conversation? Is there any possibility of broadening these conversations to include some of the "orthodox" American sectors, as well? Or, in other words, do these "orthodox" sectors have any interest in widening, opening, or rethinking their canon?

Saldívar: Yes, I believe that Chicano and Chicana writers such as Rolando Hinojosa, Américo Paredes, Tomás Rivera, Luis Valdéz, Gloria Anzaldúa, John Rechy, Helena Viramontes, Cherríe Moraga, Ana Castillo, and Sandra Cisneros, among others, belong to what many of us in Chicano/a literary and cultural studies are calling the borderlands of American culture—and to the borderlands of Greater Mexico. I will try to put this another way, because some of my comparative work attempts to grapple with what you term "heterodox" and "orthodox" American affiliations and sectors. That is, just as I see William Faulkner, the great Mississippi modernist of the 1930s, writing against President Franklin Delano Roosevelt's New Deal North and portraying his primal hero Thomas Sutpen as a proto-fascist in *Absalom, Absalom!* (1936), and Gabriel García Márquez in the radical 1960s writing both against the insularity of Colombian literary practices in *Cien años de soledad* (1967) and against the imperialist United Fruit Company's underdevelopment of the Caribbean part of Colombia, so, too, I see Hinojosa writing a series of transmodern Spanish, English, American, Mexican, and bilingual and multicultural chronicles/novels about a particular space he calls Belken County, Texas—a chronicle, I might add, that does not take the hegemonic Texas Rangers perspective on the winning of the so-called frontier.

So when Sherwood Anderson advised William Faulkner to write about "that little patch up there in Mississippi where you started from," he underlined his justification by adding, "But that's all right too. It's America too." By "America," I suppose that Anderson meant the United States, but in the some eighty years since he assured Faulkner of the full significance of creating "that little patch" called Yoknapatawpha County, Mississippi, the resulting Faulknerian chronicle has acquired hemispheric, inter-American, and global mappings and ramifications neither Anderson nor Faulkner dreamed of. Maybe the great imaginative writers Gabriel García Márquez, Rolando Hinojosa, Édouard Glissant, and Toni Morrison (who [as Chloe Ardellia Wofford] wrote her master's thesis in English on Faulkner at Cornell University in 1955) had already begun to view Faulkner's great imaginary South and that larger Global South as a kind of mirror in which they saw their own imperialized and racialized and partitioned American Global South reflected, distorted, and bent awry. It was this Global South that Hinojosa turned to in his *gran cronicón* about South Texas, and it was this Global South that the Cuban Casa de las Américas, led by Fernández Retamar, grasped, acknowledged, and published in the Cuban edition of *Klail City y sus alrededores*.

In 1973, Hinojosa published his first novel, *Estampas del valle y otras obras*, with Berkeley's alternative Quinto Sol Press, and twenty years later, in 1993, he published *The Useless Servants* with Houston's Arte Público Press, the tenth novel in his multivolume chronicle. Hinojosa is still adding narratives and poetry to this monumental chronicle.

Hinojosa's first experimental novel used the Spanish literary tradition of *estampas*, or biographical sketches. His tenth, *The Useless Servants*, a detective novel about the U.S.-Mexican borderlands, anticipated, we might say, the dynamic duo of Subcomandante Marcos and Paco Ignacio

Taíbo II in writing a hard-boiled political fiction, *Muertos incómodos (falta lo que falta)* (2005), about the Global South. Hinojosa's first books about Belken County were written in a vernacular, *norteño* Mexican and Tejano Spanish; his last six were written in a borderlands vernacular English.

So how in the world are we to place Hinojosa's work of linguistic hybridity and outernationality? As North American, minoritized, "heterodox" literature? As Greater Mexican literature? To complicate matters even more, as you suggest, Hinojosa's great second novel, *Klail City y sus alrededores*, won the highly coveted Cuban Casa de las Américas prize in 1976 as the best Latin American novel. Were Chicanos to be welcomed forever as Latin American "orthodox" subjects in Havana? Why did *Klail City y sus alrededores* win the Cuban prize? Because it used the Gulf of Mexico's oceanic *choteo* as an aesthetic? These were some of the questions I grappled with initially in my analysis of Hinojosa's work. Now, whether or not we see Faulkner, García Márquez, or Hinojosa as an American "heterodox" or "orthodox" writer is still, I think, very much an open question in the U.S. academy, although I do share your skepticism that the exceptionalist American university has any pedagogical interest in "rethinking the canon." But I hope that anyone who reads Hinojosa's ten-volume chronicle would agree with Héctor Calderón (2004, 194) of the University of California, Los Angeles, that "Hinojosa, is, to be sure, the finest expression in Mexican American literature of how the language and cultures of Spain, Mexico, [elsewhere in Latin America,] and the United States have fused to form a Texas-Mexican culture of Greater Mexico."

As far as the current conversations between Fernández Retamar's Casa de las Américas and Chicano/a literature, I can only say that many of us are trying our best to get around George Bush's, and now Barack Obama's, continuing blockade of Cuba. My colleague Ben Olguín, a professor of Chicano literature at the University of Texas, San Antonio, for example, recently traveled to Cuba "illegally" as a regular member of the famous Venceremos Brigade. Before leaving for Cuba, he asked some of us within the field of Chicano/a literary studies to contribute modest funds so he could purchase and personally hand-deliver to Casa de las Américas the most recent novels, essays, dramas, and poetry written by Chicano and Chicana writers.

"Looking Awry" at the Borders of History and Nation

González García: In recent articles published in *American Literary History, Revista Casa de las Américas, Cultural Studies,* and *Modern Fiction Studies,* you refer to remarkable readings of hegemonic narratives made in recent years. For instance, you cite Gayatri Spivak's interpretation of U.S. Latino, African American, and Native American demands in the United States as postcolonial struggles within the nation. You also comment on Amy Kaplan's analysis of Theodore Roosevelt's account of his participation in the Cuban War for Independence, which she reads in terms of a national "internal" conflict in relation to African American soldiers, showing the domestic tensions of Roosevelt's discourse manifested within the context of the war. Yet it concerns me that these readings focus on the national effects or characteristics of the imperial history of the United States. In this sense, if the nation is still used as a main frame of analysis, this may contribute to the ghostly status of the history the United States is writing "abroad," as an empire . . .

On the other hand, I wonder if the South Asian Subaltern Studies Group and Latin American Subaltern Studies Group you invoke in some of these essays have tended to use certain categories in rigid ways. That is, there seems to be a clear convention related to who the subaltern is. In this sense, it seems to me that if we think only in terms of race, class, and gender, we risk leaving outside many sectors that currently do not benefit from the hegemonic project of modernity because they would remain invisible to traditional categories of "subalternity." This is a concern related to neoliberalism and its latest effects in terms of both the growth and the reshaping of those sectors that we also could call "subaltern." Are there any new readings in this respect? Would you consider it useful to "look awry" at traditional categories of subalternity?

Saldívar: As far as Gayatri Chakravorty Spivak's and Amy Kaplan's works are concerned, all I can say is that I have found their deconstructive feminist readings on the "archives" of the cultures of British and U.S. imperialism extremely important for my own work on the general question of the subaltern and U.S. Latino/a studies. I often teach their celebrated work in my graduate seminars on the cross-genealogical roots and routes of subaltern studies, from Antonio Gramsci's *Prison Notebooks* and Michel Foucault's *The History of Sexuality* to a survey of the emergent schools of the South Asian Subaltern Studies Group (founded by the brilliant historian Ranajit Guha and including Spivak, Dipesh Chakrabarty, and Partha Chatterjee) and the equally monumental—but short-lived—Latin American Subaltern Studies Group (founded by the energetic and sharp Latinamericanist literary and cultural critics John Beverley, Ileana Rodríguez, and José Rabasa, and including Walter Mignolo, Alberto Moreiras, and Gabriela Nouzeilles). All of their work on the Global South, nepantla, and subalternity helped me think through a variety of core issues of power and race in my book.

For me, Spivak's work on the archive fever of our times and on the subaltern has helped me begin to see how the native informant is produced in the Global South. Faulkner's *Absalom, Absalom!*, for example, with

Shreve, a Canadian Northerner, insisting that Quentin from the South play the role of the native informant ("Tell me about the South"), or of Arturo Islas's *The Rain God*, where Miguel Chico also resists the tropologics and protocols of the heteronormative U.S.-Mexican border ("I don't hate Mexicans! I don't hate the Borderlands! I don't hate gays!"). I am also beginning to see Paul D in Toni Morrison's *Beloved* as grappling with this when he confronts Sethe early in the novel and badgers her with the proto-universalist statement, "Sethe, you've got two feet not four." So I obviously find Spivak's critical readings of the native informant and power very useful for all sorts of reasons.

I will now attempt to get at your second question about subaltern studies by describing how I am entering into this complex debate. Trans-Americanity, to make a long story short, analyzes the assumptions and theories behind statements by Morrison and Anzaldúa (among others) to examine the processes by which trans-American and South Asian diasporic and border writers and thinkers from the Global South establish the grammar and syntax proper to the expression of their particular meanings. Following post-structuralists and postcolonialists such as Paul de Man, Judith Butler, and Ranajit Guha, I term these processes the "creation of rhetorical form." The text investigates the enabling conditions of narrative (novels, memoirs, testimonies) by subaltern writers such as José Martí, Miguel Barnet, Víctor Martínez, Sandra Cisneros, and Arundhati Roy and the various ways in which their stories seek to create an epistemological ground on which coherent versions of the world may be produced.

González García: My question meant not to criticize the work of Spivak and Kaplan as a whole but to address a specific potential limitation related to their national frame of analysis. In your new work, "Trans-Americanity," in fact, the notion of the "unspeakable," which you introduce after Toni Morrison (or after her character Sethe), is very illuminating, given the difficulties of narrating the stories performed by "the small voices of history." If I understand it well, this notion refers to an entire dimension linked to the hidden effects of modernity, which is hidden precisely because it lacks a vocabulary to account for it as an existing phenomenon. In this sense, and in connection with my previous question, could it be also assumed that you would consider those new, still unnamed, still unspoken subalternities created by neoliberalism difficult to articulate due to this (subaltern condition of) unspeakability? If this is the case, then, do you think it is possible to borrow the syntax or the epistemological ground created in literature to begin to tell the story of these new colonial or imperial subjects (because it is mandatory that the subaltern speak)?

Saldívar: Yes, absolutely. I think all of us who are located in the human and social sciences have to work very hard to get beyond using the nation as our unit of analysis. Turning to a critique of the cultures and politics of U.S. imperialism—as Spivak and Kaplan have been doing in their work— has been a real breakthrough for mainline American studies scholars based in the United States. Now, as far as what Toni Morrison has taught me over the many years I have been discussing her novels in my seminars, let me put it this way: in reading her Pulitzer Prize–winning *Beloved*, for example, I see her allegorizing how language (maybe even diasporic literary language) seems persistently tempted to fulfill itself in one single moment, in the uniquely figural expression that would explain its inef-fable subaltern mysteries. Hence, we are, as readers of her "unspeakable" subalternist texts, constantly faced with the frustration of attempting to define something that continually resists definition. But I think your own elegant reading of what you have gleaned in the subaltern's condition of unspeakability is precisely what I am getting at. To read, then, is to question and to understand Morrison's texture and the rhetorical re-sources of her figural language, as well as to grapple with referential and formal issues before us. I am interested in seeing the aesthetic structure of subaltern knowledge in the texts written by writers like Morrison, Anzaldúa, and Roy. I think that a critical awareness of this rhetorical screen can provide us with insight into the validity of any statement that seeks to describe or prescribe what, in a novel such as *Beloved*, is real and imaginary or not yet real or imaginary.

González García: In *Border Matters* (1997), you proposed to examine the zones of geographical contact between the United States and Mexico to undermine U.S. nationalism and its traditional historiography. First, could you talk a little about what this project feels like some ten years later? What were you trying to do in this more focused book on the U.S.-Mexico borderlands? Why were you using black British cultural studies (Stuart Hall, Paul Gilroy, Kobena Mercer) to focus on *conjunto* music, corridos, rock en español, novels, performance art, folklore? Second, I wonder if another step in terms of undermining traditional historiogra-phy can involve the re-examination of the notion of "empire" as a cate-gory of analysis, because, as we know, the history of the imperial United States not only surpasses its national borders but also seems to be mainly inscribed abroad. In this sense, what categories do you use to explore overseas events such as the U.S. intervention in the Cuban War for Independence in 1898? What did you expect to achieve by looking awry at 1898? What other places in history and geography do you believe could be revisited to eventually rewrite traditional and hegemonic history?

Saldívar: In the unprecedented context of undocumented—mostly Mexi-can—migrants in the millions taking to the streets of Los Angeles, Oak-land, San Francisco, Dallas, Philadelphia, Houston, Chicago, and New York in March and April 2006 to show their dismay and disgust with immigration bills in the House and the Senate that would make them, as undocumented border crossers, into felons, let me try here to be a bit audacious in my answer. *Border Matters*, I think, was a book of its time. Today, almost ten years after its publication, I see my text as a scathing report on how cultural and political violence were used in the United States to make and maintain its borders in stark and abusive violation of the human rights of the people who cross the militarized borders between the United States (the Global North) and Mexico, Central America, and América Latina (the Global South). In *Border Matters*, however, I was both raising what I saw as the "transfrontier issue of our time" and recounting the stories (what you call the historiography) that have challenged them. Drawing on a wealth of trans-*frontera*-crossing scholarship, from Américo Paredes and Renato Rosaldo to George Lipsitz, Lisa Lowe, and Barbara Harlow, I not only drafted a critical agenda that worked across what I neologized as a "transfrontera contact zone" (in honor of the literary critic Mary Louise Pratt) but also successfully worked out the parameters of a U.S.-Mexican border writing and border thinking (in honor of Gloria Anzaldúa and Walter Mignolo) that must, at the same time, struggle toward documentation of the undocumented in the United States and contest the pervasive articulations (to use Gramsci's and Hall's language) between the moral panic about border-crossing migrations and what I saw in California as the drift into a militarized law-and-order society so virulently purveyed by the mass media and the politicians (in both the House and the Senate) who legislate other lives. Today these legislators want to make undocumented border-crossers felons.

I divided *Border Matters* into two sections. Part 1, titled "Comparative Intercultural Studies," elaborated on a selection of contributions to recent academic work and area studies development in precisely these matters; in part 2, "El Otro Lado/The Other Side," it is in post-contemporary and transmodern Tijuana and Los Angeles, Baja, and what used to be called Alta California that, "going beyond literature," I located my border-matters commentary across several disciplinary distinctions and media.

While I do not have space to get into a full-blown précis of the book's two parts, I will just say that my favorite chapters are those from part 2, where the interlocutors I am commenting on all demand "Rights for All." This account begins on what I termed "the bad edge of la frontera" (Saldívar 1997, 95) with a critical reading of Helena María Viramontes's short story "The Cariboo Cafe," about a Salvadoran mother in search of her disappeared child on the mean back streets of Los Angeles pursued by what Viramontes calls "*la polie*" (the police). It proceeds with John Rechy's fabled account of the not so "miraculous day of Amalia Gómez" in the same world city of Los Angeles, and is accompanied by the rock en español, punk, and hip-hop music of Los Illegals and (Kid) Frost, orchestrating what I recorded as "the complex sounds of mass media texts critiquing and complicating the dominant culture's linear views of immigration, the American Bildung, ethno-race and the nation" (Saldívar 1997, 122). After Los Angeles came "Tijuana Calling," set in the touristic words of the mainline travel writer Beverly Lowry of the *New York Times* re-scored in the auto-ethnography of Luis Alberto Urrea; the displaced travels of the great journalist and poet Rubén Martínez; and what I characterized as the changed and changing career choices and perspectives by Richard Rodríguez and the multimedia "happenings" and performances by the Chilango Guillermo Gómez-Peña. In the book's conclusion, I turned back to the Gilded Age, when the U.S.-Mexican borderlands—as Gloria Anzaldúa and Américo Paredes taught us—were being divided and partitioned; when the treaties were drafted and signed, the railroads were built, the historical romances were written, and monopoly capitalism was consolidated. It was time for me to reread María Amparo Ruiz de Burton's re-edited novel *The Squatter and the Don* (1885) and to see the precedents that John Gregory Bourne, a soldier-ethnologist for the Third United Cavalry, had set in his symptomatically titled article "The American Congo," published in *Scribner's* in 1894, about South Texas border culture and society. In the article, he compared the Rio Grande and the Congo River as predetermining the flows of nineteenth-century imperialist aspirations and late-twentieth-century globalizing imperatives. And it was time for me to think again about José Martí's "Nuestra América" in this context not only of hemispheric un-mappings but also in its global dimensions.

Border Thinking and Rethinking the Border
within Immigration Times and Struggle

González García: In your recent articles you define "border thinking" as "a new geopolitically located thinking from both the internal and external borders of the modern (colonial) world 'system'" (Saldívar, 2007, 339). In addition, you specify that this epistemology emerges from undocumented immigrants, migrants, *bracero* workers, refugees, and so on. How can we remap or reinterpret border thinking, taking into account the recent actions carried out by Latino immigrants in the United States, which have been described as demands for civil rights? Also, if what those immigrants are looking for is the legalization of their immigration status, in a certain (epistemic) way, that would imply leaving the border behind. Do you think this would change the notion of border thinking? What consequences do you foresee in terms of local histories and global designs? In this context, what is your reading of those who still understand América as the white and Anglophone United States?

Saldívar: I'd like to begin wrapping up by saying that some of the questions regarding border thinking were in a sense already anticipated and answered in my précis of *Border Matters* as a scathing report about human rights abuses in the United States. What I would like to do now is, with all due respect to my Latinamericanist interlocutors and friends on the left from Venezuela, Colombia, Peru, Ecuador, and Argentina who do not agree with my local views on immigration struggles in the United States—grapple with the demonstrations in March and April 2006 by a mega-social movement of undocumented border crossers mostly from Mexico and the Global South. While I understand why many of my *paisanos* from Latin America or the Global South tended to misread this movement as a newer, U.S. Latino/a–tinged call for "civil rights"—like that of African Americans of the 1950s and 1960s—or just dismissed the protests because the workers were mainly attempting to acculturate into the U.S. culture and society, my own views, given my previous work in Chicano/a studies and location in California, are a bit different.

First of all, why did so many millions of undocumented workers (and their children and families)—mostly Mexican—take to the mean streets of the major cities of the United States in March and April 2006 to intervene in the political debates over immigration policy? For me, given the prior right-wing legislative history of unconstitutional propositions in California, such as Proposition 187, it has never been a question only of "civil rights," as some argue, for this new and unprecedented social movement was not re-scoring Martin Luther King's great march on Washington in 1963. Could we say that this mega-movement was in fact an attempt to counter the almost exclusive political focus on electoral politics in California and the rest of the United States that continues to betray them?

On the other hand, it also seemed to me that these events were not entirely about Samuel Huntington's racist and melancholic fantasy that demography is destiny, as others suggested. Were these border-crossing protests then about the U.S. economy—that the mostly undocumented Mexican workers (one-sixth of Mexicans now work "illegally" in the United States) were making a performative plea that they should not be blamed entirely for having "depressed the wages" of unskilled (and legal) labor to the detriment of low-income, so-called native-born hyphenated Americans—especially African Americans and white ethnics? Is the post-contemporary immigration debate really about the politics of race, nation, and culture?

On still another level, what did it mean that these mass protests (larger than the combined populations of many Latin American countries) were coordinated and organized by activist DJs such as Renán Almendárez Coello in the new, massified U.S. public sphere—that is, on the vibrant Spanish-language mass AM and FM radio stations throughout the United

States? What did Almendárez Coello's estimated 35 million daily morning listeners hear "sonically" in the call for dissent in his radio show, which is syndicated in thirty-six cities throughout the United States? Almendárez Coello not only got people out to protest, but, according to the *San Francisco Chronicle* of August 1, 2006, he was also well on his way to getting some 1 million new Latino/a voters (a rather different imagined community) registered to vote against the anti-immigrant members of the House and Senate in the November 2006 elections.

Or was Samuel Huntington, the Harvard political scientist and Democrat who served in the Kennedy administration, right when he warned in *Who Are We?* (2004b) that unchecked Latino/a and Mexican immigration was bringing to the United States what he condemned as "alien" non-WASPish cultural values—that is, that the sacrosanct White Anglo-Saxon Protestantness of the imagined community was being threatened? Last, what might it mean that the so-called underrepresented ethnic minorities (African Americans, Hispanics, Chicanos/as, Asian Americans) are now the majority of the population of the United States? Will the so-called white Americans become a minority group? As you know, according to the 2000 Census, that is already the case in California, Texas, and New York, with Arizona and Florida soon to follow.

In 2007–8, when I was the director of the Latino/a Studies in the Global South program at Duke University, I was invited to a daylong symposium on U.S. immigration policy. Specifically, my marching orders were to respond to the rich quantitative study "Measuring Immigrant Assimilation in the United States" by my Duke colleague Jacob Vigdor. In his fascinating "quantitative index," Vigdor measured "the degree of similarity between native- and foreign-born adults in the United States" —that is, he reported to us the good news that, although "assimilation initially declined in the 1980s, . . . assimilation has actually increased slightly" over the past two years (Vigdor 2008, 2). Hence, Vigdor's quantitative index's rich snapshot suggested that the immigrant's trajectory in the United States was "not as bleak" as many recent commentators had suggested. Rather, the trajectory (and steady stability of the quantitative index) for Vigdor was truly remarkable, given the rapid growth of the immigrant population. It doubled between 1990 and 2006.

And given that these new immigrants from the Global South were by and large more distinct when they arrived in the United States than were past immigrant populations, the new immigrants, Vigdor (2008, 2) concluded, had "assimilated"—his term—more successfully and "more rapidly than their counterparts of a century ago."

Vigdor gracefully eschewed righteous polemic. His report, he claimed, neither proposed nor endorsed any public-policy responses; its sole aim was to provide careful, long-term historical information about economic, cultural, and civic assimilation. The work he was doing, however, demonstrated beyond dispute what a carefully honed analysis based on more than a century's worth of historical data on the status of immigrants in the United States can bring to immigration studies and to public-policy debates on immigration.

In my response to Vigdor, I raised the issues of methodology and interpretation that I wish his report had grappled more with. The story of "assimilation" (I prefer the political neologisms "transculturation" or "incorporation") is not just about how immigrants we receive have adapted over the past century; it is also fundamentally about the reception the United States has given them. Why has U.S. immigration policy seemed largely to start and end at the U.S.-Mexican border or at the U.S.-Canadian border? If Vigdor's quantitative index is right (immigration has stabilized over the past decades), why hasn't incorporation (through full citizenship) also increased? In the 1950s, we know, four out of five foreign-born residents in the United States held American citizenship. However, in 2004 fewer than two out of five became citizens. What accounts for this decline in incorporation? Is there something wrong with the immigrants from Mexico and the Global South, as Huntington (2004b) polemically argued? Have these new immigrants chosen not to participate? These questions, of course, assume that the decline in political incorporation in the United States stems only from the immigrants themselves. The news here is not so good.

As a comparative American studies scholar, I was somewhat surprised by Vigdor's decision to use the nation as his unit of analysis. What might have happened to his quantitative index if he had included other countries in the analysis? Are countries such as Canada, New Zealand, and Australia doing better in their attempts to incorporate immigrants? Are their immigration policies more successful in helping the new immigrants achieve incorporation through full citizenship? When I worked with Irene Bloemraad at the Berkeley Institute for Latino Public Policy, she convincingly demonstrated that we could study how cultures and society from around the hemisphere and the world create civic cohesion, unity, and political community. Bloemraad (2006, 2) suggested that,

> relative to the United States, Canada has taken a more interventionist stance toward immigrant incorporation. Canadian policies of governmental multiculturalism have supported immigrant integration and favored citizenship as the exemplary form of incorporation. Federal, provincial, and municipal units in Canada also offer more public assistance with the business of settlement, integration, and incorporation (subsidizing classes, for instance, to learn English, or programs to find jobs). The United States, in comparison, deals with immigration and engages with little outreach, and we know that the federal government provides only sustained settlement support to only recognized refugees, like it did with

Cuban Americans. Hence, how might we have explained in a comparative way, why the overwhelming majority of foreign-born residents in Canada (2001 Canadian Census Report), 72% had acquired Canadian citizenship? This was almost double the proportion of that of the United States.

I thus wanted Vigdor (using his quantitative index) to say more about the attainment of incorporation—attaining full citizenship. Differences in government intervention, settlement, and diversity policies, as Bloemraad (2006) argued, create interpretative differences that affect the political integration of immigrants. (The official promotion of citizenship by Canada's immigration ministries is part and parcel of that country's public policy of multiculturalism. Can the U.S. Department of Homeland Security handle the economic, civic, and cultural work of political incorporation?) By developing pride both in background and in connection to their multicultural community, Canada does significantly better than the United States in having more new immigrants successfully run for office. (Perhaps the United States impedes newcomers from successfully running for office by keeping power in the hands of party old-timers.)

My last point, Mónica, was to raise the historical and sociological question about what the great African American social scientist and planetary humanist W. E. B. Du Bois called the U.S. color line. How has race in the United States affected the success of assimilation? How has the black–white color line fundamentally shaped the dynamics of immigrants' incorporation into the United States? As Judith Shklar has argued elsewhere (quoted in Bloemraad 2006, 1), one cannot understand U.S. citizenship without taking into account the legacy of slavery that is predicated on race. Put more directly, has not the legacy of U.S. slavery and diaspora of the transatlantic Middle Passage (as Morrison demonstrated in *Beloved* and in *A Mercy* [2008]) not shaped ethno-racial incorporation in the United States?

González García: Could you follow this up by saying more about how it felt for you personally as a Chicano to live in North Carolina and direct the Latino Studies in the Global South program at Duke University? Samuel Huntington, whom you brought up earlier, argued in "The Hispanic Challenge" (2004a) that the proportion of Latinos/as in the Global North had exploded ; they had established what he called "beachheads" in regions such as the U.S. South, [with a population that had grown in] Arkansas, Georgia, Tennessee, Alabama, and South Carolina [by] 222 percent. In North Carolina, the number of Latinos and Latinas increased between 1990 and 2000 at an incredible rate of 449 percent.

Saldívar: Yes, among Huntington's greatest concerns in that work are the culture-clash and state fantasies he imagined between Anglo-Americans' "America" and Americanism's cultures of Latinidad. And he proposed— wrongly, I believe—that the essential element of Anglo-America was its ideological "creed" derived from the founding fathers. Even if they dream the American dream in Spanish, he wrote, U.S. Latinos/as "will be in the United States and not of it" (Huntington 2004a, 45). For Huntington, there can be "no Americano dream," for "there is only the American Dream created by an Anglo-Protestant society" (Huntington 2004a, 45). But when I lived in Durham, I saw immigrants from and in the Global South dreaming the Americano dream twenty-four hours a day. While I directed Latino/a Studies in the Global South at Duke, I helped sponsor a testimonial film on a three-part narrative by Durham's Latino Credit Union dedicated to migratory workers' financial education. Even the film's title, *Los Sueños de Angélica* (Angelica's Dreams), speaks powerfully back (in contestation) to Huntington's political and phantasmatic negative hallucinatory fears and anxieties. The central purpose of the film—the first independent U.S. Latino film made in North Carolina—was to teach the heterogeneous U.S. Latino/a communities in Chapel Hill, Durham, Raleigh, and Greensboro the processes of buying a home—and of dreaming in "Americano." Rodrigo Dorfman produced the film with monetary gifts from the U.S. Treasury Department and the Latino Credit Union. He focused on the border-crossing story of Angélica, a house-cleaner, and Roberto, a butcher by night and a construction worker by day, who discuss throughout the film whether to return to their home in the Global South or to stay in the Homeland Security state of the United States and buy their dream house. When an unexpected event occurs in Durham, everything changes for Angélica and Roberto, and they grapple with the hard realization that one of them will have to sacrifice the dreams.

Experimenting and mixing and cutting documentary and fiction, melodrama, and the telenovela format—the way the great Pedro Almodóvar stylizes and heightens all of his films—Dorfman shot *Los Sueños de Angélica* entirely in Durham, with local actors and in Spanish, moving his protagonists into the everyday life of one of the fastest and most vibrant Latino and Latina communities of the United States. And like Almodóvar, Dorfman deconstructs the border-crossing genre itself by making Roberto, the husband, the character given most to hysteria and histrionics, to which Angélica calmly replies "Díos mío—this is just like living in a telenovela." Dorfman showcased this new, brave U.S. Latinidad by plunging us into Durham's many *carniceras* (butcher shops), downtown construction-job sites (Roberto works alongside real construction workers at a new American Tobacco Historic District project in downtown Durham), bars, Catholic churches, public parks, real-estate agencies, and the Latino Credit Union. Roberto and Angélica perform U.S. Latinidad and the Americano dream (in Spanish), and Dorfman wryly thematizes a new social-movement struggle in North Carolina, triangulating the anachronistic black–white binary into a black–brown–white multiculture. The film thematizes how locally based credit unions—such as Durham's Latino Credit Union—can help improve the financial condition of migrant workers by providing them not only with checking accounts and first-home mortgages but also with a new cultural-frontist unionship based on democratic intercultural relationships: each member votes, and each member pools the money together to make more loans.

I will end this riff by suggesting, somewhat utopianly, that this megamovement of ethnic and racial triangulation might in the future take more of its cues from the recent events in Latin America and the Global South, where new indigenous leaders, as in Bolivia, were elected to office for the first time.

What did it mean that many of those who marched (as I witnessed and participated in our protests in Berkeley) cared about the immigration debates in the United States but also attempted to see beyond them? Many protestors were quoted as saying, "I used to be undocumented. I came here to the march because many of my friends and family can't."

The millions of undocumented and documented marchers not only cared about U.S. immigration reform. They were also concerned with human rights for all, with wages and better working conditions. They cared for health care, education in the public schools that their tax dollars pay for, and the environment. They were protesting because they could not go to the hospitals for care; they were protesting because they could not drive to work, because they could not get driver's licenses; they were protesting because they could not organize at work. Unlike Latino and Latina workers in Durham, they had no Latino Credit Union of their own in California.

When I was last in Mexico City, I had the opportunity to rethink these massive protests by literally millions of undocumented workers. What would the so-called three Mexican presidents (or so they claimed that Sunday night after the Mexican election) Vincente Fox, Andrés Manuel López Obrador, and Felipe Calderón have done if one-sixth of their nation's population in the United States had returned to Mexico City and protested human rights for all on their home turf? My sense is that at least two of these Mexican presidents might have called on the army to put down the uprising of workers and their families.

Not only are leftist and rightist Mexican political legislators flinching on immigration, but even President Barack Obama, our best hope and best legislator in the United States, is dropping the ball on immigration rights. In March 2009, President Obama pulled back from nominating the Chicano Thomas Saenz, the gutsy former chief counsel to Mayor Antonio Villagriosa of Los Angeles and current director of the Mexican American Legal Defense and Educational Fund (MALDEF), to run the Civil Rights Division of the U.S. Justice Department. According to the *New York Times* of March 24, 2009, Saenz, who was privately offered the job in January 2009, was rejected when the floating of his name led to "fierce outbursts" from both leftist and rightist anti-immigrant groups and blogs in the United States who detested him for being so good at what he does—that is, litigate in favor of documented and undocumented workers' rights to have rights. Saenz not only successfully led the fight to block California's Proposition 187, an unconstitutional measure to deny schooling and social services to undocumented immigrants; he also defended the rights of Latino and Latina day laborers targeted by illegal California police stings and by unconstitutional anti-solicitation ordinances. An op-ed piece in *Investor's Business Daily* (March 24, 2009) linguistically mugged him by calling him "an open borders extremist" and announced that MALDEF wanted to give California back to Mexico. José and Josefina-haters, please! "None of it was true," according to the *New York Times* (March 24, 2009), "but it was too much for [Obama's] White House." Why did President Obama reject an activist lawyer (as he once claimed to be) for the top civil rights job because he stood up for the right to have rights? President Obama needs to move away from Huntington's core "creed"—that being an undocumented worker from the Global South is un-American and, worse, an unpardonable crime. The suffering that undocumented workers in the United States receive— from raids to exploitation to camp detention, camp thinking, and absurd legislation in Arizona—is a human-rights crisis. The provisions in Arizona Senate Bill 1070, for instance, which included bizarre sections that required cops to check a person's immigration status while enforcing other laws, are totally unconstitutional. If I can paraphrase Judith Butler (2009, 94), the immigration war at home at the beginning of the twenty-first century is an effort to minimize "precariousness for some [and] to maximize it for others"—that is, for los nacionales mexicanos que se encuentran en Estados Unidos, independientemente de su condición migratoria, cuentan con derechos humanos inalienables, así como con mecanismos de protección bajo el derecho internacional, las leyes federales estadounidenses.

This is to say, my views on border thinking, immigration, and the immigration struggle are, like Subcomandante Marcos's, both utopian and dystopian.

González García: Immigration has been a complex phenomenon, and if you will allow me, I would like to pose another question regarding this matter to conclude our dialogue. As you and other remarkable scholars have noted, geographical borders, especially on the U.S.-Mexican frontier, are places where these tense processes of restructuring identities, experiences, and knowledge intensify. Is it possible to advance a reading of the current debate about immigration while also taking into account the history of the United States as an empire? In other words, what is the place of immigration within the imperial configuration of the United

States? At the same time, as we discussed earlier, other types of borders exist that have not been sufficiently explored—that is, the epistemic borders where Quijano's coloniality of power could also be illuminating in recording the local stories and epistemic sites that the empire is fueling—through neoliberalism, intervention, and war—in the bodies and daily experiences of people who remain within the limits of their nations. Would you still consider it useful to allow for the notion of border thinking to address the stories of people who, without having migrated, are yet caught in a space of in-betweenness?

Saldívar: I think it was Stuart Hall who explained the recent history of black migration to Britain and the United Kingdom best with the slogan, "We Are Here because You Were There." I think that this logic is at work with regard to U.S. immigration and U.S. empire, but with a difference. Neither China nor Greece and Rome was ever really a "global" empire. The British Empire was global to a great extent. However, according to the geographer Neil Smith (2003), the U.S. Empire is the first to be striving to be "planetary." And as Amy Kaplan (2006) has taught us, this U.S. planetary logic of empire expresses a contradictory U.S. structure of feeling—an assumed geography of privilege and exceptionalism (it never credits itself with any originary belligerence), on the one hand, and what Smith (2003, xiii) characterizes as a peculiarly "anti-geographical ideology of post-nineteenth-century Americanism," on the other.

What I think Smith is getting at is not only that today the U.S. Empire is interested in, say, the geopolitics of oil and resources, but also more precisely that the power of the U.S. Empire is in the first place exercised through what we call "the world market" and only secondarily (when necessary) in geopolitical terms. Using Smith's way of thinking about the U.S. Empire allows us to see that the country has never followed the British and European models of empire, for from its beginnings, the United States forged its own "Manifest Destiny" and its own geographical and economic expansion in the twentieth century and twenty-first century. That is why I think Niall Ferguson, the European financial historian of empire, is off-base when he argues that the U.S. Empire should model itself after the British Empire but without the errors of the British with the underside of modernity.

The U.S. Empire—in contradistinction to Europe—was built on what Smith (2003, xvii–xviii) calls a "strategic recalibration of geography with economics, a new orchestration of world geography in the pursuit of economic accumulation." What we have partly in Smith's *American Empire* and fully worked out in his mentor David Harvey's book on the American empire, *The New Imperialism* (2003), is a concern with temporal-spatial dynamics and with a healthy grounding of historical geographic materialism. They are both interested in constructing a theory of place relations, with the geographic development under (late) capitalism that they believe can explain state functions, uneven development, urbanism, and imperialism. On Harvey's view two logics are at work in the new U.S. imperialism: a global logic of capital operating in continuous time and space and a territorializing logic of states oriented to imagined collective interests. These two logics are "articulated" by the current U.S. hegemony of the U.S. Empire.

Where Quijano's great theory of the patrón de poder would surely help us in conceptualizing is precisely what you have noted as the way Americanity and capitalism built a new fixed space (landscape) in 1492, necessary for its own unique functioning, based on the creation of racial, gendered, and caste hierarchies the Iberians and British brought with them from the other side of the world to enslave indigenous and black bodies. This is what Marx called primitive accumulation—the way resources are expropriated and humans enslaved once and for all from a commons that was built up over centuries.

The U.S. Empire's accumulation by dispossession today in Latin America, the Middle East, and other parts of the world might also allow us to see how it is attempting to impose a "structural coherence" on the rest of the world. So yes, I think that this logic also foretells newer forms of border thinking around our planet in response to these new, dual logics of territory (fronteras) and capital of the U.S. Empire.

González García: Have you seen Sean San José's and Marc Bamuthi Joséph's play *Fukú Americanus*, adapted by the Campo Santo Theater Company from Junot Díaz's great novel *The Brief Wondrous Life of Oscar Wao* (2007)? Could you meditate on Americanity and talk about Díaz's theorizing of *Fukú Americanus*? What accounts for the literary buzz around Díaz and his work?

Saldívar: As you know, I am totally blown away by Junot Díaz's extraordinary imaginative work *Drown* (1996) and *The Brief Wondrous Life of Oscar Wao*. A few years ago, I had the great honor and pleasure of sharing the stage with the great young writers Junot Díaz and Edwidge Danticat as keynote speakers at a conference on the circum-Caribbean and black Atlantic diaspora organized by graduate students in Berkeley's Comparative Literature and History departments. It was a real rush trying to match literary and political wits with Díaz and Danticat that evening. Partly as a result of that experience, I have made it a point to teach as much of their work in my literature classes as possible. After I taught *The Brief Wondrous Life of Oscar Wao* in undergraduate and graduate seminars at Berkeley and at Stanford University, my students helped set me straight in my belief that Díaz may be the best American writer today. He is not only a master of imaginative and emotional effects in his texts; he is also extremely (scarily) intelligent. For instance, Díaz uses his bilanguaging imagination at his command with the nonchalance and the zest of the insider in all of his texts. There is a fascinating moment of heteroglossic erudition in *The Brief Wondrous Life of Oscar Wao*. There is Lola telling her story of her own sexual desire and of her wooing by an ethnic Italian American boyfriend in New Jersey: "I ran, off, dique because of a boy. What can I really tell you about him? He was like all boys: beautiful and callow, and like an insect he couldn't sit still. Un blanquito with long hairy legs who I met one night at Limelight. His name was Aldo. He was nineteen and lived down at the Jersey Shore with his seventy-four year old father. In the back of his Oldsmobile on University I pulled my leather skirt up and my fishnet stockings down and the smell of me was everywhere" (Díaz 2007, 61–62). Throughout the novel, English, Spanish, and Spanglish are seamlessly woven together into poetic bursts of synaesthesia. There are puns galore, Caribbean historiographic excursions about Trujillo and the great Latin American dictator novels about him by Mario Vargas Llosa and Julia Álvarez, and the sheer beautiful lyricism of the author's prose. Amid the hurly-burly of the novel's action in Paterson and New Brunswick, New Jersey, and Santo Domingo, and in one of my favorite scenes in the novel, Yunior, while out at 2 A.M., is jumped by townie morenos. Here is Yunior telling his own story of Dominican American male bravado and of his enduring love for the lovely Lola: "Wish I could say I went down swinging but these cats just laid me out. If it hadn't been for some Samaritan driving by the motherfuckers probably would have killed me. The old guy wanted to take me to Robert Wood Johnson [hospital], but I didn't have no medical, and besides, ever since my brother died of leukemia I hadn't been hot on doctors, so of course I was like: No no no. For having gotten my ass kicked I actually felt pretty good" (Díaz 2007, 166). When Yunior, an upperclassman, is mugged on the mean streets of Rutgers University, he turns again to Lola, who briefly was his girlfriend in his sophomore year, for care, and she cries when she sees his state. Lola cooks, cleans, picks up Yunior's college schoolwork, gets his medicine, and slowly nurses him back to life. Yunior says all of this nonchalantly in his best Tony Soprano-wannabe Jersey speak: "In other words, [Lola] sewed my balls back on, and not any woman can do that for a guy. Believe you me. I could barely stand, my head hurt so bad, but she would wash my back and that was what I remember most about that mess. Her hand on the sponge and that sponge on me. Even though I had a girlfriend, it was Lola who spent those nights with me" (Díaz 2007, 168). Yunior's soliloquy, which in *Fukú Americanus* is addressed to the audience, is both self-description and an announcement of his self-determination. Yunior dwells on his Dominican American attractiveness, his true fitness for love and sex with Lola: "[Lola] was a girl it was easy to care about. Lola was like the fucking opposite of the girls I usually macked on: bitch was almost six feet tall and no tetas at all and darker than your darkest grandma. Like two girls in one: the skinniest upper body married to a pair of Cadillac hips and an ill donkey. One of those overachieving chicks who run all the organizations in college and wears suits to meetings" (Díaz 2007, 168). Here Yunior thematizes himself from the start. But Yunior can only recall his first dalliance with Lola during his sophomore year in college—"I remember she was wearing sweats and a Tribe T-shirt. Took off the ring her boy had given her and then kissed me. Dark eyes never leaving mine. You have great lips she said. How do you forget a girl like that?" (Díaz 2007, 169). But Díaz deliberately gives Yunior a glimmer of humanizing weakness in this scene to suggest that at some level he is always falling in love with Lola and cannot bear that she often thinks him wholly unreliable and hyper-machista. In *Fukú Americanus*'s adaptation of this marvelous episode, Yunior is left alone on the stage. His posture and self-determination are secure, but the same security does not extend to the author/dramatist—or to Lola, for that matter—for she puts an end to the scene by refusing to sleep with Yunior that night. Lola speaks virtuously and movingly, "Yo soy prieta, Yuni, she said, pero no soy bruta" (Díaz 2007, 169). The whole point of the episode is a marvel for Díaz.

I eagerly attended [the premiere of *Fukú Americanus* in San Francisco in 2009] with my former graduate students Alma Granado, María Villaseñor, and Sara Ramírez hoping for more marvels. For the adaptation, San José, Joséph, and the Campo Santo players—like Díaz's brilliant novel—focused on the Dominican and Dominican American characters of Oscar de León (a.k.a. Wao); his grandmother La Inca; his cancer-ridden mother, Beli; his sister, Lola; and Lola's former "player" boyfriend, Yunior, who first appears as a precocious narrator in Díaz's short-story collection *Drown*. Like a surreal, topsy-turvy Shakespeare play, *Fukú Americanus* is entirely built on Díaz's rich and gritty English and Spanglish poetic languages, with the pulse of the authoritarian history of the Dominican Republic and the black Atlantic and Gulf of Mexico diaspora as backdrops. But the stage in San Francisco is hardly the Globe; the entire two-and-a-half-hour play is performed on a moveable stage the size of a Mission District barrio porch, providing the audience with an acid intimacy in the De León family romance. The play, like the novel, opens powerfully not with any of the De León family members or with Yunior but with a curse of the *fukú americanus*, an inherently theatrical planetary performativity announcing the transatlantic slave trade, the Middle Passage, exterminated native American indigenous people of the Caribbean islands, the Taínos, and the Genoese explorer Columbus who in 1492 planted the first Iberian and European colony and whom the novel and the play simply call "the Admiral." The idea of a doom or a curse looming over a family's entire genealogy, too, is pure theater of *les damnés de la terre*'s colonial wound and of the art and ideology of Gabriel García Márquez and the Global South. The title of the Campo Santo Theater Company's adaptation comes from this very curse. The Iberian,

Italian, and European advents, Yunior as narrator announces, released a demon into the world of the *damnés*: *fukú americanus*, "the Curse and the Doom of the New World" (Díaz 2007, 1). It is this planetary notion of *fukú* Americanity, if I can call it that—both large and small—that drives the plot of the novel and the play, exerting its marvels and power on both the local (individual) and world-system scale—on Columbus himself; on the Dominican Republic's dictator for life Rafael Leonidas Trujillo Molina, "also known as El Jefe, the Failed Cattle Thief, and Fuckface" (Díaz 2007, 1); on Trujillo's enemies; and on the United States and John F. Kennedy. The curse especially dooms Oscar's family in the Dominican Republic and, later, in New Jersey. In other words, in Díaz's hands, Santo Domingo and New Jersey become the primal sites of Americanity's patrón de poder and transmodernity. Oscar routinely calls Santo Domingo "the Ground Zero of the New World" (Díaz 2007, 1), and because Oscar is brutally murdered by Trujillo's police in 1995, Díaz is suggesting that the phrase "Ground Zero" refers to Hiroshima and Americanus's nuclear sublime and Cold War state fantasies, not Bush's hegemonic state fantasy of September 11, 2001, and victimhood. Díaz thus brilliantly uses the *fukú americanus* as a unit of analysis (the nation, the region, the planet) to tell his historia. One of the many geopolitical lessons Yunior, the central consciousness in the text, discovers is that in Puerto Rico the *damnés* call the curse "*fufu*," and the Haitians, he says, the *damnés*, "have some shit just like that" (Díaz 2007, 4,). Still, Díaz's spatio-temporal matrix is wider: "Santo Domingo was Iraq before Iraq was Iraq" (Díaz 2007, 4), and "Trujillo was Mobutu before Mobutu" (Díaz 2007, 3, fn. 1) For all its local circum-Caribbean particularity, Díaz's story of *fukú americanus* stands for Americanity's spatio-temporal matrix of the patrón de poder.

Yes, this matrix of Americanity weighs heavily on the life and times of Oscar, who is obese, shy, awkward, unable to talk to girls, addicted to Japanese sci-fi cinema and comic books/graphic novels such as Alan Moore's *Watchmen* (2005) and fantasy novels such as J. R. R. Tolkien's *Lord of the Rings* (1954–55), and prone to playing games like Dungeons and Dragons. Unlike Yunior, the Dominican exemplary player, Oscar is no Lothario and remains throughout the novel and the play, the narrator tells us, so very "un-Dominican"—wearing his "nerdiness like a Jedi wore his light saber" (Díaz 2007, 11, 21). Oscar passes an anguished, dyspeptic, virginal, and solitary adolescence in Paterson; once in college in New Brunswick, everyday life is much worse. At Rutgers, Oscar is baptized with a homophobic slur "Wao" when a member of his Dominican American ethno-racial cohort mishears and mispronounces the name "Oscar Wilde, surely a pejorative codeword suggesting Oscar's solitude and epistemology of the closet. And the slur sticks. He also attempts suicide. But it is also at Rutgers that Yunior—still craving Lola—becomes Oscar's roommate, and both bond over Lola and their aspirations to become

10. Photo of *Fukú Americanus,* featuring Brian Rivera and Maria
Candelario (foreground) and Ana Maria Lucero (background).
Photograph by the author.

great imaginative writers portraying their thwarted romances and "the
Great American Doom."

In other words, *The Brief Wondrous Life of Oscar Wao* and its theatrical
adaptation, *Fukú Americanus,* are themselves allegories for what Oscar
calls the "more speculative genres" (Díaz 2007, 43) and are based on
Oscar's interest in the structural unpredictability of science fiction, its
chaos theory, and Freudian–Althusserian overdetermination. Both the
novel and the play, following the historicist-science fiction dialectic that
frames them, move retrospectively and proleptically in search of origins
and causes of the *fukú americanus* curse; they attempt to geologically un-
cover scientific patterns that for the De Leóns and Yunior—the *damnés* of
Santo Domingo and New Jersey—seem like a fate condemning them to
solitude. Beli, La Inca, Oscar, and Lola all seem condemned to the curse
(*damnés de la terre*), and all of them except La Inca escape the Dominican
Republic and Trujillo's state fantasies and predations by traveling to New
York and New Jersey.

Nevertheless, it is only Oscar who willingly returns to the Dominican
Republic's "supernaturalism," for all the roots and discrepant routes of
the novel lead him back to Santo Domingo—to the authoritarianism of
Trujillo; to the politics that kept him in power; to the history of the
coloniality of power that empowered dictatorships. This, then, is how

Díaz's science fiction and history are not (or not only) two separate themes in *Fukú Americanus*. One might want finally to insist on the way in which any science-fiction reading of *The Brief Wondrous Life of Oscar Wao* and *Fukú Americanus* must eventually move into a second allegorical one, in which the wild, imaginative "speculative genres" Oscar loves to read and emulate in his own sedimented fiction stands revealed as sociopolitical content. As Yunior recalls of Oscar, "He was a hardcore sci-fi and fantasy man, believed that that was the kind of story we were all living in. He'd ask: What more sci-fi than the Santo Domingo? What more fantasy than the Antilles?" (Díaz 2007, 6).

Behind Oscar's theories of sci-fi and *lo real supernaturalismo*, behind his transmodern desire to become "the Dominican Tolkien" (Díaz 2007, 192), lie praxis, history, and human production that make a mockery of those who refuse to accept Díaz's *fukú americanus*. The characters in *Fukú Americanus* use Díaz's raw poetic language and a simple low-tech projector to dialectically explain the effects of the Trujillo dictatorship or to define Dominican American vernacular expressions such as *pariguayo*. The projector lasers on the on-stage screen that "pariguayo" is a party watcher, or an Oscar-like man who is bad with the ladies. Furthermore, Oscar's utopian attempts at Rutgers to become the first Dominican Tolkien by filling up scores of autoethnographic notebooks (like Césaire) is not Díaz's attempt to represent radical alternatives; rather, it is simply Oscar's imperative to imagine alternatives.

Notes

Preface

1. In suggesting a nuanced spatio-temporal matrix and transmodernist approach for U.S. critical studies, I use two terms and concepts that require some defining. I borrow "outernational" from the Afro Celts founder Simon Emerson and the British DJ Phil Meadley of the duo The Outernationalists, which name refers to the planetary sonics that they take to the outer limits of experimentation, with a mix of African, Indian, Arabic, and Latin American sonics. Another term recurring throughout the book is "post-contemporary," by which I mean a post-contemporary thinking that places the present within a transmodernist historical matrix, while recognizing that the contemporary itself often melts into thin air. The present is always before us.

2. "By the term field-imaginary," Pease (1990, 11–12) writes, "I mean to designate a location for the disciplinary unconscious.... Here abides the field's fundamental syntax—its tacit assumptions, convictions, primal words, and the charged relations binding them together." In *The New American Exceptionalism* (2009a, 19), Pease later exposed the field-imaginary of mainline Americanists as one that empties out and separates the realm of culture from that of politics. The "new Americanists," in contradistinction to the "old" mainline and hegemonic Americanists, Pease argues "insist on literature as an agency within the political world and thereby violate the fundamental presupposition" of the mainline liberal imagination. In *Cultures of U.S. Imperialism* (1993), he and Amy Kaplan attempted to imagine an alternative to the field-imaginary's hegemonic categories and master narratives of America by interrogating the formation of national borders in a transnational context—that is, in the name of anti-imperialism. *The New American Exceptionalism* deconstructs the meta-narratives of Ronald Reagan and George W. Bush and of Barack Obama's post-9/11 America as a state of exception and uses the multiple ways the New Americanists emerged from and continued their connections with emancipatory new social movements. Pease's work for two decades has been concerned with the irreconcilable rifts within our political culture that opened up during the transition from the end of the U.S. Cold War to the inauguration of its global war on terror.

3. According to Wallerstein, world-system analysis builds on earlier theorizing in social science such as the relational concept of the "core–periphery." The subsequent elaboration of the Cuban Revolution inspired "dependency theory" for understanding Latin America's location in the world and that it did not need to go through a phase of bourgeois revolution that had to preclude a proletarian revolution. Moreover, world-system analysis asked what unit of analysis was most appropriate—the nation or the world?—to understand what

had been called the First World, Second World, and Third World. Wallerstein (2004, 16) summarizes world-system theory as an attempt "to combine coherently concern with the unit of analysis and concern with social temporalities [such as Fernand Braudel's *longue durée*], and concern with barriers that had been created between different social science disciplines."

4. For Quijano's coloniality of power, see Laó-Montes 2001, 1–52.

5. Marcus Rediker (2007, 10) defines race and coloniality in terms and processes similar to Wallerstein and Quijano: "In producing workers for the plantation, the ship-factory also produced 'race.' At the beginning of the voyage, captains hired a motley crew of sailors, who would, on the coast of Africa, become 'white men.' At the beginning of the Middle Passage, captains loaded on board the vessel a multiethnic collection of Africans, who would in the American port, become 'black people' or a 'negro race.' The voyage thus transformed those who made it. War making, imprisonment, and the factory production of labor power and race all depended on violence . . . The traffic continued illegally for many years, but a decisive moment in human history had been reached. Abolition, coupled with its profound coeval event, the Haitian Revolution, marked the beginning of the end of slavery" but not the coloniality of power and the invention of Americanity.

6. Area studies developed in the United States after the Second World War as a new academic disciplinary category to group intellectual work and its cultures of scholarship and "traveled" to other parts of the world. The basic idea was straightforward: the area was a large territorial zone with supposed cultural, historic, and linguistic coherence, such as the Soviet Union, China, Latin America, South Asia, and, later, the United States. Given its hegemonic role after the Second World War, the United States needed knowledge about—and, therefore, specialists on—the current knowledge–power couplet of these regions. See Wallerstein et al. 1996; Chakrabarty 2000.

7. See O'Gorman 1958; Rabasa 1993.

8. For Fabian (1983), the "denial of coevalness" was the result of Eurocentrism's relocating people in a chronological hierarchy rather than in geographical places. For Mignolo (2000b, 283), Fabian's idea of the "denial of coevalness" found "its most systematic formulation in Hegel's *Philosophy of History* (1822), which remained virtually "uncontested" by critical social theorists "until the past fifty years when intellectuals engaged with the movements of liberation and decolonization put pressure on its assumptions" about the relocation of people, languages, and knowledges in time rather than space.

9. For rich personal histories of the South Asian Subaltern Studies Group and the Latinamericanist Modernity/Coloniality Research Project, see Guha 1996, 1–8; Mignolo 2001, 424–44.

10. Without the work of the Latinamericanist Modernity/Coloniality Research Project, the narrative and argument in this book would be poorer and not what they are today. Although I occasionally imagined myself as its only "dissenting" member (as sole Chicano and critical U.S. studies representa-

tive), I thank the iconic research collective for allowing me to participate in its rich meetings and discussions. Participant members of the collective, with whom I met over the past five years, are Walter Mignolo (U.S.), Aníbal Quijano (Peru), Enrique Dussel (Argentina and Mexico), Boaventura de Sousa Santos (Portugal), Catherine Walsh, (Ecuador), Libia Grueso (Colombia), Edgardo Lander (Venezuela), Fernando Coronil (Venezuela and U.S.), Javier Sanjinés (Bolivia and U.S.), Arturo Escobar (Colombia and U.S.), Margarita Cervantes-Zalazar (Cuba and U.S.), Santiago Castro-Gómez (Colombia), Oscar Guardiola (Colombia), Ramón Grosfoguel (Puerto Rico and U.S.), Agustín Laó-Montes (Puerto Rico and U.S.), and Nelson Maldonado-Torres (Puerto Rico and U.S.). See Quijano 2007, 168–78.

11. Quijano (2007, 171) argues that "coloniality of power" was conjured "together with America [and Latin America] and Western Europe, and with the social category of 'race' as the key element of the social classification of colonized and colonizer. Unlike in any other previous experience of colonialism, the old ideas of superiority of the dominant, and the inferiority of dominated under European colonialism were mutated in a relationship of biologically [biopolitically] and structurally superior and inferior." "The process of Eurocentrification of the new world," Quijano elaborates, "gave way to the imposition of such a 'racial' criteria to the new social classification of the world population on a global scale. So, in the first place, new social identities were produced all over the world: 'whites,' 'Indians,' 'Negroes,' 'yellows,' 'olives,' using physiognomic traits of the peoples as external manifestations of their 'racial' nature. Then, on that basis the new geocultural identities were produced: European, American, Asiatic, African, and much later, Oceania."

12. Magical realism often refers to the genre of an "outsize" realism associated with the Latin American *nueva narrativa* and the writers Alejo Carpentier and Gabriel García Márquez and with South Asian writers such as Salman Rushdie. While the term "magical realism" can be readily attributed to Franz Roh (1995) in his introduction to post-expressionist painting of 1925, more recently the postcolonial critics Ato Quayson and William Childers see a peculiarly "magically idealist" attitude to phenomenal reality already present in medieval Spain's genre of chivalric romance, with starting Cervantes's *Don Quixote* (Childers 2006, esp. part 2; Quayson 2006).

13. The notion of the novel as a protean genre has been advanced by Michael Holquist (1977) and Walter Reed (1981). The idea that the "novelness" of novels derives from its impulse to transcribe the dialectical tensions among the meanings of human utterances is taken in part from Mikhail M. Bakhtin's magisterial *The Dialogic Imagination* (1981).

14. See Adams 2009; Anderson 1998; Baucom 2005; Brickhouse 2004; Dimock 2009; Gilroy 1993; Gruesz 2001; Levander and Levine 2008; Rediker 2007; Roach 1996; Sollors 1998; Spivak 2007; Walcott 1986. Susan Gilman's rich comparative American adaptation studies and her zigzagging essay on Martí's and Fernández Retamar's comparative readings of Helen Hunt Jack-

son's *Ramona* and Harriet Beecher Stowe's *Uncle Tom's Cabin* first clued me into the way post-exceptionalist American studies need not conflate the rhetoric of temporality with the many idioms of space (see Gilman 2008).

1 Unsettling Race

1. Briefly, the concept of the coloniality of power was first theorized by Quijano. He argues that modern regimes of power are characterized by what he terms "coloniality," which, as distinct from colonialism, is defined not simply by a formal re-domination between empire and colony but primarily by global and national/cultural hierarchies (gendered, racialized, and sexualized) that are articulated differentially in time and space (see Quijano 1999, 2000b; see also Grosfoguel 2003; Laó-Montes 2003; Mignolo 2000b).

2. For a discussion of the twinned logics of U.S. empire (as a spatial territory) and as the cultures of U.S. new imperialism (as a de-territorialized logic of capitalism), see Harvey 2003.

3. See Althusser 1971; Judith Butler, " 'Conscience Doth Make Subjects of Us All': Althusser's Subjection," in Butler 1997.

4. The post-positivist realism the *Reclaiming Identity* scholars defend emerges from within the philosophy of science and is informed by the work of Charles Sanders Pierce, W. V. O. Quine, and Hilary Putnam, among others. I have profited from Putnam's autobiographical essay on the philosophy of science "A Half Century of Philosophy, Viewed from Within" (1997).

5. Mohanty (1997, 216) hypothesizes, "Instead of conceiving identities as self-evidently based on the authentic experiences of members of a cultural or social group . . . , or as all equally unreal to the extent that they lay any claim to the real experiences of real people because experience is a radically mystifying term . . . , we need to explore the possibility of a theoretical understanding of social and cultural identity in terms of objective social location. To do so, we need a cognitivist conception of experience."

6. As I have suggested, the coloniality of power functions to organize cross-genealogical dialogues and theoretical developments around issues central to the futures of minority studies: identity, subjectification, power regimes, epistemology, and transformative politics. Among the scholars engaged in those dialogues are Enrique Dussel, Ramón Grosfoguel, Agustín Laó-Montes, Walter Mignolo, Aníbal Quijano, Freya Schiwy, and Catherine Walsh.

7. One of the most important (and sympathetic) critiques of Quijano's coloniality of power analysis has been written by the feminist philosopher María Lugones. As she suggests, it is "politically important that many who have taken [Aníbal Quijano's] the coloniality of power seriously have tended to naturalize gender. That position is also one that entrenches oppressive colonial gender arrangements, oppressive organizations of life" (Lugones 2007, 186).

8. For far-reaching studies of the emerging problems in the intellectual and

2pinstitutional organization of academic thinking, see Mignolo 2000b; Wallerstein et al. 1996. While the Gulbenkian Commission's report is a highly analytical narrative of the social sciences over the past one hundred years and gracefully uses world-system theory, chaos and dynamic complexity theory, contingent universalism, and a timely call for enthnoracial and gender diversity in the academy to overturn Max Weber's worn-out call for a "disenchantment with the world," Mignolo's study of the historical humanities in the modern world's colonial system can be read as an exemplary corrective to the Gulbenkian Commission's call for universalizing the social sciences. Mignolo argues that the Gulbenkian Commission's position on universalism ends up subalternizing others. Briefly, the issue for Mignolo is not how to universalize the social sciences or the historical humanities but how to better locate the "colonial difference" embedded in our academic cultures of scholarship. Mignolo insists that we need to think in terms of local U.S. Latino/a and global border knowledge (*gnosis*) rather than in terms of the disciplines.

9. For an understanding of how nineteenth-century America was obsessed about vernacular varieties of English, see Jones 1999.

10. "*Nepantla*" is a word used by Nahuatl-speaking people in the sixteenth-century to define their own socio-cultural situation in the face of the Spanish conquest. As Mignolo suggests, the word "nepantla" was recorded by Diego Durán, a Dominican missionary who was writing an ethnographic history of Nahuatl-speakers from the Valley of Mexico. When Durán asked one of his informants what he thought about the difficult situation that had been created for them by the Spanish invasion, the informant is reported to have responded, "*Estamos nepantla* (We are nepantla)"—that is, "We are in-between" (personal correspondence, January 15, 1998). My emphasis on nepantla throughout the chapter is meant to function as a reminder of the "colonial difference" implicit in U.S. Latino/a studies, a translational and transnational memory that all cultural difference has to be seen in the context of power and of the relations of subalternity and domination.

11. Gloria Anzaldúa writes in "Border Arte: Nepantla, El lugar de la Frontera" that border art "depicts both the soul of the artist and the soul of the pueblo. It deals with who tells the stories and what stories and histories are told. I call this form of visual narrative *autohistorias*. This form goes beyond the traditional self-portrait or autobiography, in telling the writer/artist's personal story, it also includes the artist's cultural history" (Keating 2009, 113). In a conversation with me at the University of California, Santa Cruz, on October 17, 1990, Anzaldúa described the form of *Borderlands/La Frontera* by using the home-grown neologism "*autohistoriateoría*." I first met Anzaldúa in person in 1988 at the University of California, Santa Cruz, and began working closely with her in a series of graduate tutorials on Chicano/a literature and theory. She then asked me to be one of the primary examiners for her doctoral qualifying exams in the Literature Program.

12. Anzaldúa's imaginative work has had the great fortune of having been

218 Notes to Chapter One

treated by superb feminist and postcolonial critics. In addition to Mignolo's and Keating's work, readers can track in work by Sonia Saldívar-Hull, Chela Sandoval, Yvonne Yarbro-Bejarano, and Angie Chabram-Dernersesian an emerging debate in Chicana/o studies between psychoanalytic-deconstructive work such as Norma Alarcón's and post-postivist realist work such as Paula Moya's. For Alarcón (1996, 50), Anzaldúa's "lesbo-erotic" text not only "re-codifies the multiple names of Woman" and recuperates "a new mestiza consciousness," but it also re-situates Coatlicue through the author's own "non-conscious memory." Briefly, for Alarcón (1996, 50), Anzaldúa represents "the non-(pre)-oedipal mother" in *Borderlands/La Frontera* and in the process "gives birth to herself as inscriber/speaker of/for mestiza consciousness." More recently, Moya has responded to Alarcón's and Chela Sandoval's reading of Anzaldúa by suggesting that in their proto-post-structuralist approaches to Chicana feminism in general, and to Anzaldúa's work in particular, they have "run the risk of theorizing . . . Chicana identity in terms of ambiguity and fragmentation so that the 'Chicana' becomes, in effect, a figure for marginality and contradiction in the postmodern world. I would argue that the term 'Chicana' should not denote a principle of abstract oppositionality" (Moya 2002, 129). In contradistinction to Alarcón's and Sandoval's readings, Moya calls for a post-positivist realist approach to Anzaldúa's work based on issues of identity and experience. Thus envisaged, Anzaldúa's new mestiza consciousness for Moya can be interpreted as a form of "epistemic privilege"—that is, "a special advantage with respect to possessing or acquiring knowledge about how fundamental aspects of our society . . . operate to sustain matrices of power" (Moya 2002, 188, fn. 36). While this is not the place to respond to this debate in Chicano/a studies, I note that Anzaldúa's work engages us with another "take" on the "post"—that is, what we might call the "post-human." Throughout *Borderlands/La Frontera*, Anzaldúa asks an urgent question: how do we go about breaking down the barriers we build between the human and the animal? In contradistinction to Weber and Descartes, Anzaldúa calls for a reenchantment with the world. Specifically, her "alien" allegory builds on passages such as the following one in her autohistoriateoría: "I tremble before the animal, the alien, sub-or suprahuman, the one that has something in common with the wind and the trees, . . . that possesses a demon determination and ruthlessness *beyond the human*" (Anzaldúa 1987, 72; emphasis added).

13. For a superb scholarly sampling of Anzaldúa's imaginative and critical work spanning a thirty-year period, see Keating 2009. Keating's work is useful to readers who are unfamiliar with Anzaldúa's writings, as well as to those who have read, taught, and analyzed her work for decades.

14. I thank my former Berkeley colleague Gautam Premnath for allowing me to read his superb dissertation, "Arguments with Nationalism in the Fiction of the Indian Diaspora" (2003). I am especially indebted to his powerful suggestion that Roy politically declares herself and her characters to be "mobile republics" to get at the fundamental failure of the Indian republic to come into

its own. I read Premnath's work after I had completed the writing of this last section of the chapter, and after I had formulated my arguments that *The God of Small Things* fundamentally critiques postcolonial coloniality and nationalism through its dystopian deconstruction of kinship in Kerala and alternatively uses the erotic as a utopian form of political and cultural critique.

15. It should become clear that I am mostly in agreement with Satya Mohanty that our identities are not mere social constructions, and hence "spurious," or fixed, unchanging essences in a brutalizing world. I agree, further, with Mohanty that "we have the capacity to examine our social identities, considering them in light of our best understanding of other social facts and our other social relationships" (Mohanty 1997, 201). My reading of *The God of Small Things* is indebted to what I take to be Mohanty's significant reformulation of experience and identity dispersed throughout *Literary Theory and the Claims of History*.

16. I read Roy's critique of the bourgeois nation in *The God of Small Things* as echoing Ranajit Guha's description of the South Asian Subaltern Studies Group's project. In "On Some Aspects of the Historiography of Colonial India" (1988, 43), Guha defines the problematic of their project as "the study of [the] historical failure of the nation to come into its own, a failure due to the inadequacy of the bourgeoisie as well as of the working class to lead it to a decisive victory over colonialism and a bourgeois-democratic revolution of either the classic nineteenth-century type under the hegemony of the bourgeoisie or a more modern type under the hegemony of workers and peasants, that is a 'new democracy.'"

17. I refer, of course, to the term Orlando Patterson (1982) gives to the status of being a living being radically deprived of all rights.

18. My reading of kinship and positionality has profited immensely from Butler 2000.

2 Migratory Locations

1. For an illuminating discussion of "de-territorialization," see Deleuze and Guattari 2002, in which the authors use the term to locate the politics of exile in literature and language.

2. By the phrase "transnationally local" I mean the border contact zones where the local and global intersect (see Mignolo 2000b).

3. Page numbers for direct quotes from *Divergent Modernities* are cited in parentheses in the text. According to Román de la Campa (1999, vii), "Latin-americanism" can be defined both as a field-imaginary (like critical U.S. studies or American studies) and as a "community of discourses ... mainly [produced] in the United States, but also beyond." Like other field-imaginaries, it is currently turning toward subaltern and hegemonic mainline forms of criticism such as postcolonial studies, deconstruction, postmodernism, and boom and

post-boom discourses. In addition, I profited immensely from my conversations with the late Antonio Cornejo Polar, a colleague at Berkeley, who argued that Latinamericanism faced the post-contemporary condition that he called "diglossia"—that is, a sharp split and antagonism that divides the studies of Latinamericanist cultures produced from within Latin America and the research and studies produced from within the United States (see Cornejo Polar 1997). In this chapter, I follow Julio Ramos's argument that Latinamericanism is vitally related to the War of 1898 and to José Martí's subaltern writings in New York City.

4. Public spheres, for Habermas (1989), are both direct and mediated "critically reasoning" conversations between individuals who form public opinion and thus influence the political system.

5. *North American Scenes* is a series of chronicles on everyday life in North America, especially in New York City. Written between 1881 and 1892 for various newspapers, particularly *La Nación* (Buenos Aires), *El Partido Liberal* (Mexico City), and *La Opinión Nacional* (Caracas), these modern chronicles form what Ramos (2001, xiv) calls a "seldom studied" and "fundamental part of Martí's voluminous corpus." More significantly, *North American Scenes* constitutes, again for Ramos, "a foundational moment in the genealogy of Latin Americanist discourse, as they deploy a series of rhetorical strategies, tropes, and subject positions." See also Rotker 1998; Martí 2002.

6. Julio Ramos's study of Martí's "minor writings," like Deleuze's and Guatarri's study of Kafka's minoritized discourse, relies on a deconstruction of the canonical category of high art. Ramos rejects this hierarchic model of the canonical paradigm and instead favors a spatial, "lateral criticism" in which poetic or minor discourses are variously "inside" or "outside" the dominant discursive practices of the hegemonic culture (Ramos 2001).

7. For a range and sampling of critical reviews of Ramos's *Desencuentros de la modernidad* (1989), see, e.g., Ruben Ríos Avila, "Hacía una crítica lateral," *Puerto Rico Ilustrado* (cultural supplement to *El Mundo*), August 1990, 10–22; John Beverley, "Review of *Desencuentros de la modernidad*," *Revista Iberoamericana* 555, no. 5 (1995), 745–49; Antonio Cornejo Polar, "Review of *Desencuentros de la modernidad*," *Revista de Crítica Literaria Latinoamericana* 18, no. 34 (1991), 296; Luis Millones Figueroa, "El surgimiento de la literatura moderna en Latinoamerica," *Nuevo Texto Crítico* 8 (1991), 221; María Elena Rodríguez Castro, "El buen decir y la crítica," *Posdata* 1, no. 2 (1991); Karen Stoley, "Review of *Desencuentros de la modernidad*," *Hispanic Review* 60, no. 1 (1992), 109–111. For an extended reading of Ramos's work, see Beverley 1993. For an incisive reading of the emergence of this new trans-American criticism as a response to the limits of (North) American cultural criticism from Ralph Waldo Emerson to Richard Rorty, see Jay 1997.

8. See Weber 1950. My views here on Weber draw on Habermas (1987).

9. Drawing on the cultural work of Ángel Rama, Jean Franco, and Noé Jitrik, among others, Ramos's thesis on the uneven modernity in nineteenth-century

Latin America anticipates the views on twentieth-century Latin America in García Canclini 1990, 65: "We [in Latin America] have had an exuberant modernism with a deficient modernization."

10. For a lucid and cogent analysis of this "Occidentalism" for the Américas, see Fernández Retamar 1995d.

11. A large part of the book, which was originally published in Amsterdam in 1944, is based on notes of intense discussions between Adorno and Horkheimer in their exile in Santa Monica, California.

12. If, as Ramos suggests, Martí's writings are "minoritized discourses," we might also extend this key insight by saying that Martí's positions emerged in similar ways as U.S. ethnic and minority positions have emerged, in the words of David Lloyd (1982, 12), "in differential relation to the unifying tendencies of the state and its apparatus."

13. As opposed to "traditional intellectuals," Gramsci's "organic intellectuals" are the new progressive intellectuals needed to organize a new social class.

14. Martí's allusion to Marx anticipates Marshall Berman's view that the twentieth century oscillates between modernization and modernism, shattering the public sphere into a multitude of fragments and privatized languages. As Berman (1982, 15), puts it, "To be modern . . . is to experience personal and social life as maelstrom, to find one's world and oneself in perpetual disintegration and renewal, trouble and anguish, ambiguity and contradiction: to be part of a universe in which all that is solid melts into air. To be a modernist is to make oneself something at home in the maelstrom, to make its rhythms one's own, to move within its currents in search of the forms of reality, of beauty, of freedom, of justice, that its fervid and perilous flow allows."

15. Instead of using terms such as "mass culture" or "popular culture," Adorno (1975, 12) reminds us, "In our drafts we spoke of 'mass culture.' We replaced that expression with 'culture industry' in order to exclude from the outset the interpretation agreeable to its advocates: that it is a matter of something like a culture that arises spontaneously from the masses themselves, the contemporary form of popular art. From the latter the culture industry must be distinguished in the extreme."

16. See Retamar 1995a, 137, in which he argues persuasively that Marti "fue el anti-Gobineau, y con una visión popular, defendió exáctamente lo opuesto que el prefascita Francés, la igualdad de las razas (was an anti-Gobineau and, with his popular vision, exactly defended the opposite of the French prefascist, the sameness of races)." Fernández Retamar, of course, is alluding here to Martí's differential vision of biopolitics in "Our America" (1891), in which he claimed that "no hay odio de razas, porque no hay razas (there is no hatred of races because there are no races)." I thank Roberto Fernández Retamar for many helpful conversations while we walked around the streets of Havana, in January 1997 and for sharing with me his most recently published scholarly work on Martí.

17. For two wonderful complementary readings of the origins of the proto–

U.S. Latino/a discourses in the United States, see Brickhouse 2004; Gruesz 2002. For far-reaching imaginative and phantasmatic interpretations of José Martí in New York City's barrioscapes, see Goldman 2004; Vega 1990.

18. I have also profited from Fernández Retamar 2009.

19. According to Mónica Garcia González (2009), the Chilean Francisco Bilbao founded this two-sided Latinamericanist vision of the Américas in "Iniciativa de la América: Idea de un Congreso federal de las repúblicas" (1856).

20. See Wayman Poma de Ayala's narrative about colonial Peru, *Nueva Crónica y Buen Gobierno*; see also the dictum on the Zapatistas' website at http://www.ezln.org (accessed July 12, 2010); Mignolo 2005.

3 The War of 1898

1. For an "exceptionalist" history of the war, see Musicant 1997.

2. From Roosevelt's own pen in *The Rough Riders*, we know that his gun was in fact a revolver recovered from the sunken battleship *Maine* and was given to him by a brother-in-law in the Navy.

3. Tellingly, in his review of *The War of 1898* (1998), Theodore Draper dismisses Pérez's book as "overly simple" and "propagandistic." Worse, he red-baits Pérez for writing "as a Cuban liberationist refighting the war. . . . His concluding pages fervently praise Fidel Castro for bringing to the light the wrongs of 1898": Theodore Draper, "The Fours-Sided War," *New York Review of Books*, March 3, 1999, 44.

4. The use of the term "Smoked Yankee" by Spain and the United States defines African American soldiers as not "real Yankees." As Kaplan (2002, 229) explains, real Yankees, are after all "Anglo Saxons." Both Spanish and U.S. imperialists used "Smoked Yankee" as a category of biological race and of political history. See also Gatewood 1987.

5. Lenin 1996 (1916) remains the classic economic theory of empire.

6. Kaplan (1995, 328) writes that the "historical interpretations of American imperialism are inseparable from the debates about its existence. . . . [From the perspective that the American empire] is a contradiction in terms . . . America's foreign interventions, whether military, economic, political or cultural, have been acts of liberation, efforts to defend the oppressed from the aggressive designs of other imperialists."

7. During the race for governor of New York, H. W. Brands (1997, 372) writes, Roosevelt "fully appreciated what a coup it would be for him to receive the [Congressional Medal of Honor] during the campaign; even if arrived too late for that—and, in fact, the election came and went with no medal from Washington—it could still provide a confirmation of character that any opponent would be hard-pressed to match."

8. Ada Ferrer (1999, 230) writes that "the massive multiracial and anti-

colonial movements that transformed Cuban society between 1868 and 1898 [produced] an army which, by the final war in 1895, was said to be about 60 percent of color."

9. The phrase "the Black Legend" was first coined in 1912 by the Spanish journalist Julián Juderías in protest of the representations of Spain as a primitive (backwater) multicultural country defined by ignorance, superstition, and religious fanaticism, whose history could never recover from the "black" mark of its violent conquest of the Américas. In Roosevelt's hands, the Black Legend's shadow expresses itself in his view of the Spanish military men as "not very good shots"; as unmanly, for the Spaniards are frequently described as "running from the rifle pits"; and as "nervous" (Roosevelt 1999 [1899], 54, 82, 105). Throughout his memoir, Roosevelt "blackens" the white Spaniards fighting in Cuba not only morally but also physically to the point that he, incredibly, believes that one cannot tell the difference between the African Cuban *mambises* and the Spanish soldiers fighting his Rough Riders. "It was impossible to tell the Cubans from the Spaniards, and, as we could not decide whether these were Cubans following the Spaniards we had put to flight, or merely another troop of Spanish retreating after the first, . . . we dared not fire" (Roosevelt 1999 [1899], 57). I have profited from DeGuzmán 2005; Greer et al. 2007.

10. Kaplan emphasizes that it was W. E. B. Du Bois who first linked the shadow of the "color line" at home in the Jim Crow South and the exportation of this scientific racism abroad to the new outposts of the U.S. empire. Du Bois's famous dictum from *The Souls of Black Folk* (1990 [1903], 221), "The problem of the twentieth century is the problem of the color-line,—the relation of the darker to the lighter races of men in Asia and Africa, in America and the islands of the sea," addresses precisely this issue of imperialism and globalization at the first Pan-African Conference of 1900.

11. Roosevelt's four-volume history, *The Winning of the West*, published between 1889 and 1896, as his biographer Brands (1997, 232) notes, was largely emplotted in a "heroically nationalist" mode. Native American Indians, like Cubans, Filipinos, and Puerto Ricans, were cast by Roosevelt as "very terrible in battle," "cruel," "savage" and "bloody." As Brands explains (1997, 233), *The Winning of the West* "lacked the subtlety and nuance that were absent from all his writings (and speeches and most of his actions). Its ethnocentrism and moral self-assurance likewise were typical of the author (not to say of the age)."

12. According to the Latin American Subaltern Studies Group's "Founding Statement" (1995, 140), "The emergence of the testimonial and documentary forms [from, say, 1968 to 1979] shifts dramatically the parameters of representation away from the writer and the avant-gardes." The *testimonio*, they explain, "leads to a new emphasis on the concrete, the personal, the 'small history,' writing . . . by women, political prisoners, lumpen, and gays, raising, in the process, questions of who represents whom."

13. Throughout this section, I link Henry Louis Gates's notion of the "signifyin[g] vernacular tradition in African American literature" (Gates 1988, 51)

with Fernando Ortiz's Afro-Cuban vernacular tradition of the *choteo* (Ortiz 1924). To signify for Gates and to *chotear* for Ortiz is to engage in vernacular rhetorical games. "Signifyin[g]," according to Gates (1988, 51), is always "black double-voicedness; because it always entails formal revision and an intertextual relation." In the second half of chapter 7, on Rolando Hinojosa's *Klail City*, I return to the Cuban uses and history of the *choteo*.

14. The process by which Montejo constitutes himself as a subject and thus becomes the proper subject of his own *historia* is a classic example of what Louis Althusser (1979, 174) has termed "the interpellation of the subject" by the determining forces of ethno-racial and class formations. According to Althusser (1979, 182), an individual "is interpellated as a (free) subject in order that he shall submit freely to the commandments of the Subject, i.e. in order that he shall (freely) accept his subjection, i.e. in order that he shall make the gestures and actions of his subjection 'all by himself.' There are no subjects except by and for their subjection."

15. If the frontier was the food-stamp program of the nineteenth century for whites, the history of the possessive investment in whiteness by elites by using land rights continued well into the twentieth century. As George Lipsitz (2006) argues, home-ownership programs were largely structured on the basis of race. Only whites (regardless of financial status) could qualify for home mortgages.

16. Fidel Castro, "Broadcast to Venezuelan People," Radio Caracas, January 24, 1959, 2.

17. See Jameson (1991, 44–45), especially his thrilling reading of Michael Herr's notion of *la vida loca* in *Dispatches*—that is, the hallucinogenic excitement, the military structures of eroticism, and the drug-like intensities that feel like euphoria. I have also profited from Edna Duffy's provocative reading of Jamesonian space and speed in *The Speed Handbook* (2009).

18. Donald Pease (2009a, 89) argues that the Vietnam Wall was "erected during the second year of Reagan's presidency [and] was intended to achieve two outcomes: (1) The erasure of the negative chain of recollections associated with the Vietnam syndrome; and (2) The replacement of the Vietnam veteran, with the representation of the POW as the symbol of an imprisoned American citizenry, struggling to return to the political certitudes of World War II."

19. For my views on Johnson and the Vietnam War, I have relied on Berman 1989; Chafe 1991; Halberstam 1993; Karnow 1984.

20. Antonio Gramsci (1971, 54–55), in Hegelian, Marxist, universalist, teleological fashion, envisages subaltern history as incomplete and fragmented: "The history of subaltern social groups is necessarily fragmented and episodic. There undoubtedly does exist a tendency to (at least provisional stages of) unification in the historical activity of these groups, but this tendency is continually interrupted by activity of the ruling groups; it can therefore only be demonstrated when an historical cycle is completed and this cycle culminates in a success."

4 The "Mexican Elvis"

1. For Manuel Castells (2004, 67), the network society "is neither a network of enterprises nor an intra-firm, networked organization. Rather, it is a lean agency of economic activity, built around specific business projects, which are enacted by networks of various composition and origin."

2. U.S. Latinos and Latinas (mostly Chicanos) make up 36 percent of public high school graduates in California, whites make up 41 percent, African Americans make up 6 percent, and Asian Americans make up 16 percent. By 2010, U.S. Latinos and Latinas became the largest minority group in the United States.

3. See Omi and Winant (1994, 55–56), in which they define racial formation "as the sociohistorical process by which categories are created, inhabited, transformed, and destroyed. [It] is a process of historically situated projects in which human bodies are organized. Next we link racial formation to the evolution of hegemony, the way in which society is organized and ruled." As the Mexican Elvis, Robert Lopez brings together crisscrossed sets of racial and class categories—Southern black and white as well as Southwestern Mexican and Anglo American. My reading here relies on Neil Foley's explication of the "cotton culture" of Texas, in which he argues there is a "fusion of cotton and cattle culture, of plantation and ranch, creat[ing] a hybrid economy" (Foley 1997, 4).

4. In this chapter, I rely on the formulation of "cultural citizenship" in which Renato Rosaldo (1992, 7) uses the term both "in the legal sense (one either does or does not have a document) and also in the familiar sense of the spectrum from full citizenship to second-class citizenship."

5. According to Quijano and Wallerstein (1992, 552), "Americanity" was "the erection of a gigantic ideological overlay to the modern world [colonial] system." Thus envisaged, the Américas were fundamental to the historical formation of an internal and external coloniality of power, and "Americanity" was a foundational element of modernity. Coloniality, racism, ethnicity, and the very concept of newness, they suggest, were constitutive of the Américas from their very start. Drawing on the work of Quijano and Wallerstein, Mignolo (2000b) argues that the ethno-racial foundations of modernity can be located in the production of "Americanity" and the "coloniality of power," where their basic principles were established in the sixteenth century and altered thereafter by successive uneven colonialisms. Parallel to the ethno-racial classification of the Americas and the world, there was the classification of languages and knowledge. The epistemology of the European Renaissance was assumed to be the natural perspective from which knowledge could be described and suppressed. This same process, Mignolo emphasizes, was reiterated after the Enlightenment, when the concept of Reason opened up a new description and reason became associated with northern Europe and indirectly with whiteness (Hegel and Kant).

6. I draw on Norma Alarcón's influential insights that women of color, especially Chicanas, are "multiply interpellated"—that is, they are called by many names, constituted in and by that multiple calling ("The Theoretical Subject(s) of This Bridge Called My Back" in Calderón and Saldívar 1991, 28–39).

7. Vernon Chadwick has organized four international symposiums on Elvis Presley and cultural studies in and of the New South. My discussion of the new field of "Elvispalooza" in this chapter is indebted to Chadwick 1997.

8. Karen Schoemer, "Love That Blue Suede Sombrero: Shake, Rattle, and Roll with the Mexican Elvis," *Newsweek*, vol. 128, no. 19, November 4, 1996, 78.

9. As we know, "ethnicity" is a slippery term. For example, the Greek–English lexicon tells us that the word *"ethnos"* meant "a number of people accustomed to living together," "one's own people," and "nation." Side by side with this definition was the related word *"ethnikos,"* meaning "other people," "heathen," "pagan," "foreign," and so on. El Vez's songs voice and write themselves between ethnos and ethnikos, where he attempts to de-anthropologize himself by thematizing a staged identity.

10. In *Cuban Counterpoint* (1995, 98), Fernando Ortiz writes, "I have chosen the word transculturation [instead of acculturation] to express the varied phenomena that came about in Cuba as a result of the extremely complex transmutation of culture that has taken place here."

11. My use of the term "transmodernity" relies on the philosophical work of Enrique Dussel, who uses the term as an alternative to the Eurocentric formulation of postmodernity. As he sweepingly puts it, "The overcoming of cynical managerial reason (planetary administration), of capitalism (as economic system), of liberalism (as political system), of Eurocentrism (as ideology), of machismo (in erotics), of the reign of the white race (in racism), of the destruction in nature (in ecology), and so on presupposes the liberation of diverse types of the oppressed and/or excluded. It is in this sense that the ethics of liberation defines itself as transmodern (because the postmoderns are still Eurocentric)" (Dussel 1998, 19).

12. See Spivak 1998a, 287, in which she argues that the "contemporary division of labor is a displacement of the divided field of nineteenth-century territorial imperialism."

13. El Vez and the Memphis Mariachis, "Taking Care of Business," *GI Ay, Ay! Blues*, Big Pop, 1996.

14. Throughout this chapter, I rely on the succinct definition of the subaltern in Guha 1998, 35: "[It] is a name for the general attribute of subordination . . . whether this is expressed in terms of class, caste, age, gender, and office or in another way."

15. El Vez and the Memphis Mariachis, "Trying to Get to You," *GI Ay, Ay! Blues*.

16. El Vez and the Memphis Mariachis, "Misery Tren," *GI Ay, Ay! Blues*.

17. I have learned a great deal from Walter Mignolo's incisive essay "The Zapatistas' Theoretical Revolution: Its Gnoseological, Political, and Ethical

Consequences," in which he suggests that the Zapatistas' theoretical revolution in Chiapas is "a new way of thinking from the border between epistemological power and gnoseological privilege. . . . By gnoseology . . . I refer to any kind of knowledge, academic or not" (Mignolo 2002c, 9).

18. El Vez and the Memphis Mariachis, "JC Lowrider Superstar," *GI Ay, Ay! Blues.*

5 Making U.S. Democracy Surreal

1. Throughout this chapter, page numbers for quotes from Guinier and Torres 2000 are in parentheses in the text.

2. In thinking my way through arguments about race and colorblindness and color-consciousness in Guinier and Torres 2002, I have profited from many conversations with Michael Omi on the dilemma of racial formations in the twenty-first century. For example, Guinier and Torres might have asked more sharply some of the following questions Omi raised for me: How have those policymakers who believe in the doctrine and many idioms of colorblindness explained the state's recent willingness to destabilize colorblindness as its hegemonic "common sense"? How has terrorism posed a new dilemma for the state? When, and under what circumstances, should the state notice or not notice race? While the dominant colorblindness point of view by intellectuals and policymakers has asserted that the state should not engage in any form of race color-consciousness, the current U.S. war on terrorism has elicited quite different responses that argue for specific forms of state-sanctioned racial profiling. This is precisely the dilemma that Omi analyzes in his provisionally entitled forthcoming book *The Dilemma of Racial Formation in the 21st Century.*

3. This assimilation of differences into similarities is, as we know, for Nietzsche the figural basis of all rational discourse; it is also one of the characteristics Jacques Derrida ascribed to metaphor in "White Mythology" (1982).

4. Critical race theorists conceptualize race and law as mutually empowering. For an overview of the project, see Crenshaw et al. 1996.

5. In opposition to a positive identity that is fixed, absolutist, and self-satisfied, Adorno (1973, 406) offers a negative dialectic that proposed a critique of "every self-absolutizing particular."

6. In the most fundamental sense, U.S. Latinos/as, according to Mike Davis (2000, 54), are struggling to "reconfigure the 'cold' frozen geometries of the old spatial order to accommodate a 'hotter,' more exuberant [and magical] urbanism."

7. Paul Gilroy (2004, 9) maps this symbolic starting point by specifying the logic by which race articulated a rational irrationality; he argues that this irrational symbology can be marked by "the moment in which Kant compromised himself by associating the figure of the 'Negro' with stupidity and connecting differences in color to differences in mental capacity. From that point

on, race has been a cipher for the debasement of humanism and democracy." See also Gilroy 2004; Kant 1960.

8. See Conley 1999; see also Lipsitz 2006; Oliver and Shapiro 2006. As early as 1935, Du Bois specified how, despite their low wages, white workers were privileged in public functions and facilities, in employment as police, and voting rights, with an accompanying dominance in local schools and courts (see Du Bois 1935, 700–770).

9. Arturo Islas Papers, Stanford University, Stanford, Calif., folder 1, correspondence, 1974–75.

10. See Timothy Pfaff, "Talk with Mrs. Kingston," *New York Times Book Review*, June 15, 1980, 1.

11. My comments on Toni Morrison's voyage of the *damnés* near the end of *Beloved* profited from Baucom 2005; Fanon 1987; Gilroy 1993; Hartman 2007; JanMohamed 2005; Jimenez 2010; Kaplan 2006; Rediker 2007. I also broached the idea of the voyage of the damnés in *Beloved* and *A Mercy* in my brief and informal conversations with Toni Morrison when I was asked by Ian Baucom to serve as her faculty escort when she visited Duke University on January 30– February 2, 2008.

6 Chicano/a Literature

1. On Paredes 1958, see Saldívar 1991; on Hinojosa 1976, see Saldívar 1985, 1–20.

2. See Américo Paredes's chronicles published in *Pacific Stars and Stripe*; his poetry in *Between Two Worlds* (1991), especially "Westward the Course of Empire" and "Pro Patria"; and his short stories "Ichiro Kikuchi" and "Sugamo" in *The Hammon and the Beans and Other Stories* (1994).

3. See Paredes 1995 for a representative sampling of the folksong corpus of *danzas* and *corridos* of the lower U.S.-Mexican borderlands.

4. For rich histories of the Plan de San Diego and *los sediciosos*, see Mac-Laclan 1991; Sandos 1992.

5. Ramón Saldívar (2006, 180) suggests that Américo Paredes's novel *George Washington Gómez* "repeatedly rejects the agency of the heroic figure of the historical present, but it also offers no alternative future plot to replace the hero's action either." In other words, Paredes contrapuntally bumps up the Global North against the Global South into the very naming and interpellation of the warrior hero of the novel, George Washington Gómez—as well as Protestantism versus Catholicism, capitalism versus anarchism, and assimilation versus multicultural transculturation.

6. Paredes's marriage with Consuelo Silva collapsed during the early years of the Second World War. In 1947, Paredes met Amelia Sidzu Nagamines, the daughter of a Uruguayan mother and a Japanese diplomat father, in Tokyo, and they married in 1948.

7. Américo Paredes, "Desde Tokio (25 de julio)," *El Universal*, August 11, 1946.

8. Ibid.

9. In one of his final interviews, with Ramón Saldívar (2006, 97), Paredes said that it "was eerie and wonderful to be in Tokyo in those days.... In Tokyo business was booming. Americans had landed on enemy soil, stacked their weapons, and went shopping, souvenir hunting for kimonos, obis, silk fans, fine lace, ceremonial dolls, and fine prints. The department stores in Ginza were cleaned out very quickly, and you had to hit the side-street black market shops to find anything interesting. . . . In the side-streets and the train stations, young women offered themselves for a box of field rations or a bar of chocolate."

10. For this history, I relied on Kennedy 1999.

11. On Roberto Fernández Retamar and Casa de las Américas, see Saldívar 1991.

12. The Casa de las Américas Prize has now survived for more than four decades. When I was a judge for the Thirty-Eighth Casa de las Américas Prize in January 1997, more than five hundred manuscripts in the genres of testimonio, novel, short story, drama, and criticism were submitted. The Casa de las Américas was founded by the Cuban revolutionaries and intellectuals Haydee Santamaría and Marcia Leiseca. Just four months after the Cuban Revolution in 1959, the Casa de las Américas was created as a way to continue an intercultural exchange with the Américas and the planet in the face of the U.S. blockade of everything Cuban. I think it is safe to say that every artist and intellectual-activist who visits Cuba also has to visit the modest buildings that make up the Casa de las Américas in the beautiful Malecón district of Havana. While it may be too over the top to formulate the "deep" ideological meaning of Casa de las Américas to those in the United States and the Global North not familiar with it, my fellow *jurist*, the great Mexican feminist novelist Bárbara Jacobs, told me that for her generation of Latinamericanist imaginative writers, the Casa de las Américas was "un lugar sagrado para la cultura latinoamericana y caribeña." With its awarding of the premio extraordinario in U.S. Latino/a literature in 1997, was Casa de las Américas also attempting to annex the largest minority group in the United States: U.S. Latinos and Latinas? According to Santamaría, "Queremos que Cuba no se aisle de las formas artísticas y culturales del continente." To accomplish this, the Casa de las Américas inaugurated the first Casa de las Américas Prize in 1959. Again, as the Cuban cofounder of Casa de las Américas, Marcia Leiseca, suggested one day when we were touring Casa's archives, "La revolución cubana es determinante para la literature latinoamericana, por los menos su difusión—es la Revolución que despierta ese interés."

13. Sonia Rivera-Valdés's *Las historias prohibidas de Marta Veneranda* (1997), a winner of the Casa de las Américas Premio Extraordinario de Literatura Hispana en Estados Unidos, is a splendid collection of unified stories about the

prohibited loves of U.S. Latina women. Erudite, passionate, and critical of heteronormative subject positions, the book can be seen as joining the ground-breaking work of other women writing in the flesh, as Cherríe Moraga affirmed in *Loving in the War Years* (1983). A Cuban American resident of New York City since the 1960s, Rivera-Valdés previously published short stories in anthologies in the United States and Latin America and is now a professor of Latin American and Hispanic literature at the City University of New York. What Emilio Bejel, Pablo Armando Fernández, and I immediately appreciated was the ex-quisite manner in which a series of separate confessions (*historias*) were related to the transcriber, Marta Veneranda, creating a kind of fantastic *narrativa testimonial*. After an introduction, the feminist transcriber recedes into the background, and firsthand testimonial accounts from Cuban American and other U.S. Latina women whose sexual lives are interconnected come to the fore.

14. Alejandro Murguia's short-story collection submitted for the Casa de las Américas Prize was published in the United States under the new title, *This War Called Love: 9 Stories* (2002). One of the best stories I read while I was a judge in Cuba was Murguia's rich "Ofrendas." It follows the ritual celebration of the Día de los Muertos (Day of the Dead) in the Mission District of San Francisco, complete with the descriptions of *raza* dressed as *calaveras* and the many altars in the Mission District's barrioscapes. The slick narrator, a Latino radio show host, describes the scene this way: "Everyone in La Mission is here dressed in some kind of skeleton costume. I can't tell who's who except for the obvious beer belly of Toño's or the unmistakable broad nalgas of an ex-girl-friend" (Murguia 2002, 57–58). Amid this happening, the narrator tries to cope with his cousin's death, which occurred that morning. "On the Day of the Dead laughter is the only cure for dying," Murguia (2002, 65) laments. This melan-choly of racial formations for many U.S. Latinos mirrors the significance of the celebration of the Día de los Muertos.

15. The Klail City Death Trip series, the title of Hinojosa's *gran cronicón*, comprises *Estampas de Valle y otras obras* (1973), *Klail City y sus alrededores* (1976), subsequently published in a bilingual edition in the United States as *Generaciones y semblanzas* (1977); *Korean Love Songs* (1981); *Rites and Witnesses* (1982); *Partners in Crime* (1985); *Becky and Her Friends* (1989); *The Useless Servants* (1993); and *Ask a Policeman* and *We Happy Few* (2006).

16. My reading of Mañach's and Hinojosa's *choteo* has profited from the Cuban American literary scholar Gustavo Pérez-Firmat's ingenious essay "Rid-dles of the Sphincter" (1984).

17. Fernando Ortiz first defined his neologism "transculturation" this way: "With the reader's permission, especially if he is interested in ethnographic and sociological questions, I am going to take the liberty of employing for the first time the neologism transculturation, fully aware of the fact that it is a neo-logism. And I venture to suggest that it might be adopted in sociological terminology . . . as a substitute for the term acculturation, whose use is now spreading." Later in the passage, Ortiz concludes his keyword definition by

explaining, "I have chosen the word transculturation to express the highly varied phenomena that have come about in Cuba as a result of the extremely complex transmutations of culture that have taken place here, and without a knowledge of which it is impossible to understand the evolution of the Cuban folk, either in economic or in the institutional, legal, ethical, religious, artistic, linguistic, psychological, sexual, or other aspects of its life" (Ortiz 1995, 97–98). The cultural transmutations of vernacular culture in Cuba and Greater Mexico as forms of the choteo and transculturation, as Ortiz, Paredes, and Hinojosa all noted in their works, never transcends their subaltern positions of (trans)modernity.

7 Transnationalism Contested

1. See, e.g., "What Is the Best Work of American Fiction of the Last Twenty-Five Years?," *New York Times Book Review,* May 21, 2006, in which twenty-two books, as determined by an informal survey conducted by the *Times,* appeared on the magazine's front page. The best work of American fiction, according to the survey, was Toni Morrison's *Beloved* (1987). Of the other texts featured on the cover, not a single novel was by a U.S. Latino/a writer. The majority of novels were written by white male authors such as Philip Roth, Don DeLillo, and Cormac McCarthy, who are primarily in their seventies.

2. Cisneros's first novel and book of short stories, *The House on Mango Street* (1991) and *Woman Hollering Creek and Other Stories* (1992), respectively, have had the good fortune of being treated by exceptionally fine and rigorous literary and cultural critics: see Brady 2002; Calderón 2004; Limón 1998; McCracken 1998; Quintana 1996; Rebolledo 1995; Rosaldo 1989; Saldívar 1990; Saldívar-Hull 2000a; Sandoval 2009.

3. Incredibly, Earl Shorris (1992, 390) claimed that with *The House on Mango Street,* Cisneros "found an audience by writing in a childlike voice about a child. She confirmed what the gringos have said about Mexicans" since the U.S.-Mexican War of 1846–48.

4. According to Arif Dirlik (2007, 1), the neologism "the Global South" goes back to the 1970s. It is affiliated and entangled with other keywords that post–Second World War modernizations and movements used to describe societies (capitalist and socialist) that faced difficulties in achieving the political and economic goals of Western modernity. The Global South neologism was then popularized in reports written by the Brand Commission that advocated the infusion of capital from the Global North into the Global South to help achieve their modernization. Thus envisaged, the burden of the Global South, as Dirlik suggests, is that it has to grapple not only with hegemonic power but also with the hegemonic ideology called neoliberalism.

5. For a useful distinction between mainline American immigrants and subaltern colonized immigrants, see Grosfoguel 2003.

6. See Paul de Man's review essay "A Modern Master: Jorge Luis Borges"

(1984) in de Man 1989, 123–29. In Borges's short stories, all crimes and acts of infamy are founded on misdeeds, dissimulations, impersonations, and duplicities. For example, in "Tlon, Uqbar, Orbis Teritus," Borges writes about a fictional planet that was once glimpsed in an encyclopedia that itself turned out to be based on a false report in the Encyclopedia Britannica. In the story "The Shape of the Sword," an ignominious Irishman betrays the man who saved his life and then passes himself off for his own victim. And, of course, in "The Garden of Forking Paths," the iconic story by Borges, a Chinese hero spies on the British mostly for the satisfaction of labyrinthine dissimulation. For Borges (and for many of the characters in Cisneros's *Caramelo or Puro Cuento*), the creation of truth and beauty begins with acts of duplicity and *infamia*.

7. Through its production of *fotonovelas* and *telenovelas*, the Mexican mass media helps shape women's consciousness and their knowledge of the world. The media especially targets the subaltern working poor, who often do not have more than a grammar-school education. According to Jean Franco (1986, 137), these mass-media texts not only "plot the incorporation of women into society," but they also, more insidiously, "reinforce the serialization of women —the very factor that makes their exploitation, both as reproducers of the labor force and as cheap labor."

As Sonia Saldívar-Hull (2000a, 115–16) suggests, Tellado's readers are asked "to believe in a social fantasy in which anyone can live anywhere in the world and succeed financially. Tellado's romances urge readers to assume that their lives and customs in Latin America are universal." Gloria Anzaldúa's insight in *Borderlands/La Frontera* (1987, 17) that "*la gorra, el rebozo,* [and] *la mantilla* are symbols of my culture's 'protection' of women" underwrites many of Cisneros's critiques of the power of these symbols in *Caramelo or Puro Cuento*.

8. Sandra Cisneros has always insisted on "using simple language and colloquial speech" in her fictions as part of her ideological "vendettas against" the highbrow poetics of the Global North (personal interview with the author).

9. I owe this insight about the close relationship between the European word "vermin" and its folksy American cousin "varmaint" to Lerer 2006.

10. Throughout this chapter, I use the term "melodrama" to mean a text based on a romantic plot and developed sensationally, with little regard for convincing motivation and with an excessive appeal to the emotions of the reading audience. Melodrama literally means "a play with music" and at one time was applied to opera in a broad sense. In Cisneros's fictions, melodrama in its ethnic Mexican manifestations signifies a sharply archaic excess of sensation and sentiment, a rhetorical manipulation of the heartstrings that, for many highbrow readers, often exceeds the bounds of "good taste." Furthermore, I have profited from Linda Williams's argument that racial melodrama "endures not only as an archaic holdover of nineteenth-century stage play (and its virtuous victims and leering villains) and not only in soap operas . . . but as an evolving mode of storytelling crucial to the establishment of moral good" (Williams 2001, 12).

Thus envisaged, melodramas offer us a utopian hope that there still may be an original locus of virtue and that virtue can be achieved in individual acts.

11. For an alternative and provocative critique of the alleged stereotyping of "sordid," "degenerate," "Mexican immigrant" male characters in Cisneros's short fiction—such as the hypersexualized Juan Pedro in "Woman Hollering Creek"—see Limón 1998, 165–67. Limón argues that Cisneros's "portrait" of her Mexican immigrant male characters is "consistent with both those offered by the [Mexican] Samuel Ramos–Octavio Paz tradition and the American iconographic Mexican tradition of Western folk song, travel writing, and film. One can only wonder what happens in the consciousness of Cisneros's very many Anglo-American lay readers as they read this story in the context of a U.S. hysteria about unregulated—in every way—Mexican immigration" (Limón 1998, 166). Nowhere in Cisneros's short stories, Limón suggests, "do we find a desirable eroticized Mexican male [character], although Flavio in 'Bien Pretty' comes close" (Limón 1998, 149). I offer the faceless and nameless "Geraldo sin appellido"—to say nothing about the number of well-rounded ethnic Mexican and Chicano male characters in *Caramelo or Puro Cuento*—as other possible exceptions.

12. Throughout this chapter, I borrow Paul Gilroy's idea of "conviviality" and convivial culture. In *After Empire* (2004, xi), Gilroy uses the idea of "conviviality" as a way to refer to what he sees as "the processes of cohabitation and interaction that have made multiculture an ordinary feature of social life in Britain's urban areas and in postcolonial cities elsewhere" (xi). I agree with Gilroy's hope that "an interest in the workings of" *convivencia* will blast off "from the point 'multiculturalism' broke down."

13. As Walter Benjamin (1998, 178) suggests, "Allegories are, in the realm of thoughts, what ruins are in the realm of things." In addition, Benjamin notes that, in theater, "Allegorical characters, these are what people most see. Children are hopes, young girls are wishes and requests." This suggests a connection between spectacle and allegory.

14. I use "bare life" in Walter Benjamin's earlier and Giorgio Agamben's later senses of the term. Near the end of "Critique of Violence" (1996 [1978], 249]), Benjamin introduces the concept of "bare life" to describe the form of life attacked by legal violence and power, which "in its archetypal form is a [bare] (*bloße*) manifestation of the gods." Bare life, as I see it, is "a pure, naked form of vitality" (*convivencia*) attacked by the bare violence of law and power. Bare life is the moral form of life that distinguishes us from the gods. Legal violence (mythic) is simply the power over life and death. As Benjamin (1996 [1978], 250) argues, "Blood is the symbol of [bare] life. . . . Mythic violence is bloody power over [bare] life for its [power's] own sake." In *Homo Sacer* (Agamben 1998), "bare life" initially seems to be the equivalent of the physical life of all beings (*zoé*). But as *zoé* leaves behind the sphere of the *oikos*, the home, it enters the sphere of the polis. For Agamben "bare life" is not merely "biological life"; it is biological life (Foucault's notion of biopolitics) that has entered the

public realm and is now located at the center of politics. For Agamben, this transformation of bare life is the decisive event of modernity, for the political actor is no longer a citizen but the human body.

15. In "From a Writer's Notebook" (1987), Cisneros herself contextualizes her novel's crystallization in a seminar discussion at the Program in Creative Writing at the University of Iowa of Gaston Bachelard's *The Poetics of Space*. Julian Olivares (1988) discusses this Bachelardian influence on Cisneros. My discussion focuses more on how Cisneros uses the poetic and aesthetic spaces of the *oikos* as a way to chart Esperanza's engagement with bare life.

16. When Cisneros visited my Chicano literature seminar on October 24, 1984, when I was an assistant editor at Arte Público Press, she emphasized to my students that her novel was built around micro-chapters she neologized as "lazy poems." Cisneros, after all, considers herself a poet and novelist. Through her lazy poems, Cisneros is thus able to further pursue her option of aesthetic temporality in *The House on Mango Street*. A year earlier, Nicolás Kanellos, the director and publisher of Arte Público, had asked me to proofread the galleys for Cisneros's *The House on Mango Street*. The novel did not warrant any of my editorial hints.

18. I have used Russell Berman's erudite reading of Walter Benjamin's "Theses on the Philosophy of History" (1969) to help me formulate part of my reading of Cisneros's *The House on Mango Street*. According to Berman (2007, 18), Benjamin's "theses" are meant to criticize mainline historicism's inability to empathize with the past, and hence has no real lack of motivation to redeem it, and, as Benjamin was writing at the height of Hitler's assault on Europe, traditional socialism's assumption that progress neatly unfolds in history. Benjamin's third perspective is, of course, the one famously called "historical materialism." By linking distant moments in time through a profound empathy, through empty space, Berman suggests, this empathy takes on a revolutionary character by disrupting the regularity of quotidian temporality. Thus, in "Theses on the Philosophy of History," Berman (2007, 18) argues, Benjamin "pursues . . . the option of aesthetic temporality." Like Benjamin, Cisneros's protagonist Esperanza, I suggest, appeals to the aesthetic ability to overcome the separation of time, to allow for critical empathy, and to escape traditional historicism's determinism.

18. "Barriology" and "barrioization" were neologisms formulated by Albert Camarillo (1979) to refer to the socio-historical processes by which by the mid-nineteenth century in Southern California the ethnic Mexican populations were barriozed by Anglo-American segregation and hegemony.

19. Ten years earlier, in a journalistic piece entitled "Problemas de la novela?," written for *El Heraldo*, Gabriel García Márquez complained,

> There ha[d] not yet been written in Colombia a novel evidently and fortunately influenced by Joyce, Faulkner or Virginia Woolf. And I say "fortunately" because I don't think we Colombians can be an exception at this point to the play of influences. In her prologue to *Orlando* Virginia Woolf

admits her influences. Faulkner himself could not deny those exerted upon him by Joyce. There is something—especially in the management of time—in common between Huxley and, again, Virginia Woolf. Franz Kafka and Proust are everywhere in the literature of the modern world. If we Colombians are to take the right path, we must position ourselves inevitably within this current. The lamentable truth is that it has not happened yet and there is not the slightest sign of it ever happening. (Gabriel García Márquez's "Problemas de la novela?," *El Heraldo*, April 24, 1950)

This article, as Gerald Martin (2009, 135) notes, "casts scorn on most fiction being written in Colombia at the time." I have also profited immensely from Dopico (forthcoming) in understanding Fernando Botero's presence in García Márquez's *Cien años de soledad*.

20. Late in *Caramelo or Puro Cuento*, after Celaya has transferred from Immaculate Conception, the Catholic high school in San Antonio, to Davy Crockett, the South Side's vocational high school, she reveals her loathing for her possible life chances and futures as either a "farmer," or a "beautician" by expressing her desire to travel, make movies, and take university classes "like anthropology and drama" (Cisneros 2003, 352). I have borrowed the neologism *"anthropoeta"* from my conversations with Renato Rosaldo and Ruth Behar, ethnographers who are also published poets and blur generic boundaries in their experimental ethnographies.

21. Celaya, in fact, rejects becoming a native informant of sorts by rejecting the many idioms of high art offered to her by telling us a tale embroidered, like a Mexican *rebozo*, and modeled on Mexican telenovelas and melodrama.

22. Late in the novel, and in one of her telling and erudite footnotes to *Caramelo or Puro Cuento*, Cisneros (2003, 409 fn.) suggests how the transnational telenovelas emulate Mexican bare life and not the other way around: "A famous chronicler of Mexico City stated Mexicans have modeled their storytelling after the melodrama of a TV soap opera. But I would argue that the *telenovela* has emulated Mexican life. Only societies that have undergone the tragedy of a revolution and a near century of inept leadership could love with such passion the *telenovela*, storytelling at its very best since it has the power of a true Scheherazade—it keeps you coming back for more. In my opinion, it's not the storytelling in *telenovelas* that's so bad, but the insufferable acting." Moreover, as Mexicans and Russians know very well, Cisneros continues, "The greatest *telenovela* screenwriter of all [is] la Divina Providencia," who emplots the mass-mediated story "with more plot twists and somersaults than anyone would ever think believable" because "their twin histories" confirm it. "Only the elderly," she wryly concludes the footnote, "who have witnessed a lifetime of astonishments, would ever accept the [historias] as true. Conversely, it is only those who haven't witnessed and experienced a 'lifetime of astonishments' who find the historias in *telenovelas* as 'ridiculous,' 'so naively unbelieveable,' 'preposterous,' and 'ludicrous,' and so 'ill-conceived.' " Celaya, of course, learns these interpretative lessons from Soledad, her Awful Grandmother.

23. Throughout this chapter, I use "critical theory" and "critical reading" inter-changeably as terms that seek to analyze the social organization of arts, politics, and the ordinary ways of life to imagine alternative social formations and to establish the grounds on which to dispute the value of existing social forms.

24. That is, Celaya's Awful Grandmother and her mother, Zoila, pass on to her phantasmatic oral tales (*cuentos*) as antidotes to Mexico's misogynist and censorious treatment of women.

25. To paraphrase the astute reading of what Thomas Ferraro (1993, 159) calls "courageous daughtering" in Maxine Hong Kingston's *The Woman Warrior* (1975), Celaya's battle against patriarchy for her (great)-grandmothers requires courageous grand-daughtering.

26. In Celaya's description of the way in which, of the two terms of equiva-lence, one comes to serve as the expression of the other (the silk expresses its value in the rebozo), the caramelo rebozo serves as the material in which that value is expressed. We can also begin to see a Marxist dialectical expression of the doctrine of metaphor as tenor and vehicle. Does the very irreversibility of the equation by which the two objects are affirmed as being the "same" in value introduce a temporal process into this structure? And is this compatible with the Reyes's family tradition (as Celaya announces in the prologue/disclaimer) of the generation of the narrative out of the metaphorical "healthy lies" and the subsequent allegorical forms that result from this structural tendency?

27. For a superb history of Amerindian writing without words, see Mignolo 1995.

28. The reader of *Caramelo or Puro Cuento* must avoid assuming that the passages highlighted earlier represent authoritative expressions of Cisneros's own theories of language, de-colonial thinking, and philology. At one point in the novel or another, Celaya, Soledad, the Awful Grandmother's Ghost, Ino-cencio, and Zoila all express distinct complementary or even contradictory opinions. This multiplicity of voices is one indication of the dialogical and dialectical nature of Cisneros's border thinking.

29. According to John L. Austin, vows and promises are complex examples of what he initially called performative utterances (a variety of a speech act). Austin's notion of the speech act in which he distinguishes performative utter-ances as "doings" from constative utterances as "sayings" can help the reader map out some of the linguistic and thematic patterns that characterize the speech acts of Celaya and Soledad, the Awful Grandmother. In *How to Do Things with Words* (1975), Austin replaced his performative–constative couplet with the new "illocutionary–prelocutionary" dyad. See also Pratt 1977.

30. See the reading of Archie Bunker's rhetoric in de Man 1979, 10.

31. In "Introduction to the Structural Analysis of Narrative" (1977), Roland Barthes classified narrative episodes into two broad groups, which he called "cardinal functions" and "catalyses." Celaya varies the terminology here, pre-ferring (like the splendid theorist of the novel Franco Moretti) to use the terms turning points and "fillers." Turning points, Moretti suggests, are decisions

among different courses of action, and fillers literally "fill up" the space between one decision and the next. Fillers may nuance and enrich the overall structure of the narrative, but they do not modify the alternatives established by the turning points. Fillers, Moretti argues, represent "good manners, possibility—a general awakening of the everyday." Further, they "rationalize narrative—make it regular and steady." I thank Franco Moretti for allowing me to read his unpublished essay "Fillers" (2001).

32. Anyone with the slightest familiarity with deconstruction will see that I have generally been attempting to follow the literary theorist Paul de Man's idea of reading, for "deconstruction is not something we have added to the text but it constituted the text in the first place. A literary text simultaneously asserts and denies the authority of its own rhetorical mode, and by reading the text as we did we were only trying to come closer to being as rigorous a reader as the author had to be in order to write the sentence in the first place. Poetic writing is the most advanced and refined mode of deconstruction: it may differ from critical or discursive writing in the economy of its articulation, but not in kind." See the iconic "Semiology and Rhetoric" in de Man 1979, 17. In addition, in my reading of *Caramelo Or Puro Cuento*, I have dialectically combined and used Marx's critical transcoding insights on value, Mignolo's decolonial theory of colonial semiosis, Austin's distinguishing between performative and constative speech acts of various kinds, and de Man's rehearsing of the Austinian oppositions in terms of "grammar" and "rhetoric."

References

Adams, Rachel. 2009. *Continental Divides: Remapping the Cultures of North America.* Chicago: University of Chicago Press.

Adorno, Theodor. 1973. *Negative Dialectics,* trans. E. B. Ashton. New York: Seabury.

———. 1975. "Culture Industry Reconsidered." *New German Critique* 6 (Fall), 1–12.

Adorno, Theodor, and Max Horkheimer. 1972. *Dialectic of Enlightenment,* trans. John Cumming. New York: Continuum.

Agamben, Giorgio. 1998. *Homo Sacer: Sovereign Power and Bare Life,* trans. Daniel Heller-Roazen. Stanford: Stanford University Press.

Alarcón, Norma. 1991. "The Theoretical Subject(s) of *This Bridge Called My Back* and Anglo American Feminism." *Criticism in the Borderlands: Studies in Chicano Literature, Culture, and Ideology,* ed. Héctor Calderón and José David Saldívar, 28–39. Durham: Duke University Press.

———. 1996. "Anzaldúa's Frontera: Inscribing Gynetics." *Displacement, Diaspora, and Geographies of Identity,* ed. Smadar Lavie and Ted Swedenburg, 35–58. Durham: Duke University Press.

Alcoff, Linda Martín. 2000. "Who's Afraid of Identity Politics?" *Reclaiming Identity: Realist Theory and the Predicament of Postmodernity,* ed. Paula M. L. Moya and Michael R. Hames-García, 312–44. Berkeley: University of California Press.

Alegría, Fernando. 1986. *Nueva historia de la novela hispanomericana.* Hanover, N.H.: Ediciones del norte.

Aleman, Jesse. 1998. "Chicano Novelistic Discourse: Dialogizing the Corrido Paradigm." *Multi-Ethnic Literature of the United States* 23, no. 1, 49–64.

Althusser, Louis. 1971. "Ideology and Ideological State Apparatuses (Notes towards an Investigation)." *Lenin and Philosophy and Other Essays,* trans. Ben Brewster, 127–86. New York: Monthly Review.

Anderson, Benedict. 1983. *Imagined Communities: Reflections on the Origins and the Spread of Nationalism.* London: Verso.

———. 1998. *Specters of Comparison: Nationalism, Southeast Asia, and the World.* New York: Verso.

Anzaldúa, Gloria. 1987. *Borderlands/La Frontera: La Nueva Mestiza.* San Francisco: Aunt Lute.

———. 1993. "Border Arte: Nepantla, El Lugar de la Frontera." *La Frontera/The Border: Art about the Mexico/United States Border Experience,* ed. Natasha Bonilla Martinez. San Diego: Centro Cultural de la Raza, Museum of Contemporary Art.

Austin, John L. 1975. *How to Do Things with Words.* Oxford: Oxford University Press.

Baker, Houston A., Jr. 1987. *Blues, Ideology, and Afro-American Literature: A Vernacular Theory.* Chicago: University of Chicago Press.

Bakhtin, Mikhail M. 1981. *The Dialogic Imagination: Four Essays*, ed. Michael Holquist. Austin: University of Texas Press.

Barnet, Miguel, and Esteban Montejo. 1966. *Biografía de un cimarrón*. Havana: Editorial Letras Cubanas.

———. 1994. *Biography of a Runaway Slave*, trans. W. Nick Hill. Willimantic, Conn.: Curbstone.

Barthes, Roland. 1977. "Introduction to the Structural Analysis of Narrative." *Image, Music, Text*, trans. Stephen Heath, 79–124. New York: Hill and Wang.

Barth, John. 1986. "A Few Words about Minimalism." *New York Times*. December 28. 1.

Baucom. Ian. 2005. *Specters of the Atlantic: Finance Capital, Slavery, and the Philosophy of History*. Durham: Duke University Press.

Bederman, Gail. 1996. *Manliness and Civilization: A Cultural History of Gender and Race in the United States, 1880–1917*. Chicago: University of Chicago Press.

Behar, Ruth. 1996. *The Vulnerable Observer: Anthropology That Breaks Your Heart*. Boston: Beacon.

Beiteks, Edvins. "Latinos Fighting America's Wars." *San Francisco Examiner* (April 29, 1999): C1 and C8.

Benjamin, Walter. 1969. "Theses on the Philosophy of History." *Illuminations*, trans. Harry Zohn, 253–64. New York: Schocken.

———. 1996 (1978). "Critique of Violence." *Walter Benjamin's Selected Writings: Volume 1, 1913–1926*, ed. Marcus Bullock and Michael W. Jennings. Cambridge: Harvard University Press.

———. 1998. *The Origin of German Tragic Drama*, trans. John Osborne. London: Verso.

Benveniste, Émile. 1971. "The Correlation of Tense in the French Verb." *Problems in General Linguistics*, trans. M. E. Meek, 205–15.: Coral Gables: University of Miami Press.

Berman, Larry. 1989. *Lyndon Johnson's War: The Road to Stalemate in Vietnam*. New York: W. W. Norton.

Berman, Marshall. 1982. *All That Is Solid Melts into Air: The Experiences of Modernity*. New York: Penguin.

Berman, Russell A. 2007. *Fiction Sets You Free: Literature, Liberty, and Western Culture*. Iowa City: University of Iowa Press.

Beverley, John. 1993. *Against Literature*. Minneapolis: University of Minnesota Press.

———. 1999. *Subalternity and Representation: Arguments in Cultural Theory*. Durham: Duke University Press.

Binder, Wolfgang, ed. 1985. *Partial Autobiographies: Interviews with Twenty Chicano Poets*. Erlangen, Germany: Verlag Palm.

Bloemraad, Irene. 2006. *Becoming a Citizen: Incorporating Immigrants and Refugees in the United States and Canada*. Berkeley: University of California Press.

Bloom, Harold. 1997. *The Anxiety of Influence: A Theory of Poetry*. New York: Oxford University Press.

Bonacich, Edna, and Richard Applebaum. 2000. *Behind the Label: Inequality in the Los Angeles Apparel Industry*. Berkeley: University of California Press.

Bradbury, Malcolm. 1988. "Neo-realist Fiction." *Columbia Literary History of United States,* ed. Emory Elliott, Martha Banta, Terence Martin, Marjorie Perloff, David Shea. New York: Columbia University Press.

Brady, Mary Pat. 2002. *Extinct Lands, Temporal Geographies: Chicana Literature and the Urgency of Space.* Durham: Duke University Press.

Brands, H. W. 1997. *TR: The Last Romantic.* New York: Basic.

Brickhouse, Anna. 2004. *Transamerican Literary Relations and the Nineteenth-Century Public Sphere.* Cambridge: Cambridge University Press.

Brown, Wendy. 1995. *States of Injury: Freedom and Power in Late Modernity.* Princeton: Princeton University Press.

Butler, Judith. 1990. "The Force of Fantasy: Feminism, Mapplethorpe, and Discursive Excess." *Differences* 2, no. 2, 105–25.

———. 1997. *The Psychic Life of Power: Theories of Subjection.* Stanford: Stanford University Press.

———. 2000. *Antigone's Claim: Kinship between Life and Death.* New York: Columbia University Press.

———. 2009. *Frames of War: When Is Life Grievable?* New York: Verso.

Butler, Judith, Ernesto Laclau, and Slavoj Žižek. 2000. *Contingency, Hegemony, Universality: Contemporary Dialogues on the Left.* New York: Verso.

Calderón, Héctor. 2004. *Narratives of Greater Mexico: Essays on Chicano Literary History, Genre, and Borders.* Austin: University of Texas Press.

Calderón, Héctor, and José David Saldívar, eds. 1991. *Criticism in the Borderlands: Studies in Chicano Literature, Culture, and Ideology.* Durham: Duke University Press.

Camarillo, Albert. 1979. *Chicanos in a Changing Society: From Mexican Pueblos to American Barrios in Santa Barbara and Southern California, 1848–1930.* Cambridge: Harvard University Press.

Carpentier, Alejo. 1949. "Prólogo." *El reino de este mundo* (The Kingdom of This World). Havana: Ediciones Unión.

———. 1967. "De lo real maravilloso americano." *Tientos y diferencias,* 103–21. Montevideo: Arca.

———. *Explosion in a Cathedral.* 1979, trans. Harriet De Onís. New York: Avon Books.

———. 1979. *The Lost Steps,* trans. John Sturrock. New York: Harper Colophone Books.

Carver, Raymond. 1989. *What We Talk About When We Talk About Love: Stories.* New York: Vintage.

Casaus, Victor. 1982. *Giron en la memoria.* Havana: Editorial Letras Cubanas.

Castells, Manuel. 1997. *The Power of Identity* (*The Information Age: Economy, Society, and Culture*), vol. 2, 2d ed. London: Blackwell.

———. 2001. *The Internet Galaxy: Reflections on the Internet, Business, and Society.* New York: Oxford University Press.

Chadwick. Vernon. 1997. "Introduction: Ole Massa's Dead, Long Live the King of Rock 'n' Roll." *In Search of Elvis: Music, Race, Art, Religion,* ed. Vernon Chadwick, ix–xxvi. Boulder: Westview.

Chafe, William. 1991. *The Unfinished Journey: America since World War II*. New York: Oxford University Press.

Chakrabarty, Dipesh. 1997. "The Time of History and the Times of the Gods." *The Politics of Culture in the Shadow of Capital*, ed. Lisa Lowe and David Lloyd, 35–60. Durham: Duke University Press.

———. 1998. "Reconstructing Liberalism? Notes toward a Conversation between Area Studies and Diasporic Studies." *Public Culture* 10, no. 3, 457–82.

———. 2000. *Provincializing Europe: Postcolonial Thought and Historical Difference*. Princeton: Princeton University Press.

———. 2007. "A Small History of Subaltern Studies." *A Companion to Postcolonial Studies*. ed. Henry Schwartz and Sangeeta Ray, 467–85. Oxford: Blackwell.

Chanady, Amaryll. 1995. "The Territorialization of the Imaginary in Latin America: Self-Affirmation and Resistance to Metropolitan Paradigms." *Magical Realism: Theory, History, Community*, ed. Lois P. Zamora and Wendy Faris, 125–44. Durham: Duke University Press.

Chatterjee, Partha. 1995. *The Nation and Its Fragments: Colonial and Postcolonial Histories*. Princeton: Princeton University Press.

Chavez, Denise. 1986. *The Last of the Menu Girls*. Houston: Arte Público Press.

Childers, William. 2007. *Transnational Cervantes*. Toronto: University of Toronto Press.

Cisneros, Sandra. 1987. "From a Writer's Notebook." *Americas Review* 15, 69–73.

———. 1991. *The House on Mango Street*. New York: Vintage.

———. 1992. *Woman Hollering Creek and Other Stories*. New York: Vintage.

———. 1994a. *La Casa en Mango Street*, trans. Elena Poniatowska. New York: Vintage.

———. 1994b. *Loose Woman*. New York: Alfred A. Knopf.

———. 2003a. *Caramelo or Puro Cuento*, New York: Vintage.

———. 2003b. *Caramelo or Puro Cuento*, trans. Liliana Valenzuela. New York: Vintage Español.

Clifford, James. 1997. *Routes: Travel and Translation in the Late Twentieth Century*. Cambridge: Harvard University Press.

Clifford, James, and George B. Marcus, eds. 1986. *Writing Culture: The Poetics and Politics of Ethnography*. Berkeley: University of California Press.

Coronil, Fernando. 1995. "Transculturation and the Politics of Theory: Countering the Center, Cuban Counterpoint." Introduction to Fernando Ortiz, *Cuban Counterpoint: Tobacco and Sugar*, trans. Harriet de Onís. Durham: Duke University Press.

———. 1997. *The Magical State: Nature, Money, and Modernity in Venezuela*. Chicago: University of Chicago Press.

Cronin, William. 1995. "Frederick Jackson Turner." *A Companion to American Thought*, ed. Richard Wightman Fox and James T. Kloppenberg, 691–92. Oxford: Blackwell.

Conley, Dalton. 1999. *Being Black, Living in the Red: Race, Wealth, and Social Policy in America*. Berkeley: University of California Press.

Cornejo Polar, Antonio. 1997. *Mestizaje e híbridez: Los riegos de las metáforas*. La Paz: Universidad Mayor de San Andrés.

Crenshaw, Kimberlé, Neil Gotanda, Garry Peller, and Kendall Thomas. 1996. *Critical Race Theory: The Key Writings That Formed the Movement.* New York: New Press.

Darío, Rubén. 2009. *Autobiografía de Rubén Darío.* Barcelona: Linkgua.

Davis, Mike. 2000. *Magical Urbanism: Latinos Reinvent the U.S. Big City.* New York: Verso.

De Acosta, José. 1590. *Historia natural y moral de Indias.* Seville: Casa de Iuan de Leon.

De Ayala, Felipe Guama Poma. 1980. *El Primer Nueva Crónica y Bueb Gobierno.* Madrid: Siglo Veintiuno.

DeGuzmán, María. 2005. *Spain's Long Shadow: The Black Legend, Off-Whiteness, and Anglo-American Empire.* Minneapolis: University of Minnesota Press.

De la Campa, Román. 1999. *Latin Americanism.* Minneapolis: University of Minnesota Press.

De la Mora, Sergio. 2004. *Cinemachismo: Masculinities and Sexuality in Mexican Film.* Austin: University of Texas Press.

Deleuze, Gilles, and Félix Guattari. 1977. *Anti-Oedipus: Capitalism and Schizophrenia,* trans. Robert Hurley, Mark Seem, and Helen R. Lane. New York: Viking.

———. 2002. "What Is a Minor Literature?" *Kafka: Towards a Minor Literature,* trans. Dana Polan, 16–27. Minneapolis: University of Minnesota Press.

de Man, Paul. 1979. *Allegories of Reading: Figural Language in Rousseau, Nietzsche, Rilke, and Proust.* New Haven: Yale University Press.

———. 1989. *Critical Writings, 1953–1978,* ed. Lindsay Waters. Minneapolis: University of Minnesota Press.

Derrida, Jacques. 1982. "White Mythology." *Margins of Philosophy,* trans. Alan Bass, 207–71. Chicago: University of Chicago Press.

———. 1992. "Force of Law: The 'Mystical' Foundation of Authority." *Deconstruction and the Possibility of Justice,* ed. Drucilla Cornell, Michel Rosenfeld, and David Gray Carlson, 3–67. New York: Routledge.

———. 1994. *Specters of Marx: The State of the Debt, the Work of Mourning, and the New International.* New York: Routledge.

Díaz, Junot. 1996. *Drown.* New York: Riverhead.

———. 2007. *The Brief Wondrous Life of Oscar Wao.* New York: Riverhead.

Dimock, Wai Chee. 2009. "Hemispheric Islam: Continents and Centuries for American Literature." *American Literary History* 21, no. 1 (Spring), 28–52.

Dirlik, Arif. 2007. "The Global South: Predicament and Promise." *Global South* 1, no. 1 (January), 12–23.

Doctorow, E. L. 1980. *Loon Lake.* New York: Random House.

———. 1985. *World's Fair.* New York: Random House.

———. 1989. *Billy Bathgate.* New York: Random House.

———. 1997. *Ragtime.* New York: Modern Library.

———. 2002. *The Book of Daniel.* New York: Random House.

———. 2005. *The Long March.* New York: Random House.

Dopico, Ana María. Forthcoming. *Houses Divided: Social Crisis and Genealogical Fantasies in Novels of the Americas.* Durham: Duke University Press.

Dorfman, Rodrigo. 2007. *Los Sueños De Angélica.* Durham: Melloweb.

Drinnon, Richard. 1980. *Facing West: The Metaphysics of Indian-Hating and Empire-Building.* New York: New American Library.

Du Bois, W. E. B. 1935. *Black Reconstruction.* New York: Harcourt Brace.

———. 1986 (1903). *The Souls of Black Folk.* New York: Vintage.

Duffy, Edna. 2009. *The Speed Handbook: Velocity, Pleasure, Modernism.* Durham: Duke University Press.

Ellison, Ralph. 1995 (1952). *Invisible Man.* New York: Vintage.

Fabian, Johannes. 1983. *Time and the Other: How Anthropology Makes Its Object.* New York: Columbia University Press.

Fanon, Frantz. 1987. *Les damnés de la terre.* Paris: Gallimard.

Faulkner, William. 1990. *Absalom, Absalom!* New York: Vintage International.

Fernández Retamar, Roberto. 1989. "Calibán: Notes toward a Discussion of Culture in Our América." *Calibán and Other Essays,* trans. Edward Baker and Roberto Márquez, 3–45. Minneapolis: University of Minnesota Press.

———. 1995a. "Del anticolonialismo al antimperialismo." *Nuestra América: Cien años y otros acercamientos a Martí.* Havana: Editorial 51-Mar.

———. 1995b. "Modernismo, 98, subdesarrollo." *Para el perfil definitivo del hombre,* 2d ed., 120–127. Havana: Editorial Letras Cubanas.

———. 1995c. "Para leer a Che." *Para el perfil definitive del hombre,* 2d. ed., 168–87. Havana: Editorial Letras Cubanas.

———. 1995d. "Naturalidad y novedad en la literatura martiana." *"Nuestra América": Cien años y otros acercamientos a Martí,* 15–53. Havana: Editorial SI-MAR.

———. 1995e. "Nuestra América y Occidente." *Para el perfil definitivo del hombre,* 2d ed., 112–50. Havana: Editorial Letras Cubanas.

———. 2009. "Martí in His (Third) World," trans. John Beverley with Miguel Linás. *Boundary 2* 36, no. 1 (Spring), 61–94.

Ferraro, Thomas. 1993. *Ethnic Passages: Literary Immigrants in Twentieth-Century America.* Chicago: University of Chicago Press.

Ferrer, Ada. 1999. "The Silence of Patriots: Race and Nationalism in Martí's Cuba." *José Martí's "Our America": From National to Hemsipheric Cultural Studies,* ed. Jeffrey Belnap and Raul Fernández, 228–52. Durham: Duke University Press.

Flores, Ángel. 1995 (1955). "Magical Realism in Spanish American Fiction." *Magical Realism: Theory, History, Community,* ed. Lois P. Zamora and Wendy Faris, 109–18. Durham: Duke University Press.

Foley, Neil. 1997. *The White Scourge: Mexicans, Blacks, and Poor Whites in Texas Cotton Culture.* Berkeley: University of California Press.

Foucault, Michel. 1980. "Two Lectures." *Power/Knowledge: Selected Interviews and Other Writings, 1972–1977,* ed. Colin Gordon, 78–108. New York: Pantheon.

———. 1982. "The Subject and Power." *Michel Foucault: Beyond Structuralism and Hermeneutics,* ed. Hubert L. Dreyfus and Paul Rabinow, 208–26. Chicago: University of Chicago Press.

———. 1984. "What Is Enlightenment? *The Foucault Reader*, ed. Paul Rabinow, 32–50. New York: Pantheon.

———. 1998. *The History of Sexuality: The Will to Knowledge.* London: Penguin Books.

Franco, Jean. 1986. "The Incorporation of Women: A Comparison of North American and Mexican Popular Culture." *Studies in Entertainment: Critical Approaches to Mass Culture*, ed. Tania Modeliski, 119–38. Bloomington: Indiana University Press.

Frost, Kid. 1990. *hispanic causing panic.* Virgin Records. 2–91377.

Galarza, Ernesto. 1977. *Barrio Boy: The Story of a Boy's Acculturation.* Notre Dame, Ind.: University of Notre Dame Press.

García, Ignacio. 1999. "Unfinished Letter to Terry." *Aztlán and Viet Nam: Chicano and Chicana Experiences of the War*, ed. George Mariscal, 133–36. Berkeley: University of California Press.

García Canclini, Néstor. 1990. *Culturas híbridas: Estraegias para entra y salir de la modernidad.* Mexico City: Grijalbo.

García Márquez, Gabriel. 1967. *Cien años de soledad.* Buenos Aires: Editorial Sudamericana.

———. 1990. *The General in His Labyrinth*, trans. Edith Grossman. New York: Alfred A. Knopf.

———. 1992a. *De Europa y América: Obra periodística 3, 1955–1960.* Barcelona. Mondadori.

———. 1992b. "Dos o tres cosas sobre 'La Novela de la Violencia,' Octubre de 1959." *De Europa y América: Obra periodística 3, 1955–1960,* 646–52. Barcelona. Mondadori.

———. 1992c. "La literatura colombiana, un fraude a la nación, Abril de 1960." *De Europa y América: Obra periodística 3, 1955–1960,* 662–67. Barcelona: Mondadori.

Gates, Henry Louis, Jr. 1988. *The Signifying Monkey: A Theory of Afro-American Literature.* New York: Oxford University Press.

Gatewood, Willard. 1987. *Smoked Yankees: Letters from Negro Soldiers.* Fayetteville: University of Arkansas Press.

Ghosh, Amitav. 2005. *The Hungry Tide.* New York: Houghton Mifflin, Harcourt.

Gillman, Susan. 2008. "Otra vez Caliban/Encore Caliban: Adaptation, Translation, American/World Literature." *American Literary History* (February), 187–209.

Gilroy, Paul. 1987. *"There Ain't No Black in the Union Jack": The Cultural Politics of Race and Nation.* Chicago: University of Chicago Press.

———. 1993. *The Black Atlantic: Modernity and Double Consciousness.* Cambridge: Harvard University Press.

———. 2004. *After Empire: Melancholia or Convivial Culture?* London: Routledge.

Goldman, Francisco. 2004. *The Divine Husband: A Novel.* New York: Atlantic Monthly.

González Echevarría, Roberto. 1977. *Alejo Carpentier: The Pilgrim at Home.* Ithaca: Cornell University Press.

González, Mónica García. 2009. "Transepistemología subalterna en Rubén Darío y José Martí: Estéticas modernistas y modernidades imperialistas en Chile y Nueva York." Ph.D. diss., University of California, Berkeley.

González, Mónica García, ed. 2006. *Lucero.* Special issue: *Cartografías subalternas, heterogéneas/trans-americanas: Remapeando la idea de América* 17.

Gramsci, Antonio. 1971. *Selections from the Prison Notebooks,* ed. and trans. Quintin Hoare and Geofrey Nowell Smith. New York: International.

Greer, Margaret, Walter Mignolo, and Maureen Quilligan, eds. 2007. *ReReading the Black Legend: The Discourses of Religious and Racial Differences in the Renaissance Empires.* Chicago: University of Chicago Press.

Grosfoguel, Ramón. 2003. *Colonial Subjects: Puerto Rico and Puerto Ricans in a Global Perspective.* Berkeley: University of California Press.

Grosfoguel, Ramón, Nelson Maldonado-Torres, and José David Saldívar, eds. 2005. *Latin@s in the World-System: Decolonization Struggles in the 21st Century U.S. Empire.* Boulder: Paradigm.

Gruesz, Kirsten Silva. 2002. *Ambassadors of Culture: The Transamerican Origins of Latino Writing.* Princeton: Princeton University Press.

Guevara, Ernesto. 1996. *Episodes of the Cuban Revolutionary War, 1956–58.* ed. Mary Alice Water. New York: Pathfinder.

Guha, Ranajit. 1983. *Elementary Aspects of Peasant Insurgency in Colonial India.* Delhi: Oxford University Press.

——. 1988. "On Some Aspects of the Historiography of Colonial India." *Selected Subaltern Studies,* ed. Ranajit Guha and Gayatri Spivak, 1–7. New York: Oxford University Press.

——. 1996. "The Small Voice of History." *Subaltern Studies* 9, 1–8.

——. 1997. *Dominance without Hegemony: History and Power in Colonial India.* Cambridge: Harvard University Press.

——. 1998. "Preface." *Selected Subaltern Studies,* ed. Ranajit Guha and Gaytri Chakravorty Spivak, 3–34. New York: Oxford University Press.

Guinier, Lani, and Gerald Torres. 2002. *The Miner's Canary: Enlisting Race, Resisting Power, Transforming Democracy.* Cambridge: Harvard University Press.

Gunder Frank, Andre. 1967. *Capitalism and Underdevelopment in Latin America: Historical Studies of Chile and Brazil.* New York: Monthly Review Press.

Gutiérrez, Ramón. 1991. *When Jesus Came, the Corn Mothers Went Away: Marriage, Sexuality, and Power in New Mexico, 1500–1846.* Stanford: Stanford University Press.

Habell-Pallan, Michele. Forthcoming. "Personal Interview with El Vez." *Americas Review.*

Habermas, Jürgen. 1983. "Modernity—An Incomplete Project," trans. Seyla Benhabib. *The Anti-Aesthetic: Essays on Postmodern Culture,* ed. Hal Foster. Port Townsend, Wash.: Bay Press.

——. 1987. *The Philosophical Discourse of Modernity: Twelve Lectures,* trans. Frederick G. Lawrence. Cambridge: MIT Press.

——. 1989. *The Structural Transformation of the Public Sphere: An Enquiry into a Category of Bourgeois Society.* Cambridge: MIT Press.

Halberstam, David. 1972. *The Best and the Brightest.* New York: Ballantine.

Hames-García, Michael. 2000. "Who Are Our Own People?: Challenges for a Theory of Social Identity." *Reclaiming Identity: Realist Theory and the Predicament of Postmodernism.* ed. Paula M. L. Moya and Michael R. Hames-García, 102–32. Berkeley: University of California Press.

Haraway, Donna. 1991. "A Cyborg Manifesto: Science, Technology, and Socialist Feminism in the Late Twentieth Century," 149–81. *Simians, Cyborgs, and Women: The Reinvention of Nature.* New York: Routledge.

Hartman, Saidiya. 2007. *Lose Your Mother: A Journey along the Atlantic Slave Route.* New York: Farrar, Straus, and Giroux.

Harvey, David. 2003. *The New Imperialism.* New York: Oxford University Press.

Hernández, Gilbert, and Jaime Gilbert. 1982–2009. *Love and Rockets.* Fotonovela series. Seattle: Fantagraphics.

Herr, Michael. 1991. *Dispatches.* New York: Vintage.

Herrera-Sobek, María. 1999. "Silver Medals." *Aztlán and Viet Nam: Chicano and Chicana Experiences of the War,* ed. George Mariscal, 232–33. Berkeley: University of California Press.

Hinojosa, Rolando. 1973. *Estampas de Valle y otras obras.* Berkeley: Quinto Sol.

———. 1976. *Klail City y sus alrededores.* Havana: Fondo Editorial Casa de las Américas.

———. 1977. *Generaciones y semblanzas,* trans. Rosaura Sánchez. Berkeley: Editorial Justa.

———. 1981. *Korean Love Songs.* Arte Público.

———. 1982. *Rites and Witnesses.* Houston: Arte Público.

———. 1985. *Partners in Crime: A Rafe Buenrostro Mystery.* Houston: Arte Público.

———. 1989. *Becky and Her Friends.* Houston: Arte Público.

———. 1993. *The Useless Servants.* Houston: Arte Público.

———. 2006a. *Ask a Policeman.* Houston: Arte Público.

———. 2006b. *We Happy Few.* Houston: Arte Público.

Holquist, Michael. 1977. *Dostoevsky and the Novel.* Princeton: Princeton University Press.

Huntington, Samuel. 2004a. "The Hispanic Challenge." *Foreign Policy* (March–April), 30–45.

———. 2004b. *Who Are We?: The Challenges to America's National Identity.* New York: Simon and Schuster.

Igarashi, Yoshikuni. 2000. *Bodies of Memory: Narratives of War in Postwar Japanese Culture, 1945–1970.* Princeton: Princeton University Press.

Islas, Arturo. 1984. *The Rain God: A Desert Tale.* Palo Alto: Alexandrian.

———. 1990. *Migrant Souls.* New York: William Morrow.

———. 1996. *La Mollie and the King of Tears.* Albuquerque: University of New Mexico Press.

James, C. L. R. 1963. *The Black Jacobins: Toussaint L'Ouverture and the San Domingo Revolution.* New York: Vintage.

Jameson, Fredric. 1991. *Postmodernism, or, The Logic of Late Capitalism.* Durham: Duke University Press.

———. 2002. *A Singular Modernity: Essay on the Ontology of the Present.* New York: Verso.

———. 2005. *Archaeologies of the Future: The Desire Called Utopia and Other Science Fictions.* New York: Verso.

JanMohamed, Abdul. 2005. *The Death-Bound Subject: Richard Wright's Archaeology of Death.* Durham: Duke University Press.

JanMohamed, Abdul, and David Lloyd, eds. 1990. *The Nature and Context of Minority Discourse.* New York: Oxford University Press.

Jay, Paul. 1997. *Contingency Blues: The Search for Foundations in American Criticism.* Madison: University of Wisconsin Press.

Jimenez, Teresa G. 2010. "They Hatch Alone: The Alienation of the Colonial American Subject in Toni Morrison's *A Mercy.*" *Berkeley Undergraduate Journal* 22(2). Retrieved from: http://escholarship.org/uc/item/ods156ew on August 18, 2011.

Jones, Gavin. 1999. *Strange Talk: The Politics of Dialect Literature in Gilded Age America.* Berkeley: University of California Press.

Kant, Immanuel. 1960. *Observations on the Feeling of the Beautiful and the Sublime,* trans. John T. Goldthwait. Berkeley: University of California Press.

Kaplan, Amy. 1992. "Left Alone with America: The Absence of Empire in the Study of American Culture." *Cultures of U.S. Imperialism,* ed. Amy Kaplan and Donald E. Pease, 3–21. Durham: Duke University Press.

———. 1993. "Black and Blue on San Juan Hill." *Cultures of United States Imperialism,* ed. Amy Kaplan and Donald E. Pease, 219–36. Durham: Duke University Press.

———. 1995. "Imperialism and Anti-imperialism." *A Companion to American Thought,* ed. Richard Wightman Fox and James T. Klopenberg, 328–30. Cambridge: Blackwell.

———. 1998. "Manifest Domesticity." *American Literature* 70, 581–606.

———. 2002. *The Anarchy of Empire in the Making of U.S. Culture.* Cambridge: Harvard University Press.

Kaplan, Amy, and Donald E. Pease, eds. 1993. *Cultures of United States Imperialism.* Durham: Duke University Press.

Kaplan, Sara. 2006. "Unspeakable Thoughts, Unthinkable Acts: Toward a Black Feminist Liberatory Politics." Ph.D. diss., University of California, Berkeley.

Karnow, Stanley. 1991. *Vietnam: A History.* New York: Penguin.

Keating, AnaLouise, ed. 2009. *The Gloria Anzaldúa Reader.* Durham: Duke University Press.

Kelley, Robin D. G. 1997. *Yo Mama's Disfunktional!: Fighting the Cultural Wars in Urban America.* Boston: Beacon.

Kennan, George F. 1950. *American Diplomacy, 1900–1950.* Chicago: University of Chicago Press.

Kennedy, David. 1999. *Freedom from Fear: The American People in Depression and War, 1929–1945.* New York: Oxford University Press.

Kingston, Maxine Hong. 1975. *The Woman Warrior: Memoirs of a Girlhood among Ghosts.* New York: Vintage Books.

———. 1980. *China Men.* New York: Alfred A. Knopf.

Klein, Kerwin Lee. 1997. *Frontiers of Historical Imagination: Narrating the European Conquest of Native America, 1890–1990.* Berkeley: University of California Press.

LaCapra, Dominick. 1996. *Representing the Holocaust: History, Theory, Trauma.* Ithaca: Cornell University Press.

Laclau, Ernesto, and Chantal Mouffe. 2001. *Hegemony and Socialist Strategy: Towards a Radical Democratic Strategy,* 2d ed. New York: Verso.

Laó-Montes, Agustín. 2003. "Introduction." *Mambo Montage: The Latinization of New York City,* ed. Agustín Laó-Montes and Arlene Dávila, 1–55. New York: Columbia University Press.

Latin American Subaltern Studies Group. 1995. "Founding Statement." *The Postmodernism Debate in Latin America,* ed. José Aviedo, John Beverley, and Michael Aronna, 135–46. Durham: Duke University Press.

Leal, Luis. 1995 (1967). "Magical Realism in Spanish American Literature." *Magical Realism: Theory, History, Community,* ed. Lois P. Zamora and Wendy Faris, 119–24. Durham: Duke University Press.

Lenin, Vladimir I. 1996 (1916). *Imperialism: The Highest Stage of Capitalism,* ed. James Malone. London: Pluto.

Lerer, Seth. 2006. *Inventing English: A Portable History of the Language.* New York: Columbia University Press.

Levander, Caroline, and Robert Levine. 2008. *Hemispheric American Studies: Essays beyond the Nation.* New Brunswick: Rutgers University Press.

Limón, José E. 1992. *Mexican Ballads, Chicano Poems: History and Influence in Mexican-American Social Poetry.* Berkeley: University of California Press.

———. 1998. *American Encounters: Greater Mexico, the United States, and the Erotics of Culture.* Boston: Beacon.

Lipsitz, George. 2006. *The Possessive Investment in Whiteness: How White People Profit from Identity Politics,* rev. ed. Philadelphia: Temple University Press.

Lloyd, David. 1999. "Foundations of Diversity: Thinking the University in a Time of Multiculturalism." Unpublished ms. in author's possession.

Lott, Eric. 1996. *Love and Theft: Blackface Minstrelsy and the American Working Class.* New York: Oxford University Press.

Lott, Tommy. 1994. "Black Cultural Politics: An Interview with Paul Gilroy." *Found Object* (Spring), 1–46.

Lowe, Lisa. 1996. *Immigrant Acts: On Asian American Politics.* Durham: Duke University Press.

Lugones, María. 2007. "Heterosexualism and the Colonial/Modern Gender System." *Hypatia* 22, no. 1 (Winter), 186–209.

Lyotard, Jean-François. 1984. *The Postmodern Condition,* trans. Geoff Bennington and Brian Massumi. Minneapolis: University of Minnesota Press.

MacLaclan, Colin M. 1991. *Anarchism and the Mexican Revolution: The Political Trials of Richard Flores Magon in the United States.* Berkeley: University of California Press.

Maldonado-Torres, Nelson. 2008. *Against War: Views from the Underside of Modernity.* Durham: Duke University Press.

Mañach, Jorge. 2009. *Indagación Del Choteo.* Barcelona: Linkgua ediciones.

Marcos, Subcomandante, and Paco Ignacio Taibo II. 2006. *Muertos Incómodos (Falta lo que Falta).* Mexico City: Joaquin Mortiz.

Marcus, Greil. 1991. *Dead Elvis: A Chronicle of Cultural Obsession*. New York: Doubleday.

Mariscal, George, ed. 1999. *Aztlán and Viet Nam: Chicano and Chicana Experiences of the War*. Berkeley: University of California Press.

Martí, José. 1946. *Cartas á Manuel A. Mercado*. Mexico City: Universidad Autónomo Nacional.

———. 2001. *Obras completas de José Martí*, 26 vols. Havana: Centro de Estudios Martianos.

———. 2002. *Selected Writings*, ed. and trans. Esther Allen. New York: Penguin.

Martin, Gerald. 2009. *Gabriel García Márquez: A Life*. New York: Viking.

Martínez, Victor. 1992. "Shoes." *Caring for a House*, 12. San José: Chusma House.

———. 1996. *Parrot in the Oven: Mi Vida*. New York: Joanna Cotler.

Marx, Karl. 1976. *Capital, Volume 1*, trans. Ben Fowkes. London: Penguin-NLB.

———. 1978. "The Communist Manifesto." *The Marx–Engels Reader*, ed. Robert C. Tucker, 469–500. New York: W. W. Norton.

Masuo, Sandy. 1995. "El rey está muerto: Viva El Vez!" *Options* 62, 82–85.

McClary, Susan. 2000. *Conventional Wisdom: The Content of Musical Form*. Berkeley: University of California Press.

McCracken, Ellen. 1998. *New Latina Narrative: The Feminine Space of Postmodern Ethnicity*. Tucson: University of Arizona Press.

Menchú, Rigoberta. 1984. *I, Rigoberta Menchú: An Indian Woman in Guatemala*. ed. Elisabeth Burgos-Debray; trans. Ann Wright. London: Verso.

Mignolo, Walter. 1995. *The Darker Side of the Renaissance: Literacy, Territoriality, and Colonization*. Ann Arbor: University of Michigan Press.

———. 2000a. "The Larger Picture and the Historical Argument: Hispanics/ Latinos/as/Americans in the Colonial Horizon of Modernity." *Hispanics/ Latinos in the United States: Ethnicity, Race, and Rights*, ed. Jorge Gracia and Pablo De Grieff, 99–125. London: Routledge.

———. 2000b. *Local Histories/Global Designs: Coloniality, Subaltern Knowledges, and Border Thinking*. Princeton: Princeton University Press.

———. 2001. "Coloniality of Power and Subalternity." *The Latin American Subaltern Studies Reader*, ed. Ileana Rodriguez, 424–44. Durham: Duke University Press.

———. 2002a. "The Geopolitics of Knowledge and the Colonial Difference." *South Atlantic Quarterly* 101, no. 1, 57–96.

———. 2002b. "Rethinking the Colonial Model." *ReThinking Literary History: A Dialogue on Theory*, ed. Linda Hutcheon and Marío J. Valdés, 155–93. New York: Oxford University Press.

———. 2002c. "The Zapatistas' Theoretical Revolution: Its Gnoseological, Political, and Ethical Consequences." *Review* 25, no. 3, 245–76.

———. 2005. *The Idea of Latin America*. Oxford: Blackwell.

Mohanty, Satya P. 1997. *Literary Theory and the Claims of History*. Ithaca: Cornell University Press.

———. 2000. "The Epistemic Status of Cultural Identity: On *Beloved* and the Postcolonial Condition." *Reclaiming Identity: Realist Theory and the Predica-*

ment of Postmodernism. ed. Paula M. L. Moya and Michael R. Hames-García, 29–66. Berkeley: University of California Press.

Montejano, David. 1987. *Anglos and Mexicans in the Making of Texas, 1836–1986.* Austin: University of Texas Press.

Moraga, Cherríe. 1983. *Loving in the War Years: Lo Que Nunca Pasó por Sus Labios.* Boston: South End Press.

Moretti, Franco. 1998. *Atlas of the European Novel, 1800–1900.* London: Verso.

———. 2001. "Fillers." Unpublished essay in the author's possession.

Morrison, Toni. 1987. *Beloved.* New York: Vintage.

———. 1992. *Playing in the Dark: Whiteness and the Literary Imagination.* New York: Vintage.

———. 2004. *Sula.* New York: Vintage.

———. 2008. *A Mercy.* New York: Knopf.

Moya, Paula M. L. 2000. "Postmodernism, 'Realism,' and the Politics of Identity: Cherríe Moraga and Chicana Feminism." *Reclaiming Identity: Realist Theory and the Predicament of Postmodernism,* ed. Paula M. L. Moya and Michael R. Hames-García, 67–101. Berkeley: University of California Press.

———. 2002. *Learning from Experience: Realist Theory and Chicano/a Identity.* Berkeley: University of California Press.

Moya, Paula M. L., and Michael R. Hames-García, eds. 2000. *Reclaiming Identity: Realist Theory and the Predicament of Postmodernism.* Berkeley: University of California Press.

Murguia, Alejandro. "Tropics of Desire." *This War Called Love: Nine Stories.* San Francisco: City Lights.

Musicant, Ivan. 1997. *Empire by Default: The Spanish-American War and the Dawn of the American Century.* New York: Henry Holt.

Nava, Michael. 1992. *The Hidden Law.* New York: HarperCollins.

O'Gorman, Edmundo. 1958. *La invención de América: El universalismo de la cultura occidental.* Mexico City: Universidad Autonóma de México.

Olivares, Julian. 1988. "Sandra Cisneros's *The House on Mango Street* and the Poetics of Space." *Chicana Creativity and Criticism: Charting New Frontiers in American Literature,* ed. Maria Herrera-Sobek and Helena María Viramontes, 160–69. Houston: Arte Público.

Oliver, Melvin, and Thomas Shapiro. 2006. *Black Wealth/White Wealth: A New Perspective on Racial Inequality,* 2d ed. New York: Routledge.

Omi, Michael, and Howard Winant. 1994. *Racial Formation in the United States: From the 1960s to the 1990s,* 2d. ed. New York: Routledge.

Ortiz, Fernando. 1924. *Glosario de afronegroísmos.* Havana: Imprenta El Siglo XX.

———. 1995. *Cuban Counterpoint: Tobacco and Sugar,* trans. Harriet de Onís. Durham: Duke University Press.

Paredes, Américo. 1953. "Ballads of the Lower Border." M.A. thesis, University of Texas.

———. 1958. *"With His Pistol in His Hand": A Border Ballad and Its Hero.* Austin: University of Texas Press.

———. 1990. *George Washington Gómez: A Mexicotexan Novel*. Houston: Arte Público.

———. 1991. *Between Two Worlds*. Houston: Arte Público.

———. 1994. *The Hammon and the Beans and Other Stories*. Houston: Arte Público.

———. 1995. *A Texas-Mexican Cancionero: Folksongs of the Lower Border*. Austin: University of Texas Press.

Patell, Cyrus. 1999. "Comparative American Studies: Hybridity and Beyond." *American Literary History* 11, 166–86.

Patterson, James T. 1996. *Grand Expectations: The United States, 1945–1974*. New York: Oxford University Press.

Patterson, Orlando. 1982. *Slavery and Social Death*. Cambridge: Harvard University Press.

Paz, Octavio. 1990. *La hija de Rappaccini*. Mexico City: Eva.

Pease, Donald E. 1990. "New Americanists: Revisionist Interventions into the Canon." *Boundary 2* 17, no. 1 (Spring), 1–37.

———. 2009a. *The New American Exceptionalism*: Minneapolis: University of Minnesota Press.

———. 2009b. "Re-thinking 'American Studies after U.S. Exceptionalism." *American Literary History* 21, no. 1 (Spring), 19–27.

Pérez, Emma. 1999. *The Decolonial Imaginary: Writing Chicanas into History*. Bloomington: Indiana University Press.

Pérez, Louis, Jr. 1998. *The War of 1898: The United States and Cuba in History and Historiography*. Chapel Hill: University of North Carolina Press.

Pérez-Firmat. Gustavo. 1984. "Riddles of the Sphincter: Another Look at the Cuban Choteo." *Diacritics* 14, no. 4 ((Winter), 67–77.

Pérez-Torres, Rafael. 2006. *Mestizaje: Critical Uses of Race in Chicano Culture*. Minneapolis: University of Minnesota Press.

Polkinhorn, Harry, Alfred Velasco, and Malcolm Lambert, eds. 1983. *El Libro de Caló: Pachuco Slang Dictionary*. San Mateo, Calif.: Atticus.

Pratt, Mary Louise. 1977. *Toward a Speech Act Theory of Literary Discourse*. Bloomington: Indiana University Press.

———. 1981. "The Short Story: The Long and the Short of It." *Poetics* 10, 175–94.

Premnath, Gautum. 2003. "Arguments with Nationalism in the Fiction of the Indian Diaspora." Ph.D. diss., Brown University.

Putnam, Hilary. 1997. "A Half Century of Philosophy, Viewed from Within." *American Academic Culture in Transformation: Fifty Years, Four Disciplines*, ed. Thomas Bender and Carl E. Schorske, 193–226. Princeton: Princeton University Press.

Quayson, Ato. 2006. "Fecundities of the Unexpected: Magical Realism, Narrative, and History." *The Novel, Volume 1: History, Geography, and Culture*, ed. Franco Moretti, 726–58. Princeton: Princeton University Press.

Quijano, Aníbal. 1999. "Modernity, Identity, and Utopia in Latin America." *Boundary 2* 2, 140–55.

———. 2000a. "Colonialidad del poder y clasificación social." *Journal of World-System Research* 1, no. 3, 342–88.

——. 2000b. "Coloniality of Power, Eurocentrism, and Latin America." *Nepantla* 1, no. 3, 533–80.

Quijano, Anibal, and Immanuel Wallerstein. 1992. "Americanity as a Concept, or the Americas in the Modern World-System." *International Social Science Journal* 29, 549–57.

Quintana, Alvina. 1996. *Home Girls: Chicana Literary Voices*. Philadelphia: Temple University Press.

Rabasa, José. 1993. *Inventing America: Spanish Historiography and the Formation of Eurocentrism*. Norman: University of Oklahoma Press.

——. 1997. "Of Zapatismo: Reflections on the Folkloric and the Impossible in a Subaltern Insurrection." *The Politics of Culture in the Shadow of Capital*, ed. Lisa Lowe and David Lloyd, 399–431. Durham: Duke University Press.

Rama, Angel. 1996. *The Lettered City*, trans. John Charles Chasteen. Durham: Duke University Press.

Ramos, Julio. 1989. *Desencuentros de la modernidad en América Latina: Literatura y política en el siglo XIX*. Mexico City: Fondo de Cultural Económica.

——. 2001. *Divergent Modernities: Culture and Politics in Nineteenth-Century Latin America*, trans. John D. Blanco. Durham: Duke University Press.

Rebolledo, Diana Tey. 1995. *Women Singing in the Rain: A Cultural Analysis of Chicana Literature*. Tucson: University of Arizona Press.

Rechy, John. 1992. *The Miraculous Day of Amalia Gómez*. New York: Little Brown.

Rediker, Marcus. 2007. *The Slave Ship: A Human History*. New York: Viking.

Reed, Walter L. 1981. *An Exemplary History of the Novel: The Quixotic versus the Picaresque*. Chicago: University of Chicago Press.

Ríos, Alberto. 1996. *The Iguana Killer: Twelve Stories of the Heart*. Albuquerque: University of New Mexico Press.

——. 1999. "The Vietnam Wall." *Aztlán and Viet Nam: Chicano and Chicana Experiences of the War*, ed. George Mariscal, 280–81. Berkeley: University of California Press.

Rivera-Valdés, Sonia. 1997. *Las historias prohibidas de Marta Veneranda*. Havana: Fondo Editorial Casa de las Américas.

Roach, Joseph. 1996. *Cities of the Dead: Circum-Atlantic Performance*. New York: Columbia University Press.

Robertson, Roland. 1992. *Globalization: Social Theory and Global Culture*. London: Sage.

Roh, Franz. 1925. *Nach-Expressionismus, Magische Realismus: Probleme der nuesten Europasischen Maleri*. Leipzig: Kinkhardt and Biermann.

——. 1995. "Magical Realism: Post Expressionism." *Magical Realism: Theory, History, Community*, ed. Lois P. Zamora and Wendy Faris, 15–31. Durham: Duke University Press.

Roosevelt, Theodore. 1889–96. *The Winning of the West*, 4 vols. New York: G. P. Putnam's Sons.

——. 1994. "The Strenuous Life." *Theodore Roosevelt: An American Mind*, ed. Mario R. DiNunzio, 184–90. New York: Penguin.

——. 1999. *The Rough Riders*. New York: Modern Library.

Rosaldo, Renato. 1991. "Fables of the Fallen Guy." *Criticism in the Borderlands: Studies in Chicano Literature, Ideology, and Culture*, ed. Héctor Calderón and José David Saldívar, 84–96. Durham: Duke University Press.

———. 1989. *Culture and Truth: The Remaking of Social Analysis*. Boston: Beacon.

———. 1992. "Cultural Citizenship: Attempting to Enfranchise Latinos." *La Nueva Visión* 1, no. 2, 7.

Rotker, Susana. 1998. "The (Political) Exile Gaze in Martí's Writing on the United States." *José Martí's "Our America": From National to Hemispheric Cultural Studies*, ed. Jeffrey Belnap and Raul Fernández, 58–76. Durham: Duke University Press.

Roy, Arundhati. 1996. *The God of Small Things*. New York: Farrar, Straus, and Giroux.

Ruiz de Burton, María Amparo. 1995. *The Squatter and the Don*, ed. Beatriz Pita and Rosaura Sánchez. Houston: Arte Público Press.

Rushdie, Salman. 2006. *Midnight's Children*. New York: Random House Trade.

Said, Edward W. 1975. *Beginnings: Intentions and Method*. Baltimore: Johns Hopkins University Press.

Saldívar, José David. 1991. *The Dialectics of Our America: Genealogy, Cultural Critique and Literary History*. Durham: Duke University Press.

———. 1996. "Las fronteras de Nuestra América: Para volver a trazar el mapa de los Estudios Culturales Norteamericanos." *Revista Casa de las Américas* 204 (July–September), 3–19.

———. 1997. *Border Matters: Remapping American Cultural Studies*. Berkeley: University of California Press.

———. 2000a. "The Location of Américo Paredes's Border Thinking." *Nepantla* 1, no. 1, 191–95.

———. 2000b. "Looking Awry at 1898: Roosevelt, Montejo, Paredes, and Mariscal." *American Literary History* 12, no. 3, 386–406.

———. 2001. "Migratory Locations: Subaltern Modernity and Inter-American Cultural Criticism." Introduction to Julio Ramos, *Divergent Modernities: Culture and Politics in Nineteenth-Century Latin America*, xi–xxxiv. Durham: Duke University Press.

———. 2007. "Unsettling Race, Coloniality, and Caste in Anzaldúa's *Borderlands/ La Frontera*, Martinez's *Parrot in the Oven*, and Roy's *The God of Small Things*." *Cultural Studies* 21, nos. 3–4 (March–May), 339–67.

———. 2008a. "The Hybridity of Culture in Arturo Islas's *The Rain God*." *Critical Mappings of Arturo Islas's Fictions*, ed. Frederick Luis Aldama, 21–38. Tempe, Ariz.: Bilingual.

———. 2008b. "Making Democracy Surreal: Political Race and the Miner's Canary." *American Literary History* 20, no. 3 (Summer), 609–21.

———. 2008c. "Los orígenes transnacionales de la literatura chicana: El itinerario de Américo Paredes en Asia y el Pacífico." *Revista Casa de las Américas* 252 (July–September), 76–83.

Saldívar, José David, ed. 1985. *The Rolando Hinojosa Reader: Essays Historical and Critical*. Houston: Arte Público.

Saldívar, Ramón. 1990. *Chicano Narrative: The Dialectics of Difference.* Madison: University of Wisconsin Press.

———. 2006. *The Borderlands of Culture: Américo Paredes and the Transnational Imaginary.* Durham: Duke University Press.

———. 2009. "Asian Américo: Paredes in Asia and the Borderlands, a Response to José E. Limón." *American Literary History* 21, no. 3 (Fall), 584–95.

Saldívar-Hull, Sonia. 2000a. *Feminism on the Border: Chicana Gender Politics and Literature.* Berkeley: University of California Press.

———. 2000b. "Introduction to the Second Edition." Introduction to Gloria Anzaldúa, *Borderlands/La Frontera: The New Mestiza,* 2d ed., 1–13. San Francisco: Aunt Lute.

Sánchez, George J. 1993. *Becoming Mexican American: Ethnicity, Culture, and Identity in Chicano East Los Angeles, 1900–1945.* New York: Oxford University Press.

Sánchez, Rosaura. 1995. *Telling Identities: The Californio Testimonio.* Minneapolis: University of Minnesota Press.

Sandos, James. 1992. *Rebellion in the Borderlands: Anarchism and the Plan de San Diego, 1904–1923.* Norman: University of Oklahoma Press.

Sandoval, Anna Marie. 2009. *Toward a Latina Feminism of the Americas: Repression and Resistance in Chicana and Mexicana Literature.* Austin: University of Texas Press.

Shorris, Earl. 1992. *Latinos: A Biography of the People.* New York: Avon.

Smith, Neil. 2003. *American Empire: Roosevelt's Geographers and the Prelude to Globalization.* Berkeley: University of California Press.

Sollors, Werner, ed. 1998. *Multilingual America, Transnationalism, Ethnicity, and the Languages of American Literature.* New York: New York University Press.

Spivak, Gayatri Chakravorty. 1988a. "Can the Subaltern Speak?" *Marxism and the Interpretation of Culture,* ed. Cary Nelson and Lawrence Grossberg, 271–313. Urbana: University of Illinois Press.

———. 1988b. "Subaltern Studies: Deconstructing Historiography." *Selected Subaltern Studies,* ed. Ranajit Guha and Gayatri Chakravorty Spivak, 3–34. New York: Oxford University Press.

———. 1995. "Teaching for the Times." *Decolonization of the Imagination: Culture, Knowledge, and Power,* ed. Jan Nederveen Pieterse and Bhikhu Parekh, 177–202. London: Zed.

———. 2007. *Other Asias.* London: Wiley-Blackwell.

Stone, Robert. 1997. *Dog Soldiers.* New York: Mariner Books.

———. 1981. *A Flag for Sunrise.* New York: Knopf.

Suárez, Luis. 1978. "El periodismo me dio conciencia político," La Calle (Madrid), ed. Alfonso Rentería Mantilla, 195–200, *Gabriel García Márquez habla de García Márquez en 33 grandes reportajes.* Bogota: Rentería Ediciones.

Turner, Frederick Jackson. 1920 (1893). "The Significance of the Frontier in American History." Address to the American Historical Association, Chicago. Published in 1920 as *The Frontier in American History.* New York: Henry Holt.

Vega, Bernardo. 1990. *Memories of Bernardo Vega: A Contribution to the History of the Puerto Rican Community,* ed. Cesar A. Iglesias, trans. Juan Flores. New York: Monthly Review.

Vigdor, Jacob L. 2008. "Measuring Immigrant Assimilation in the United States." Report no. 63, Center for Civic Innovation Report, Manhattan Institute, New York.

Viramontes, Helena María. 1985. *The Moths and Other Stories.* Houston: Arte Público.

Walcott, Derek. 1986. "The Sea Is History." *Collected Poems: 1948–1984,* 364–67. New York: Farrar, Straus, and Giroux.

Wallerstein, Immanuel. 1974. *The Modern World-System, Volume 1: Capitalist Agriculture and the Origin of the European World-Economy in the Sixteenth-Century.* New York: Academic Press.

——. 2004. *World-Systems Analysis: An Introduction.* Durham: Duke University Press.

Wallerstein, Immanuel, Calestous Juma, Evelyn Fox Keller, Jürgen Kocka, Dominique Lecourt, Valentin Y. Mudimbe, Kinhide Mushakoji, Ilya Prigogine, Peter J. Taylor, and Michel-Rolph Trouillot. 1996. *Open the Social Sciences: Report of the Gulbenkian Commission on the Restructuring of the Social Sciences.* Stanford: Stanford University Press.

Webb, Walter Prescott. 1935. *The Texas Rangers: A Century of Frontier Defense.* Boston: Houghton Mifflin.

Weber, Max. 1950. *The Protestant Ethic and the Spirit of Capitalism,* trans. Talcott Parsons. New York: Scribner's.

White, Richard. 1994. "Frederick Jackson Turner and Buffalo Bill." *The Frontier in American Culture: Essays by Richard White and Patricia Nelson Limerick,* ed. James R. Grossman, 7–66. Berkeley: University of California Press.

Williams, Linda. 2001. *Playing the Race Card: Melodramas of Black and White from Uncle Tom to O. J. Simpson.* Princeton: Princeton University Press.

Williams, Raymond. 1983. *Keywords: A Vocabulary of Culture and Society,* rev. ed. New York: Oxford University Press.

Wofford, Chloe Arcella. 1955. "Virginia Woolf's and William Faulkner's Treatment of the Alienated," M.A. thesis, Cornell University.

Zaldívar, Alfredo. 1994. *Soy un tauro perdido y otras poemas.* Havana: Vigía ediciones.

Zamora, Lois P., and Wendy Faris, eds. 1995. *Magical Realism: Theory, History, Community.* Durham: Duke University Press.

Žižek, Slavoj. 1992. *Looking Awry: An Introduction to Jacques Lacan through Popular Culture.* Cambridge: MIT Press.

Index

Page numbers in italics refer to illustrations.

JOSÉ DAVID SALDÍVAR is a professor of comparative literature and the chair and director of the Program in the Center for Comparative Studies in Race and Ethnicity at Stanford University. He is the author of *Border Matters: Remapping American Cultural Studies* (1997) and *The Dialectics of Our America: Genealogy, Cultural Critique, and Literary History* (Duke, 1991). He edited *The Rolando Hinojosa Reader: Essays Historical and Critical* (1985) and co-edited (with Ramón Grosfoguel and Nelson Maldonado-Torres) *Latin@s in the World-System: Decolonization Struggles in the Twenty-First Century U.S. Empire* (2005) and (with Hector Calderón) *Criticism in the Borderlands* (Duke, 1991).

Library of Congress Cataloging-in-Publication Data

Saldívar, José David.
Trans-Americanity : subaltern modernities, global coloniality,
and the cultures of greater Mexico / José David Saldívar.
p. cm. — (New Americanists)
Includes bibliographical references and index.
ISBN 978-0-8223-5064-4 (cloth : alk. paper)
ISBN 978-0-8223-5083-5 (pbk. : alk. paper)
1. America—Study and teaching (Higher) 2. America—Civilization.
3. America—Research. 4. Interdisciplinary research.
I. Title. II. Series: New Americanists.
E16.5.S25 2012
970—dc23   2011021962